Lecture Notes in Computer Science 8605

Commenced Publication in 1973
Founding and Former Series Editors:
Gerhard Goos, Juris Hartmanis, and Jan van Leeuwen

Alessandro De Gloria (Ed.)

Games and Learning Alliance

Second International Conference, GALA 2013
Paris, France, October 23–25, 2013
Revised Selected Papers

 Springer

Editor
Alessandro De Gloria
University of Genova
Genova
Italy

ISSN 0302-9743   ISSN 1611-3349 (electronic)
ISBN 978-3-319-12156-7   ISBN 978-3-319-12157-4 (eBook)
DOI 10.1007/978-3-319-12157-4

Library of Congress Control Number: 2014953269

LNCS Sublibrary: SL3 – Information Systems and Applications, incl. Internet/Web, and HCI

Springer Cham Heidelberg New York Dordrecht London

Printed on acid-free paper

Springer is part of Springer Science+Business Media (www.springer.com)

Preface

The second GALA Conference was held during October 23–25 at the Dassault Systèmes (Paris). The Serious Games Society supported and organized the conference along with the Games and Learning Association, the Network of Excellence on Serious Games funded by the European Union under the Seventh Framework Programme. The conference has been devoted to Serious Games (SGs) and aimed at gathering, building, and nurturing an expert community on SGs which involves academic, industrial developers, teachers, and corporate decision makers, to promote knowledge share, technology transfer, and business development. SGs aim at improving learning processes by providing attractive, motivating, and effective tools. So far, effectiveness of SGs has been shown by recent studies (e.g., [1, 2]), but the potential of SGs in education is still far to be fulfilled. Furthermore, there is a growing need for scientific and engineering methods and tools for efficiently building games as means that provide effective learning experiences (e.g., [3–5]). An effective application of SGs for education and training demands appropriate metrics, analytics, tools, and techniques for in-game user assessment. This can be achieved in particular by measuring elements such as learning outcomes and engagement, considering the twofold nature of SGs as compelling games that achieve precise educational goals (e.g., [6, 7]). Recent technological advances have brought what was once expensive, specialized Human–Computer Interaction (HCI) equipment located in research labs, to our family rooms and classes at an affordable cost. Devices such as stereo cameras, eye trackers, tablets and smartphones, pointing devices, motion sensors, sensors related to the central and peripheral nervous systems (e.g., galvanic skin response, heart rate, neuronal activity) [8, 9], amongst others, not only provide innovative interaction methods and techniques, but also present opportunities to develop innovative solutions for continuous user monitoring and assessment (e.g., [10–12]). All in all, design of SGs is a very complex activity, involving different constraints, targets, and disciplines, which is being investigated but is still far from maturity [13–15]. This book reports the studies presented during the conference, addressing the above-mentioned call for paper indications. The book is divided into two parts. The first and main part includes three SG research tracks: design, technology, and application. The second part reports the results of the Workshop "Acquiring 21st Century Skills: gaining insight in the design and applicability of a serious game with 4C-ID" and presents short papers describing the posters exhibited during the conference.

The first research track is dedicated to SG design. The first paper describes the gamification process in a safety and energy-efficiency application context, while the second describes a location-based SG for promoting citizens' preparedness to flooding situations. The third article presents two case studies of SGs for supporting music research, while the fourth gives an overview of the conceptual development and technical implementation of an early staged prototype combining a business simulation and an SG. Learning analytics (LA) are discussed in the next two papers, the first paper devoted to a practical experience on using LAs in educational games and the second stressing the importance of the game log files for developing LAs. The last paper of the track deals with the relationship between entertainment games and SGs and what SG designers may learn from entertainment game design. The second research track is devoted to the technology applied in SGs. The first paper presents an accessible multiplatform game engine for a new version of the eAdventure educational game authoring platform. The second paper proposes an agent paradigm as a methodological tool to guide the design of SGs in the social field. The next article presents the F1 game, used to demonstrate how learning takes place in the domain of the Formula 1. An additional paper shows the learning path for solving learning difficulties in the use of money and other basic business activities by kids with cognitive disabilities. Two studies deal with significant enabling technologies. The Haptic technology is presented as a provider of a physical control layer that could enhance the immersion of virtual reality. Voice emotion recognition, on the other hand, is presented in the context of improving learning through webcams and microphone. The flow experience and how it can facilitate the game evaluation and design process is discussed in another paper, while the last article in the track presents the perspective of executive functions and discusses how they can help provide a more coherent approach to understanding the cognitive benefits of playing games. The third track of the research part is dedicated to SG applications. The first paper presents a business simulation game with an agent-based deliberative model of consumer behavior, while second paper deals with the evaluation of team collaboration in digital entertainment games. A cultural heritage application is considered in the next paper, presenting the key features, design solutions, and game mechanics of the Fort Ross Virtual Warehouse SG, while a subsequent study presents a Game-Based Learning MOOC for entrepreneurship. A case study presents how to deal with cultural awareness in a game concerning deployment of troops in Afghanistan. Another study provides a handy toolkit for evaluating the effectiveness of a SG for cultural awareness and heritage. The next paper investigates the gambling interactive experience, understanding how games of chance are structured and how they are related to cognitive errors and biases that occur in both frequent and infrequent gamblers. Another article describes a player-specific conflict handling ontology. The last paper in the track presents a compelling case for the use of games as a method for carrying out useful computational work by players in order to define new tools for designing SGs.

The second part of the book starts with the presentation of a workshop exploring how a widely applied instructional design model, 4C-ID, can ease the uptake of SGs by offering teachers a model fitting their background to assess games on the applicability in their learning contexts. The final part of the book collects short papers describing the exhibited posters, addressing a wide range of topics, from user profiling to knowledge convergence measure and from design to description of new SGs in different application fields.

In summary, as the above description may have shown, we are confident that a variety of stakeholders in the field of SGs—industrial developers, researchers, teachers, corporate decision makers, etc.—may find in this book a rich material for their work and inspiration for their activities.

References

1. Connolly, T.M., Boyle, E.A., MacArthur, E., Hainey, T., Boyle, J.M.: A systematic literature review of the empirical evidence on computer games and serious games. Comput. Educ. **59**(2), 661–686 (2012)
2. Wouters, P., van Oostendorp, H., van Nimwegen, C., van der Spek, E.D.: A meta-analysis of the cognitive and motivational effects of serious games. Comput. Educ. **60**(1), 412–425 (2013)
3. Greitzer, F.L., Kuchar, O.A., Huston, K.: Cognitive science implications for enhancing training effectiveness in a serious gaming context. ACM J. Educ. Res. Comput. **7**(3), 2:1–2:16 (2007)
4. Marfisi-Schottman, I., Labat, J.-M., Carron, T.: Building on the case teaching method to generate learning games relevant to numerous educational fields. In: IEEE International Conference on Advanced Learning Technologies (iCALT 2013), Beijing, China, 15–18 July 2013
5. Bellotti, F., Berta, R., De Gloria, A., D'Ursi, A., Fiore, V.: A serious game model for cultural heritage. ACM J. Comput. Cult. Herit. **5**(4) (2012)
6. Howell, K., Glinert, E., Holding, L., Swain, C.: How to build serious games. Commun. ACM **50**(7), 44–49 (2007)
7. Doucet, L., Srinivasan, V.: Designing entertaining educational games using procedural rhetoric: a case study. In: Proceedings of 5th ACM SIGGRAPH Symposium on Video Games, Los Angeles, CA, July 2010 (2010)
8. Berta, R., Bellotti, F., De Gloria, A., Pranantha, D., Schatten, C.: Electroencephalogram and physiological signal analysis for assessing flow in games. IEEE Trans. Comput. Intell. AI Games **5**(2), 164–175 (2013)
9. Ninaus, M., Kober, S.E., Friedrich, E.V.C., Dunwell, I., de Freitas, S., Arnab, S., Ott, M., Kravcik, M., Lim, T., Louchart, S., Bellotti, F., Hannemann, A., Thin, A.G.G., Berta, R., Wood, G., Neuper, C.: Neurophysiological methods for monitoring brain activity in serious games and virtual environments: a review. Int. J. Technol. Enhanced Learn. (IJTEL) **6**(1), 78–103 (2014)
10. Bellotti, F., Kapralos, B., Lee, K., Moreno-Ger, P., Berta, R.: Assessment in and of serious games: an overview. Adv. Hum. Comput. Interact. (2013). Article ID 136864. doi:10.1155/2013/136864
11. Shute, V.J, Ke, F.: Games, learning, and assessment. In: Ifenthaler, D., Eseryel, D., Ge, X. (eds.) Assessment in Game-Based Learning: Foundations, Innovations and Perspectives, pp. 43–58. Springer, New York (2012)
12. el Blanco, Á., Serrano-Laguna, Á., Freire, M., Martínez-Ortiz, I., Fernández-Manjón, B.: E-learning standards and learning analytics. Can data collection be improved by using standard data models? In: Proceedings of the IEEE Engineering Education Conference (EDUCON), pp. 1255–1261 (2013). doi:10.1109/EduCon.2013.6530268
13. Bellotti, F., Berta, R., De Gloria, A.: Designing effective serious games: opportunities and challenges for research. Special Issue: Creative learning with serious games. Int. J. Emerg. Technol. Learn. (IJET) **5**, 22–35 (2010)

14. Arnab, S., Lim, T., Carvalho, M.B., Bellotti, F., de Freitas, S., Louchart, S., Suttie, N., Berta, R., De Gloria, A.: Mapping learning and game mechanics for serious games analysis. Br. J. Educ. Technol. (2014). doi:10.1111/bjet.12113
15. Ritterfeld, U., Cody, M., Vorderer, P. (eds.) Serious Games: Mechanisms and Effects. Routledge, New York (2009)

October 2013   Alessandro De Gloria

Organization

General Chair

Alessandro De Gloria   University of Genoa, Italy

General Co-chair

Jean Menu   Serious Game Lab, France

Workshop and Tutorial Chair

David Wortley   Gamification and Enabling Technologies, UK

Program Committee

Aida Azadegan	University of the West Scotland, UK
Albert Angehrn	INSEAD, France
Alessandro Berni	NATO, Italy
Ana Paiva	INESC-ID, Portugal
Andreas Oikonomou	University of Derby, UK
Anthony Brooks	Aalborg University, Denmark
Audrius Jurgelionis	Fraunhofer, Germany
Baltasar Fernández-Manjón	Complutense University of Madrid, Spain
Bianca Falcidieno	CNR IMATI, Italy
Brian Goldiez	University of Central Florida, USA
Carmen Padron	ATOS, Spain
Carolina Islas Sedano	University of Eastern Finland, Finland
Christos Gatzidis	Bournemouth University, UK
Damien Djaouti	IRIT, France
Daniel Burgos	UNIR, Spain
David Wortley	Gamification and Enabling Technologies, UK
Dirk Ifenthaler	Open Universities Australia, Australia
Donald Brinkman	Microsoft, USA
Erik Duval	Katholieke Universiteit Leuven, Belgium
Erik van der Spek	Technical University of Eindhoven, The Netherlands
Fabrizia Mantovani	Università di Milano Bicocca, Italy
Francesco Bellotti	University of Genoa, Italy
Francisco José Gallego Durán	University of Alicante, Spain

Frank Dignum	University of Utrecht, The Netherlands
George Lepouras	University of Peloponnese, Greece
Igor Mayer	Technical University of Delft, The Netherlands
Ioana Stanescu	Carol I National Defence University, Romania
Ion Roceanu	Carol I National Defence University, Romania
Ivan Lombardi	Catholic University Sacred Heart, Italy
J.C. Hertz	Author of Joystick Nation, USA
Jannicke M. Baalsrud Hauge	Bremer Institut für Produktion und Logistik GmbH, Germany
Johann Riedel	University of Nottingham, UK
Josef Froschauer	Vienna University of Technology, Austria
Kam Star	Playgen, UK
Katerina Mania	Technical University of Crete, Greece
Kristian Kiili	Tampere University of Technology, Finland
Kurt Debattista	University of Warwick, UK
Kyung-Sik Kim	Dankook University, South Korea
Leonardo Caporarello	SDA Bocconi School of Management, Italy
Lucia Pannese	imaginary, Italy
Marcello Carrozzino	Institute for Advanced Studies Lucca, Italy
Margarida Romero	Esade, Spain
Maria Magdalena Popescu	Carol I National Defence University, Romania
Marius Preda	Institut National des Télécommunications, France
Mark McMahon	Edith Cowan University, Western Australia
Matthias Rauterberg	Technical University of Eindhoven, The Netherlands
Michael Derntl	RWTH Aachen University, Germany
Michael Kickmeier-Rust	Technical University of Graz, Austria
Michela Mortara	CNR, Italy
Miguel Encarnação	University of Louisville, USA
Milos Kravcik	RWTH Aachen University, Germany
Muriel Ney	Imag, France
Nahum D. Gershon	MITRE, USA
Nathalie Charlier	Katholieke Universiteit Leuven, Belgium
Norman Badler	University of Pennsylvania, USA
Ole-Ivar Holthe	Geelix, Norway
Olivier Irrmann	Aalto University, Finland
Pablo Moreno-Ger	Complutense University of Madrid, Spain
Panagiotis Petridis	Serious Games Institute, UK
Paolo Riva	Università di Milano Bicocca, Italy
Per Backlund	Högskolan i Skövde, Sweden
Peter Van Rosmalen	Open University of the Netherlands, The Netherlands
Rafael Bidarra	Delft University of Technology, The Netherlands
Ralph Klamma	RWTH Aachen University, Germany
Riccardo Berta	University of Genoa, Italy

Rob Nadolsky	Open University of the Netherlands, The Netherlands
Rosa Maria Bottino	National Research Institute, Italy
Rui Prada	INESC-ID, Portugal
Sandy Louchart	Heriot-Watt University, UK
Sara de Freitas	Coventry University, UK
Simon Egenfeldt-Nielsen	Serious Games Interactive, Denmark
Staffan Bjork	Chalmers, Sweden
Stephen Lane	University of Pennsylvania, USA
Steve Ellis	NASA, USA
Sung Hyun Cho	Hongik University, South Korea
Tanya Krzywinska	Brunel University, UK
Theo Lim	Heriot-Watt University, UK
Travis Ross	Indiana University, USA
William Fisher	Quicksilver, USA
Wim Westera	Open University of the Netherlands, The Netherlands
Yiorgos Chrysanthou	University of Cyprus, Cyprus

Local Arrangements Committee

Patricia Doherty	Dassault Systèmes, France
Caroline Freyther	Dassault Systèmes, France
Claudia Schoke	Dassault Systèmes, France
Elisa Lavagnino	University of Genoa, Italy

Publications Chair

Riccardo Berta	University of Genoa, Italy

Communication Chair

Francesco Bellotti	University of Genoa, Italy

Administrative Chair

Patricia Doherty	Dassault Systèmes, France
Elisa Lavagnino	University of Genoa, Italy

Contents

SG Applications

SG Design

Energy-Efficient and Safe Driving
Using a Situation-Aware Gamification
Approach in Logistics

Roland Klemke[1(✉)], Milos Kravcik[2], and Felix Bohuschke[3]

[1] Center for Learning Sciences and Technology, Open Universiteit Nederland,
Valkenburgerweg 177, Heerlen, The Netherlands
roland.klemke@ou.nl
[2] Advanced Community Information Systems (ACIS), Informatik 5,
RWTH Aachen University, Aachen, Germany
kravcik@dbis.rwth-aachen.de
[3] Humance AG, Goebenstraße 10-12, 50672 Cologne, Germany
fbo@humance.de

Abstract. Safety and energy-efficiency is the main aim of every reasonable driver. But often there is too much relevant information a driver has to take into account and evaluate. A useful support can be provided by technology that can observe the driver's situation, analyze it, and offer individualized information and services to the driver. Moreover, by means of gamification mechanisms drivers can receive valuable feedback and motivation to improve their behavior. This paper presents such a situation-aware gamification approach in logistics, which has been elaborated in the LogiAssist project and enhanced in the TEGA game. A first user study indicated the general usefulness of this approach and revealed also several shortcomings. These results imply that this synergy of various technologies provides a promising opportunity for further investigation and development.

1 Introduction

Truck drivers are working in an environment of permanent pressure: schedules for freight delivery are tight, transportation rules for special goods are complex, and legal regulations require conformity to a number of rules. Drivers need to pay attention to a number of information channels, ranging from internal truck related information, navigation information, traffic information, incoming information about route or destination changes.

Even though safety and energy-efficiency are declared to be problems of a high societal relevance and importance, adherence to safety regulations and energy saving driving styles are hard to achieve in this situation. Drivers simply have too many other things to look at. Traditionally, education for truck drivers is performed in driving schools and specialized trainings [1]. However, especially in the field of driving safety training, traditional training approaches show little effect [2]. Improvements, which have been proposed to the training situation of truck drivers, include improved training programs [3], the use of driving simulations [2], or the use of complex logistic

© Springer International Publishing Switzerland 2014
A. De Gloria (Ed.): GALA 2013, LNCS 8605, pp. 3–15, 2014.
DOI: 10.1007/978-3-319-12157-4_1

processes [4]. The integration of training and learning into the driver's workplace with the help of situation aware assistive technology and gamification aspects has not been reported so far.

The LogiAssist project aims to improve the situation for truck drivers by providing a community-based infrastructure for a number of assistance functionalities and educational services tailored to the needs of truck drivers [5]. Observing driver's current situation and performing a rule-based situation analysis, LogiAssist provides individualized information and services to the driver.

Part of the LogiAssist infrastructure is a gamified component called TEGA (Telematic Ecologic GAme). TEGA uses a portion of the observed situation model and extracts driving style related information from it (e.g. frequency of using the brake, driving speed, gear used, fuel consumption). This information is compared to idealistic data about an optimal driving style. Based on the deviations and matches found, hints, goals, and achievements are assigned to the driver.

The aim of this paper is to explore, in how far the situation-aware assistance approach of LogiAssist can be extended by a gamification approach, which motivates drivers to improve their ecologic and economic driving style. This paper is focused on the technical feasibility of this approach and discusses a first realization of the TEGA approach as an extension of the LogiAssist framework. Consequently, we discuss some related work and present the LogiAssist background. We describe the general situation observation and analysis approach of the LogiAssist rule engine and describe the gamification approach used for TEGA. After introducing the outcomes of a user study, we conclude the paper.

2   Related Work

The problem addressed in this paper consists of several different dimensions that need to be considered, including quantified self, energy awareness, situational awareness, game-based learning and gamification. In the following we briefly introduce each of them.

The movement called Quantified Self [6] is being followed by people wanting to track regularly their physiological data in order to achieve certain benefits. It is aimed at various aspects of a person's daily life, including inputs (e.g. food), states (e.g. mood), and performance (e.g. physical, mental). It is based on different kinds of data collected from available sensors, which can be visualized in order to enable self-monitoring and discovery of correlations. This kind of self-reflection can lead to a desired behavior change. An important aspect of the quantified self movement is the sharing of measured data in order to compare individual results with community results [7].

One important area where more reflection is required in order to change behavior of people in a right way is energy consumption. It has been shown that clear instantaneous direct feedback is necessary to effectively control fuel use and to reduce its demand [8]. So appropriate feedback is crucial for learning of behavioral patterns as well as it is useful for understanding and control of energy use.

Situational awareness is required in order to provide relevant hints in concrete circumstances. User experience plays a key role in the development of recommender systems [9]. This implies that in addition to the more traditional content-based and collaborative approaches, contextual ones become equally important. Nevertheless, understanding the current situation of the user is a challenging task, as the current context and user preferences change dynamically all the time, reflecting various cues and constraints, like the time, location, task, mood, company of other people, etc. Therefore context-aware recommender systems [10], which adapt relevant recommendations to the specific user situation, became a special area of interest for researchers and developers. For instance, it has been shown that users prefer a context-aware mobile recommender system to a similar one without contextual information [11]. For the sake of this paper we use the terms context or situation as synonyms, which describe the system user's situation comprising physical information (location, direction, speed, vehicle related information), work related information (destination, working time), routing information (borders, points of interest), and personal information (community).

Within the past decade, studies have demonstrated that commercial as well as educational games support constructivist learning and teaching, i.e. constructive, situated and social learning [12, 13], and match the determinants of intrinsic motivation [14] especially, when mobile games are used [15]. Game-based learning approaches particularly make sense if the content to be learned is dry and only somewhat interesting, if the considered target group is rather difficult to motivate for learning, and/or if the target group does not have the necessary competencies to deal with other self-learning material (e.g. the competence to act or learn self-directed) [16].

While game-based learning refers to the application of games, which have been explicitly created for learning in certain contexts, gamification refers to the use of game mechanics and game design elements to everyday activities. Some observations revealed that the use of gamification approaches can help to engage users and motivate a desired behavior in non-game contexts [17]. One of the principles of gamification is to provide rewards (e.g. points, badges, levels, progress bars, virtual currency) for players when they have accomplished desired tasks [18]. Gamification can be applied in various situations. Individual elements of game design, so called design-patterns can be used to construct games [19]. With this regard, four elements are typical for games: goals, rules, feedback, and voluntary participation. Another crucial element is competition, which motivates and stimulates players by comparing them with the others and promoting the most successful ones [20]. Of course, these principles do not represent a general remedy and must be applied carefully, depending on the particular learning objectives, context, and users. For instance learners' collaboration can also be very motivating and effective. There are also other relevant concerns regarding gamified learning, like addiction, development of utilitarian mentality, or extrinsic instead of intrinsic motivation. Nevertheless, there is also evidence of positive outcomes when these different aspects of the learning experience have been carefully balanced [21].

3   Base Framework: LogiAssist Services

In logistics, mobile systems are used to coordinate and optimize transportation processes. Tracking and routing information as well as communication systems are used to support truck drivers. Different available systems comprise various peripheral devices, such as navigation systems, tachographs, or radio devices.

A consistent approach combining these different approaches is missing. The LogiAssist project aims to address these issues by offering a set of functionalities, services and applications, which help drivers in their day-to-day business. The LogiAssist tools and services provide the basis for the development of the gamification approach. Individual services offered by LogiAssist comprise:

- Navigation and routing support with special features for truck drivers (e.g. avoid routes with limitations with respect to dangerous goods).
- Community features with recognition of nearby friends.
- Medical service with routing to nearby physicians with special services for truck drivers (based on DocStop data).
- Telematic services around vehicle related information (e.g. combining fuel status information with information about nearby gas stations).

In addition, LogiAssist provides a wide range of learning and training offers, tailored to the needs of truck drivers:

- Language training for cross-national traffic.
- Information and training materials about the handling of dangerous goods.
- Health-related training materials (nutrition, gymnastics, and exercise).
- Driving license and special licenses related content.

These LogiAssist tools are combined through a situation-aware system, which recognizes different user situations, analyses them and reacts accordingly, by offering specific user outputs and interactions. LogiAssist combines information from heterogeneous sources to model the user's current situation. The information about the user's situation is then used to provide personalized assistance and learning services to the user. Consequently, the above-mentioned services can be individualized to the needs of the current driver.

Figure 1 shows the registration screen and the main screen of the LogiAssist core app, which gives access to all connected services. More detail on LogiAssist can be found in [5]. In the following sections we will describe, how the situation observation and analysis in LogiAssist works and how it can be used to create the gamification service for energy-aware and safe driving.

4 Situation Observation and Analysis

LogiAssist provides an infrastructure, which constantly monitors the driver's situation based on a set of predefined context parameters in order to offer specific, situation-related assistance. Typical situations, which require assistance functionalities, comprise:

- Recognition of national borders to be crossed soon, which triggers the delivery of hints on different rules applying in the country to enter.
- Driving time related hints to nearby rest areas, including also community related information on possible friends to meet there.

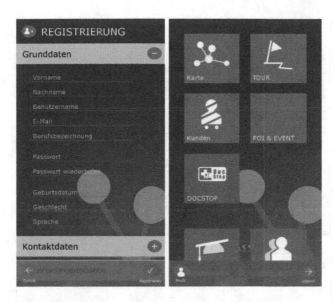

Fig. 1. LogiAssist registration and core app providing access to different assistance functions and educational services

- Detection of driver license related information (e.g. expiration of a specific certificate) offering access to relevant educational material during breaks.

Figure 2 shows the main elements of the rule engine architecture. The situation observation and analysis in LogiAssist is centered around a core context model, which represents the current situation in terms of a set of context parameters. A context monitor component constantly observes the context parameters and updates the context model correspondingly. The rule management component detects all changes in the context model and performs a rule-based situation analysis. When rules are found, which match the current situation, the action manager handles the execution of rule specific actions. The following paragraphs detail, how the situation observation and analysis works.

The context parameters observed by the context monitor cover a variety of different aspects:

- Technical parameters retrieved via the vehicle's CAN-bus (Controller Area Network is a serial bus protocol to connect individual systems and sensors) infrastructure (such as speed, gear used, fuel consumption), which is connected to the LogiAssist system using a Squarell-Box (multi source vehicle data interface) with a Bluetooth-adapter.
- Driver related parameters retrieved via the LogiAssist app (such as GPS position, destination, traffic information, routing information).
- Infrastructural parameters retrieved via the LogiAssist backend infrastructure (such as community information, profile information).

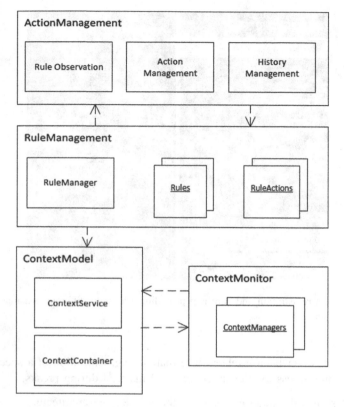

Fig. 2. Architecture of the situation observation and analysis

Rules as defined in the rule management comprise the definition of a specific set of context parameters, which describe the situation in which a rule triggers and a set of actions to be performed in such a case. The rule also defines a rule priority, ensuring that e.g. security relevant actions are handled prior to others.

The action management takes care of the rules that have been triggered and starts the corresponding actions. Rules are handled in order of their priorities and their trigger time. Different types of actions are offered by the LogiAssist system:

- Background actions (e.g. status updates to the backend infrastructure).
- Non-intrusive user interface updates (e.g. status updates for map displays).
- Intrusive user interface updates (e.g. warning messages on screen).
- Blocking user interface updates (e.g. warnings/hints requiring user interaction for acceptance or denial of a route change).

Figure 3 shows the last variant of a blocking user interface update. In this case a low fuel status requires taking a detour in order to be able to reach a proposed gas station. The user has to confirm the suggestion provided or continue at own risk.

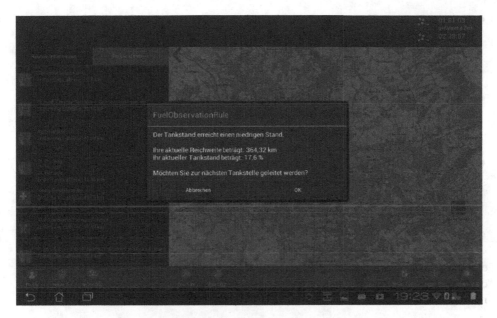

Fig. 3. Example of a blocking user interface update with required interaction

5 Gamification Approach in TEGA

With the above described infrastructure, LogiAssist can offer a range of situation-aware services to the driver. However, the goals of LogiAssist go beyond assistance functionalities: In the field of energy efficient and safe driving, LogiAssist aims to provide learning and training services to drivers in a manner that is motivating, non-intrusive, and effective at the same time.

In order to support these goals, we performed a student development project at RWTH Aachen, where a group of computer science students participating in the course "Hightech Entrepreneurship and New Media" (HENM 2012/2013)[1] consequently got the task to design and implement a gamified application (TEGA) with the following gamification elements:

- *Level system:* Users gain experience by using the app – the level does not depend on the economic driving style, but simply on the frequency of use of the app. This way, continuous use of the app is awarded with leveling up.

---

[1] The course "Hightech Entrepreneurship and New Media" combines tutorials and lectures on the development of complex information products with practical experience in start-ups (in this case Humance AG) solving concrete IT related tasks. An important part of the course is the development of soft skills, including presentation, planning and cooperation in a team, as well as communication with the customer. Integrated into the concept of this course is the procurement of useful information for start ups in high-tech branches, taught by practitioners. The outcomes of the project are presented in a public presentation at the end of the course.

- *Scoring system:* Users gain points by using an economically friendly driving style. The scores gained are calculated through a weighted combination of fuel consumption, speed, RPM (revolutions per minute), and the carbon emission over a certain travel distance. Only, when the driver performs better than a defined threshold, the score is increased.
- *Reward/Achievement system:* Users can receive badges and titles by reaching certain goals – goals comprise for example: driving at constant speed over a period of time or reducing average fuel consumption by 5 %, 10 %, or 15 %. Goals are defined using rules, which the user has to meet to gain the corresponding badge.
- *Ranking system:* Users can compare their driving style with others: as an additional motivator, users can publish their achievements and scores to a social network. The leaderboard displays the scores and badges of different users in a high-score list. To be visible in a high score list, users have to be connected as friends in the underlying LogiAssist community portal.

The LogiAssist infrastructure (see Fig. 4) is used to support these gamification elements by adding appropriate context parameters to the LogiAssist context model and context monitor and by modeling corresponding rules within the LogiAssist rule manager:

- As LogiAssist already requires users to register, the LogiAssist community services are used for TEGA by providing login services and access to user profiles.

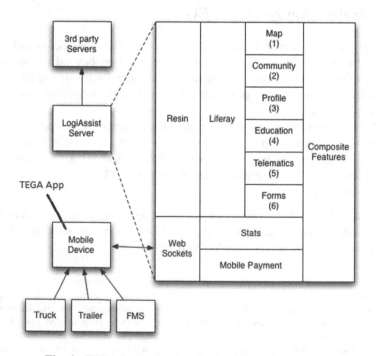

Fig. 4. TEGA integration into the LogiAssist infrastructure

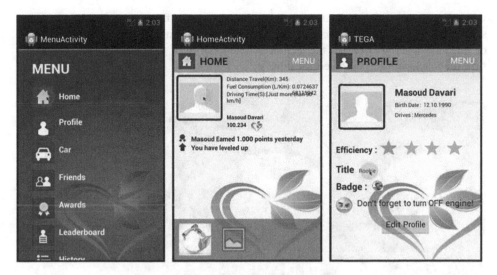

Fig. 5. Screenshots of the TEGA app

- LogiAssist's situation observation and analysis module is used to identify key parameters of the driving style, which are retrieved using LogiAssist's connection to the vehicle's infrastructure.
- LogiAssist's rule management component is extended with rules representing the goals necessary for badges.

The TEGA app is then used as a front-end to display gamification results, profile information, and social information. Figure 5 displays core screenshots of the TEGA app, showing the main screen giving access to various areas, the home screen, which gives access to latest gamification updates (recent scores and level information), and the profile view displaying overall achievements and gamification results (action statistics, level information, and score information).

In the current implementation stage, the TEGA app works as a standalone app, which is connected to the LogiAssist framework to access the LogiAssist services (user profiles, situation analysis, rules). Once the TEGA app is started and connected to the LogiAssist backend, the gamification results (scores, levels, achievements) are displayed in the TEGA app.

Low intrusiveness in TEGA is achieved by not requiring the user to actively interact with the system, when she is driving. Once, the app is started, it begins to record and analyze the driving related information. The display is continuously updated, so that information is always displayed to the user.

6 User Study

While the LogiAssist infrastructure is already available for public access via the Google play store for the Android platform, the TEGA app is currently implemented as a first functional prototype for Android. A first small scale user study has been performed with pilot users, which indicates the general usefulness of the approach, while it at the same time reveals some shortcomings to the user interface approach of TEGA. The aim of this first study was to test the technical functionality of the prototype and to gather first feedback on the perceived usefulness.

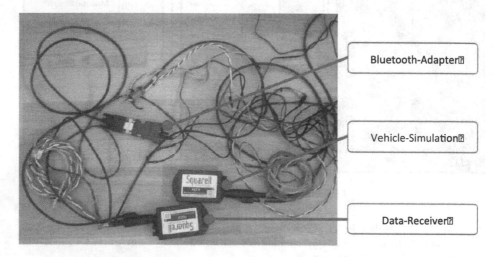

Bluetooth-Adapter

Vehicle-Simulation

Data-Receiver

Fig. 6. Hardware setup for simulated TEGA test-drives

For security reasons and as it was not possible to get access to real vehicle hardware during the student project, the study has been performed using simulated test-drives. Figure 6 shows the hardware setup used for these test-drives, including a Bluetooth-adapter, which is connected to a data-receiver (Squarrell-box). The data-receiver receives simulated CAN-bus data from the vehicle simulation (second Squarrell-box). The vehicle simulation is realized using test drive datasets, which can be loaded into the vehicle simulation box. This data is then used to provide realistic CAN-bus data to the data-receiver box.

The TEGA app receives the test-drive data from the data-receiver box via the Bluetooth adapter and performs the analysis accordingly. This setup enables us to perform user tests in predefined test-drives, which gives us the opportunity to concentrate on user interface aspects of the tool without the need to actually perform test drives. Vehicles equipped with Squarrell hardware have not been available at test time.

While performing the test-drives, the gamification rules and corresponding thresholds could be tested and adjusted. This functional testing was carried out during the development process and lead to improvements of the game mechanism applied to TEGA.

Furthermore, first feedback on the TEGA approach could be gathered by exposing the simulated drives to a limited number of test users (four students not involved in the team project). At this stage, we collected qualitative feedback from the test users.

While the rule-based gamification approach generally works and was accepted by the users, the TEGA app needs to be less intrusive by operating mainly in the background, only notifying the user of achievements and scores. Especially, the use of audio notification for achievements or leveling information was mentioned to be more appropriate than on-screen notifications. Furthermore, the underlying goals for achievements to be unlocked and scores to be gained have to be communicated to the user in a more explicit way.

7 Conclusion

In this paper we presented the LogiAssist approach to monitor the current situation of truck drivers, analyze it, and provide relevant information and services to them. This has been enhanced by the TEGA gamification approach to motivate and stimulate potential users.

The general infrastructure as provided by the LogiAssist framework for situation-aware assistance can be flexibly utilized to support a number of assistance functionalities. Beyond immediate support functionality, we have demonstrated that this framework can also be the basis for a gamification-based approach towards energy-efficient and safe driving.

The rule-based approach of situation-awareness implemented in the LogiAssist framework was extended to support the gamification aspects required for the TEGA approach, including:

- Rules, which detect the energy-efficiency of the driver's driving style could be modeled – these use the data gathered through the vehicle's infrastructure.
- Gamification elements such as scores, levels, achievements, and badges were modeled as results of rule triggers. The user profile was extended with the gamification outcomes in order to be able to share the gamification results with other users.
- Through the connection of TEGA and LogiAssist to a community-based infrastructure, an additional competitive element was added to the gamification approach by maintaining a rank list of participants.

A more thorough study involving the actual integration of the TEGA app in a vehicle, which has to be equipped with the Squarrell-box and the Bluetooth-adapter has yet to be performed in order to test usability and effectiveness of the TEGA approach under real life conditions. As future steps, we plan to complement the TEGA approach with specific training advices based on the individual driver's driving style. This way, we aim to combine the game progress with specific instructions relevant to the driver at hand.

Furthermore, we intend to integrate the TEGA gamification approach into the core LogiAssist app. This way, the existing learning and assistance functionality of LogiAssist and the gamification approach of TEGA can be seamlessly combined to offer a consistent user experience.

Acknowledgments. We want to thank the participating Students of the HENM 2012/2013 course for their contributions. The LogiAssist project is co-funded by *Ministerium für Wirtschaft, Mittelstand und Energie des Landes Nordrhein-Westfalen* in their programme *Logistik.NRW*.

References

1. Horn, B.E., Tardif, L.P.: Licensing and training of truck drivers-new and continuing challenges. IATSS Res. **23**, 16–25 (1999)
2. Fisher, D.L., Laurie, N.E., Glaser, R., Connerney, K., Pollatsek, A., Duffy, S.A., Brock, J.: Use of a fixed-base driving simulator to evaluate the effects of experience and PC-based risk awareness training on drivers' decisions. Hum. Factors J. Hum. Factors Ergon. Soc. **44**(2), 287–302 (2002)
3. Nagatsuka, Y.: Are licensed drivers "perfect drivers"? Getting a driver's license and driver training: current situation in Japan. IATSS Res. **23**(HS-042 888) 93–99 (1999)
4. Rothe, J.P. (ed.): Driving Lessons: Exploring Systems that Make Traffic Safer. University of Alberta, Edmonton (2002)
5. Scheffel, M., Kirschenmann, U., Taske, A., Adloff, K., Kiesel, M., Klemke, R., Wolpers, M.: Exploring LogiAssist - the mobile learning and assistance platform for truck drivers. In: Accepted for 8th European Conference on Technology Enhanced Learning (EC-TEL 2013), 17–21 September 2013, Paphos, Cyprus (2012)
6. Wolf, G., Carmichael, A., Kelly, K.: The quantified self. TED (2010). http://www.ted.com/talks/gary_wolf_the_quantified_self.html
7. Swan, M.: Sensor mania! The Internet of Things, wearable computing, objective metrics, and the Quantified Self 2.0. J. Sens. Actuator Netw. **1**(3), 217–253 (2012)
8. Darby, S.: The effectiveness of feedback on energy consumption. A Review for DEFRA of the Literature on Metering, Billing and direct Displays, 1–21 (2006)
9. Konstan, J.A., Riedl, J.: Recommender systems: from algorithms to user experience. User Model. User-Adap. Inter. **22**(1–2), 101–123 (2012)
10. Adomavicius, G., Tuzhilin, A.: Context-aware recommender systems. In: Ricci, F., Rokach, L., Shapira, B., Kantor, P.B. (eds.) Recommender Systems Handbook, pp. 217–253. Springer, US (2011)
11. Baltrunas, L., Ludwig, B., Peer, S., Ricci, F.: Context relevance assessment and exploitation in mobile recommender systems. Pers. Ubiquit. Comput. **16**(5), 507–526 (2012)
12. Gee, J.P.: What video games have to teach us about learning and literacy. Palgrave Macmillan, Basingstoke (2007). Revised and Updated Edition
13. Prensky, M.: Digital Game-Based Learning: Practical Ideas for the Application of Digital Game-Based Learning. Paragon House, St. Paul (2007)
14. Carstens, A., Beck, J.: Get ready for the gamer generation. TechTrends **49**(3), 22–25 (2010)
15. Douch, R., Savill-Smith, C.: The mobile learning network: the impact of mobile game-based learning. In: Proceedings of the IADIS Int'l Conference on Mobile Learning 2010, Porto, Portugal, pp. 189–197 (2010)
16. Schmitz, B., Czauderna, A., Klemke, R., Specht, M.: Game based learning for computer science education. In: Proceedings of Computer Science Education Research Conference, pp. 81–88. ACM, Heerlen (2011)
17. Deterding, S., Sicart, M., Nacke, L., O'Hara, K., Dixon, D.: Gamification. using game-design elements in non-gaming contexts. In: Proceedings of the 2011 annual conference extended abstracts on Human factors in computing systems, pp. 2425–2428. ACM (2011)
18. Muntean, C.I.: Raising engagement in e-learning through gamification. In: Proceedings of 6th International Conference on Virtual Learning ICVL, pp. 323–329, October 2011
19. Kelle, S., Klemke, R., Specht, M.: Effects of game design patterns on basic life support training content. Educ. Technol. Soc. **16**(1), 275–285 (2013)

20. Reeves, B., Read, J.L.: Total Engagement: Using Games and Virtual Worlds to Change the Way People Work and Businesses Compete. Harvard Business Press, Boston (2009)

21. Bellotti, F., Berta, R., De Gloria, A., Lavagnino, E., Antonaci, A., Dagnino, F. M., Ott, M.: A gamified short course for promoting entrepreneurship among ICT engineering students. In: 2013 IEEE 13th International Conference on Advanced Learning Technologies (ICALT), pp. 31–32. IEEE (2013)

Learning Analytics and Educational Games: Lessons Learned from Practical Experience

Ángel Serrano-Lagunaa[⊠], Javier Torrentea, Borja Maneroa,
Ángel del Blancoa, Blanca Borro-Escribanoa, Iván Martínez-Ortiza,
Manuel Freirea, and Baltasar Fernández-Manjón

Complutense University of Madrid, C/Profesor José García Santesmases, 9,
28040 Madrid, Spain
aserrano@e-ucm.es

Abstract. Learning Analytics (LA) is an emerging discipline focused on obtaining information by analyzing students' interactions with on-line educational contents. Data is usually collected from online activities such as forums or virtualized courses hosted on Learning Management Systems (e.g. Moodle). Educational games are emerging as a popular type of e-learning content and their high interactivity makes them potential sources for relevant educational user data. However, it is still uncertain how to deploy and combine these two incipient technologies, as multiple challenges remain unresolved. This paper reports on our practical experience using LA to improve assessment of experimental research on educational game-based instruction. In the last year, we conducted four experiments evaluating game-based instruction under different conditions (using three adventure games and a puzzle game respectively) in 13 educational institutions including schools, universities and vocational training organizations. A LA system was used to track interaction around six hundred students. In these experiences, we encountered several problems in each of the steps of the process, from issues related to the design of the experiment and the game to different technical and practical problems, derived from the very diverse conditions of the facilities and policies of each institution (computer laboratories, computers hardware, software installed, irregular Internet access), which hinders the data collecting process (e.g. the system had to deal with high latency Internet connections and backup plans had to be devised for collecting data when no Internet access was available). We present the lessons learned and propose guidelines from a technical and practical perspective for the design of experimental research using both LA systems and educational games.

1 Introduction

This paper aims to be a practical guide for researchers interested in conducting experimental research on educational gaming who might also want to explore the opportunities that embedding a learning analytics system provides to improve the research. Building on our experience, we identify potential issues that can arise while conducting this kind of research, and also provide recommendations to tackle them. Some of the issues discussed are technical, related to the implementation and

A. De Gloria (Ed.): GALA 2013, LNCS 8605, pp. 16–28, 2014.
DOI: 10.1007/978-3-319-12157-4_2

deployment of the technology, while others are rather logistical, operational and related to the design of the experiments.

The field of learning analytics (LA) refers to the collection, analysis and visualization of large amounts of data related to educational processes. In its heart, LA aims to harness the power of big data and data-mining techniques to improve the assessment of the learning processes. LA also can create new opportunities for adaptive and personalized learning, which has remained an unfulfilled promise of the e-learning field for years. As an incipient new era of online learning, promoted by Massive Online Open Courses (MOOCs) comes upon our shoulders, LA could find the perfect conditions to make an impact in education in the next few years [1].

As any big data system, LA requires gathering a wealth of data from different sources. It usually uses data generated from tracking students' interactions with the online platform used to support learning (e.g. a Learning Management System like Moodle or Sakai). For example created posts, pages and resources accessed or time spent on each piece of content. Research in the LA field is currently exploring how to leverage other data sources to improve the effectiveness of the paradigm. One of the proposals is to use educational games, which are another pushing educational technology. Although educational games are still far from reaching massive adoption due to unresolved limitations [2–4], their effectiveness to improve learning is accepted among the academic community [5], as attributed benefits to educational games like increased student motivation, improved engagement and better knowledge acquisition have been recently backed up with experimental research [6–9]. Serious games can pose an advantage to feed LA systems as they are inherently highly interactive pieces of software which can produce massive user data.

Achieving a successful synergy between serious games and learning analytics poses significant challenges that are added to the difficulties of designing and conducting experimental research in education. In the next sections we will present an overview of our recent research and discuss the issues found and the solutions we came up with.

2 Overview of Games Used in the Experiences

During the last year, we have conducted 4 experimental research studies using educational games. In round numbers, 4 games have been deployed at 13 educational institutions including universities, high schools and vocational training institutions, involving more than 600 students.

The four games were independently developed and cover different knowledge areas. Three of them were conversational point-and-click games developed with the eAdventure platform [10, 11], while the fourth was programmed from scratch.

Experiments carried out with these games followed a similar process. In a starting phase, the games were designed. The games were implemented and then internally tested. Once the games were polished and ready for distribution, they were deployed to conduct experiments in several educational institutions. During the experiments, students completed a pre-test to measure initial levels of motivation and knowledge on the subject. Then they played the game while the LA system collected data gathered from their interaction with the game. At the end of the session, students completed a post-test. Differences between pre and post tests were measured to estimate effect of instruction.

Next subsections briefly introduce each experiment and the games used.

2.1 The Big Party

The Big Party [12] is an eAdventure game (Fig. 1) that aims to teach persons with different levels of cognitive disabilities life management skills related to personal hygiene, safety, social interaction and transportation. The goal of the game is to reach a party organized by the player's company for all the staff. To complete the game, players must find their way through different common situations of daily life until they reach the venue of the party. This game was played by 19 players of different ages and with different levels of cognitive disabilities.

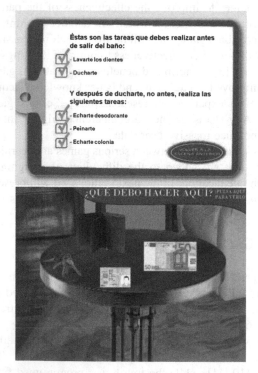

Fig. 1. Screenshots of the game "The Big Party".

2.2 Lost in Space <XML>

This puzzle, level-based game (Fig. 2) was designed to teach XML syntax to students with different programming backgrounds. In the game, players control a spaceship they must lead to a target point by writing little XML documents with instructions (e.g. move spaceship two units forward, rotate 90°, shoot, etc.). 89 students from computer science and social science studies played this game distributed in two different settings.

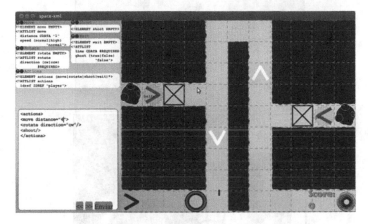

Fig. 2. Screenshot from the game "Lost in Space <XML>".

2.3 La Dama Boba

The game La Dama Boba [13] is an eAdventure game (Fig. 3) that was designed to motivate youngsters on classic theater plays. This goal is achieved making avatars interesting to players, by incorporating different theater techniques within their personalities and including the elements that can be used as audiovisual contents, such as music, scenery and dressing.

The game is based on the equally named comedy by the Spanish playwright Lope de Vega, wrote in 1613. The player becomes Laurencio, the main male character of the comedy, and has to live the story through his eyes. As the plot unveils, several minigames about grammar and literature are also introduced.

This game has been deployed in 9 different high schools in Madrid where 370 students aged from 11 to 15 played it.

2.4 Donations

Donations is an eAdventure game-like simulation (Fig. 4) developed in collaboration with the Spanish National Transplant Organization (ONT). This game simulates the process that the ONT staff follow for deceased donation management. These steps are (1) organ and donor evaluation, (2) the organ distribution and (3) the organ transportation. The game was developed to facilitate instruction of new personnel within the organization as well as to support transferring this successful workflow to other transplant coordinators. The game has been evaluated by 150 students in three training courses.

Fig. 3. Screenshots of the game La Dama Boba. Character design inspired in customs by Agatha Ruiz de la Prada for an adapted version of the play.

3 Designing and Planning the Experiment

Our experiments are oriented to evaluate the impact that using videogames has on the learning process. Mainly, we try to measure the educational gain (knowledge acquired by the students as a consequence of the intervention) and changes in the motivation towards the subject of interest (e.g. literature or computer programming).

In this section we provide a set of considerations we take when designing the experiments.

3.1 Instruments for Measuring Variation in Knowledge and Motivation

We use a twofold approach to measure variations of motivation and educational gain. First we use questionnaires to perform an external analysis of the learning process. This type of analysis does not consider how or what makes learning happen; instead, it just focuses on the outputs. Second, GLEANER, a LA system [14], is used to perform an internal evaluation of the process, gathering insight on what aspects of the game promote learning.

Several instances of the questionnaire are used along the experiment to have multiple values to compare with. At least the questionnaire is used twice: a pre-test that

Fig. 4. Screenshots of the game Donations. Main central office of the ONT and action of organ evaluation.

is administered just before students start playing and a post-test administered after the intervention, but it can be used more times for longer or longitudinal experiments. The results of different measures of the questionnaires are compared (e.g. pre-test Vs post-test) to determine the effect of the game.

A thorough design of the questionnaire is strongly recommended. The questions included in the test must tackle exactly what it is meant to be measured in the study. We combine several strategies to iteratively design and refine our questionnaires. First, we identify the aspects that we want to capture, usually distributed in three or more sections: demographics (e.g. age, gender, video game preferences, etc.), knowledge on the subject, and motivation towards the subject and/or evaluation of the experience (for post-tests only). Second, we write a set of candidate questions exploring different wordings and evaluation scales for each of the aspects. We also design several questions oriented to measure aspects that are difficult to capture because they cannot be observed, like the knowledge or motivation. This allows us to build subscales that aggregate all the questions related to the same aspect to generate a variable that is more powerful for statistical analysis. Third, the candidate questions are distributed for iterative review among an internal team of experts in educational games and also experts in the knowledge area. Finally, one or more testing sessions are organized where the instruments and questionnaires are piloted with a group of selected students.

As a preferred format, we use 7-point Likert questions for subjective aspects (e.g. motivation) as this allows sometimes applying parametric statistical methods for analysis. For objective aspects (e.g. knowledge) we tend to use multiple-option questions to simplify evaluation.

3.2 Group Comparison

It is essential to compare the effect of game-based instruction to traditional instruction to allow drawing valid conclusions at the end of the study [2], especially if the same questionnaire is used at different points of the experiment, which introduces bias in the variation measured.

For that purpose, we distribute students in at least two groups: experimental and control. Students in the experimental group attend the session where the game is played. Students in the control group attend a traditional instruction session, which is usually a lecture driven by an experienced teacher. In some cases we use a third group where the best possible instruction is delivered to the student, which is usually driven by experts in the field using (perhaps) special equipment. All groups must use the same pre and post tests to measure variation. This allows discussing the effectiveness of the game comparing to bottom and top lines.

3.3 Duration of the Experiment and Logistics

Our experiments are designed to require an intervention of maximum 50 min, which is the typical schedule slot in education. All instruments and also the game must be designed to respect this constrain.

Longer exposure to instruction is desirable, but it is hard to achieve in many educational organizations as logistics and organizational costs for an experiment like these, which are already high, increase. It must be noted that in many cases the experiment will require taking up most of the computer resources of the institution for a while. Computer clusters in schools usually have less than one computer per student (around 20 computers per cluster) to minimize costs, which implies that students usually work in pairs. If the game under evaluation is designed for individual use, it will be needed to use two computer clusters if possible, or to split students in the experimental group in two turns, requiring to have access to the cluster for a longer period.

Some institutions will not meet these requirements. In that case, a different kind of experiment must be planned, following a qualitative approach. Students can play the game in groups, and the sessions would be recorded for later analysis. These data can be combined with interviews or debriefing sessions.

3.4 Getting Support from the Educational Institution

It is essential to get support from the educational organization where the experiment will take place to ensure that researchers are given access to facilities, students and personnel. Also researchers must make sure that the institution understands all the requirements for the experiment. In our experience, we have observed that sometimes researchers' and institutions' interests conflict. On the one hand, researchers want to have the facilities and support required to conduct an experiment that is as controlled and well designed as possible to ensure that the conclusions obtained are valid. On the other hand, the institution has usually tight schedules and organizing an experiment like these has a considerable impact for them. Having strong institutional support will help researchers finding a balance between both perspectives that benefits the goals of the research.

A possible strategy to get better institutional support is to make the institution and its staff understand that getting involved in the experiment adds value to all the stakeholders involved. Principals and administrative staff can be enticed by the idea of participating in a pilot study that improves innovation in the institution. Motivated teachers or early adopters may be interested in having new software available to improve their instruction for free.

3.5 Maximize Control to Reduce Error Rates

Researchers should supervise all the important parts of the experience and ensure they are in control. People out of the research can unintentionally bias the results of the experiment. In this regard, understanding teachers' perspectives before the experiment can help to foresee potential problems and develop mitigation plans. In our experience we discovered that some teachers are worried about how their students will perform compared to other institutions. In this sense, they felt their work as teachers being under examination. These teachers unintentionally tended to give students more clues to solve the tests, introducing bias.

If the experience requires randomized allocation of students in groups that will receive different instruction, we suggest not leaving the entire responsibility to the teacher, or at least researchers should supervise the process. Teacher used to consider playing the game as a reward for the best students, and this could bias data.

3.6 Ethical and Legal Issues

Ethical and legal issues must always be considered, especially when the target audience include minors. Privacy of data collected must be ensured. For that reason, we use anonymization techniques and anonymous questionnaires. To pair questionnaires and results within the game, each student is given a unique code that the write on paper tests and also introduce in the games to identify data sent to the LA system.

All students should receive the same treatment and have access to the same content. For that reason, we usually let students in control group play the games once the experiment is complete and all data have been collected. Also students in the experimental group are given traditional instruction after the experience.

3.7 Workflow

For the reader's convenience, in this section we provide a summary of the workflow with all the activities conducted in these experiments.

- Make an initial design of experiment, materials and game. This will help know the requirements of your experiment.
- Start recruitment. Approach institutions that may be interested in participating. This process may be long and tedious, until the desired number of participants is ensured for the project. Contact institutions, get their attention and explain your needs. Make sure to explain that they have the opportunity of participating in a research project for free (teachers are used to companies offering different services for the schools, and tend to refuse them immediately).
- Meeting the teachers that will participate. Normally, in a school, there are several teachers for a single subject. The meeting must be planned to involve the maximum number of teachers. Explain the requirements and schedule activities according to the needs of the institution. Also get information about the facilities of the institution, special requirements, etc.
- Refine or adapt the design of the experiment and materials to fit the needs or limitations of each institution, if necessary.
- Install the software and revise the computers in advance. We strongly recommend testing the computers and to install the game in advance as not all the institutions have maintenance plans for the computers. All software and computers must be installed and ready before the experiment takes place.
- The day of the experiment. We suggest a minimum of two researchers to carry out the experience. They should arrive ten minutes in advance. One researcher will lead the experimental group and check that the computer facilities are ready. The other researcher will lead the control group and supervise all activities conducted by teachers.
- Post-mortem activities. After the experiment, link data collected from questionnaires and data obtained from the LA system and analyze the results. Then, conduct debriefing sessions and interviews with teachers involved to get insight on their impressions about the experience and present the results obtained.

4 Designing and Implementing the Game

In this section we provide an overview of technical issues that must be considered when designing and implementing the game to ensure that (1) data collected from LA will be of interest and (2) the game is as easy to deploy as possible to meet the varying conditions and requirements of the institutions.

4.1 Designing the Game for Learning Analytics

Educational game design is a complex activity and it is not our intention to delve into all the considerations that make a game both educational and entertaining. For further reading on this matter we would recommend some of the articles that can be found in the literature [15, 16]. Instead, in this section, we elaborate on the requirements that a game design must meet to allow effective use of LA.

In short, the game must interlace mechanics oriented to facilitate building new knowledge with mechanics oriented to assess the new knowledge acquired. This behavior is frequently present in video games where players acquire new skills throughout a game level and at the end they have to apply these skills in a new way to defeat a final "boss".

We did not consider this issue when we designed The Big Party. The game was linear and students did not have to apply any new piece of knowledge acquired. We learned from this experience, and the following games were designed having two phases: one to let the student build new knowledge, one to assess. The Table 1 shows a summary with each game and how the two phases were distributed.

Table 1. Description of the learning and assessment phases

Game	Educating phase	Assessment phase
Lost in Space < XML>	Phase presenting a new power-up (representing a new syntax structure to be learned)	Phases not presenting any new power-up (players must use structures already learned)
La Dama Boba	Several text screens explaining literature concepts, mini-games about grammar and spelling	Direct questions at the end of the game, mini-games repetition. Final assessment is shown to the player
Donations	First phase, where players are guided through all the donation process, allowing them to commit mistakes and correcting them	Second phase, where players go through all the donation process, with no help and no mistakes allowed

4.2   Game Technical Requirements

The game must be implemented using a technology that can be easily deployed using the computers of the institution(s) where the experiment will be held. Having a detailed description of the settings can be used to make an informed decision on the appropriate technology. However, it is not always possible to get this information. Our recommendation is to choose a technology that is lightweight, flexible and easy to deploy across platforms (Windows, Linux and Mac). In our games, we use two technologies that meet this requirement: Java, and the Web Browser (HTML plus JavaScript).

Educational institutions may also have different hardware configurations. Especial attention must be placed on the dimension of the displays and audio support. While some institutions may have modern high definition displays, others may support low resolution applications. Similarly, some institutions may provide headsets while in others sound may be disabled. For these reasons, we use an 800×600 resolution which works well in low resolution screens and which also looks nice in larger screens. We also design the games so that they can be played with or without sound.

4.3   Tracking System Requirements

This section presents some of the technical considerations to bear in mind when deploying a videogame that communicates with a LA system.

The game must establish communication with a remote server and also univocally identify the player in a way that allows pairing data collected through all the instruments of the experiment. If a good Internet connection is available identification can be done on the server side. However, in many educational institutions Internet access is not reliable or bandwidth is insufficient. To deal with these situations, an offline alternative must be designed. For example, the game can store the information locally and the identification can be done using a code provided by the researchers. After the experiment researchers can collect the files storing tracking information and upload it manually to the LA system.

The server is in charge of receiving and storing the traces. To facilitate the analysis of the data, the server must store not only the traces but also the user id, game id, session id (continuous period of time where the user plays the game), user's group and learning activity/experience. These metadata allows the researcher to contextualize the statistical analysis of the data giving other variables to the analysis.

Depending on the size of the experiment and the data collected, the data traffic generated can be significant. Hence, it is needed to prepare the server to manage quite high workloads efficiently. The server must minimize the response time, and must use a storage system specifically optimized for writing loads of data. For that purpose, it is handy to use a NoSQL database (e.g. Apache Cassandra, Apache HBase, MongoDB, etc.) because they are particularly optimized for writing throughput. However it is possible to use a traditional relational database system, usually by mixing clustering and sharding techniques. Note that the storage system used to store the traces received by the tracking system may not be the same used to analyze the data, that is, the received data can transformed to another representation (e.g. graph, relational, etc.) and stored into another database that can facilitate the analysis of the data.

Finally, in order to minimize the response time and to avoid the collapse of the tracking system, it is usually needed to throttle the requests to the tracking system (limit the number of request per second) and limit the amount of data to be sent per request. This request throttling requires a close collaboration between the client and the server, on one hand the server can control (even dynamically) the number of allowed request per second and notifies with an especial error that the game has reached this limit or that the request cannot be currently processed, and on the other hand the client must be aware of this error conditions and resend the request after a certain amount of time.

It is desirable to have a tool to monitor the client-server communication during the experiment. This allows adapting the settings to deal with any technical issue that may prevent correct data collection. Ideally, this tool gives real time feedback on the communication and summary statistics. In our case, we had a service that showed how many students were playing and its identifiers, allowing us to visually confirm that the number of students playing were the same as the number of users that server was receiving traces for.

To help to interpret part of the collected data, it can be helpful to write notes about observations made during the experience, associated to concrete student identifiers.

For example, we observed that most high school girls carefully read screen texts, while most boys don't. Something that we confirmed after analyzing traces with the time-stamps to know the time expend in those screens that include instructions for the game.

5 Final Remarks

Probably the most important recommendation, according to our experience, is to follow a careful process to design and execute the experiment. All the aspects are important - from the design of the game to the wording of the questionnaires. To achieve success attention must be placed on all the details. Also it is important to be prepared for unexpected situations and to have a backup plan for carrying out the experiment.

References

1. Johnson, L., Adams, S., Cummins, M.: NMC Horizon Report: 2012 K-12 Edition, p. 44. The New Media Consortium, Austin (2012)
2. Hays, R.T.: The effectiveness of instructional games: a literature review and discussion. Naval Air Warfare Center, Orlando, FL (2005)
3. Johnson, L., Adams Becker, S., Cummins, M., Estrada, V., Freeman, A., Ludgate, H.: NMC Horizon Report: 2013 Higher Education Edition, Austin, Texas, USA (2013)
4. Pivec, P.: Game-based Learning or Game-based Teaching? Becta (2009)
5. Hwang, G.-J., Wu, P.-H.: Advancements and trends in digital game-based learning research: a review of publications in selected journals from 2001 to 2010. Br. J. Educ. Technol. **43**(1), E6–E10 (2012)
6. Connolly, T.M., Boyle, E.A., MacArthur, E., Hainey, T., Boyle, J.M.: A systematic literature review of empirical evidence on computer games and serious games. Comput. Educ. **59**(2), 661–686 (2012)
7. Sadler, T.D., Romine, W.L., Stuart, P.E., Merle-Johnson, D.: Game-based curricula in biology classes: differential effects among varying academic levels. J. Res. Sci. Teach. **50**, 479–499 (2013)
8. Tuzun, H., Yilmazsoylu, M., Karakus, T., Inal, Y., Kizilkaya, G.: The effects of computer games on primary school students' achievement and motivation in geography learning. Comput. Educ. **52**(1), 68–77 (2009)
9. Warren, S.J., Dondlinger, M.J., McLeod, J., Bigenho, C.: Opening the door: an evaluation of the efficacy of a problem-based learning game. Comput. Educ. **58**(1), 397–412 (2012)
10. Moreno-Ger, P., Burgos, D., Martínez-Ortiz, I., Sierra, J.L., Fernández-Manjón, B.: Educational game design for online education. Comput. Hum. Behav. **24**(6), 2530–2540 (2008)
11. Torrente, J., Del Blanco, Á., Marchiori, E.J., Moreno-Ger, P., Fernández-Manjón, B.: <e-Adventure>: introducing educational games in the learning process. In: 2010 Conference on IEEE Education Engineering (EDUCON), pp. 1121–1126 (2010)
12. Torrente, J., del Blanco, Á., Moreno-Ger, P., Fernández-Manjón, B.: Designing serious games for adult students with cognitive disabilities. In: Huang, T., Zeng, Z., Li, C., Leung, C.S. (eds.) ICONIP 2012, Part IV. LNCS, vol. 7666, pp. 603–610. Springer, Heidelberg (2012)

13. Manero, B., Fernández-Vara, C., Fernández-Manjón, B.: E-learning a Escena: De La Dama Boba a Juego Serio. IEEE-RITA **1**(1), 51–58 (2013)
14. Serrano, A., Marchiori, E.J., del Blanco, A., Torrente, J., Fernandez-Manjon, B.: A framework to improve evaluation in educational games. In: Proceedings of the 2012 IEEE Global Engineering Education Conference (EDUCON), pp. 1–8 (2012)
15. Salen, K., Zimmerman, E.: Rules of Play: Game Design Fundamentals. MIT Press, Cambridge (2003)
16. Ak, O.: A Game Scale to Evaluate Educational Computer Games. Procedia - Social Behav. Sci. **46**, 2477–2481 (2012)

Designing Games with a Purpose for Data Collection in Music Research. Emotify and Hooked: Two Case Studies

Anna Aljanaki[1](✉), Dimitrios Bountouridis[1], John Ashley Burgoyne[2],
Jan Van Balen[1], Frans Wiering[1], Henkjan Honing[2],
and Remco Veltkamp[1]

[1] Utrecht University, Princetonplein 5, 3508 TB Utrecht, The Netherlands
{A.Aljanaki,A.Bountouridis,J.M.H.VanBalen,F.Wiering,
R.C.Veltkamp}@uu.nl
[2] University of Amsterdam, Science Park 105, 1098 XG Amsterdam
The Netherlands
{J.A.Burgoyne,Honing}@uva.nl

Abstract. Collecting ground truth data for music research requires large amounts of time and money. To avoid these costs, researchers are now trying to collect information through online multiplayer games with the underlying purpose of collecting scientific data. In this paper we present two case studies of such games created for data collection in music information retrieval (MIR): Emotify, for emotional annotation of music, and Hooked, for studying musical catchiness. In addition to the basic requirement of scientific validity, both applications address essential development and design issues, for example, acquiring licensed music or employing popular social frameworks. As such, we hope that they may serve as blueprints for the development of future serious games, not only for music but also for other humanistic domains. The pilot launch of these two games showed that their models are capable of engaging participants and supporting large-scale empirical research.

1 Introduction

Music Information Retrieval, or MIR, is a fast-developing interdisciplinary scientific field that treats music with data-mining techniques. These research methods often entail the collection of large ground-truth datasets. For some tasks, such as tonality or chord labeling, musical experts are needed to perform the annotation task. For other tasks, such experts are unnecessary and sometimes even undesirable. This is the case, for instance, when annotating music with tags or emotions, or measuring music similarity, because for these tasks researchers are more interested in variation in listeners' perception in general, as opposed to the theoretically more consistent opinions of experts. This second category of tasks is well suited for crowdsourcing data collection, for instance by using serious games.

Serious games, i.e., games that have non-entertainment purposes, have found multiple applications in health-care [5], education [8], and professional training [16]. Serious games are often perceived as a type of edutainment [17], for which there can be

A. De Gloria (Ed.): GALA 2013, LNCS 8605, pp. 29–40, 2014.
DOI: 10.1007/978-3-319-12157-4_3

a diversity of goals: acquiring new skills, theoretical knowledge application in a simulation of a real world situation, or even informing oneself about a particular political situations. Serious gaming comprises all games that pursue goals other than entertainment [17]. In this paper, we will concentrate on non-educational type of serious games, which normally have the purpose of gathering data from participants as a form of crowdsourcing. These games are called 'games with a purpose' (or GWAPs). Such games are created in order to provide a framework where humans perform tasks that computers cannot (yet) solve alone. The most prominent example is, perhaps, the ESP game – a GWAP for image labeling [1]. The data collected by ESP game have been used to improve image search and image recognition algorithms. In the field of MIR there are many tasks where human-computer collaboration is necessary. In this paper we are presenting two GWAPs that were created to collect metadata for music: Emotify, for emotional annotation of music, and Hooked, for studying musical catchiness.

1.1 Motivation

There are several reasons why games with a purpose are especially suitable for data collection in the realm of music. Firstly, for many tasks involving music, the common-sense expertise that every adult music listener possesses is sufficient, regardless of whether these listeners have had formal training in music. Secondly, listening to music is pleasant and self-rewarding. Most people enjoy listening to music, and therefore it is easy to create engagement. The third reason is that sometimes it is simply infeasible to collect data in other ways. Musical tasks are usually very time-consuming and the responses are subjective, and thus music experiments require a lot of time to complete and large numbers participants to control for presence of the effect(s) in question. It is sometimes possible to hire people to do the tasks in a way that Mechanical Turk [15] does, or alternatively to involve volunteers like The Open Mind Initiative [19] did, but these strategies can be very expensive because of the time-consuming nature of the tasks in first case or face the difficulty of verifying the accuracy of the results in second case. Games with a purpose, in contrast, are designed in such a way that the winning strategy is to provide the most correct and precise result possible. It is not possible to exclude vandalism or errors entirely when dealing with human-provided data, but as designers of GWAPs, we tried to minimize the risks, and we will discuss the techniques that we employed for that below.

2   Related Work

The term and concept of 'gaming with a purpose' was first suggested by Luis von Ahn, a pioneer in the area of human-based computation games [1], who introduced the ESP game in 2004. The ESP game is a competitive two-player game, whereby people provide labels for the pictures and score points by guessing the same answer. Google purchased a license to create its own version of the game in 2006. In 2008, a similar game called TagATune was created to enable music annotation with tags [12]. TagATune was designed to produce tags that would be much less subjective than those one could obtain from social music websites like last.fm. In TagATune, a player is randomly paired with a partner, both of whom must label a short (thirty-second) musical excerpt with a series of tags. Based on their opponent's tags, players must guess whether they and their opponent have listened to the same song or not. In such a setup, tags referring to personal musical taste or subjective associations with music will naturally be avoided by players, as such tags are unlikely to provide useful information to a random opponent. MajorMiner and HerdIt! [2, 14] are similar to TagATune in design and purpose, but HerdIt! uses Facebook as a platform and supports multiplayer games.

Apart from GWAPs that collect textual annotations, some GWAPs for music have also collected other metadata, such as emotional annotations (MoodSwings) [10]. In MoodSwings, players jointly listen to the same musical fragment and provide continuous annotations by pointing with a mouse at a certain location on the screen, where the screen presents a two-dimensional representation of an emotional model.

3 Emotify: Collecting Emotion Annotations

Many MIR research areas are stimulated by music industry demand, and automatic music emotion recognition is one of them. It is easy and natural for people to organize music by emotion: witness the popularity of *stereomood.com*, a website where people collaborate to create emotion-based playlists. There is a need for technology that could automate this process. Automatic music emotion recognition relies on ground truth data, however, and there are no sizeable public datasets that could be used for training of the algorithms. The tags that can be collected from social music tagging websites, for example, lack consistency.

Moreover, there are two distinct goals for automatic music emotion recognition that need to be handled differently. The first task is automatic selection of background music: music to accompany a film or a commercial, with a requirement to express a certain emotion. Secondly, a musical piece might be selected as a means of mood regulation, for instance in music therapy settings or as a background for physical exercises. In the first case, music expresses a certain emotion; in the second case, music induces an emotion in listeners. The second case – *induced emotion* – is in the scope of our article and the game in question.

3.1 Emotify: Design Decisions

When discussing related work, we mentioned MoodSwings, a game for emotional annotation of music. MoodSwings focuses on *perceived* emotion (as opposed to *induced* emotion), which is also apparent in their choice of emotional model and their method of data collection. In our game, in contrast, we are trying to collect *induced* emotion annotations. For a game with a purpose, induced emotion creates a design problem. A standard type of player engagement in GWAPs is making players compete over giving the most standard answer possible (which is also supposed to be the correct one). In case of *induced* emotion there is no correct answer, and it would be misleading to encourage the listener to look for one. Induced musical emotion is by its nature personal and subjective.

This is why we introduced a different fun element than competition. We decided to create engagement by providing a feedback on player's answers in the manner of a psychological quiz. In addition, we decided to use a social network in order to give the player a possibility to compare his musical tastes and perception to those of his or her friends in the social network. There were three feedback elements in the game.

- **Continuous** feedback: A score calculated as a correlation of the player's answers to the averaged answers of other players. This score is recalculated after every answer and averaged over all answers.
- **Final** feedback: A histogram of the player's emotional responses for songs that player liked and for songs that the player disliked. This feedback was provided only after completing 10 songs, and thus we stimulated user to continue by promising a reward.
- **Playlist** feedback: Feedback on every song to which the player listened. Players had the possibility to listen to the whole song (not just the initial one-minute excerpt), and to see a detailed comparison to other players.

We hope that by designing such a feedback scheme, we encouraged players to give sincere and serious answers and at the same time provide a reward for their contribution.

3.2 Game Flow

We created two versions of the game: one as a Facebook application (http://apps.facebook.com/emotify/) and another as a stand-alone version (http://emotify.org/). Figure 1 shows a screenshot of the game interface. We chose to launch the game on the Facebook applications platform for several reasons. Firstly, it provides a possibility to gather background information (age group, gender, location) about the player without additional questionnaires. Secondly, it simplifies game dissemination. Thirdly, it gives the player a possibility to involve people known to the player, as it might be more interesting to be compared to a friend than it would be to people with whom one is not acquainted. Moreover, Facebook has already successfully hosted serious games, such as the Rapport Game for common-sense knowledge collection [11, 20].

The gameflow is as follows.

1. The player authenticates through Facebook (or alternatively, enters the game from the stand-alone website) and provides personal details: age, gender, musical preferences, first language, level of English, and current mood.
2. The player is randomly assigned to one of four musical genres (rock, pop, classical and electronic music) and can switch to any other if he or she so wishes. The player may also switch at any later time.
3. In every genre, the player is presented with a random sequence of musical excerpts, each one minute in length. If a player is invited by a friend through Facebook, he or

she is presented with the same sequence as the player who sent the invitation. This constraint is necessary in order to enable comparison between them.

4. After listening to the one-minute fragment, the player selects up to three emotions from a list of nine. This limitation should encourage player to think more carefully about the choices he or she makes.
5. The player also may indicate whether he or she liked or disliked the music and whether he or she knows the song. The player may also provide a new emotion definition if none of the nine correspond to what he or she is feeling.
6. At any time, it is possible to skip listening and go to another song or another genre.
7. There is a countdown from 10 to 1, saying that after 10 fragments the player will receive final feedback on his or her emotional perception of music. The countdown should encourage players to listen to at least 10 fragments to earn a "reward". Players may continue after listening to 10 fragments, but we prefer them not to do so, because understanding emotional content of music requires concentration and sensitivity, which is difficult to maintain for long periods of time.

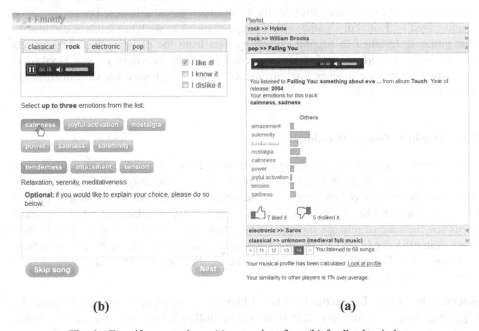

(b)   (a)

Fig. 1. Emotify screenshots: (a) game interface (b) feedback window

3.3   Discussion

Emotify was launched on the 1st of March 2013, and in the 4 months following the game launch, 1285 players played it. On average, they listened to 8 songs, and spent 13 min and 40 s playing the game ($SD = 12.62$). The actual time spent in the game differed a lot depending on the player. As we were advertising a game through online media, there were many players who merely examined the game and quit almost immediately, but there were also devoted players who spent a lot of time listening to music. Overall, the players gave positive feedback to the game and were motivated by the reward scheme the game provided.

The data collected since game launch is openly accessible[1] will be regularly updated.

4 Hooked: A Serious Game for What Makes Music Catchy

Many listeners, even those without musical training, experience the pleasant feeling of recalling a song to memory after hearing a few seconds of its "hook". Similarly, listeners are immediately able to identify whether a new song will be "catchy". Understanding hooks and catchiness is valuable not only for studying musical memory, but also for MIR tasks such as recommendation and similarity. Nonetheless, little research has been conducted on these notions, perhaps due to the fuzziness of their definition and a lack of experimental data. From a cognitive point of view, we solve the first issue by defining a hook simply to be the most salient, easiest-to-recall fragment in a piece of music [9] and catchiness as the long-term musical salience. The second issue is addressed by Hooked, a game with a purpose aimed at studying musical catchiness. Our game is designed to support collecting data from the players, similar to serious games such as Foldit [7]. However, in contrast to the previous games, Hooked is developed for mobile devices, making use of their social nature for viral distribution and discovery.

4.1 Hooked: Design Decisions

Two scientific needs drove the design of Hooked. First, we needed to be able to work with well-known music, in order to capture fragments that truly remained in the participants' memories over the long term. Secondly, because each participant has his or her own listening history, we needed to be able to support a large number of participants for the sake of reliable statistics. Three tasks are central to how we transformed these scientific needs into entertaining gameplay paradigms: recognition, verification, and prediction. We will discuss them first outside the context of the game overall, and later as a unified game experience.

Recognition Task. The recognition task plays the most important role in the game by triggering long-term memory. It is based on the following premise: the easier a music fragment to recall after a long period of time, the catchier it should be. Therefore, we devised a "game-based" – thus featuring "goals" – quiz-style game. Following the "drop-the-needle" paradigm, a piece of music starts playing from a random point in the middle while players are asked to recognize it within a fixed timeframe (e.g., $N = 10$ s). The theoretical literature on hooks suggests that hooks should coincide with the

---

[1] http://www.projects.science.uu.nl/memotion/emotifydata

beginning of major structural sections (e.g., a new verse or chorus) [3], thus in our game, the starting points for each song are limited to manageable subset. Once the music starts playing, players are given two options ("Yes" and "No") corresponding to the prompted question "Do you know this song"? While the player listens to the music, points are counting down, penalizing players who listen longer than necessary. Based on that fact, penalizing players for "taking their time" actually motivates them to act as quickly as possible whenever their long-term memory is triggered by a hook. It should be noted that choosing "No" does not affect the player's score, since we do not want to encourage guessing. Figure 2 illustrates the recognition gameplay as implemented for iOS devices.

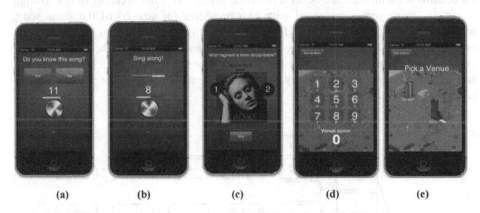

(a)   (b)   (c)   (d)   (e)

Fig. 2. Screenshots from the prototype. (a) The recognition task: a song starts from the beginning on an internal musical section, chosen at random, and the player must guess the song as quickly as possible. (b) The sound then mutes for a few seconds while the player is asked to follow along. When the sound comes back players must verify that the song is playing back from the correct place. (c) Occasionally, players instead must do the reverse: predict which of two sections is catchiest. (d) Ten recognition tasks constitute a level and groups of ten levels form a "Venue". (e) The player is asked to complete all "Venues" and their corresponding levels.

Verification Task. The recognition task by itself is only valid for controlled environments. In addition, from a gameplay perspective, such a trivial task presents no interest for the player. Therefore, we needed a complementary task to verify the correctness of the player's answer. An initial implementation made use of the typical music trivia paradigm where players are asked to identify, or select from a number of options, the artist name, title or year of release of the song in hand. However, such an approach has two major drawbacks: it introduces context and it assumes that listeners always remember these facts about songs they know. Adding context would make guessing a viable option, which makes the game easier. Knowing a song on the other hand, and therefore recalling it musically, does not imply knowing its title or composer.

Our approach is based on the observation that once a music piece has been fully recalled to memory, players should be able to follow along even after playback stopped. Therefore, as soon as the player hits "Yes" in the recognition task, the sound is muted while the song keeps playing for a fixed amount of time (e.g., $M = 3$ s). During this time, the player is asked to sing along (Fig. 2b). When the sound returns there are two possible scenarios. Sometimes, the music will continue playing from the correct place. Other times, the playback can be offset by predefined number of seconds (e.g., $D = -15$ s). The player is then asked whether the music is playing from the correct place with the following question: "Is this what should be playing now"? A correct answer rewards the player with $N - response\_time$ points, whereas an incorrect answer subtracts $N - response\_time$ points from his or her current score.

Prediction Task. Both of the aforementioned tasks were designed considering the notion of hook as a musical stimulus that eases recall. The prediction task, on the other hand, aims at capturing the listener's informal intuition of what is catchy or not. During this task, the player is presented with two fragments (of size N) of the same song, accompanied by its title, artist and album cover (Fig. 2c). The latter "metadata" are used to trigger the player's memory in case the musical stimuli fail. The player is asked to listen to both fragments and pick the one that he or she considers catchier. In the next part we describe how such a survey question can be meaningfully integrated inside the general game context.

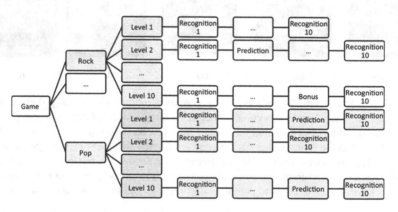

Fig. 3. The hierarchical layering of "Hooked!". The game is decomposed into "Venues", which themselves contain 10 levels each. Each level is completed after 10 recognition tasks, interrupted by prediction tasks and "bonus" rounds. Predictions appear with a chance of 20 % while "bonus" rounds with a chance of 10 %.

4.2 Hooked: Inside an Entertainment Game Context

The recognition-verification couple and the prediction tasks are independent tasks, i.e., no interaction between them occurs. Merging such data collection tasks inside a game structure was therefore challenging, especially considering that players are unaware of the underlying scientific questions they are helping to address. For them, Hooked should be consistent with the current entertainment standards offered by popular mobile games. The next paragraphs describe our gameplay design approach and the incorporation of a social element.

Hierarchical Leveling. One of currently popular mobile leveling schemes is based on the hierarchical arrangement of levels. At the top of the hierarchy, levels are grouped based on a common feature (e.g., scenery). These clusters, typically referred to as "episodes", commonly serve an underlying storyline progression. Episodes contain a fixed number of enumerated levels, which remain unavailable until all preceding levels have been successfully completed. Our game employs a similar structure. Instead of "episodes", however, we use the metaphor of "venues", which contain similar music in terms of either genre (e.g., pop or rock) or time (e.g.,'80 s or'90 s). Each "venue" contains 10 levels, and each level consists of at least 10 recognition tasks. A level is complete if more than 6 recognition answers are correct. In order to increase difficulty as the player progresses, we prompt the player with older and less popular music at each new level. The corresponding features, release date and popularity (the so-called "hotness" feature) are available from the Echo Nest service [6].

Bonus Rounds. As we previously mentioned, prediction tasks act as survey questions outside the game context. Incorporating them meaningfully was solved with "bonus" levels. Recognition tasks can be interrupted by prediction tasks. Each time a player completes a prediction task, the chosen fragment is stored in a special pool. The recognition task enters a bonus round periodically (unless the fragment pool is empty) for double points. The prompted fragment is randomly selected from the pool. Therefore, if the player picks the catchiest fragment in the prediction task, he or she will have higher chances to recall the song in the "bonus" level. Consequently, the player is motivated to perform the prediction task thoroughly. Figure 3 illustrates the hierarchical layering of Hooked, including predictions tasks and bonus rounds.

Wildcards. Wildcards are a common scheme for increasing a depth of the gameplay and keeping players motivated. Our game rewards players with wildcards after "combo" recognition tasks (e.g., 5 correct recognitions in a row). Wildcards can be used during later recognition rounds for revealing the album cover of the prompted song, decreasing the mute time M, multiplying the gained points by a factor, and other strategies to help score more points.

Social Elements. Interaction between players, centered on the social nature of the mobile phone, has generated much interest among game designers in the past years. Due to the scientific purposes of our games, incorporating a social element aims at viral distribution and discovery, thereby attracting a large number of players and statistically useful scientific data. Two frameworks were investigated: Facebook Games and Apple's Game Center. The first offers a convenient protocol for invites and social bragging on the news feed (e.g., "Check out my score on Hooked!"). The second offers a more direct interaction between players, such as turn-based and real-time matches, in addition to common leaderboards. As such, our current implementation employs Game Center to increase the game's depth and sophistication.

Hooked uses leaderboards and achievements as the primary step of social inter-action. Players with a high score appear on the common leaderboard of the Game Center platform. Achievements are rewards for completing certain tasks and appear on player's Game Center profile. The most challenging interactions, however, are turn-based matches. Players can invite each other to a game of recognition tasks in a turn-based fashion. Our game allows challenges of up to two players. Each player must complete a recognition task before passing his turn to the other player. The prompted song for both players is the same, to ensure fairness. At the end of ten recognition tasks, the player with the higher score is announced to be the winner.

5   Hooked and Emotify: Musical Material and Game Settings

One of the most challenging tasks for serious musical games is acquiring a large set of licensed music data. Emotify and Hooked solve this problem in different ways. For Hooked, we needed music that would be widely recognizable for the majority of players; for Emotify, well-known music was, to the contrary, undesirable.

In order to avoid licensing problems, Hooked uses Spotify's iOS library, which offers a catalogue of around 20 million tracks [18]. In addition to its increased popularity and high audio streaming speeds, Spotify is partnered with Echo Nest such that the Echo Nest Analyzer can be applied conveniently to any item in the Spotify corpus. We use this link to obtain estimates of the start times of the major structural sections, year of release, and "hotness" for each song. Therefore, the Spotify–Echo Nest coupling presents a unique combination of vast and well-documented music data, proving to be an excellent choice for the back end of serious musical games.

As the main component serving our scientific purposes, the recognition task should be parameterized to separate catchy sections from the rest. Therefore the choice of mute time M, maximum recognition time N and offset D were of great importance. A pilot version, comprising of 32 songs and 20 participants, was run during the months May–June 2013 for that purpose. The configuration $M = 3$, $N = 10$ and $D = -15$ yielded the most statistically significant recognition time differences between sections [4].

In case of Emotify, the main purpose of the game is to collect induced emotion annotations. For musical perception, familiarity of the music has certain consequences, as associations with the music already known to listener might create an undesirable additional emotional response. This is why we decided to make use of relatively little-known music by the recording label Magnatune [13]. This label releases music under Creative Commons licenses, which permits free use of its music for non-commercial purposes.

6   Discussion

In this article, we presented two musical games with a purpose: Emotify and Hooked. While Emotify has already been launched, Hooked is still in the pilot stage. Discussing the data collected by the games and scientific value of this data is out of the scope of this article; for more information on these questions, we refer readers to [4]. The games that we presented are serious games created for the purpose of data collection, or GWAPs, but in contrast with other GWAPs, they do not force players to compete to guess the correct answer. Emotify rewards players by giving feedback on their own input and comparing their answers to other players' input; Hooked stimulates players by awarding points for the correct answers. Hooked collects data in an indirect way by measuring players reaction time, whereas Emotify's data come from direct self-assessment. Furthermore, Emotify and Hooked use two distinct musical corpora and two different distribution channels: web-browsers and mobile devices.

Emotify uses social networks as a platform. We faced some limitations, however, when using the Facebook application platform. The Emotify game tried to use invitations to involve new players into the game, but the acceptance rate of the invitations was very low: of the invitations sent by players of Emotify, only 6 % were accepted. Moreover, people were reluctant to use the Facebook version of the game. After running the pilot of the game on Facebook, we launched an independent website for hosting the game, and both the Facebook version and the independent website were advertised together. Having a choice, more than 90 % of the players preferred to use the independent website. Hooked, on the other hand, uses mobile devices, a familiar platform with its own interaction patterns. As a consequence, users sometimes attempted to employ typical tactile gestures (e.g., pans or swipes) on the game elements. This resulted in some initial confusion, but with a few minutes of experience, the overall gameplay impression was clearly positive. All the participants in the pilot found the game rather addictive and fun. It should be noted that most participants showed rapid learning rate, meaning that their responses times were gradually decreasing as the game became more familiar to them.

7 Conclusion

We presented two case studies of serious musical games with a purpose. Data gathering inside a gameplay context has been addressed by two separate paradigms, each one employing a unique approach for transforming scientific needs into valid game practices. Two social interaction models have also been investigated: an invitation-based Facebook model and a competitive, turn-based match model. Preliminary investigations showed that data collected by the means of these GWAPs is of sufficiently high quality to support academic research [4].

Emotify and Hooked offer valuable insights regarding musical games and help to answer questions about music material acquisition, approaching player-participants, viral distribution, and more. In particular, they illustrate the importance of thinking outside the social-media box – an enormous proportion of players preferred *not* to integrate their serious gaming with social media – and the importance of including a modular and regular reward structure even for tasks like music that players normally enjoy. The approach described in this paper could also be used to build non-musical serious games.

References

1. von Ahn, L., Dabbish, L.: Labeling images with a computer game. In: Proceedings of the SIGCHI Conference on Human Factors in Computing Systems, New York, NY, USA, pp. 319–326 (2004)
2. Barrington, L., O'Malley, D., Turnbull, D., Lanckriet, G.: User-centered design of a social game to tag music. In: Proceedings of the ACM SIGKDD Workshop on Human Computation, New York, NY, USA, 7–10 (2009)

3. Burns, G.: A typology of 'hooks' in popular records. Popular Music **6**(1), 1–20 (1987)
4. Burgoyne, J.A., Bountouridis, D., Van Balen, J., Honing, H.: A game for discovering what makes music catchy. In: Proceedings of the 14th International Conference on Music Information Retrieval, Curitiba, Brazil (2013)
5. Deponti, D., Maggiorini, D., Palazzi, C.E.: DroidGlove: an android-based application for wrist rehabilitation. In: International Conference on Ultra Modern Telecommunications Workshops, pp. 1–7 (2009)
6. EchoNest. http://echonest.com/
7. Foldit. http://fold.it/portal/
8. Gaggi, O., Galiazzo, G., Palazzi, C., Facoetti, A., Franceschini, S.: A serious game for predicting the risk of developmental dyslexia in pre-readers children. In: 21st International Conference on Computer Communications and Networks (ICCCN), pp. 1–5 (2012)
9. Honing, H.J.: Lure(d) into listening: the potential of cognition-based music information retrieval. Empir. Musicol. Rev. **5**(4), 121–126 (2010)
10. Kim, Y., Schmidt, E., Emelle, L.: MoodSwings: a collaborative game for music mood label collection. In: Proceedings of the 9th International Conference on Music Information Retrieval, Philadelphia, PA, USA, pp. 231–236 (2008)
11. Kuo, Y., Lee, J.C., Chiang, K., Wang, R., Shen, E., Chan, C., Hsu, J.: Community-based game design: experiments on social games for commonsense data collection. In: Proceedings of the ACM SIGKDD Workshop on Human Computation, Paris, France, pp. 15–25 (2009)
12. Law, E.L.M., von Ahn, L., Dannenberg, R.B., Crawford, M.: TagATune: a game for music and sound annotation. In: Proceedings of the 8th International Conference on Music Information Retrieval, pp. 361–364 (2007)
13. Magnatune. http://magnatune.com/
14. Mandel, M., Ellis, D.: A web-based game for collecting music metadata. J. New Music Res. **37**(2), 151–165 (2008)
15. Mechanical Turk. https://www.mturk.com/mturk/
16. Microsoft Flight Simulator. http://www.microsoft.com/games/fsinsider/
17. Ratan, R., Ritterfeld, U.: Classifying serious games. In: Ritterfeld, U., Cody, M., Vorderer, P. (eds.) Serious Games: Mechanisms and Effects, pp. 10–24. Routledge, New York (2009)
18. Spotify. http://spotify.com
19. Stork, D.G.: The open mind initiative. IEEE Intell. Syst. Appl. **14**(3), 19–20 (1999)
20. Taktamysheva, A., Krause, M., Smeddinck, J.: Serious questionnaires in playful social network applications. In: Anacleto, J.C., Fels, S., Graham, N., Kapralos, B., Saif El-Nasr, M., Stanley, K. (eds.) ICEC 2011. LNCS, vol. 6972, pp. 436–439. Springer, Heidelberg (2011)

Learning Analytics in Serious Gaming: Uncovering the Hidden Treasury of Game Log Files

Wim Westera[✉], Rob Nadolski, and Hans Hummel

Open University of the Netherlands, Valkenburgerweg 177,
6419 AT Heerlen, The Netherlands
{wim.westera, rob.nadolski, hans.hummel}@ou.nl

Abstract. This paper presents an exploratory analysis of existing log files of the VIBOA environmental policy games at Utrecht University. For reasons of statistical power we have combined student cohorts 2008, 2009, 2010, and 2011, which led to a sample size of 118 students. The VIBOA games are inquiry-based games, which offer a lot of freedom of movement. Our premise is that this freedom of movement is accompanied by behavioural variability across individuals, which may influence the efficiency of learning. Descriptive statistics of our sample revealed such variability of diverse game parameters. We have identified "switching behaviour", defined as the number of game objects (videos, resources, locations) accessed per unit time, as a relevant behavioural pattern. Multiple regression analysis showed that switching rates of videos and locations explain 54 % of the variance of learning efficiency (defined as final score per unit time). Both the model and the model coefficients were significant beyond the 0.001 level. The same switching variables also account for 45 % of the variance of total time spent. Predictive models of final score weren't found. We conclude the paper by critically evaluating our findings, making explicit the limitations of our study and making suggestions for future research that links learning analytics and serious gaming.

1 Introduction

Serious games are outstanding examples of adaptive systems as they continuously adjust their responses to the learners' actions for preserving favourable game play. Although many serious games retain somewhat of the user's history in log files, the actual use of logging data is quite limited. Adaptive game responses seldom build on the user's history of consecutive actions, but instead tend to use a static set of criteria, very similar to a simple checklist. Similarly the assessment of learning progress is based on closures and performance milestones. From a game developer's perspective this situation is understandable, since the only relevant thing would be to check whether the player achieves sufficient performance milestones within the constraints of the game rules. However, from an educator's perspective, if not a research perspective, the players' logging history could be beneficial for building detailed user models, analysing the process of learning or tracing bottlenecks in game play. For preserving the efficiency of learning it is highly relevant to gain insights in the activities and

© Springer International Publishing Switzerland 2014
A. De Gloria (Ed.): GALA 2013, LNCS 8605, pp. 41–52, 2014.
DOI: 10.1007/978-3-319-12157-4_4

behaviours needed for the player to reach these performance milestones: e.g. did the learner achieve the milestone in an efficient and well-considered way, or was it a thoughtless trial and error style that took a lot of time without achieving any learning gains? Various authors [1, 2] explain the difference between a performance orientation and a learning orientation: while game play tends to focus on performance, which is linked with an attitude of achieving milestones and score (in many cases under time constraints), learning requires opportunities for reflection, repetition, self-evaluation, pauses, and even the preparedness to make mistakes. Hence, the process of gaming may readily counteract the process of learning. Having completed a serious game successfully doesn't necessarily imply successful learning. This uncertainty about the effectiveness of learning will be larger as games offer more freedom of movement to the learners. In well-structured drill and practice games, e.g. in arithmetic, learning gains are likely to coincide with performance gains. In recent years, however, serious games have been based more and more on open approaches associated with contextualized problem solving, adventure games, inquiry-based learning and competence learning. These approaches all offer large degrees of freedom and heavily rely on self-directed learning, self-regulation and other 21st century skills relevant for today's knowledge workers [3, 4]. In such contexts the freedom of movement is likely to display more behavioural variability across different individuals. So far, however, very little is known about the actual in-game behaviours of learners and how these behaviours relate to learning achievements. Game logging data are a treasury of information, which could be exploited for distilling more details about the players' learning achievements based on their wanderings and trajectories through the network of game state nodes.

This paper provides an exploratory study of existing log files of serious games that were used by 118 master students in environmental sciences students at Utrecht University. For practical reasons the study is constrained to a retrospect study: the logging files date back to 2008–2011. Our aim is to explore to what extent the logging data of these particular games would be helpful to reveal meaningful patterns, variables and relationships. We will first briefly explain the emerging research field of learning analytics and connect this with new developments of user tracking in serious games. We will describe our serious games and their context of use. Next we will describe the type of logging data that are available and explain what primary variables will be used for the analysis. Finally the results are presented and critically evaluated.

2   Learning Analytics

Analysing learner log data is closely related to the wider framework of learning analytics, which is generally defined as using the ever-growing amounts of data about learners' activities and interests for improving learning outcomes [5]. A related term is educational data mining [6]. While the focus of educational data mining is on methods for extracting the data, learning analytics concerns the development and application of predictive models in instructional systems [7]. Although student metrics have been used for decades to improve student throughputs and education workflows, in recent years datasets have grown larger and have become more easily accessible because of the use of Learning Management Systems such as Moodle and Blackboard for the online delivery of learning content. Many of these tools include student tracking functions that automatically log and aggregate student activity data as well as user profile data, access statistics and test results. At an institutional level a best practice is provided by the Signals project at Purdue University, which demonstrates how educational data mining and predictive modelling can be used for obtaining higher grades and retention rates than were observed in control groups [8, 9]. New developments such as open educational resources and MOOCS [10] will yield big sets of learner data and support their analysis. Although learning analytics is generally qualified as an opportunity for improving the quality and effectiveness of learning, important concerns are raised because analytics could severely disempower and demotivate learners when they are provided with continuous feedback about their knowledge and performance gaps as compared with other students [11]. Also the capturing of unstructured personal traces across different platforms, social networks and contexts goes with some principle barriers linked with privacy protection and other legal issues [5].

3 Serious Gaming and Logging

As Gee [12] pointed out many video games are based on the growth of the players' mastery of knowledge and skills, and therefore incorporate tracking methods that allow for continuous adaptation of difficulty levels, hints and challenges to their achievements and progress. Some games provide learner support services based on playing behaviour, e.g. scaffolding, hinting, micro-feedback, meta-level feedback [13, 14]. Social gaming companies, such as Zynga, use player tracking for predicting what users want and will do next in a game to find out how to make games more fun and get users more engaged [7]. In most serious games, however, the logging is mainly used for triggering events and new episodes in the game flow and game narrative, but is seldom used for the accommodation of user modelling and personalised learning. Although user tracking is a predominant and well-exploited mechanism for adaptive gameplay, the player's full history of states is greatly underused, because most games reflect a discrete time Markov chain, which assigns only a limited role to state history and process memory. Serrano-Laguna et al. [15] notice that logging data in games are highly underexploited. They suggest that logging of interactions in a game could in principle be used for automated assessment as an alternative for intermediate tests or questionnaires, which are often perceived as unwanted interruptions of game play. A comprehensive approach for in-game assessment was given by Shute et al. [16], which entails the combination of Evidence-Centered Assessment [17] and Bayesian score models [18]. Its ingredients include a competency model, a learner model, an evidence model (providing clues for evidence) and a task model. Reese and colleagues [19] report about the CyGaMEs project, which quantifies game play activity to track timed progress toward the game's goal and uses this progress as a measure of player learning. Westera et al. [4] point at using game logging data for strategic feedback rather than tactic or micro-level feedback, in order to nourish the learners' self-directedness, self-evaluation and reflection.

4   Serious Gaming Context: Environmental Policy Games for a Master of Science Degree

Our analysis focuses on a series of 5 online serious games in the domain of environmental sciences that were jointly developed by the Open University of the Netherlands, Utrecht University, and Radboud University Nijmegen. The games are implemented on the EMERGO game engine (www.emergo.cc) and linked together in a single game run that takes about 50 hours of study. Students preparing for their Master of Science degree adopt the role of an environmental consultancy trainee at the (fictitious) VIBOA consultancy agency. In this role they are confronted with authentic environmental policy problem cases (1. Wadden Sea, 2. Wind energy, 3. Lake Naarden, 4. Micro pollution, 5. River management). Guided by inquiry-based gaming scenarios the students individually have to make a thorough analysis of the problems by consulting various stakeholders (video-based interviews with experts) and by collecting and combining relevant information from reports, scientific papers, texts of law, formal documents and other sources. They have to apply scientific methodologies and theories, and finally deliver a report for proposing well-substantiated policy measures. The game narrative and feedback is closely linked with the work conditions at the environmental consultancy office. In Fig. 1 a screenshot of the online game shows a scene from a (videotaped) meeting at the VIBOA environmental consultancy office.

The games include 4 pre-tests which are used for self-testing of prior knowledge before entering a game. Each of the games offers large degrees of freedom to the students as to what approach to develop, who to interview, or what sources to use. Occasionally, incoming notifications or (pseudo) email messages provide new information, announce new events, provide hints or prompt for certain actions. The first game is an introductory game. The examination is based on the students' reports about games 2, 3, 4 and 5.

Fig. 1. Screenshot of the VIBOA environmental consultancy game

We've retrieved logging data of student cohorts from Utrecht University. For reasons of statistical power we have combined cohorts of 2008, 2009, 2010, and 2011, all playing the games under the same internal and external conditions (e.g. preparation, time frames, intermediate assessments, examinations). After exclusion of students who failed to obtain a final score (e.g. dropouts), we ended up with a sample of 118 students (46 % male, 54 % female) including 7 people who failed in one year but re-enrolled in the subsequent year.

5 Logging Data and Principle Variables

The observations that we will be able to make are constrained by the type of logging data that we have available. The EMERGO educational game engine is an open source web-based game authoring and run-time delivery environment composed of diverse functional components. These components are linked together by the game logic. Since each component has its own separate logging system, we have implemented a logging aggregator, which integrates the distributed data into a joint logging file. The logging file records all meaningful student actions such as visiting a location, opening an information resource (document, URL, picture, graph, etc.), accessing a video, asking a video-interview question, accessing a pre-test, answering a pre-test question and some more. Also system responses are recorded. All actions go with a timestamp. Figure 2 displays a specimen of the aggregated log file.

name	time	component	tag	id	key	value	system/user	userdata	data
Student XXX	21436	script Windenergie	timer	TI_Start Deeltoets 2	finished	true	system	none	none
Student XXX	21439	gesprekken	map	theoretisch kader en onderzoekmethode	outfolded	true	user	none	none
Student XXX	21454	gesprekken	question	Vanuit welk theoretisch perspectief op belei opened	true	user	none	none
Student XXX	21454	gesprekken	question	Vanuit welk theoretisch perspectief op belei outfoldable	true	system	none	none
Student XXX	21454	gesprekken	question	Vanuit welk theoretisch perspectief op belei selected	true	user	none	none
Student XXX	21454	gesprekken	fragment	OGB-WND-SAG-INT-006	opened	true	system	none	OGB-WND-SAG-INT-006.flv
Student XXX	21457	script Windenergie	timer	TI_Start Deeltoets 2	finished	true	system	none	none
Student XXX	21463	gesprekken	question	Welke methoden of modellen heb je in dit o opened	true	user	none	none
Student XXX	21463	gesprekken	question	Welke methoden of modellen heb je in dit o outfoldable	true	system	none	none
Student XXX	21463	gesprekken	question	Welke methoden of modellen heb je in dit o selected	true	user	none	none
Student XXX	21472	gesprekken	question	Was de toepassing van de methoden en mod opened	true	user	none	none
Student XXX	21472	gesprekken	question	Was de toepassing van de methoden en mod outfoldable	true	system	none	none
Student XXX	21472	gesprekken	question	Was de toepassing van de methoden en mod selected	true	user	none	none
Student XXX	21472	gesprekken	fragment	OGB-WND-SAG-INT-009	opened	true	system	none	OGB-WND-SAG-INT-009.flv
Student XXX	21475	gesprekken	question	Heb je zelf een nieuwe methode of methodi opened	true	user	none	none
Student XXX	21475	gesprekken	question	Heb je zelf een nieuwe methode of methodi outfoldable	true	system	none	none
Student XXX	21475	gesprekken	question	Heb je zelf een nieuwe methode of methodi selected	true	user	none	none
Student XXX	21475	gesprekken	fragment	OGB-WND-SAG-INT-010	opened	true	system	none	OGB-WND-SAG-INT-010.flv
Student XXX	21478	gesprekken	component	component	opened	false	system/user	none	none
Student XXX	21478	gesprekken	conversation	WND INTERVIEW SUSANNE AGTERBOSCH	opened	false	system/user	none	none
Student XXX	21478	gesprekken	conversation	WND INTERVIEW SUSANNE AGTERBOSCH	finished	true	user	none	none
Student XXX	21478	locaties NIEUW	location	LOC-Terug naar Hal	accessible	true	system	none	none
Student XXX	21478	script Windenergie	condition	IF_OGB-WND-SAG-interview_AFGEROND	opened	true	system	none	none
Student XXX	21478	script Windenergie	action	THEN_LOC Terug naar Hal_TOEGANKELIJK	opened	true	system	none	none

Fig. 2. Specimen of the aggregated log file

A brief explanation of the log file: the "time" column displays the timestamps expressed in seconds, the "component" column refers to the EMERGO software component involved, the "id" column refers to a specific authored game content object that is addressed, "key" and "value" represent the action exerted, the "system/user" column refers to the actor (either the user or the system, or both). For instance, at time 21454 the user selects a question to ask to an expert, whereupon the system responds by playing the Flash video file OGB-WAD-SAG-INT-006.flv, which contains the recorded answer of the expert.

From the logging data we were able to derive descriptive statistics (e.g. means, standard deviations, variances) of a wide range of variables. For this first explorative study we have confined ourselves to a basic set of variables that are retrievable for each student with simple queries:

T Total time spend
N_L Number of locations (re-)visited
N_R Number of information resources accessed
N_V Number of videos accessed
N_P Number of pre-test answers given, including improvements
S_P Pre-test score (initial answers only)
S_F Final assessment score assigned by the examiner on the basis of submitted reports.

Locations are spaces in the game environment, for instance "rooms" where the players may find specific information or where they may talk to an expert (video interviews). Resources include relevant papers, reports, letters or other documents, URLs, graphs etcetera that are made available in the game. Videos can be any recorded file including expert interviews, instructional videos, archived TV-programs or documentaries. The pre-test scores S_P are based on the initial answers of the students to the pre-test items (40 items in total). Since students were allowed to change their answers, we used their initial answers to obtain a metric of prior knowledge. The final assessment scores S_F are the only data not derived from the logging, but they are assigned by the examiner on the basis of the reports the final report about the respective games.

In view of the inquiry-based gaming environment and the freedom of moment for students we focused our study on the following research questions:

- To what extent can we identify different gaming behaviours?
- To what extent can behavioural characteristics be predictors of the final assessment scores?
- To what extent can pre-test scores be predictors of final assessment scores?

6 Results

We used MS-Excel for filtering the log files of 118 students (up to 700,000 records) and used SPSS for statistical processing. Few outliers were traced (in all cases at most two outliers with z-score >3), which were kept in the sample.

6.1 To What Extent Can We Identify Different Gaming Behaviours?

In Table 1 some of the key figures of the logging analysis are summarized.

Table 1. Descriptive statistics of the logging data

	Average per student	Standard deviation	Coefficient of variation
Total time T	53.8 h	24.6 h	0.44
Pre-test score S_P	6.6	1.2	0.18
Final score S_F	6.6	1.5	0.24
Resources accessed N_R	180	96	0.54
Videos accessed N_V	120	42	0.35
Locations accessed N_L	156	61	0.39
Pre-test answers N_P	65	42	0.65

Total time required for the 5 games is about 54 h. The standard deviation of 24 h indicates considerable spread among students. Similar large spreads are observed in the amounts of accessed resources, videos, locations and pre-test answers, indicating substantial variability of playing behaviours. Note that the games provide access to a limited set of resources (89), videos (100), locations (23) and pre-test questions (40). So, many of these are revisited. Some locations re-occur in all games and have to be re-opened in each game. It should be noted that the pre-tests and the final test are not equivalent: the pre-tests are a simple check of basic knowledge required for entering the games, while the final test covers all contents covered by the games.

For analysing the coherence of variability across different behavioural indicators we calculated correlations between the access numbers N_R, N_V and N_L. We omitted pre-test questions N_P because the pre-tests are preceding the actual game play. Table 2 shows the results.

Table 2. Correlations of accessed resources, locations and videos

Variables		Correlation r	p-value
Accessed resources N_R	Accessed locations N_L	.489	<.001
Accessed resources N_R	Accessed videos N_V	.447	<.001
Accessed videos N_V	Accessed locations N_L	.351	<.001
Access rates resources N_R/T	Access rates locations N_L/T	.500	<.001
Access rates resources N_R/T	Access rates videos N_V/T	.484	<.001
Access rates videos N_V/T	Access rates locations N_L/T	.576	<.001

We found moderate correlations of $r_{R,L} = .489$, $r_{R,V} = .447$ and $r_{V,L} = .351$ all at a significance level of $p < 0.001$. In view of the variance of total time T we replaced the access numbers N_R, N_V and N_L with the access rates N_R/T, N_V/T and N_L/T, respectively. Here we found slightly higher correlations of $r_{R/T,L/T} = .500$, $r_{R/T,V/T} = .484$ and $r_{V/T,L/T} = .576$, all of which are likewise highly significant ($p < 0.001$). It demonstrates that all variables point at the same direction, be it that the variability of one rate variable explains between about 23 % and 33 % (r-squared) of the variability of another rate variable. This signals some behavioural consistency between the access rates of resources, videos and locations. Both the correlation and the variance identify the students' "switching" behaviours as a likely behavioural trait.

6.2   To What Extent can Behavioural Characteristics Be Predictors of the Final Assessment Scores?

Given the observed variability of "switching" behaviours we have looked into predictive regression models that use the switching rates N_R/T, N_V/T and N_L/T as predictors of learning gains. Regarding these time-based activity rates we expressed the learning gains as scores per unit time S_F/T (this represents the efficiency of learning). Table 3 shows the results of the multiple regression analysis (hierarchical forced entry).

Table 3. Hierarchical regression analysis of learning efficiency and switching behaviours

Model	Video switching rates N_V/T included	Location switching rates N_L/T included	Resources switching rates N_R/T included	R^2	p-value
Learning efficiency S_F/T	yes	no	no	.430	<.001
Learning efficiency S_F/T	yes	yes	no	.540	<.001
Learning efficiency S_F/T	yes	yes	yes	.545	<.001

We found that the overall model has an explanatory power of $R^2 = .545$ ($F(3,114) = 45.6$, $p < 0.001$) which means that more than half of the variability of scores can be explained by the variability of switching behaviours. In the model hierarchy the adjusted R^2 increased from 0.430 (videos only: $F(1,116) = 87.5$, $p < 0.001$) to 0.540 (videos and locations: $F(2, 115) = 27.5$, $p < 0.001$) and 0.545 (videos, locations and resources: $F(3,114) = 1.3$, $p < 0.249$). It follows that only videos and locations contribute significantly to the model. Regression coefficients in the reduced model are $b_1 = 0.037$ ($t(117) = 5.5$, $p < 0.001$) for the video rate and $b_2 = 0.022$ ($t(117) = 5.2$, $p < 0.001$) for the location rate. It means that switching behaviour as based on video access rates and location access rates is a predictor (54 %) of learning efficiency.

High learning efficiency, however, isn't equivalent with high final score, because the latter may also depend on total time spent. To what extent is switching behaviour a predictor of total time spent? Do fast switchers study faster? Multiple regression analysis with switching behaviours N_V/T and N_L/T as predictors for total time T produce a significant model with $R^2 = 0.445$ ($F(2,115) = 46.0$, $p < 0.001$) and standardized coefficients $b_1 = -0.431$ ($t(117) = -5.1$, $p < 0.001$) and $b = -0.318$ ($t(117) = -3.7$, $p < 0.001$). This suggests that the variance of switching behaviours can account for 45 % of the variance of total time spent. The negative signs of the regression coefficients indicate that high switching rates correspond with low T.

Unfortunately, a combined model of using switching behaviours and total time spent T for predicting final scores S_F failed to produce meaningful outcomes. This is consistent with the very weak correlation that we've observed between scores S_F and total time spent T ($r = 0.182$, $p = 0.049$). Apparently other factors are predominant in final scores.

6.3 To What Extent Is Prior Knowledge a Predictor of Final Assessment Scores?

Having low levels of prior knowledge means that a learner has to make more efforts for achieving the same learning outcome. Alternatively, making the same learning effort as learners with sufficient prior knowledge would procure lower final scores. This line of reasoning suggests a model with pre-test score and total time as predictors of final score. Also the learning would be proportional with learning efficiency. As has been explained above learning efficiency is partly predicted by switching behaviours. Regressions with the current dataset, however failed to confirm a combined model of switching and pre-test score to predict final score. Also, simplified models using fewer predictors failed to produce meaningful outcomes. We've also used the number of answers N_P given in the pre-tests, which is possibly an indicator of ignorance or trial and error behaviour, as a predictor. But N_P didn't contribute significantly to the regression statistics.

7 Discussion and Conclusion

In this study we analysed existing logging files of the VIBOA environmental policy games at Utrecht University. The freedom of movement that these inquiry-based learning games offer seems to be accompanied by substantial behavioural variability across different individuals. Descriptive statistics of our sample of 118 subjects revealed such variability of the number of accessed locations N_L, the number of accessed videos N_V, the number of accessed resources N_R, the number of pre-test answers N_P given, and the time T spent to the games. On average the game's (written) resources are opened twice, while videos tend to be opened only once. An explanation might be in the very modality of the objects: written resources are randomly accessible, while video has a temporal nature. It takes time to review a video, while a written resource could be re-accessed easily for looking up things. A technical issue may even have concealed the true rate of resource consultation, because in contrast with videos and locations all resources automatically open in a new browser window, which can be re-consulted by the player without making the game engine aware of this (therefore we didn't make extensive use of the resource variable N_R in our analyses). We found moderate but significant cross-correlations of N_R, N_V and N_L and even higher values between the access rates N_R/T, N_V/T and N_L/T, respectively, suggesting the relevance of a behavioural trait that could be identified as "switching behaviour". Multiple regression analysis showed that a model which uses video access rates N_V/T and location access rates N_L/T as predictors explains 54% of the variance of learning efficiency. Both the model and the model coefficients were significant beyond the

0.001 level. The sample size of 118 subjects is well above the minimum requirements according to Greens [20] rules of thumb (50 + 8 k, and 104 + k with k the number of predictors), which strengthens the reliability of the outcome. We also were able to produce a reliable and significant model of switching behaviours $N_{V/T}$ and $N_{L/T}$ predicting total time T. The silent but reasonable assumption here is that the dependent variable T is not necessarily required for determining the switching rates. So the switching rates are supposedly inherent individual traits that can be determined independently from total time T. Alternatively, the model can be transformed to use T square as the dependent variable by multiplying both hands of the model with T. Our efforts to establish a predictive model for final score failed. We found only a very weak correlation between scores and time. Also we weren't capable of demonstrating any relationships between the pre-test results and the final scores.

In view of the statement that there are "lies, damned lies and statistics", which is generally attributed to former British Prime Minister Benjamin Disraeli, we need to critically evaluate the significance of our findings. First of all this study is handicapped by having only log data and final scores available, while additional background profiles of students fail. Also, we had to do without tailored pre-tests and post-tests, questionnaires, direct observations, and a randomised trial with experimental groups and a control group. Second, our starting point of associating the learners' increased freedom of movement with increased behavioural variability may be valid as such, but what is actually meant with freedom of movement and how it is expressed both in a qualitative and quantitative way is open to debate. Third, while we were able to identify switching behaviour as a relevant explanatory factor, we didn't provide an appropriate interpretation and theoretical foundation of this variable and a connection to cognitive states. Switching behaviour could be conceived as either a positive trait reflecting focused attention and efficient behaviours or a negative trait associated with impatience, superficiality or disorientation. As can be derived from Table 1 the average switching rates are typically 10 items per hour and are nothing like the frequent clicking that is common in social media and entertainment games. Fourth, the generalisation of the findings in this study is not straightforward because (naturally) all data are inherently tied to the specific game contents, game design and group of users. A different game play using different resources, videos, locations or any other game object will inevitably produce different effects and relationships.

A disclaimer putting these comments in perspective is that the purpose of our study was to explore to what extent the logging data of these particular games would be helpful to reveal meaningful patterns, variables and relationships. Even without the opportunity of collecting additional user information (e.g. profiles, appreciations, attitudes) or assigning different user groups to different conditions we have demonstrated the rich potential of game logging data and brought some relevant phenomena to the surface. Next steps in research call for developing and validating metrics for expressing game conditions such as freedom of movement, and use patterns such as switching behaviour, and make theoretical foundations for these in order to allow for empirical research and generalisation of findings. Exactly serious gaming could become an exemplary case of exploiting learning analytics.

References

1. VandeWalle, D., Brown, S.P., Cron, W.L., Slocum, L.W.: The influence of goal orientation and self-regulation tactics on sales performance: a longitudinal field test. J. Appl. Psychol. **84**, 249–259 (1999)
2. Fisher, S.L., Ford, J.K.: Differential effects of learner effort and goal orientation on two learning outcomes. Pers. Psychol. **51**, 397–420 (1998)
3. Redecker, C., Punie, Y., Ferrari, A.: eAssessment for 21st century learning and skills. In: Ravenscroft, A., Lindstaedt, S., Kloos, C.D., Hernández-Leo, D. (eds.) EC-TEL 2012. LNCS, vol. 7563, pp. 292–305. Springer, Heidelberg (2012)
4. Westera, W., Nadolski, R., Hummel, H., Wopereis, I.: Serious games for higher education: a framework for reducing design complexity. J. Comput. Assist. Learn. **24**(5), 20–432 (2008)
5. Shum, S.B., Ferguson, R.: Social learning analytics. Educ. Tech. Soc. **15**(3), 3–26 (2012)
6. Baker, R.S.J.D., Yacef, K.: The state of educational data mining in 2009: a review and future visions. J. Educ. Data Min. **1**(1), 3–17 (2009)
7. Bienkowski, M., Feng, M., Means, B.: Enhancing teaching and learning through educational data mining and learning analytics: an issue brief. SRI international U.S. Department of Education, Office of Educational Technology, Washington (2012). http://www.ed.gov/edblogs/technology/files/2012/03/edm-la-brief.pdf
8. Arnold, K.E.: Signals: applying academic analytics. Educause Q. **33**(1), 10–15 (2010). http://www.educause.edu/ero/article/signals-applying-academic-analytics
9. Pistilli, M., Arnold, K.: Course signals at Purdue: using learning analytics to increase student success. In: 2nd International Conference on Learning Analytics and Knowledge. Vancouver (2012)
10. Long, P.D., Siemens, G.: Penetrating the fog: analytics in learning and education. Educause Rev. **46**(5), 31–40 (2011). http://www.educause.edu/ero/article/penetrating-fog-analytics-learning-and-education
11. Boyd, D., Crawford, K.: Six Provocations for Big Data, A Decade in Internet Time: Symposium on the Dynamics of the Internet and Society. Oxford Internet Institute, Oxford (2012). http://papers.ssrn.com/sol3/papers.cfm?abstract_id=1926431
12. Gee, J.P.: What Video Games Have to Teach Us About Learning and Literacy. Palgrave Macmillan, New York (2003)
13. Westera, W., Hommes, M.A., Houtmans, M., Kurvers, H.J.: Computer-supported training of psychodiagnostic skills. Interact. Learn. Environ. **11**(3), 215–231 (2003)
14. Kickmeier-Rust, M.D., Albert, D.: Micro adaptivity: protecting immersion in didactically adaptive digital educational games. J. Comput. Assist. Learn. **26**, 95–105 (2010)
15. Serrano-Laguna, A., Torrente, J., Moreno-Ger, P., Fernández-Manjón, B.: Tracing a little for big improvements: application of learning analytics and videogames for student assessment. Procedia Comput. Sci. **15**, 203–209 (2012). http://www.sciencedirect.com/science/article/pii/S1877050912008344
16. Shute, V.J., Ventura, M., Bauer, M., Zapata-Rivera, D.: Melding the power of serious games and embedded assessment to monitor and foster learning: flow and grow. In: Ritterfeld, U., Cody, M., Vorderer, M. (eds.) Serious Games: Mechanisms and Effects, pp. 295–321. Routledge, New York (2009)
17. Mislevy, R.J., Steinberg, L.S., Almond, R.G.: On the structure of educational assessment. Measur. Interdisc. Res. Perspect. **10**, 3–62 (2003)
18. Pearl, J.: Probabilistic Reasoning in Intelligent Systems: Networks of Plausible Inference. Kaufmann, San Mateo (1988)

19. Reese, D.D., Seward, R.J., Tabachnick, B.G., Hitt, B., Harrison, A., McFarland, L.: Timed report measures learning: game-based embedded assessment. In: Ifenthaler, D., Eseryel, D., Ge, X. (eds.) Assessment in Game-Based Learning: Foundations, Innovations, and Perspectives. Springer, New York (2013)
20. Green, S.B.: How many subjects does it take to do a regression analysis? Multivar. Behav. Res. **26**, 499–510 (1991)

Generating Computational Models for Serious Gaming

Wim Westera[✉]

Open University of the Netherlands,
Valkenburgerweg 177, 6419 AT Heerlen, The Netherlands
wim.westera@ou.nl

Abstract. Many serious games include computational models that simulate dynamic systems. These models promote enhanced interaction and responsiveness. Under the social web paradigm more and more usable game authoring tools become available that enable prosumers to create their own games, but the inclusion of dynamic simulations remains a specialist's job involving knowledge of mathematics, numerical modeling and programming. This paper describes a methodology for specifying and running a specific subset of computational models without the need of bothering with mathematical equations. The methodology comprises a knowledge elicitation procedure for identifying and specifying the required model components, whereupon the mathematical model is automatically generated. The approach is based on the fact that many games focus on optimisation problems that are covered by a general class of linear programming models. The paper thus sketches the principles of a creativity tool that removes barriers for harvesting the creative potential of teachers and students.

1 Introduction

For over 30 years games and simulations have been used in training and education. Their application is motivated by the engaging interactions and authentic experiences they offer (e.g. [1, 2]). In 1970 Abt [3] introduced the term 'serious games' to indicate games for job training, such as the training of army personnel or insurance salesmen. Serious games now span everything from learning to advancing social causes, and from promoting better health to marketing and cultural engagement [4, 5]. So far, the adoption of games for learning in formal education has been quite limited. Among adoption barriers are the limited availability of games and technologies, costs of games, limited time and resources for implementing games, the intrinsic complexity of games and their design, the unfamiliarity of teachers with games, the supposed conservative culture of education, limited empirical evidence for the effectiveness of games, and difficulties of integrating games into the curriculum [6–12].

Still, in recent years game-based learning has gained popularity among educators and learners, as the costs of multimedia and graphics went down. Various affordable game authoring tools have become available ranging from simple puzzle creation tools to full 3D programmable engines. Game engines have become popular tools in programming courses [13–15]. Some game engines are particularly tuned to education and

© Springer International Publishing Switzerland 2014
A. De Gloria (Ed.): GALA 2013, LNCS 8605, pp. 53–63, 2014.
DOI: 10.1007/978-3-319-12157-4_5

learning, e.g. EMERGO [6], Emperor [16], e-Adventure [17], Starlogo and Scratch (MIT). Hu [18] lists a number of special requirements for educational games. Nadolski et al. [19] identified over 500 game engines and showed that many engines allow for educational scenarios: the key of serious games is in game design rather than game technology. Playing a game means engaging in a process and learning by doing while influencing the process in a favourable way.

Many games include computational models that simulate dynamic systems, which procure enhanced interaction and responsiveness. Well-known examples are in management and business games, where computational models cover the dynamics of supplies, customer flows, production processes, and sales revenues. Other examples are in social simulations, ecology or system evolution games, surveillance games, traffic and logistics games and many other types of games. Games that comprise such dynamic models provide immediate and relevant feedback, which enables players to learn from their successes and mistakes.

A common tendency of today's social web is that users become active contributors of content, while they are supported by online authoring tools and services that have become publicly available. Teachers and students increasingly produce and use their own videos, web pages and interactive stories. Although more and more free game authoring tools have become available online, self-authored (serious) games are scarce and hardly exceed the level of simple multiple choice quizzes or puzzle games. Moreover, whatever brilliant ideas teachers or students may have for creating a serious game, the development of an appropriate computational model for enhanced dynamics and interactions seems to remain a specialist's job that inevitably requires knowledge of mathematics, numerical modeling and programming.

This paper addresses this problem by providing a methodology for specifying a computational model without going into mathematical equations. The methodology comprises a knowledge elicitation procedure for identifying and specifying the required model components, whereupon the mathematical model is automatically generated. The approach is based on the fact that many games focus on optimisation problems that are covered by a general class of linear programming models. The notion of linear programming is not so much about programming but refers to a mathematical problem solving method, which is applicable to a wide range of optimisation problems in different domains and contexts, including operations research, and non-zero sum games [20–22]. Quite some simulation modeling software based on linear programming is available on the market, e.g. Vstep, FlexSim, and Siemens Plant Simulation, but in all cases these tend to specialise in particular domains such as vehicle simulation, logistics, manufactory planning, crop simulation, and process automation, which are hard to be used by non-specialists. Also, they are closed solutions that don't allow for interfacing with external software. The elicitation methodology proposed in this paper brings the model parameters, model coefficients and model logic to the surface in a pragmatic way, without requiring computational modeling skills. The approach benefits from the generic nature of linear programming and the wide spectrum of optimisation problems that it covers. In addition, various algorithms such as the simplex method [23] are available for solving linear programming problems. The optimum solutions that these algorithms provide can be used as a pedagogical benchmark for providing guidance and feedback to learners involved in optimisation tasks. The paper is a setup as follows.

First we will summarise the formal basics of linear programming. Second we will show how the linear programming framework can be linked with simulation modeling. Finally we will describe the elicitation approach and explain its implications for serious game design.

2 Linear Programming

Many processes in business, economy and nature can be described as linear programming problems. Linear programming refers to a mathematical methodology for minimising or maximising linear functions (e.g. minimising costs, maximising profits) subject to linear constraints (e.g. limited resources, limited time). In their elementary form such models reflect conversion processes or mappings that link a set of input variables to a set of output variables (cf. Fig. 1).

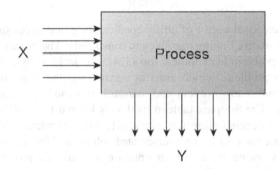

Fig. 1. A black-box system with input vector X and output vector Y

Linear programming problems may have very different manifestations, but all rely on the same mathematical methodology, which offers optimal solutions. Below we will list some problem examples (e.g. [21]):

- Diet problems: Compose a menu of food products (inputs) at minimum costs, which preserves the minimal daily doses of nutrients, e.g. proteins, vitamins, minerals, calories and so on (outputs).
- Shipping problems: Optimising the transportation of products from a series of warehouses (inputs) to a series of markets (outputs), while fulfilling market demands.
- Activity planning problems: Distributing a factory's resources (inputs) e.g. machines, money, energy, or staff to activities (outputs) that produce highest profits.
- Staff assignment problems: Allocating staff (inputs) to production activities (outputs), taking into account the people's different effectiveness on different tasks.

These examples cover a wide range of optimisation problems that can be varied by changing the number of inputs and outputs, choosing different types of processes, or linking multiple problems together.

2.1 Mathematical Description

The standard minimum problem has the following formal structure: Find the n-vector
X (X_1, X_2, ..., X_n) that minimises the objective function O given by

$$O = \sum_{j=1}^{n} c_j \cdot X_j \tag{1}$$

Minimisation is required under m functional constraints given by

$$\sum_{j=1}^{n} A_{ij} \cdot X_j \geq p_i \tag{2}$$

Also, n nonnegativity constraints apply:

$$X_j \geq 0 \tag{3}$$

Here c_j is an n-dimensional vector of utility coefficients, p_i are m constraint coefficients
and A_{ij} is an m × n matrix linking variables to constraints. The equations represent the
standard minimum problem in canonical form [24]. It is technically equivalent with the
standard maximum problem, which aims at maximising the objective function. For
both the standard minimum problem and standard maximum problem solution algorithms are available. The Simplex tableau method is known for its efficiency, although
occasionally cycling degeneration may occur [21, 24]. Calculated solutions could be
used as a benchmark for evaluating user-created solutions. Herein lies its educational
potential: learners working on a task to optimise a simulated process could receive
informative feedback how well they do as compared with the calculated optimum.
Below we will further detail the relevant process variables and coefficients that have to
be specified and explain how practical problems can be translated into standard form.

2.2 Connecting Input and Output Variables

In accordance with Fig. 1 we assume a process or mechanism that connects an input
vector X = (X_1, X_2, ..., X_m) with an output vector Y = (Y_1, Y_2, ..., Y_n). These
variables reflect the amounts of each input and output, e.g. (1) the amounts of food
products and nutrients, (2) the quantities of product shipped from a harbour or shipped
to a market, (3) the amount of resources allocated to different activities, or (4) the
amount of time that people are allocated to tasks, and so on. The distinction between
inputs and outputs is not essential: allocating people to tasks is technically the same as
allocating tasks to people.

The characteristics of the process are covered by an m × n matrix a_{ij}, which
interconnects the two vectors X and Y. For explaining the nature of these intercon-
nections we need to distinguish between two separate problem classes, each of which
require a different approach. The classes differ by the type of interventions users are
allowed to make, while dealing with the optimisation problem: (1) Adjusting the vector

X (or Y), or (2) Adjusting the matrix a_{ij}. Below we will subsequently elaborate the model descriptions of the two problem classes.

2.3 Model Class 1: Adjusting the Vector X (or Y)

In this problem class the user has to adjust the input variable X to arrive at an optimal output Y. Examples are:

- The activity planning problem: The user decides upon the input resources X_i that produce the best output Y;
- The diet problem: The user decides upon the amounts of food products X_i that offer required nutrients Y_j.

Amount Attribution. The process reflects a mapping of X onto Y, that is, it converts inputs X into outputs Y, which is defined by the elements of matrix a_{ij}. It assumes that each input variable X_i is related to each output variable Y_j by an amount a_{ij}, which describes the attribution of input variable X_i to the output variable Y_j. This is expressed as follows:

$$Y_j = \sum_{i=1}^{m} a_{ij} \cdot X_i \tag{4}$$

In the diet case a_{ij} would describe the amount of nutrient Y_j contained in one unit of food product X_i.

Assigning Value. The amount of a variable may differ from its value. Indeed kilograms or cubic meters are different from Euros or Dollars. Since many optimisation problems are based on value rather than amounts, we have to incorporate value rates. Mostly (but not necessarily) these will be monetary values (money). We introduce the input value rate VX_i, which is the (monetary) value of one unit of input X_i. In the activity planning problem VX_i would be the value (or costs) of one unit of the factory's resource X_i. In the diet problem VX_j would be the value (or costs) of one unit of food product X_i. Alternatively, one might want to define and use the values VY_j.

Objective Function. The total value VX_{total} is the summed value of inputs given by:

$$VX_{total} = \sum_{i=1}^{m} X_i \cdot VX_i \tag{5}$$

This total value is likely to be the objective function to be minimised or maximised in the problem solution, e.g. the total costs of a factory's resources. Alternatively, output values VY_{total} may be calculated likewise, e.g. the profits of products' sales. Note that in some cases, users may be required to optimise total amounts rather than total values. If so, the value rates VX or VY are set to unity.

Functional Constraints and Nonnegativity Constraints. Constraints refer to lower or upper boundaries that apply to the input or output variables. We distinguish the following cases of functional constraints:

1. Inputs are subjected to an upper limit:

$$X_i \leq b_i \, for \, i = 1, \ldots, m \tag{6}$$

2. Inputs are subjected to a lower limit:

$$X_i \geq c_i \, for \, i = 1, \ldots, m \tag{7}$$

3. Outputs are subjected to an upper limit:

$$Y_j \leq d_j \, for \, j = 1, \ldots, n \tag{8}$$

4. Outputs are subjected to a lower limit:

$$Y_j \geq e_j \, for \, j = 1, \ldots, n \tag{9}$$

These constraints of inputs and outputs can be understood in terms of supplies and demands: e.g. limited supplies available (constraint 1), reducing supplies (constraint 2), avoiding overproduction (constraint 3), and meeting output demands (constraint 4). In addition we have the following nonnegativity constraints:

5. All inputs are nonnegative:

$$X_i \geq 0 \, for \, i = 1, \ldots, m \tag{10}$$

6. All outputs (amounts) are nonnegative:

$$Y_j \geq 0 \, for \, j = 1, \ldots, n \tag{11}$$

Note that in all cases the input and output vectors represent amounts of entities, which cannot be negative.

Conversion to Standard Form. The vector problem of minimisation can now be summarised as follows. Determine an input vector X that has to be adjusted to optimise the objective function given by Eq. (5), e.g. the costs of the food menu under the functional constraint of Eq. (9), e.g. minimum daily doses of nutrients, and the non-negativity constraint of Eqs. (10) and (11). This is in accordance with the standard minimum form. Similar considerations hold for maximisation problems.

2.4   Model Class 2: Adjusting the Matrix a_{ij}

In this class of problems the user adjusts the coefficients a_{ij} rather than X_i or Y_j for producing an optimal solution. Examples:

- The shipping problem:
  Distributing product quantities from various warehouses to different markets reflects decisions about the attributions a_{ij}, viz. the amount of product to be shipped from a location X_i to a destination Y_j;
- The staff assignment problem:
  Allocating staff X_i to tasks Y_j, while taking into account the productivity differences between people at different tasks.

Amount Attribution. The matrix problems reflect the allocation of each input element X_i onto the output vector Y: amounts of input entities X_i are distributed over the outputs Y_j. This means that Eq. (4) is no longer valid for describing the attribution of input vector X to output variable Y_j. Instead this attribution is given by:

$$X_i = \sum_{i=1}^{m} a_{ij} \tag{12}$$

and

$$Y_j = \sum_{j=1}^{n} a_{ij} \tag{13}$$

Assigning Value. Each attribution a_{ij} decided upon by the user goes with a value that is determined by a value rate matrix Va_{ij}, indicating the (monetary) value per unit of a_{ij}. In the shipping problem Va_{ij} would be the value (or costs) per unit product shipped from warehouse i to market j. In the job allocation case Va_{ij} would be the value per unit of time that person X_i is allocated to job Y_j.

Objective Function. The total value Va_{total} of all decisions is then given by Eq. (14).

$$Va_{total} = \sum_{i=1}^{m} \sum_{j=1}^{n} a_{ij} \cdot Va_{ij} \tag{14}$$

This is likely to be the objective function to be minimised or maximised, for instance total value of all shipping, or total value of job allocations. Note that in some cases, the problem may require optimisation of total amounts rather than monetary value. If so, the value rates Va_{ij} are all set equal to unity.

Constraints. Constraints refer to lower or upper boundaries that apply to input or output variables. Options are given by Eqs. (6)–(11).

Conversion to Standard Form. The problem description of this model class can be demonstrated to correspond with the standard form: it reflects minimisation (or maximisation) of an objective function, cf. Eq. (14), subject to functional and nonnegative constraints.

3 Model Elicitation

For producing a computational model without bothering about mathematical complexities we have developed a procedure that supports game authors at expressing their ideas and at the same time extracts the nature, the variables and the coefficients needed for the model description. Table 1 lists the high level model decisions that have to be taken, including the intervention variable, the objective dimension, the optimisation criterion and the constraints.

Table 1. Successive decisions to be taken

Decisions	Options	Number of options
Intervention variable	X, Y, a_{ij}	3
Objective dimension	X, Y	2
Optimisation criterion	minimise, maximise	2
Constraints on Y	lower, upper, both, none	4
Constraints on X	lower, upper, both, none	4
Total number of options		192

It follows that the total number of options is 192 (neglecting the dimensionalities m and n of X and Y, respectively), which means that the mathematics described above allow for the specification of 192 different model types. Based on this set of decisions we have developed a structured elicitation procedure, which comprises a sequence of standardised questions, e.g.:

- "What type of process do you want to define?" (discriminating between matrix and vector model)
- "How would you qualify the output of your process?" (making explicit the sort of outcome)
- "What different types of outputs do you consider?" (extracting outputs Y_j and associated labels)
- "What units would you use to express the respective output types?" (required standards for calculations)
- "What is the value of one unit of Y_j?" (converting amounts to monetary values)
- Etcetera.

A prototype of the elicitation procedure was implemented as an Excel form. A formative test procedure included interviews with five volunteers. Model elicitation took typically 20 to 30 min. After each interview weaknesses in the elicitation procedure were identified and discussed, whereupon the form was improved. After completion of an elicitation session, the Excel prototype generated the model, which allowed for testing and making adjustments (cf. Fig. 2).

Figure 2 shows the Excel-representation of a fictitious shoe factory using 4 inputs (materials: leather, rubber, string, sewing rope) constrained to upper limits (e.g. limited supplies) and 4 outputs (running shoes, tennis shoes, soccer shoes, golf shoes) aiming for maximizing total output value by deciding about the output volumes.

		LIMITS		running shoes	tennis shoes	soccer shoes	golf shoes
materials				166,5	125,75	240	60
leather	(cow)	200	3	20	15	12	15
rubber	(kg)	20	5	20	15	40	0
string	(meter)	1500	2	2	1	1	5
sewing rope	(meter)	1500	5	0,5	0,75	0,4	1
		upper limit		pair	pair	pair	pair
								Total value of shoes
		Value		313500	4725	1467	810	320502

Fig. 2. Example screenshot of the Excel simulation prototype.

4 Discussion and Outlook

The implementation of the elicitation procedure and the associated mathematics in the Excel prototype was quite straightforward. The model was tested against a wide range of input conditions and proved to produce the required outputs, which demonstrated the feasibility of the approach. Test persons lacking any mathematical background were pleased to see how their verbalised ideas were immediately brought to life as a working simulation model. Also, the prototype made use of Excel's equation solver, which provided approximate solutions of the optimisation problem. This yields a benchmark for player performance that can be used for providing feedback to gamers.

Two main findings led to a readjustment of the elicitation procedure. First, although test persons demonstrated to be able to specify process models, it turned out to be very hard for them to imagine any process just from scratch. It was very difficult for them to make substantiated choices, for example between a matrix model and a vector model, even though quite common terms were used to guide the decision (e.g. "allocation", "production", "composing"). Specifying constraints also appeared quite difficult. Adding instructional materials appeared helpful, but not in all cases. Secondly, from the tests we found that the elicitation procedure sometimes produced degenerated models, that is, the models either don't allow for solutions, have trivial solutions, or don't reflect an optimisation problem. For instance, in case of upper limit output constraints any output minimisation problem will have a trivial solution of zero output. Analysis has shown that 154 out of the 192 model options that follow from the decision tree (cf. Table 1) are degenerate models. This leaves 36 valid model types, which can all be covered by a basic set of 12 model templates. For avoiding degenerate models we aim to use this basic set of templates as a starting point for guiding the elicitation process. We will attach concrete examples to each of the templates in order to promote a better understanding and informed decision making by game authors.

The approach explained in this paper allows for the easy extraction of model variables, coefficients and relationships, provided that the optimisation process fits in the class of linear programming problems. This opens up possibilities for developing simplified computational model builders that can be used for creating models in games and simulations. A next step would be the development of an authoring tool that implements the elicitation dialogue and model composition as a user-friendly, computer-guided service, preferably using sprites and other graphical objects for visualising the process. It should also contain a Simplex equation solver for making available a performance feedback reference. So far the problem set explained in this paper reflects single-shot problems that don't take into account progression over time. However, there are two ways to transform the approach into a time-dynamic challenge. First, in a game or simulation environment players may be asked to continue their optimisation task and repeatedly enter new inputs to find a better solution. Adding time constraints and associated scores may help enhancing the dynamic experience. Second, the models can be easily adapted to allow for a progressive accumulation of variables, e.g. sales, supplies, costs over time, which would reflect a history that contributes to the narrative of the player's performance in a game. Such accumulation may be well understood as a discrete time Markov chain, which would preserve the linear programming model as single shot, while only reformulating the constraints and objective function in the course of time. In addition, problem cases need not be restricted to a single linear problem core but could be composed of multiple cascaded or interlinked processes, each covering a single problem issue: outputs of one process acting as inputs of follow-up models in the process chain. In all cases standard linear programming models remain the heart of the description. Eventually, there are no principal barriers for using an elicitation dialogue for more complex linear, probabilistic or even nonlinear (e.g. exponential, logarithmic or power law) models.

References

1. Aldrich, C.: The Complete Guide to Simulations and Serious Games: How the Most Valuable Content Will Be Created in the Age Beyond Gutenberg to Google. Pfeiffer, San Francisco (2009)
2. David, M.M., Watson, A.: Participating in what? Using situated cognition theory to illuminate differences in classroom practices. In: Watson, A., Winbourne, P. (eds.) New Directions for Situated Cognition in Mathematics Education. Springer, New York (2010)
3. Abt, C.: Serious Games. Viking Press, New York (1970)
4. Michael, D., Chen, S.: Serious Games: Games that Educate, Train and Inform. Thomson Course Technology, Boston (2006)
5. Klopfler, E., Osterweil, S., Salen, K.: Moving Learning Games Forward; Obstacles, Opportunities and Openness. MIT - The Education Arcade, Boston (2009). http://education. mit.edu/papers/MovingLearningGamesForward_EdArcade.pdf
6. Westera, W., Nadolski, R., Hummel, H., Wopereis, I.: Serious games for higher education: a framework for reducing design complexity. J. Comput.-Assist. Learn. **24**(5), 420–432 (2008)
7. Kapp, K.M.: The Gamification of Learning and Instruction: Game-Based Methods and Strategies for Training and Education. Pfeiffer, New York (2012)
8. Arnab, S., Berta, R., Earp, J., de Freitas, S., Popescu, M., Romero, M., Stanescu, I., Usart, M.: Framing the adoption of serious games in formal education. Electron. J. e-Learn. **10**(2), 159–171 (2012). www.ejel.com
9. Westera, W.: The eventful genesis of educational media. Educ. Inf. Technol. **17**(3), 345–360 (2012)

10. Proctor, M.D., Marks,Y.: A survey of exemplar teachers' perceptions, use, and access of computer-based games and technology for classroom instruction. Comput. Educ. **62**, 171–180 (2012). http://dx.doi.org/10.1016/j.compedu.2012.10.022
11. Lean, J., Moizer, J., Towler, M., Abbey, C.: Simulations and games use and barriers in higher education. Act. Learn. High. Educ. **7**(3), 227–242 (2006). doi:10.1177/1469787406069056
12. Kebrichi, M.: Factors affecting teachers' adoption of educational computer games: a case study. Br. J. Educ. Technol. **41**(2), 256–270 (2010). doi:10.1111/j.1467-8535.2008.00921
13. Jeon, J., Kim, K., Jung, S.: A study on the game programming education based on educational game engine at school. J. Educ. Learn. **1**(2), 282–287 (2012). doi:10.5539/jel.v1n2p282
14. Berigel, M.: Learning programming through game design: a case study. Int. Online J. Commun. Mark. Technol. **1**(1), 32–44 (2012). http://www.iojcmt.net/ojs/index.php/IOJCMT/article/view/4
15. Kumar, B.: Gamification in education - learn computer programming with fun. Int. J. Comput. Distrib. Syst. **2**(1), 46–53 (2012). http://www.cirworld.com/index.php/IJCDS/article/view/IJCDS218
16. Kiili, K., Ojansuu, K.: Emperor: game engine for educational management games. In: Kommers, P., Richards, G. (eds.) Proceedings of World Conference on Educational Multimedia, Hypermedia and Telecommunications 2005, pp. 1775–1782. AACE, Chesapeake (2005)
17. Torrente, J., Vallejo-Pinto, J.A., Moreno-Ger, P., Fernández-Manjón, B.: Introducing accessibility features in an educational game authoring tool: the <e-adventure> experience. In: Proceedings of the 11th IEEE International Conference on Advanced Learning Technologies (ICALT 2011). IEEE, Athens (2011)
18. Hu, W.: A common software architecture for educational games. In: Zhang, X., Zhong, S., Pan, Z., Wong, K., Yun, R. (eds.) Edutainment 2010. LNCS, vol. 6249, pp. 405–416. Springer, Heidelberg (2010). http://dx.doi.org/10.1007/978-3-642-14533-9_42
19. Nadolski, R.J., Hummel, H.G.K., Slootmaker, A., Van der Vegt, W.: Architectures for developing multiuser, immersive learning scenarios. Simul. Gaming **43**(6), 825–852 (2012)
20. Adler, I.: On the equivalency of linear programming problems and zero-sum games. Int. J. Game Theory 17(April) (2012). doi:10.1007/s00182-012-0328-8
21. Ferguson, T.S.: Linear Programming, A Concise Introduction. United States Naval Academy, Annapolis (2008). http://engine4.org/l/linear-programming---united-states-naval-academy-w2532-pdf.pdf
22. Anderson, D., Sweeney, D., Williams, T.: Quantitative Methods for Business. West Publishing Company, St. Paul (1995)
23. Dantzig, G.B.: Linear Programming and Extensions. Princeton University Press, Princeton (1963)
24. Murty, K.G.: Linear Programming. Wiley, New York (1983)

COmBI naTion: The Fusion
of Serious Gaming and COBIT

Martin Fritsch[1(✉)], Sascha Müeller-Feuerstein[1], and Rainer Groß[2]

[1] Ansbach University of Applied Sciences,
Residenzstrasse 8, 91522 Ansbach, Germany
{martin.fritsch,sascha.mueller}@hs-ansbach.de
[2] Georg Simon Ohm University of Applied Sciences,
Kesslerplatz 12, 90489 Nuremberg, Germany
rainer.gross@ohm-hochschule.de

Abstract. This paper describes the conceptual development and prototypical implementation of a business simulation for the IT governance framework COBIT. In the first part the concept of serious games will be explained and the benefits and challenges of a simulation developed this way will be shown. The second part illustrates IT governance and the structures of COBIT. In the third part the contents for the COBIT simulation are selected and transferred into an optimized simulation model. The paper concludes with an overview of the conceptual development process of the business simulation and the technical implementation of an early staged prototype.

1 Introduction

Games are an essential element of daily life nowadays. Mostly played in spare time they are able to bond their players for many hours, but how do they manage this? The answer is because of the use of elements of challenge, fantasy and curiosity. Games intend to take their players into a virtual world where they can engage a special role, accept tough challenges and, last but not least, learn something new. All these attributes predestine games for an adoption of learning efforts [2–6]. The potential to make complex tasks simple, respectively to experience such tasks at all, is an invaluable advantage which still needs much more research effort.

In the field of modern IT solutions the implementation of appropriate strategies for the integration of *IT governance* is essential for most enterprises. The relevance of the *Control Objectives for Information and Related Technology* (COBIT) framework is consistently increasing to support the needs of different divisions of an enterprise [10]. Especially the management and control of the underlying IT systems and their interaction with the functional divisions of the enterprise lead to new challenges that need to be solved through the use of COBIT [10] and serious games.

This is where the idea of a COBIT simulation comes into play: Business simulations are intended to simplify complex processes which appear in the daily business. At the same time they shall focus and emphasize important key messages. Specifically designed simulations facilitate the transfer of the processes into a secured (digital) environment and offer the chance to experience complex tasks in a save and motivation-funded virtual reality [9]. To reach this goal a few rules, which focus on both,

© Springer International Publishing Switzerland 2014
A. De Gloria (Ed.): GALA 2013, LNCS 8605, pp. 64–76, 2014.
DOI: 10.1007/978-3-319-12157-4_6

didactical principles and contentual problems have to be observed [5–16]. In the next sections these guidelines will be explained, applied and finally used to generate a conceptual simulation model which supports the use of the COBIT framework to implement IT governance in an enterprise.

To sum up: The goal of this project is to develop a business simulation, based on the principles of serious gaming, which communicates important COBIT contents in a didactical and professionally well-founded method.

2 Principles of a Business Simulation

When a business simulation is realized as a computer-aided simulation game, it is classified in the field of *Digital Game Based Learning (DGBL)* or *Serious Games*. Ganguin describes these approaches as a concept to use computer games for educational purposes respectively for processes of learning and creation [5].

The adoption of serious games in the field of complex contexts offers many advantages for the knowledge transfer [8–16]:

- *Fantasy*: Educational games happen in a non-real world where the players can act in different roles.
- *Rules and Targets*: A business simulation follows clearly structured rules and educational goals.
- *Sensory Attraction*: Visual and aural impulses increase the interaction between simulation and player and positively influence the understanding of the delivered contents.
- *Challenges and Risks*: A consistently customizable level of complexity provides an optimal adoption to the skills of the attendees.
- *Curiosity and Engagement*: Serious games use the natural curiosity of human beings. This facilitates the motivation to learn complex correlations.
- *Control and Security*: Simulations enable the players to slide into different roles in the virtual world without the consequences of a wrong decision.

Schwan comments extensively on these assets of serious games but does not respond to the challenges of applying these concepts when building a simulation-based educational game [16]. Conventional COBIT training programs focus mostly on important contents of the framework and their implementation. Knowledge transfer through the use of a serious game requires a rethinking off from the pure content to the kind of transferring complex contexts without adulterating the substances [9]. Therefore a simulation drafted after these principles has to be tested throughout the whole development process. It is very important that the learning contents are implemented in an appropriate way for the motivation of its future players.

3 IT Governance Based on COBIT

The *Information Systems Audit and Control Association* (ISACA) released the first version of COBIT in 1996. It was planned as a framework for supporting IT revisers and IT governance agents. Since 2012 version 5 of COBIT is available which focuses even more on the support of the business objectives by the IT department of the enterprise. COBIT 5 rests upon the following five principles [10]:

- *Principle 1*: Meeting stakeholders needs
- *Principle 2*: Covering the enterprise end-to-end
- *Principle 3*: Applying a single, integrated framework
- *Principle 4*: Enabling a holistic approach
- *Principle 5*: Separating governance from management

Based on the principle of separation of governance and management, guidelines and the implementation of these can be explicitly distinguished: Governance guarantees that the needs of the stakeholders are recorded, reviewed and transferred into reasonable business objectives. Management plans, establishes, operates and monitors activities to meet the guidelines of the governance. This differentiation is also reflected in the COBIT process reference model, which consists of the domains *Governance* and *Management*. The governance domain contains five processes, which are based on the principles of *Evaluate*, *Direct* and *Monitor*. The management domain is divided into four sub domains, which are, corresponding to COBIT's idea of management, called *Plan*, *Build*, *Run* and *Monitor*. Overall this domain holds 32 processes [10].

All processes contain one high-level and several more detailed *Control Objectives* that describe the expected results of the corresponding process. The fulfilment of the control objectives is measured by *Key Performance Indicators* (KPIs) and *Key Goal Indicators* (KGIs), which are also defined for each process respectively. This strict hierarchical top-down approach ensures that enterprises that implement IT governance and IT management based on the principles of the COBIT framework are able to align IT activities and IT investments to the business needs in an optimal way.

4   Related Work

At the moment there is only one alternative solution in the field of COBIT simulations, which will be described and evaluated in the next section. Yet, this educational game is not a modern computer-based simulation and we decided to examine the *IT Infrastructure Library* (ITIL) simulation *Fort Fantastic*, developed by *Business Games and Simulations Labs* [3], as well. This analysis was intended to generate helpful functional and didactical suggestions for the development of the planned business simulation.

4.1   The COBIT Games – A COBIT-Simulation

The COBIT Games is an educational game realized as a board game. It was developed by ISACA and the authors of the COBIT framework - the *IT Government Institute* (ITGI) [13], see Fig. 1.

In this business simulation the players are supposed to prepare the imaginary city Concordia to host the Olympic Games. Concordia consists of six districts, which represent the different divisions of an enterprise. These divisions shall be prepared with the fulfillment of different actions for the forthcoming Olympic Games.

Fig. 1. The COBIT Games [7]

The developers decided to implement the contents of the entire COBIT framework in a lightly abstracted virtual world overlaid by an abstracted idea (preparation of Concordia for the Olympic Games). It is a turn-based game, uses haptic elements (e.g. game cards and tokens) and is applied mostly in the context of training sessions.

Particularly the approach of abstraction and the turn-based realization can be considered as very relevant for our planned COBIT business simulation. The lack of focus on didactical relevant parts of COBIT, the low level of abstraction and the strongly limited applicability of board games in general indicates that there is still enough potential for the development of a computer-based COBIT simulation.

4.2 Fort Fantastic – An ITIL-Simulation

Fort Fantastic [3] is a partly computer-aided business simulation that is enriched with haptic elements. It arranges complex contexts like e.g. IT service management based on ITIL or leadership in a playful way. BuGaSi Labs chose managing a theme park as the optimal scenario for content abstraction. This scenario allows the transfer of extensive IT processes to a non-expert group of participants, e.g. employees of other departments. It also reduces the time of preparation of a simulation run to only a few hours.

The unique learning effect results on the one hand from the chosen simulation model which shows the complex tasks of the park management only in a very well-directed way, and on the other hand from the concept of the simulation. This concept focuses on problem-oriented learning by intensive interaction in a group of players and real time interaction with the simulation software, see Fig. 2.

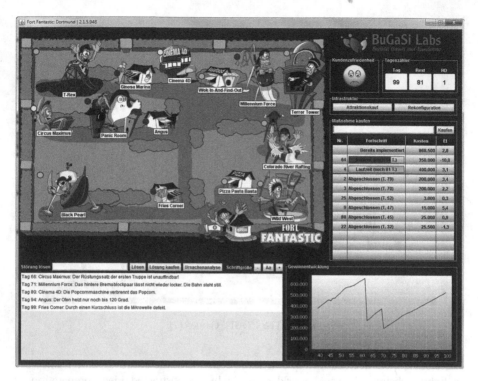

Fig. 2. Fort Fantastic [3]

The necessary group size (at least five participants), the competition between the different teams and the mixture of haptic elements (game cards and manuals) in combination with a computer-aided simulation are important characteristics of Fort Fantastic. In consequence there are several organizational conditions, e.g. adequate rooms or a common appointment for a huge amount of employees that have to be met in order to play the simulation.

In summary it can be concluded that Fort Fantastic is a successful example for a modern business simulation realised as a serious game. It demonstrates also that especially the simulation concept is the key to successful serious game development.

5   Transformation of the Contents into a Simulation Model

The learning-target-oriented selection of the simulation content is an important factor to determine the learning outcomes of a business simulation. The COBIT framework is very complex in its structure [11]. For a highly-abstracted business simulation it was important so select only contents of the framework which maximize the learning success when the simulation is played.

5.1 Selection of the Content for the Simulation

The reduction to the fundamental elements can result in significant benefits for the construction of the simulation:

- *Reduction of time*: The large framework gets disassembled into smaller pieces. These pieces can be integrated into the simulation in a more target-oriented way.
- *Consideration of the principles of serious games*: The reduced scope of contents can be adapted in a better way to the principles of serious games (*cf.* Sect. 2).
- *Higher quality*: By realizing the benefits described by Schwan [16] a higher usability and sustained yield can be expected.

The close bonds and the wide scope of the COBIT framework require a special strategy for the selection of the simulation contents. For the productive use of COBIT all dependencies of the framework have to be preserved during the selection process.

COBIT is divided into several processes, which consist of a variable amount of control objectives. These circumstances require an appropriate selection procedure. For filtering out the relevant contents for the simulation a combined top-down/bottom up approach was applied [12]. In order to rate the objectives relevance, their integration in all processes of the framework was analyzed.

COBIT processes and Control Objectives	Relevance	Comment
PO1: Define a Strategic IT Plan		
PO1.1: IT Value Management	o	IT Value Management is highly complex
PO1.2: Business-IT Alignment	++	Essential content for modern IT -> Important for simulation
PO1.3: Assessment of Current Capability and Performance	++	Relevant for determination of the IT alignment
PO1.4: IT Strategic Plan	+	Important but simulation is more tactical oriented
PO1.5: IT Tactical Plans	++	Realizable in an abstract way with simulation model
PO1.6: IT Portfolio Management	++	Relevant for priorization and alignment of IT
PO2: Define the Information Architecture		
PO2.1: Enterprise Information Architecture Model	-	Implementation of this model not reasonable
PO2.2: Enterprise Data Dictionary and Data Syntax Rules	-	Because of abstraction of IT and data not suitable
PO2.3: Data Classification Scheme	-	No direct access to data in the simulation
PO2.4: Integrity Management	-	Data integrity not essential in simulation

Fig. 3. Ranking of COBIT contents for the simulation

Figure 3 shows an excerpt of the content ranking-table for the control objectives and their corresponding processes. The validation was divided into four levels: very high (++), high (+), medium (o) and low relevance for the business simulation. For the rating of the objectives the integration of the processes into the whole COBIT framework was analyzed on the one hand. On the other hand all control objectives were reviewed in terms of their didactical and functional feasibility in a productive simulation. The necessary principles for the ranking were extracted from accessory-literature for practical implementation of IT governance in an enterprise [12].

This approach allowed us to reduce the whole simulation content to only 29 control objectives distributed in ten processes. These processes cover every sub domain of the management domain of COBIT (*cf.* Sect. 3). Despite this reduction, the entire structure, all monitoring tools and thereby the complete functionality and usability of the framework could be kept coherent in the business simulation.

5.2 Preparation of the Simulation Model

For the serious game three different simulation scenarios were developed. The game-contents for the abstraction of the COBIT processes were outlined in a very rudimental way before the virtual worlds were compared with each other. The following list shows the virtual worlds and a brief explanation of the role the players can adopt in the simulation:

- *Zoo scenario:* The group of players has to deal with the role of a zookeeper, stay in coordination with the director of the zoo and manage resources like employees, animals as IT services and others. The scope of this scenario was kept small on purpose to simplify the development of the serious game. But this smaller focus may lead to additional challenges if the model has to be extended in the future to cover more COBIT contents.
- *Pirate scenario:* The playgroup has to act as a young admiral in a pirate bay with pirate ships, different harbors as enterprise divisions, and the crew as IT employees and so on. In this scenario a very wide scope was chosen to ensure there is enough extension-potential if the abstracted COBIT contents of the simulation would increase over its lifetime.
- *Hotel scenario:* The players act in the role of a building contractor who tries to realize the requests of a hotel chain owner in an optimal way. The hotels of the chain represent the different divisions of a fictive enterprise. In this scenario a medium-wide scope was preferred. This offers on the one hand enough potential for the extension of the simulation contents and on the other hand a more efficient development of the serious game itself.

After the development of the three described game scenarios their capability to illustrate the abstracted COBIT contents was verified. It turned out that the best suiting game concept was the hotel scenario with a total amount of 31 scoring points, followed by the pirate simulation with 29 and the zoo scenario with 21.

Subsequent to the selection process the gaming content for the hotel scenario was formulated in a more detailed way to cover all necessary COBIT contents (*cf.* Sect. 5.1). The building contractor has to deal with many challenges, e.g. the construction of new attractions (abstracted IT services in the game), the maintenance of continuous operations in the hotels (IT continuity management), or the coordination of his employees during a simulation turn (strategic IT management). At the same time the players get confronted with different skills of their staff, the required construction site equipment for the completion of a building project or other unforeseen occurrences (IT change and resource management). During a simulation turn the hotel chain owner represented by the simulation logic monitors the performance of the playgroups in regular intervals. The resulting rating of the attained achievements motivates the players and stimulates the adaption of the gaming contents [5–9].

Following the structure of COBIT it was necessary to design a simulation scenario which provides all content, selected in Sect. 5.1, in an abstract way. Furthermore it had to be ensured, that the different domains of the framework (*cf.* Sect. 3) are communicated in a self-explanatory and playful game scenario to the players. In order to guarantee the integrity of the model it was repeatedly compared with the previously defined simulation contents and optimized iteratively.

6 Development of the Simulation Concept

Based on the simulation model a game concept for the business simulation was formulated. In this context the specification of the simulation structure, the necessary roles with their associated responsibilities and the analysis of the turn achievements had to be defined.

6.1 The Structure of the COBIT Simulation

An essential element of the simulation is the operative execution of IT projects. Along the targets of COBIT also a strategic plan has to be set up by the players. For the evaluation of the turn results a summary of important business indicators is needed. For this reason a trisection of the simulation turn offered the best solution:

1. *Strategic Stage*: The group of players defines which strategy they want to implement during the operational stage at the beginning of a new simulation turn. In this context budget-, resource- and capacity-specifications have to be considered.
2. *Operational Stage*: In this stage of the simulation the developed strategic plan has to be implemented. Incidents and short-term change requests complicate the fulfillment of the plan.
3. *Evaluation Stage*: At the end of a simulation turn all activities are reviewed on the base of predefined indicators and presented to the players.

Figure 4 illustrates how the different gaming contents of the three stages are interdependent to each other. Furthermore the matching between the abstracted parts of the serious game and the corresponding contents of the COBIT framework are illustrated.

6.2 Roles and Responsibilities in the Simulation

In the first version of the business simulation only essential roles will be implemented. Their mapping to COBIT [11], their functions during a simulation turn and their corresponding persona in the educational game are shown in Fig. 5.

In the current iteration of the game, all virtual roles – except the one of the building contractor – will be engaged by the simulation logic. A later remapping to real life players may be an option for the future.

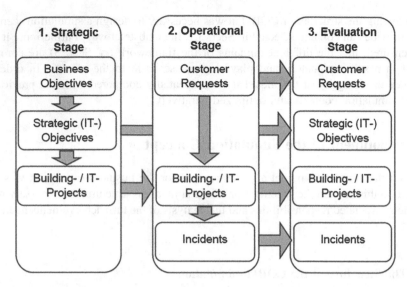

Fig. 4. Structure of a game round in the COBIT simulation

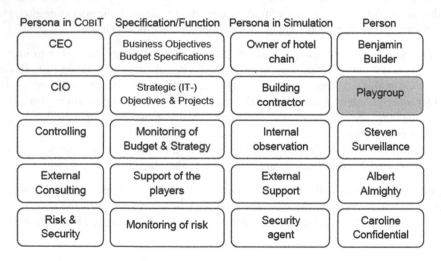

Fig. 5. Roles in the COBIT simulation

6.3   Analysis of the Round Achievements

To offer a COBIT-conform analysis of the round achievements the domain *Monitor & Evaluate* and all *Key Goal Indicators (KGIs)* of the selected *Control Objectives* for the simulation were reviewed. The review evaluated four KGIs as suitable for the result analysis [11]. These indicators form the basis for several algorithms and permit the calculation of the round achievements. The detailed configuration of the result is shown in Fig. 6.

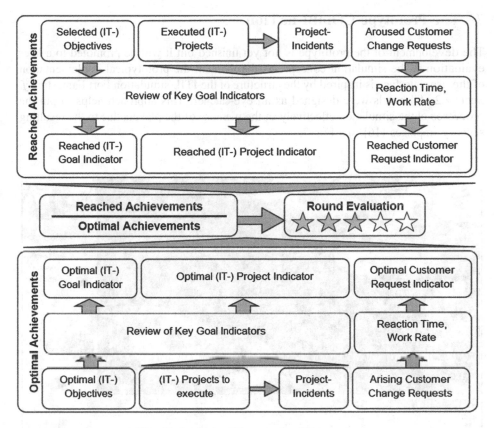

Fig. 6. Analysis of the round achievements

For the round achievement three different factors will be calculated. They consist of four different indicators from the sectors of *IT objectives*, *IT projects*, *Project-Incidents* and *Customer Change Requests*. All described sub-indicators are merged into an *(IT-) Goal-*, *(IT-) Project-* and *Customer-Request-Indicator*. For each of them, a reached and an optimal factor will be calculated and set in relation to the other. The business ratio for the reached factor rests upon the realized projects, the fulfillment of the planned goals and the handling-rate of the event-based incidents and change requests during the operational stage of the simulation turn. The optimal factor is calculated on the basis of an ex ante defined storyboard, where the trainer stores all important events for the simulation run.

After the calculation the achievements are communicated to every team of players by the simulation logic. Afterwards the results are compared to the achievements of the other groups. A collective *evaluation of the Best Practices* by the trainer closes the simulation turn to increase the adaption of the learning-contents of the simulation for a later operation in an enterprise.

7   The Prototype COmBI naTion

The development of the prototype is not yet finished but it will be promoted to a later evaluation of the simulation concept. At the moment the prototypical implementation of the user interface is inspired by the structure of the ITIL simulation Fort Fantastic, *cf.* Sect. 4.2. All hotels were designed as an eye-catcher. This approach helps to pin the processes of the simulation effectively in the memory of the players due to the resulting sensory impulses [16], *see* Fig. 7.

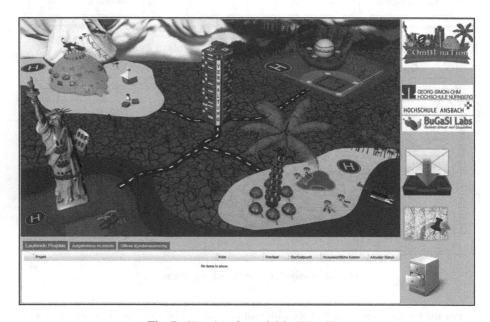

Fig. 7. User interface of COmBI naTion

The remaining parts of the user interface (UI) were designed in a functional and intuitive way. In the lower section three tabs with running projects, aroused incidents and expressed customer requests are presented to the teams. All of these have to be solved in the current simulation turn. In the right column the necessary icons for the management of activities of the operational stage, e.g. the planned building projects or the strategy to reach the objectives of the hotel chain, are located.

The simulation game is completely computer-based and accessible via a web front end. Therefore the players are location-independent and an execution of the simulation with regional separated teams is feasible. The implementation of the prototype is based on the server-side simulation framework *SUBWAY* [4] that was developed in cooperation with BuGaSi Labs. For the web UI the *Google Web Toolkit* [17], *Smart GWT* [14] and the *GWT Platform* [1] were used.

8 Conclusion

The ongoing integration of modern IT solutions in enterprises requires a successful implementation of IT governance, as it is essential for business.

The conceptual design of this business simulation shall enable its players to experience the complex COBIT processes in terms of a highly-abstracted and motivating serious game. The possibility for the players to experience the needs of the business and the efficiency of a modern IT department composes an important basis for the integration of a sophisticated alignment strategy between IT and business to enable all available potentials in the worldwide competition. The prototypical implementation of the simulation concept is not yet finished. However, the preliminary results of the COmBI naTion project demonstrate that the comprehensive contents of the COBIT framework may be implemented into a business simulation in an adequate didactical way from the actual point of view. A later evaluation of the prototype and the underlying concept will show if our simulation can support the understanding and implementation of the complex interdependencies in the field of IT governance in an enterprise.

All in all both the use of business simulations and the development of them under didactical principles provide an enormous potential of knowledge transfer [15] and deserves much more research effort.

References

1. Beaudoin, P.: A complete model-view-presenter framework to simplify your next GWT project (2011). http://code.google.com/p/gwt-platform, 31 May 2013
2. Betrancourt, M.: The animation and interactivity principles in multimedia learning. In: Mayer, R.E. (ed.) The Cambridge Handbook of Multimedia Learning, pp. 287–296. Cambridge University Press, New York (2005)
3. BuGaSi Labs: Fort Fantastic – The Simulation (2012). http://www.fortfantastic.com/index.php/en/the-simulation, 01 July 2013
4. Centmayer, M.: Subway – Konzeption und Entwicklung eines Client-Server Simulations-Frameworks für Educational und Business Games. Ansbach 2012 (2012)
5. Ganguin, S.: Computerspiele und lebenslanges Lernen – Eine Synthese von Gegensätzen. Verlag für Sozialwissenschaften, Wiesbaden (2010)
6. Dickey, M.: Game design narrative for learning: appropriating adventure game design narrative devices and techniques for the design of interactive learning environments. Educ. Tech. Res. Dev. **54**(3), 245–263 (2006)
7. Hardy, G.: ITGI to Release COBIT 4.1 and Associated Publications. COBIT Focus – The newsletter dedicated to the COBIT user community, vol. 2 (2006)
8. Holzinger, A.: Basiswissen Multimedia. Band II: Lernen – Kognitive Grundlagen multimedialer Informationssysteme. Vogel, Würzburg (2001)
9. Hugger, K.: Digitale Lernwelten: Konzepte, Beispiele und Perspektiven. Verlag für Sozialwissenschaften, Wiesbaden (2010)
10. Information Systems Audit and Control Association (ISACA): COBIT 5. Rolling Meadows 2012 (2012)
11. IT Governance Institute (ITGI) (2007a) COBIT 4.1. Rolling Meadows 2007 (2007)

12. IT Governance Institute (ITGI) (2007b) COBIT Control Practices – Guidance to achieve Control Objectives for successful IT Governance. 2nd edn. Rolling Meadows 2007 (2007)
13. IT Preneurs: The COBIT Games – How is the Game played (2010). http://www.cobitgames. com/how_to_play.php, 31 May 2013
14. Jivan, S.: Sanjiv Jivan's J2EE Blog – SmartGWT 1.0 Released! (2008). http://www.jroller. com/sjivan/entry/smartgwt_1_0_released, 31 May 2013
15. Picot, A., Zahedani, S., Ziemer, A.: Spielend die Zukunft gewinnen – Wachstumsmarkt Elektronische Spiele. Springer, Heidelberg (2008)
16. Schwan, S.: Game Based Learning – Computerspiele in der Hochschullehre (2006). e-teaching.org
17. Smeets, B., Boness, U., Bankras, R.: Beginning Google Web Toolkit – From Novice to Professional. Apress, Berkeley (2008)

The Move Beyond Edutainment:
Have We Learnt Our Lessons
from Entertainment Games?

Aida Azadegan[1(✉)], Jannicke Balsrud Hauge[2], Francesco Bellotti[3],
Riccardo Berta[3], Rafael Bidarra[4(✉)], Casper Harteveld[5],
Johann C.K.H. Riedel[6(✉)], and Ioana Andreea Stanescu[7]

[1] School of Computing, University of the West of Scotland,
Paisley PA1 2BE, UK
aida.azadegan@uws.ac.uk
[2] Bremer Instutut für Produktion und Logistik an der Universität Bremen,
Hochschulring 20, 28359 Bremen, Germany
baa@biba.uni-bremen.de
[3] University of Genoa, Via Opera Pia 11a, 16145 Genoa, Italy
{franz,berta}@elios.unige.it
[4] Delft University of Technology,
Mekelweg 4, 2628 CD Delft, The Netherlands
r.bidarra@tudelft.nl
[5] Northeastern University,
University 60 Huntington Ave., Boston, MA 02115, USA
c.harteveld@neu.edu
[6] Nottingham University Business School,
Jubilee Campus, Wollaton Rd, Nottingham NG8 1BB, UK
johann.riedel@nottingham.ac.uk
[7] Carol I National Defence University, Bucharest, Romania
ioana.stanescu@adlnet.ro

Abstract. Serious games (SGs) have been used in the education of students and
professionals for decades, but still have not reached their full potential, despite
the large consensus they have gained recently. The entertainment game industry
is a rapidly developing phenomenon, with a high market potential, enabled and
enhanced by technological innovation. The question examined in this paper is:
Did serious game designers learn from Entertainment Game (EG) designers in
building a successful game? This paper presents three case study examples of
games that have good learning outcomes to explore this question. This paper
discusses the salient aspects and the differences between the examples and
suggests how SGs could learn more from successful EGs.

1 Introduction

Entertainment Games (EGs) are defined as games that are developed and applied in
different contexts and settings solely for the purpose of entertainment. This contrasts to
SGs, which are (digital) games designed for purposes other than mere entertainment

© Springer International Publishing Switzerland 2014
A. De Gloria (Ed.): GALA 2013, LNCS 8605, pp. 77–89, 2014.
DOI: 10.1007/978-3-319-12157-4_7

[1, 6]. For example, SGs with educational purpose include explicit learning objectives and aim to achieve specific learning outcomes. This asks for a different design process, one that pays particular attention how educational content is represented and learning takes place. Yet, SGs also require the qualities that hallmark EGs.

SGs are required to learn from the entertainment industry in order to develop a captivating and engaging game environment. To do so, SG designers were asked to take the following criteria into account [5]:

- **Engagement:** The design should encourage wider and repeated use, and amplify learning opportunities and strategic thinking among users. Earlier work [8–10] on what makes players so engaged with games resulted in the identification of five factors: challenge, fantasy, curiosity, control, and interpersonal motivation.
- **Quality:** The design should have appealing visuals and graphics and an intuitive interface. Although at first, emphasis was placed on using the cutting edge in the game industry, the rise of the casual games industry and the low SG budget models led to adopting standards that are at least equal to those of casual games.
- **Balance:** The design should have models with the right amount of accuracy and have a solid integration of the educational material with gameplay. Others have later elaborated on this need for a well-balanced design, based on their own experiences in designing SGs [6].

Not much later after Rejeski's and Sawyer's report, Gee [11] published his now seminal book on what we can learn from EGs. He listed 36 principles, which range from the active, critical learning principle to the insider principle. As Gee describes, some of the best games have implemented the best theories on learning. So although EGs may not have been intentionally designed for an educational purpose, by learning from EGs and harnessing their identified principles in the development of SGs (or other educational activities), learning through SGs becomes more meaningful and effective.

Unfortunately, few to none SGs developed in the last decade have reached the viral diffusion power of EGs. *Whyville* [12] and *Quest Atlantis* [13] are one of the few exceptions. This is a possible indicator that we have been unable to achieve the desired engagement. This could be due to many factors and we should keep in mind that many SGs have a much more limited target group, but it at least begs the question if we actually have been able to implement the target qualities which were posited as initial conditions for making SGs learn from EGs. In this paper we have taken an intro-spective approach to the question if we, as SG designers, have learned from EGs in building successful educational games. We have taken three of our own case studies to explore this: *ELU*, *Seconds* and *Levee Patroller*. Each of the responsible authors reflected on the development by discussing the major successes and failures with regards to the target qualities that each, as an SG should learn from EGs, and the results are discussed in the next section. Based on this, we draw a number of lessons that the SG community can use in the next decade of SG development.

2   Case Studies of Serious Games

2.1   ELU: An Interactive TV Serious Format

The first example is from the *ELU* project. The *ELU* experience is an interesting example of the added value provided by introducing gaming mechanics into existing processes and materials to create new educational supports [14]. The idea is to build a SG format for interactive Television (iTV) by enhancing existing TV movies and videos through play-along digital games. *ELU* developed an iTV application format and corresponding development and deployment tools. At a high level, the *ELU* format involves:

- A linear AudioVisual (A/V) stream–the original video
- Non-linear interactive contents on the video that users control

The idea is to exploit a linear story (that can be viewed also by non-interactive users) and provide enhancements to improve the interactive user's experience. The *ELU* format allows multimedia content designers to build an interactive program as a sequence of educational units, named cards, that are displayed either at full-screen or partially overlapping the A/V program (or including it as a quarter picture). Each card provides one or more services, such as Multimedia Pages (MP), Interactive Edutainment Elements (quizzes, games, questionnaires, etc.), or a Virtual Teacher (VT). Cards may be synchronized with the A/V stream and are triggered at a specified time or may be asynchronous with the A/V stream.

Fig. 1. Snapshot of an *ELU* application with the Navigation Bar in the bottom of the screen, a PerformanceMeter and a ProgressBar at the top of the screen.

For every single application, the cards' flow is specified by the multimedia content designer, who is responsible for writing a script program through an ad hoc designed high-level language. The script specifies the cards (see also below), the user interaction possibilities and user profile elements according to which different personalization options are provided (e.g., in terms of card flow, contents and appearance). User profiling and assessment are fundamental aspects of serious gaming [15]. In the *ELU* system, the user profile is characterized by the learners' competences that are tracked and estimated in real-time by the system. This is achieved as the designer specifies the mapping between the user choices/responses/actions and the related competency levels [14].

In a typical program, synchronous cards are only partially overlapping the video, as the viewer should also continue following the A/V stream, while asynchronous cards appear at full-screen. Synchronous cards are typically aimed at strengthening the message of the A/V stream, helping the learner to better understand it, also through personalization, while asynchronous cards are typically available at the end of the movie, as summative tests, or to provide more information.

Another important aspect concerns the provision of feedback to the player about his performance and position in the learning space [16]. The *ELU* iTV application includes a *Progress Bar* module that is displayed on the top of the screen and schematizes the sequences of the cards in the program (Fig. 1). When a card has been completed, its outcome is shown as a green tick or red cross. Performance feedback is provided immediately just after the end of every interactive element (e.g., quiz or game). The system provides various possible types of user feedback–from jingles to VT comments, to a complete display of results and corrections–that may be chosen by authors for different needs. The overall user performance level is displayed through the *Performance Meter* that shows the player's global performance, obtained by summing the score of the cards. Performance is expressed as a percentage of the maximum score (Fig. 1, on the black stripe, on the bottom right), in order to provide an objective value.

TVSerGames is the library of game templates from which the *ELU* play-along games are instantiated (Fig. 2 shows some examples from the interactive version of Walt Disney's Snow White movie). We group them in three clusters:

- **Games and Quizzes:** *Quiz*: sequences of questions and answers; *VisualQuiz*: Q&As in images; *Couples*: join the matching elements; *RightPlace*: put icons in their right place; *RightOrder*: order a sequence of items; *Puzzle*: build an image from shuffled pieces; *Memory*: remember the cards; *Stop it!* stop the animation at the right time to answer the question; *RepeatedTrials*: statistic outcomes from experiments.
- **Simulation:** *Stock Exchange simulation*: statistics and business.
- **Clusters:** *Menu*: Cluster of games from a menu (with the replay option); *Millionaire*: Millionaire-like difficulty-escalation game/quiz cluster.

Qualitative and quantitative results on a test group of 40 university students from Italy and Latvia show the potential of the system for informal education [14]. For example, on the experience questionnaire, users reported high values for pleasantness (3.9, on a 0-5 scale), enjoyment (3.7) and usefulness (3.5) of the application.

The *ELU* system reflects some important elements of the learning principles defined by Gee [11]. First of all, the system is highly and intrinsically multimodal (No. 3 and 20), adding multimedia interactivity to video clips. As apparent from Fig. 2, the cards also involve a strong interaction with texts that is not purely verbal (No. 18).

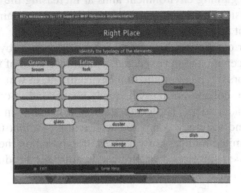

Fig. 2. Snapshot of two synchronous games (*VisualQuiz* and *TextQuiz*) played along the Disney Snow White movie and one asynchronous games played at the end of the movie stream (*RightPlace*)

The achievement principle (No. 11) is highly addressed through the above presented feedback elements, such as the *Progress Bar* and the *Performance Meter*.

Also, the *ELU* iTV format, that can be instantiated in several different serious games, structurally supports three fundamental Gee's principles, such as:

- The multiple routes principle (No. 16), in particular for the runtime automatic personalization and for the possibility of the user to choose different options and games;
- The incremental principle (No. 24), which is again supported through the personalization and multiple path options;
- The transfer principle (No. 29), which concerns in particular the games available in the menu shown at the end of the video, where users have more time to play, applying the concepts addressed during the video.

The *ELU* format supports all the Malone and Lepper's individual motivational factors [8–10]. While challenge, curiosity and fantasy depend on the actual game contents and graphics, the control factor is supported by the fact that the SGs spur the user to take decisions both on the path and the choices available for assessment.

Concerning the interpersonal factors, the iTV technology is typically unidirectional. Thus cooperation, competition and recognition is not possible through that medium alone. In order to allow users to have a reference, their performance is stated as a percentage with respect to the optimum. To achieve a full support of the interpersonal factors, other means such as ancillary (mobile) web applications should be considered.

2.2   Seconds: A Role Playing Game to Improve Decision-Making Skills

Seconds is a role and simulation based, multi-player game used to train students in decision-making [17]. It has been developed for workshop settings, using a blended learning concept. The gaming environment aims at increasing the awareness of how a participant's own decision-making impacts the supply chain, training strategic thinking and applying different methods for strategic decision-making. *Seconds* is scenario based, and the teacher can define the starting level of difficulty by using an authoring tool for adapting the scenarios to the expected competence level of the participants. The gaming scenario mirrors a typical production environment, in which complex products have to be produced in collaboration (own supply chain) and in competition (different supply chain) with stakeholders. The game features a generic simulation model, with reduced complexity and accuracy compared with reality, so that the students do only need to cope with a limited numbers of variables. It is based on the disjunction of time and space and has been developed at Bremer Institut für Produktion und Logistik (BIBA) for use at the University of Bremen (Fig. 3).

Fig. 3. GUI in the Seconds game

The figure above shows the graphical user interface (GUI). It gives players the information they need to take decisions. In *Seconds* curiosity and fantasy (see Sect. 1) of the players are fostered through only providing a starting scenario. The path of the game depends on the co-creation of players, which leads to a high degree of engagement. This is in line with Gee's idea on empowered learners and his "insider principle" (No. 36). By actively letting the students influence the gaming scenario and the outcome, they are encouraged to design their own learning experience and support active learning (No. 1).

The interface also indicates the performance of each player, by showing graphs on cost-benefit, profit, quality of delivery etc. These indicators are both used for giving immediate feedback to the students on their achievements (No. 11), as well as an element for motivation. The student and the "supply chain" team that at given points have achieved the "best" performance indicators are the winner. Players have lost the game when they get bankrupt. Teams can continue after a player's bankruptcy, but need to find a new supplier. These indicators also help players control the game and commit them to the game play (No. 7). As the scenario advances, players can improve skills, and thus achieve better quality and price. Their improvement is based on their performance in the game and their experience. Players can observe this, either by looking at the KPI as numbers or at a graphical presentation. In this way, the KPI changes will show players their success or failure. The game is designed to support co-operation. The success of each player depends on their ability to build products in production networks.

During game- the game	---	--	-	-/+	+	++	+++
The game helps in understanding theory	1	2	3	4	5	6	7
		2	1	2	21	17	27
The game is suitable for awareness of decisions	1	2	3	4	5	6	7
			1	1	21	19	28
The game supports Understand the theory	1	2	3	4	5	6	7
			1	4	9	35	21
The game mediates the complexity of SC	1	2	3	4	5	6	7
		1	1	9	19	21	19
The game supports applying theory	1	2	3	4	5	6	7
		1	1	3	35	15	15

Fig. 4. Example of evaluation results of Seconds for 2012–2013 classes

Around 300 students played *Seconds*, mostly in groups of around 24 students. The learning outcomes have been evaluated through questionnaires, analysis of student lab reports, as well as observations by facilitators/teachers and by examining the results in the database later. The current learning results are good, but the game has undergone continuous changes in order to increase the usability and the learning outcome. Several former students, now working in the field of Supply Chain Management (SCM), report that what they experienced and learned within the game has been useful and transferable to their new working environment (No. 29). Figure 4 shows some of the results from the students' questionnaire from years 2012 and 2013. The complexity of the GUI is still an issue, and for some scenarios we also see a need for a more accurate underlying simulation model. We have been analysing why several SGs need to have hand-on practice sessions and use facilitators, whereas EGs do not. One main outcome is that many SGs have focused too much on the learning outcome and thus have an unbalanced design concept. This is also the case for *Seconds*. Another observation is that if the starting scenario does not fit the competence level of the students, it has a major negative impact on the engagement level and motivation.

If the starting scenario is too complex (i.e. requires a higher level of SCM understanding than the students have), they are not able to take strategic decisions based on the feedback delivered by the game and take their decisions intuitively (No. 15).

2.3   Levee Patroller: A 3-D Action Game to Make Sense of Flood Risks

Levee Patroller is a single-player 3D first person game, aimed at training levee (or dyke) patrollers working for Dutch water boards, which play a crucial role in national security [18]. In the game, a trainee has to locate every levee failure occurring within the domain entrusted to him, report about it and possibly, depending on the state of the failure, return to the location to see if it has worsened. The game was designed to be used in workshops during which playing the game is combined with a lecture on levee inspection, or in workshops that focus completely on the game. It is played against the clock, ending either when all the emerging failures have been satisfactorily found, reported and handled, or when the player's negligence leads to a levee breach that floods the whole region. The game was developed in 2007 by Delft University of Technology, Deltares and several Dutch Water Boards [18].

Adhering to the SG criteria mentioned in Sect. 1, the developers made use of the cutting edge game technology at that time, the commercial game 3D engine "Unreal Engine 2". Throughout the development, the designers spent much effort and dedication into making a well-balanced game, which led to a SG design philosophy [6]. For example, the designers made sure that all the aspects of the learning environment were interactive, which is in accordance to Gee's active, critical learning principle (No. 1). When players want to know the length of a crack, they do not get a popup screen with information. Instead, they have to actively measure the crack by placing a "measuring marker" on one end of the crack and a second marker at the other end. Making the failures appear randomly in scenarios ensured a challenge. This further increased the repeatability of the game, which is importance for letting players practice with the game (No. 12).

Unfortunately, the game ended up being used primarily for demonstrations during workshops. In an effort to apply the game as envisioned, significant evidence was found [19]. After three weeks of distance training with the game, participants starting with limited practical experience performed as well as experts (No. 4) and their learning transferred to real world situations (No. 29). It was also engaging (No. 7): 80 % of the 147 participants played almost all exercises and spent over 10 h voluntarily and enjoyed doing this. During interviews and discussion, participants mentioned that

Fig. 5. Screenshot from Levee Patroller showing a levee failure

the game helped them to identify what it means to be a levee patroller and became better aware of their knowledge regarding the topic (Fig. 5).

These are unexpectedly positive results, yet the study highlighted many short-comings. First, participants complained about the difficulty and incomprehensibility of navigating the menus. The game clearly did not fulfill the quality standards of interface design. Second, the game had little interpersonal motivation and certainly lacked an affinity space (No. 35) in which players could converse about the game. Participants indicated that they wanted to have more interaction among each other. Third, participants indicated that they had trouble understanding the vocabulary of the game and found the learning curve of the game too steep, despite the inclusion of a tutorial. Fourth, the game applied no differentiation among and adaptation to players, meaning that some players experienced frustration and others boredom. Although more short-comings are discussed in detail elsewhere [19], the final shortcoming we want to highlight is that of feedback (No. 27). The game has several sorts of feedback. The feedback during a scenario was not direct enough as players had difficulty in under-standing what they did right or wrong. Then players often skipped or did not under-stand how to read the feedback at the end of the scenario.

3 Discussions

Both SGs and EGs rely on the innovative fusion of digital technologies and cultural creativity [3]. Even if EGs and SGs answer to different objectives and performance criteria, there are significant lessons that SG communities can learn from the EG industry, as well as significant resources that can be adapted for reusability between the two communities. In this paper we introspectively assessed whether the games we have developed abide by the SG criteria posed at the beginning of the 21st century; in doing this, we illustrated how we can learn from EGs in developing SGs. Such an assessment is inherently limited and biased. The games presented here are a small slice of all the SGs that have been developed and we cannot draw conclusions on behalf of all of them. However, for the SG field to mature and become as pervasive in society as EGs, it is important to reflect on what has been done and how we can move forward into the next decade of SG development. We see this paper as the start of an important discussion and encourage others to reflect on their games too. The criteria and insights discussed here will foster this discussion.

As for the three cases, each one of them found success, providing evidence for games' educational potential in different domains and through different types of games. The three cases widely differ on their topic, target group and implementation. *ELU* uses existing game formats (i.e., quizzes) on top of video material for children; *Seconds* is an interactive spread sheet simulation for SCM students; and *Levee Patroller* is a fully immersive 3-D action game for practitioners dealing with flood risks. Based on the reflections, it becomes clear that all cases tapped into the affordances offered by games, such as multimodality, feedback, active learning, scores and progression indicators, rewards and practice opportunities, and integrated the educational content into the game, which is a step forward compared to most edutainment titles [3]. *Seconds* and *Levee Patroller* differ from *ELU* in providing players an opportunity to become part of a "semiotic domain," that of SCM and levee inspection, respectively. Players become acquainted with the vocabulary and practices and learn to think like a supply chain manager or levee patroller. *ELU*, on the other hand, includes scaffolding, personalization and incremental progression, aspects that the other cases are lacking. And unlike *ELU*, *Seconds* and *Levee Patroller* reported interface problems in addition to problems with the learning curve. The fact that *Seconds* as well as *Levee Patroller* needed hands-on practice sessions to be used is an indicator that these games are not intuitive enough. This might be due to the increased complexity of these types of games, which require more iterations and development efforts to be done right. Nevertheless, these observations show that in terms of quality and balance these SGs still lack behind compared to EGs. We think this is general problem. SGs rarely re-enter the development cycle and their performance is usually assessed based on a singular development attempt. Largely due to limited budgets, SGs are because of this not thoroughly redesigned. Even if multiple iterations are made, such as with *Levee Patroller*, this is far less than the necessary number of iterations made by EGs to be competitive (e.g., *Angry Birds*: it was Rovio's 46th attempt to develop an entertainment game, and they almost went bankrupt in the process). SGs also need good quality Human-Computer Interaction to be really successful.

Except for *Seconds*, which is a multiplayer game, *ELU* and *Levee Patroller* lack any social features, which are important in today's EGs. In fact, all three failed to build what Gee coined "affinity space" surrounding the game. This is a space where learning happens about the game outside of playing the game itself and this is considered instrumental, if not crucial, for deep learning to occur. *Seconds* and *Levee Patroller* may have a debriefing, but if a community of learners emerges surrounding a game, this will have a much stronger effect, on learning and also on the game's longevity and dissemination. This lack is largely attributable for problems in structurally implementing SGs and the constraints SGs work with such as having a specific target group. EGs exploit global networks of production and distribution, and although they need to consider local cultural practices, tastes and social structures if they are to succeed across major markets, most SGs focus on specific cultural practices and rarely benefit of massive market production and distribution, which can lead to obscurity and failure in large-scale dissemination and the building of a community. Of course, if SGs are reasonably successful, they can gain a certain level of popularity and can be deployed on a larger scale, even if the GUI has not been refined. Very few SGs have made this leap. Most have remained prototypes and are used in forced evaluations or in local practices only.

4 Conclusions and Future Work

In reflecting on whether we have learned our lessons from the entertainment industry, it becomes clear that in developing SGs we got the 'basics' right. We moved away from edutainment and started tapping into the affordances that games offer by providing instant feedback, allowing for multiple routes to progress, and so on. It further becomes clear that although we know what is needed, it is still not as refined, user-friendly, and geared toward the player compared to EGs, as illustrated by the interface and balance issues reported in the cases. The more complex the game, the more likely this will be the case. Various causes account for this: limited budget and time, few iterations and difficulty balancing the multiple objectives needed for SGs [6]. Another insight is that the games failed to build a learning community, largely due to being able to implement the games in any structural way. This means the SG community learned from previous mistakes and from the entertainment industry, but SG designers can still learn a lot more from EGs.

So what does the SG community need to do in the next decade? First, as stressed in the previous section, we encourage others to reflect on their SGs and join this discussion. Hearing that SGs are "awful" or "bad" compared to EGs is not very helpful. We need to know what is exactly wrong with them and take the necessary steps to make sure future SGs do abide by the ideals once set forth. Second, we need to learn more about how EG developers balance their games and we need to prioritize usability and user experience as part of the development. Methods and insights from Game User Research (GUR) and game analytics should be considered for achieving this [2], as they provide heuristics for how games can be fine-tuned. Successful EG designers rely heavily on this (i.e., the large success *Candy Crush Saga* is based on analysing player data). Third, customization and personalization require more attention. This is needed to enable teachers to personalize the game according to the students' performance or implementing specific educational and technical requirements related to pedagogical constructs, learners' assessment and standardization [7]. It would further extend the use of a particular SG beyond a local practice, which is important for larger-scale distribution and dissemination. Fourth, as a community SG developers need to start finding a way of sharing best practices and insights. The community is fragmented [4], largely because it is applied in so many different domains and contexts. It does not have dissemination platforms and venues of the likes of 'Gamasutra' and the 'Game Developers Conference', places where many EG designers share and discuss their experiences. In Europe the Games and Learning Alliance (GaLA) network attempts to change this and in North America the Learning Game Network with its Playful Learning initiative is trying to accomplish this, but currently we are still far away from a thriving, collaborative community. Fifth, we need to start moving beyond the stage of (experimental) research to proof that SGs work, and instead work on issues of implementation, business models and community building, which are essential for having sustainable products.

For achieving these goals in the next decade, future work should especially consider bridging the gaps between the SG community and the EG industry, and between academia and industry, with the purpose of enabling joint game development efforts that would benefit all communities. In addition, other areas of interest for collaboration can include content interoperability standards, architectures to support interoperability, procedural level construction and networking protocols. The release of *SimCityEdu* in Fall 2013, the educational version of the latest *SimCity* franchise, which has been developed in collaboration with Electronic Arts, is a hopeful promise that we are moving into this direction.

Acknowledgments.   The research reported in this paper has been partially supported by the European Union, particularly through the projects GaLA: The European Network of Excellence on Serious Games (FP7-ICT) www.galanoe.eu and ELU: Enhanced Learning Unlimited (FP6-IST-027866).

References

1. Michael, D., Chen, S.: Serious games: Games that Educate, Train, and Inform. Thomson Course Technology, Boston (2006)
2. Seif El-Nasr, M., Drachen, A., Canossa, A. (eds.): Game Analytics: Maximizing the Value of Player Data. Springer, London (2013)
3. Bernhaupt, R. (ed.): Evaluating User Experience in Games: Concepts and Methods. Springer, London (2010)
4. Spires, H.: 21st Century Skills and serious games: preparing the N generation. In: Annetta L.A. (ed.) Serious Educational Games: From Theory to Practice, pp. 13–24. Sense Publishers, Rotterdam (2008)
5. Sawyer, B.: Serious Games: Improving Public Policy Through Game-based Learning and Simulation. WoodrowWilson International Center for Scholars, Washington (2002)
6. Harteveld, C.: Triadic Game Design: Balancing Reality, Meaning and Play. Springer, London (2011)
7. Stanescu, I.A., Warmelink, H.J.G., Lo, J., Arnab, S., Dagnino, F., Mooney, J.: Accessibility, reusability and interoperability in the european serious game community. In: Proceedings of the 9th International Scientific Conference eLearning and Software for Education, Bucharest (2013)
8. Malone, T.W.: Toward a theory of intrinsically motivating instruction. Cogn. Sci. **5**(4), 333–369 (1981)

9. Malone, T.W., Lepper, M.: Intrinsic motivation and instructional effectiveness in computer-based education. In: Snow, R., Farr, M. (eds.) Aptitude Learning and Instruction, pp. 152–188. Lawrence Erlbaum Associates, London (1987)
10. Malone, T.W., Lepper, M.: Making learning fun: a taxonomy of intrinsic motivation for learning. In: Snow, R., Farr, M. (eds.) Aptitude Learning and Instruction, pp. 223–253. Lawrence Erlbaum Associates, London (1987)
11. Gee, J.: What video games have to teach us about learning and literacy. Palgrave Macmillan, New York (2003)
12. Kafai, Y., Fields, D.: Connected Play: Tweens in a Virtual World. The MIT Press, Cambridge (2013)
13. Barab, S., Thomas, M., Dodge, T., Carteaux, R., Tuzun, H.: Making learning fun: Quest Atlantis, a game without guns. Educ. Technol. Res. Devel. 53(1), 86–107 (2005)
14. Bellotti, F., Berta, R., De Gloria, A., Ozolina, A.: Investigating the added value of interactivity and serious gaming for educational TV. Comput. Educ. 57(1), 1137–1148 (2011)
15. Bellotti, F., Kapralos, B., Lee, K., Moreno-Ger, P., Berta, R.: Assessment in and of Serious Games: an overview. Hindawi Advances in Human-Computer Interaction (2013)
16. Björk, S., Holopainen, J.: Patterns in Game Design. Charles River Media, Hingham (2005)
17. Baalsrud Hauge, J., Braziotis, C.: Enhancing the student's learning on supply chain management through the application of a business game In: Proceedings of the 17th International Symposium on Logistics, ISI 2012, Centre of concurrent Enterprise, Nottingham University Business School. Nottingham, pp. 683–689 (2012)
18. Harteveld, C., Guimarães, R., Mayer, I., Bidarra, R.: Balancing pedagogy, game and reality components within a unique serious game for training levee inspection. In: Hui, K.-C., Pan, Z., Chung, R.C.-K., Wang, C.C., Jin, X., Göbel, S., Li, E.C.-L. (eds.) EDUTAINMENT 2007. LNCS, vol. 4469, pp. 128–139. Springer, Heidelberg (2007)
19. Harteveld, C.: Making Sense of Virtual Risks: A Quasi-Experimental Investigation into Game-Based Training. IOS Press, Amsterdam (2012)

Flooded: A Location-Based Game for Promoting Citizens' Preparedness to Flooding Situations

Sondre Johan Mannsverk, Ines Di Loreto, and Monica Divitini[✉]

Norwegian University of Science and Technology (NTNU),
Trondheim, Norway
ines.di_loreto@utt.fr, divitini@idi.ntnu.no

Abstract. With the global climate changes we can expect an increased occurrence of floods, even in areas not previously affected by flooding. Having the possibility to add to the traditional crisis management organization workforce also a higher number of citizens is thus very important. Despite of this, the general public seems to be ignorant of the possibility and consequences of a major flood. In this paper we present a game for promoting citizens' preparedness to flooding situations, called Flooded. Flooded was designed using current flooding management elements, but having as main objective citizens' sensitizations. Results of the evaluations show that the game was successful in promoting flood awareness, especially in terms of increasing the player's knowledge of the local territory, but that a proper briefing and debriefing session is required to facilitate learning, retention and reflection.

1 Introduction

Over the last 35 years, the frequency of natural and man-caused disasters has increased five-fold and the damage caused has multiplied by approximately 8 times [1], making preparedness to crisis management a priority for all European countries [2]. In this scenario, having the possibility to add to the traditional crisis management organization workforce also a higher number of citizens is very important. However, training for crisis is challenging because of the complexity of the work to be performed during a real crisis, but also because of its sporadic and discontinuous nature. To address the complexity of training and complement real life training for citizens we propose to make use of serious games (i.e., games with other purposes than pure entertainment). Serious games can help participants not only to learn basic procedures but also to see things differently (and act differently) from the way they are used to act in real life. In particular in this paper we present a game for promoting citizens' preparedness to flooding situations, called Flooded. Flooded was designed using current flooding management elements, but having has main objective citizens' sensitizations. Preparedness to flooding was chosen as a subject as it's a kind of emergency that (i) continue to occur across a region; (ii) requires preparedness mechanisms that can be used also in other kind of natural disasters. In more details:

© Springer International Publishing Switzerland 2014
A. De Gloria (Ed.): GALA 2013, LNCS 8605, pp. 90–103, 2014.
DOI: 10.1007/978-3-319-12157-4_8

(i) Flooding causes enormous damages all over the world every year. In the period 1975–2001, flood events killed over 175,000 persons and affected more than 2.2 billion persons [3]. In addition to loss of lives, flooding causes material damage of billions of US dollars every year [4].

(ii) Managing flooding and the risk of flooding are keys to reduce loss of lives and material damages. To manage and re-duce flood risks a variety of strategies are being used. Forecasting and warning is used to predict when a flood is coming and to let the public know that they need to prepare. The construction of flood protection is important to reduce the impact of an impending flood, and involves building dams and levees and other protective measures [5]. A key element of flood management is the use of volunteers to help with flood protection [6]. However to recruit volunteers the public needs to be aware that flood preparedness require citizen's participation. A major issue in this regard is that people will only prepare if they feel that it is personally relevant which is not yet the case [7]. The general public seem to be ignorant of the possibilities and consequences of a major flood, and few considers moving away from areas that could be affected by flooding, with many seemingly displaying a "This cannot happen to me" attitude [8]. The increased chance of flooding, the severe consequences of major flood and the low level of awareness of citizens makes it clear that there is a need to improve the flood preparedness of citizens [9]. In this paper we describe our first attempt to use serious games to promote citizens' preparedness to flooding situations.

The rest of this paper is structured as follow. Next Section describes the state of the art of games linked with flooding preparedness. Section 3 draws some design challenge we had to address when creating our game. Section 4 describes the Flooded, a location based game for promoting citizens preparedness to flooding situations. Section 5 reports on the game evaluation. Finally, in Sect. 6 we return on the design challenges to see if the game was able to satisfy them or not.

2 State of the Art

In a previous paper on collaborative serious games for crisis management [10] we listed the elements constituting crisis management training. Limited time for decision-making, the importance of considering local optimum and global optimum (the best local decision is not necessarily the best global decision), the use of communication and collaboration, and a good territory knowledge where identified as important elements for crisis training. In the same paper we also analyzed ten serious games in the context of crisis management and found out that they had several limitations. In particular none of the analyzed game has a good connection with an actual territory, and soft skills training (e.g., communication styles during a crisis, team management and coordination, time management, stress management) was not structured. For this paper we will focus in particular on these categories when analyzing the related works (see Table 1). When doing research for the related work no serious games were found that aimed directly to promote flood preparedness. Only two serious games were found in the context of flood management, FloodSim [11] and Levee Patroller [12]. FloodSim is a simulation developed to help raise awareness of flooding issues, while Levee Patroller is a game developed to train to inspect levees. FloodSim is a relatively short and simple simulation, with basic game elements that allows the players to make strategic decisions in the context of flood management. The gameplay is linked to the territory, in the sense that the players can see an overview of a simulated flood in different cities in the UK, but it does not allow the players to actually explore the territories. In addition the game has no collaborative elements. The results of the evaluation of FloodSim, showed that the game was successful in increasing awareness at the basic level [13]. Levee Patroller aims to train the appropriate inspection skills. The motivation for creating the game was that failures of levees are quite rare, which made it difficult for the "levee patrollers" to learn from experience. A game was therefore created to simulate levee failure, to teach the patrollers to detect them. A case-study of Levee Patroller showed that the game was useful in promoting flood defense [14]. To go over the exploration of the territory limitation we decided to analyze also location based games. Only one location-based game was found in the context of crisis management, Code Red: Mobile, but as it was poorly documented in terms of game dynamics and mechanics, it was not investigated. No true location-based games were found in the context of flood preparedness or management. We analyzed then location-based games more in general. We used then previous state-of-the- arts, internet search and previous knowledge of existing location-based games and identified 20 location based games. Only 6 were selected as interesting for our research (for a more detailed analysis see [15]). Geocaching [16] was selected as it is the most well-known location-based game. It is an outdoor game where the players hide and locate containers, like a treasure hunt where the players use GPS. Although Geocaching does not require the players to collaborate, as locating a geocache requires the participants to search for and find a physical object, working together makes the game easier [17]. Floracaching [18] was selected as it had similar dynamics to Geocaching, but with a specific learning goal. In Floracaching the players search for plants identified by a GPS coordinate. Frequency 1550 [19] was selected as it combines exploration in a city environment with learning. The game takes place in six areas that represents Amsterdam anno 1550 and uses both a group of players going on the streets with mobiles and players using desktops. The game was developed as a research pilot by the Waag Society with the aim of increasing the players' awareness and knowledge of history, and their motivation for history. Savannah [20] was selected as it was the one of the most cited location-based games. Savannah is a location-based game pro-totype designed to teach players about lion behavior. The game is played with the combination of a handheld computer and a GPS receiver, rather than with a mobile phone. Shadow Cities [21] was selected as an example of "normal" game (a game created for pure entertainment purposes). Shadow Cities is a location-based multiplayer game for iPhone. In Shadow Cities, players turn into mages with magical powers, and their neighborhood turn into a magical game world. The players' goal is to explore and conquer their city and other cities all over the world. Finally, The Hidden Park [22] was primarily selected because it features an editor for expanding the game to new areas. The game turns local parks into fantasy worlds where the players must run around to solve puzzles using clues. It utilizes the iPhone's GPS, camera and speaker to immerse the players into the game world. The goal of the players is to prove the existence of magical animals in the park, to stop it from being over-run by greedy developers. Table 1 shows the different aspects of the described games. As we can see the games targeting flood do not involve territory exploration and the games involving territory exploration, having different purposes from flooding sensitization do not show the additional characteristics useful for this kind of games. For example, there is no explicit training of soft skills such as being able to pass the right information to the right person at the right time.

Table 1. Summative table for game analysis

Game	General soft skill	Collaboration	Territory exploration
FloodSim	–		
Levee Patroller	–	X	
Geocaching	–	X	X
Frequency 1550	–	X	X
Floracaching	–		X
Savannah	–		X
Shadow Cities	–	X	X
The Hidden Park	–		X

3 Design Challenges

From the previous two Sections we can underline in particular two main design challenges to take into account when designing a game targeting citizens' preparedness to flooding issues.

Increasing preparedness: Flood preparedness is used to describe any precautionary measures taken against impending flood(s). To increase the preparedness of citizens the most effective strategy is to inform them of the consequences of a flood [7]. The first step to promote flood preparedness is to sensitize citizens to the dangers and consequences of a flood. Awareness of appropriate actions to take in case of flood warnings is also vital [23]. A key element is knowing where and when to evacuate. To know where to evacuate the citizens must be aware of their local area. They need to know where it is safe to go and how to get there. For a citizen to be effectively prepared for a flood he needs to have the required soft skills (collaboration, communication, and the like). This includes listening and correctly responding to flood warnings, and communicating effectively when helping with flood management. We can then summarize all these aspect as:

- **Challenge 1:** Sensitizing about dangers of flooding.
- **Challenge 2:** Importance of doing the right action (before, during, and after a flooding).
- **Challenge 3:** Importance of territory monitoring/exploration.
- **Challenge 4:** Importance of soft skills (collaboration, communication, and the like).

A game in this context should then provide the necessary elements to promote and improve these qualities. As we can see from Table 1 none of the analyzed Serious Games target soft skills, collaboration, and territory exploration as a whole.

Create Engagement: The main purpose of a serious game is to train or sensitize people. But if the game is not engaging, people would not want to return to play, highly diminishing its impact. It can also lead to people learning less when playing the game, as they have less motivation to do well. This is a very important element when trying to sensitize people about an issue, like in our case. Finding motivational aspects that can engage people to play our game is thus an important element. It is worth to note that the game should feature engaging gameplay, which does not necessarily means that it needs to be fun.

In the following section we will describe the game design we created in order to address the above listed design challenges while in Sect. 5 we will describe the first results of its evaluation.

4 Flooded Game Design

As flooding is a territory based problem, being able to support this aspect becomes really important in order to have a good sensitization approach. Flooded is then a location-based mobile game to be played in the player's local territory. The game world is the real world represented through Google maps. In the map the players can see their own position, game objects, and the position of other players. The game is composed of three different phases. The first phase represents the time just before a flooding, the central phase depicts when the flood is hitting, while the final phase represents the time after the flood has hit. The players will have to help predicting and managing the flood before it hits, can see what happens when a flood occurs, and then they will have to act in the flooded area. Breaking the flooding in phases helped us in creating a more immersive gameplay experience and in enlarging the number of learning and sensitization objectives. The game dynamics mixes cooperation and competition. Three out of the four total quests allow the players to collaborate to achieve a common goal. They are all global quests, in the sense that the players all interact with the same game world and have the same objectives. A simple reward system has been implemented to give the players an additional extrinsic motivation to play. The players get points for doing correct actions, but can also lose points if they do something wrong. In addition the game uses a leveling system based on the player's current points. Each level represents a rank and when the player gains a level he is promoted to a new rank. If the player fails too many times, he is demoted to a lower level. The game is connected to Facebook through the built-in friends' functionality. This aspect is used to facilitate a more social experience, allowing the player to play with friends. The game has also a messaging functionality for facilitating communication between the players during the current game session.

4.1 The Quests More in Detail

The game features four different quests used to teach different aspects of flooding preparedness, and based on real world practices.

Quest 1: Flood Protection. In areas with a flooding history it is vital to learn how to protect the area to minimize the possible damage. In the *Flood Protection* quest the players must collaborate to place (virtual) sandbags at key locations to protect the area. The main learning objective of this quest is to teach the player not only that placing sandbags is a suitable strategy for flood protection, but also that a good sandbag placement can help to improve survival possibilities. This element is used to address challenges 1 and 2 (sensitizing about dangers of flooding and about the importance of doing the right action at the right time). In order to obtain this learning goal, the intensity of the flood happening in the second phase is dependent from the player's performance in this quest. Players will then be able to see the consequences of good or poor flood protection, depending on how they performed in this part. In order to minimize the effects of the flooding the players need to cover a significant section of the river with sandbags. This means that they will have to physically walk through the area in order to place the sandbags. This element is used to address challenge 3 (the importance of territory monitoring/exploration). In addition each player does not have enough sandbags to do this coverage of the territory alone. In order to cover the entire area at the best of their possibilities, players will have thus to coordinate, in order to decide who will cover a particular part of the territory. This element is used to address challenge 4 (the importance of soft skills training). This quest has a time limit of eight minutes to add real time stress to the quest. When the time runs out the players are presented with the group's flood protection score calculated taking into account how much of the area the players were able to protect (100 % is a perfect score). In order to calculate this protection score the sandbag distance from the river and the proximity with other sandbags are taken into account. Distance from the river is an important factor, as the closer the sandbag walls are placed the more of the area they are able to protect. Sandbag walls also need to be placed near other sandbag walls to be effective as a single wall is not capable of protecting much by itself.

Quest 2: Monitor the territory. Measuring the water level of a river is important to be able to predict if the river is about to overflow. In this quest, the players are asked to measure the depth of the water at different points along the river (challenge 1). If they encounter a critical rise in water level they must start an evacuation of the area (challenge 2). The main learning objective of this quest is to teach players that measuring the water level can be used for predicting floods. They will also be sensitized about the fact that an early flood warning is important to be able to evacuate in time. Finally, the players must move along the river to measure the water, which promotes exploration of the territory (addressing challenge 3). From a practical point of view, the quest consists in five check points along the river bank where the players must measure and submit the water level. The quest has a time limit of 7 min. As for the first quest, to be able to measure the water level at all the check points before the time runs out the players must split up and cover different parts of the territory (challenge 4). Coordination can be done through face-to-face communication, messaging, or by observing where the other players are on the map. If the players encounter a critical water level in different check points they are instructed to start an evacuation (triggering the evacuation quest for all the players) (Fig. 1).

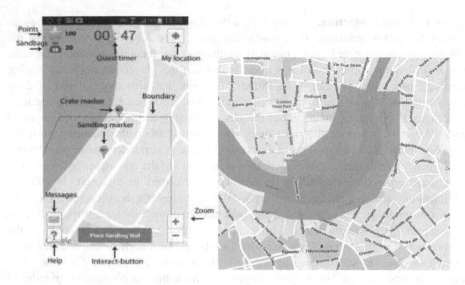

Fig. 1. (a) Main screen; (b) A maximum impact flood

Quest 3: Evacuation. When a flood warning is given, the appropriate action is to evacuate the area and go somewhere with a higher elevation. In this quest the players must run to an evacuation zone (displayed on the map) before the time runs out (challenges 1, 2, 3). If they are not able to reach the evacuation zone, they will die. By reaching the zone in time they are rewarded with points. The main learning goal is to teach that evacuation is the right course of action when a flood warning is issued. Players will also get sensitized to the geography of their local area as they have to move to a location with a higher elevation. This can make them aware of where it is smart to go if a real flood occurs.

During the Flood. This is a passive moment in the game as once the flood hits the river will overflow and the player will not have the possibility to stop it. The flooding is represented on the map as a transparent blue color that broadens the actual river (Fig. 1(b)). How much the river overflows is dependent from how well the players were able to perform in the previous quests. When the flood hits, if a player is into a flooded zone, he will die. This emotional aspect is used to sensitize about the dangers of flooding and the impact of flood protection.

Quest 4: Search and rescue. In this quest the players will look for missing people by exploring different zones. The missing people are non-player characters (NPCs) and they can be dead, injured or dehydrated (challenge 1). The NPC remains hidden until the players are within 25 m of his location. When the players get close enough they can interact with the NPCs to discover their condition. Once done, they must notify the correct authorities about the situation (for examples describing which kind of help the NPC needs, or if the NPC is dead). Obviously, to have a better chance of finding all the missing people the players should coordinate about who goes where (challenge 4). Again, because the players must physically search the area to find people, they could learn more about their local area (challenge 3). It's worth to note that if a player walks into a flooded area he dies (challenge 2).

Short Technical Description: The prototype is a standalone Android application. To play the game the players need to login with their Facebook account. Connection to Facebook is realized through the Facebook Android API v3.0, which supports basic methods to login, get user data and retrieve friends list and profile pictures, to name a few. As the game is location-based, it requires a displayable map of the player's current location, as well as any relevant game-related locations, such as quest objects and other players. The map functionality is implemented using the Google Maps Android API v2, which offers easy access to most of Google Maps' features. By using the API, map markers and the player's current position can be added to the map. The API also provides zoom and panning functionality. Quest and player data are stored in a MySQL. PHP scripts are used for fetching, updating, and inserting data. When a PHP fetch script is called, data is returned as JSON objects. Gson, a Java library, is used for converting the JSON representation to Java Objects that can be understood by the application. When a player does an action in the game, such as placing a sandbag wall, a request is sent to the server to update the database. In addition to updating the database, the server notifies the other players' devices of the action. The other players' maps are subsequently updated. To support this functionality, Google Cloud Messaging (GCM) is used.

5 Evaluation

The evaluation was performed in 2 iterations, with 8 players in total. Both evaluations lasted 1 h with around 30 min used for gameplay. The participants were all in their mid-twenties and with no physical handicap, which meant that they all had a good understanding of using mobile devices and had no major issue with the physicality of the game. The evaluation involved a game session where the volunteers played the game, a short questionnaire, and a focus group. More quantitative data were collected tracking players' movements and actions during the game. While the players were playing their GPS data were sent to the server's database. This was done to visually recreate the path they took while playing the game. An observer shadowed all the players and GOPro cameras were used to record the players' actions.

In the rest of this section we describe the results of the evaluation for each quest. The description is based on observations, video analysis, survey results and GPS data analysis. In the following section we will return on the design challenges to have a more summative understanding about the Flooded potential for promoting citizens preparedness to flooding situations.

Flood protection: The results regarding this first quest were somewhat contrasting. Some players felt it was not intuitive and realistic to spread the sandbags along the entire river, due to the limited amount of sandbags they had. Another player commented on their approach: "*We decided to place them on a line along the river bank.*" This is a coherent solution, however as they did not sufficiently spread their placement - which left parts of the river bank uncovered – they got a low score. When they were asked if they understood what they should have done differently to get a better result, one of the players correctly answered that they should have spread the sandbag walls more to cover more of the area. We will return on the importance of this post-game reflection phase later in the paper.

Monitor Territory: All the players understood the goal of the quest and how to complete it. They also understood that they were able to start an early evacuation if they found a critical water level. A player commented: "*We looked at the normal and the current water level and if there was a big difference it meant that a flood was about to arrive.*" When asked if they understood that their performance in the Monitor Territory quest (and early flood warning) gave them more time in the evacuation-quest, one of the players answered: "*It's logical when you reflect about it after you've played it. But when you're playing it's not that apparent.*" He also stated that he felt the focus group discussion was necessary for him to understand the connection. Again it's underlined the need for having a debriefing-session after the game session to increase the learning potential of the game.

Evacuation: In the first evaluation none of the players was able to reach the evacuation zone in time, however they were all able to find the zone on the map, and they understood the placement was due to its high elevation and distance from the river. When asked if they understood what they should do if a real flood warning occurred they answered: "*Get out (of the area)!*" In the second evaluation three of the players were about one to two minutes away from reaching the zone. The last player was able to reach the zone at the last second. Unfortunately for him, the GPS did not update in time for him to survive. He commented: "*I was there. I ran and I saw that I had one second left exactly when I reached the zone, but it didn't update in time. I was going to do a MacGyver and throw myself into the zone.*" When discussing the fact that the GPS did not update instantaneously caused him to fail the quest, he said: "*It was a bit my fault, I could have ran a bit more, but it was so hot.*"

Search and rescue: During the first evaluation one of the players was stuck in the flooding during this quest. This fact seemed to have a huge impact on him: "*If you make bad preparations you will most likely die if there's a flood. It's a good lesson.*" In the second evaluation, the players were able to find three of the four NPCs, but only successfully interacted with one of them. They mentioned that they saw two other NPCs on their map, but they were unable to reach them before the time ran out. The players felt they could have achieved a better result, as illustrated by one comment: "*I think we would have made it if we were in better shape and spread out. The steep hills from the river and towards the evacuation zones made it difficult.*" Another player died (in the game) because he tried to walk into the flood to interact with an NPC that was already dead. He said that he thought he could have saved him. When we asked him if he did not understand that walking into the flood would be a bad idea, he answered: "*Well, when you say it like that... I did not really think too much about it when I did it, but in retrospect it was obviously not a smart decision. It (the fact that he died) made me stay out of the flood for the remainder of the quest.*" When asked if they understood the connection between the flood protection quest and the search and rescue-quest, one player commented: "*I think the level of flooding was based on the* *flood protection score. If we had been able to protect the area better, we could potentially save even more people.*" When we told him that this was the correct interpretation he added: "*I did not get it while we were playing, but when I reflected about it now I understood. I think the way the quests are connected is good, but when I saw the flood was coming, I thought: 'But what was the point of the sandbags then? The flood is coming either way.' I did not really get the true consequences when I was playing.*"

6 Design Challenges and the Experimentation

In Sect. 3 we described the design challenges a game for promoting citizens preparedness to flooding situations should confront with. In this section we will discuss the experimentation results to see how much the current Flooded game design met these challenges.

Regarding preparedness. The game should place the players in a situation that mimics a real life flood. As it is a game, it is impossible to create a completely realistic experience, but it should at least be a decent simulation of reality. The game design contains several features that aim to achieve an acceptable level of realism. The players should get a feeling of stress while playing the game, similarly to how it would be in a real flood. It is important, though, that the stress is not too high as this could demotivate the players from playing. As the main goal of the players is to understand and manage the flood, it is important that the actions they perform in the game make sense in terms of real life crisis management.

Challenge 1: Sensitization. Three of the players felt the game made them more aware of the dangers of flooding, two were neutral. The other players mentioned that they did not feel the game increased their own awareness of the dangers of flooding, because they already knew of the dangers. However, they felt the game would be useful in this regards for others (that had less awareness). A player commented regarding the first quest: "*It made me think about what a good placement of a sandbag wall might be, which is something I've never done before.*"

Challenge 2: Actions to take. The less successful quest in this regard is the first one. As we can see from the players' reaction the way it was constructed wasn't good enough to create the illusion of a complete immersion. The evacuation quest was regarded with more interest: "*It can educate people on where it is smart to go when a flood arrives, to push them to go to an elevated area.*" One player felt that the game was slightly too unrealistic, in regards to the fact that material damages are not part of the game, and that this weakens the flood awareness aspect.

Challenge 3: Territory knowledge: A vital part of understanding the risks of a flood is to have knowledge of one's local area. As an example, by knowing what the river looks like in normal times, people can be more aware when the water level has increased, and possibly predict that a flood is imminent. For a location-based game to be effective in teaching this knowledge, the players must be given objectives that allow for, and preferably encourages, exploration of their local environment. Logs of the players' GPS data were used to determine how much they had actually explored. The players' movement during the second evaluation is shown in Fig. 2(a). All the players walked more than 2 km during the evaluation. The results seem to indicate that the game is useful in pushing exploration. In the questionnaire most of the players agreed that the game had made them more familiar with the local area. One of the players experienced firsthand importance of knowing the territory. *"While I was trying to evacuate, Google maps lured me into a dead end. On the map it showed a path you could take to get to the main road. But there was a 5 m tall wall blocking it"* (see Fig. 2(b)). When asked if he learned something from this he answered: *"Now I know where not to go if I have to evacuate from this area in real life."* Two other players answered in the questionnaire that the game had made them more familiar with the area they played in. The others were neutral. They said that they were already very familiar with the area, as one of them had lived in a house close to the river bank for two years, while the other had worked as a postman in the area. The players felt that the game had learning potential if it was in an area they had no familiarity with. One comment was: *"I think it is very useful if you want to get to know a new area. You are forced to move around and go to places that you otherwise would not."*

Fig. 2. (a) The players' movements; (b) A player walking into a dead end

Challenge 4: Soft skills. In a learning sense, the advantage of having collaborative tasks instead of individual tasks is that people working in groups can capitalize on each other's resources and skills. They can construct new knowledge through the social interaction, or increase their common knowledge by sharing a mutual understanding. Collaborative tasks can also have an effect on the general enjoyment of doing the task, as it facilitates a more social experience. In Flooded the players used each other's locations to decide where to go. Although this is not collaboration in the conventional sense, it is form of instinctive coordination that can happen if the players' are aware of each other's location. When asked how they decided where to go, one player commented: *"I looked at the position of the others, and went in the opposite direction."* Another added: *"Because we were so few people and had so little time it was pretty obvious what would be smart to do."*

Two of the players went together for the entire duration of the game session. They were communicating face-to-face when deciding where to go and where to place sandbag walls. One player tried to get help from the others by sending a message, "How do I search a zone?", but there were no response from the others. The players said that the lack of time was the reason that they did not use messaging for collaboration. A player commented: "*I did not use it, but I probably should have. The lack of time made it difficult. But I feel the fact that we could communicate is a part of the potential of the game. It is very cool that you can communicate, it makes the game more realistic.*" As an example of how it could be useful, a player commented (to another): "*I probably should have used it during the monitor territory-quest, since you were far away from me and I did not know which you would take.*"

To summarize, the game dynamics demonstrated to be adapted to the main objective (promoting citizens preparedness to flooding situations). In particular for the sensitization about flooding issues and the territory exploration worked very well. On the other hand there is a need for a more realistic representation of the consequence of a flood to pass a better sense about of which action to take in these situations. Also the social dynamics need to be improved to create a better experience.

Engagement. All the players agreed that the game was engaging. It is also interesting to note that the all answered that they would like to play the game again, both in the same area and in a different area. One of goals of Flooded was to try to put the players in stressful situations, both to mimic how stressful it's a real flood but also to make the game more engaging. It is important, though, that the positive stress, which is a feeling of excitement that can motivate you, outweighs the negative stress, which is a feeling of not being able to handle the situation. None of the players felt they game was stressful in a demotivating way. One of the players said: "*The time aspect was motivating, both negatively and positively. It was stressful after a while; I didn't really grasp the gravity of the situation at the beginning. I just walked calmly to the crate. And when I was measuring water, suddenly the flood was coming and I had to get out of there and had just a few minutes to do so. This was both stressful and engaging.*" Another one added: "*For my part, the fact that I had limited time was enough to engage me. The fact that you had a timer worked really well, and motivated me instantly to do my best.*" But also other aspects motivated the players. One player said: "*It was exciting! I didn't know what the next objective would be.*" Several players mentioned that the leaderboard and point system made it more engaging. When asked if they thought location-based games could be fun, the general consensus seemed to be that the game had to be multi-player: "*It can be a fun activity if you are many playing together.*" When asked if they were motivated to do their best, the views were somewhat split. On the one hand everyone felt the game was engaging, but the fact that they had to run was a demotivating factor for two of the players. "*I don't have the stamina to run.*" one of the players answered. The other added: "*If I knew I was going to run and did not wear jeans and bring a backpack, I would have made a better effort.*"

To summarize, the game dynamics demonstrated to be very engaging. From the game design point of view the right balance between the serious and the engaging part seems to be obtained. In particular the time stress element played a good role in connection with the territory exploration part.

7 Conclusion and Future Works

In this paper we have described the design and evaluation of Flooded, a game to promote citizens' flood preparedness. Results of the evaluations show that the game has a good potential for promoting flood awareness, especially in terms of increasing the player's knowledge of the local territory. However a proper briefing and debriefing session is required to facilitate learning, retention and reflection. The feedbacks from the players suggest that the game was highly successful in creating an engaging experience and the most interesting and engaging aspect for the players was the location-based aspect. This element compensate for the lack of realism of some of the quests. On the other hand a more intelligent way to facilitate collaboration needs to be implemented. A good solution in terms of usability would be to integrate a Voice over IP-solution. This would enable the players to talk to each other instead of having to type on a phone's limited screen. For the future, we plan to introduce the needed changes and extend the experimentation to be able to draw more stable guidelines for creating this kind of games.

Acknowledgments. The work is co-funded by NFR-VERDIKT 176841/SIO FABULA (http://teseolab.org).

References

1. New legislation on Disaster Response Capacity. http://ec.europa.eu/commission_2010-2014/georgieva/hot_topics/european_disaster_response_capacity_en.htm
2. EU Decision on Union Civil Protection Mechanism. http://ec.europa.eu/echo/files/about/COM_2011_proposal-decision-CPMechanism_en.pdf
3. Jonkman, S.N.: Global perspectives on loss of human life caused by floods. Nat. Hazards **34**(2), 151–175 (2005)
4. Kundzewicz, Z.W., Jun, X.: Towards an improved flood preparedness system in china. Hydrol. Sci. J. **49**(6), 941–944 (2004)
5. Middelkoop, H., Van Asselt, M., Van'T Klooster, S.A., Van Deursen, W., Kwadijk, J.C.J., Buiteveld, H.: Perspectives on flood management in the rhine and meuse rivers. River Res. Appl. **20**(3), 327–342 (2004)
6. Suzuki, I.: Roles of volunteers in disaster prevention: implications of questionnaire and interview surveys. In: Ikeda, S., Fukuzono, T., Sato, T. (eds.) A Better Integrated Management of Disaster Risks: Toward Resilient Society to Emerging Disaster Risks in Mega-Cities, pp. 153–163. Terra Scientific Publishing Company and National Research Institute for Earth Science and Disaster Prevention, Tokyo (2006)
7. Terpstra, T.: Flood preparedness: thoughts, feelings and intentions of the Dutch public. University of Twente (2010)
8. Krasovskaia, I., Gottschalk, L., Sælthun, N.R., Berg, H.: Perception of the risk of flooding: the case of the 1995 flood in Norway. Hydrol. Sci. J. **46**(6), 855–868 (2001)
9. Takao, K., Motoyoshi, T., Sato, T., Fukuzondo, T., Seo, K., Ikeda, S.: Factors determining residents' preparedness for floods in modern megalopolises: the case of the tokai flood disaster in Japan. J. Risk Res. **7**(7–8), 775–787 (2004)

10. Di Loreto, I., Divitini, M., Mora, S.: Collaborative serious games for crisis management: an overview. In: WETICE 2012 - IEEE International Conference on Collaboration Technologie and Infrastructures. Track on Collaborative Technology for Coordinating Crisis Management
11. http://playgen.com/play/floodsim/
12. http://www.deltares.nl/en/software/1782755/levee-patroller
13. Rebolledo-Mendez, G., Avramides, K., de Freitas, S., Memarzia, K.: Societal impact of a serious game on raising public awareness: the case of Floodsim. In: Proceedings of the 2009 ACM SIGGRAPH Symposium on Video Games, pp. 15–22. ACM (2009)
14. Harteveld, C.: A playful approach to flood defence. In: Proceedings of the International Symposium on Flood Defence (2008)
15. Mannsverk, S.J.: Flooded - A Location-Based Game for Promoting Citizens' Flood Preparedness. Master report, IDI-NTNU- Norwegian University of Science and Technology (2013)
16. http://www.geocaching.com/
17. Vitale, J.L., McCabe, M., Tedesco, S., Wideman-Johnston, T.: Cache Me If You Can: Reflections on Geocaching from Junior/Intermediate Teacher Candidates (2012)
18. http://networkednaturalist.org/floracaching/
19. Huizenga, J., Admiraal, W., Akkerman, S., Dam, G.T.: Mobile game-based learning in secondary education: engagement, motivation and learning in a mobile city game. J. Comput. Assist. Learn. 25, 332–344 (2009)
20. Facer, K., Joiner, R., Stanton, D., Reid, J., Hull, R., Kirk, D.: Savannah: mobile gaming and learning? J. Comput. Assist. Learn. 20(6), 399–409 (2004)
21. http://www.shadowcities.com/
22. http://www.thehiddenpark.com/
23. Burningham, K., Fielding, J., Thrush, D.: It'll never happen to me: understanding public awareness of local flood risk. Disasters 32(2), 216–238 (2008)

SG Technology

Development of a Game Engine for Accessible Web-Based Games

Javier Torrente$^{(\boxtimes)}$, Ángel Serrano-Laguna,
Ángel del Blanco Aguado, Pablo Moreno-Ger,
and Baltasar Fernández-Manjón

UCM, Madrid, Spain
jtorrente@e-ucm.es

Abstract. The Web is rapidly shifting towards more dynamic and interactive content. One clear example is the increasing use of web-based digital games. However, the more interactive a piece of content is, the more difficult it is to make it universally accessible. Besides, users are increasingly demanding ubiquitous access to the content and applications they use (including games), resulting in a need for ensuring that Web content is also multiplatform. These trends are adding an extra technology challenge for ensuring content accessibility. In this paper we describe our technical approach to create an accessible multiplatform game engine for the new version of the eAdventure educational game authoring platform (eAdventure 2.0). This approach integrates accessibility as a core design principle instead of adding accessibility features *a posteriori*. We expect this to facilitate the creation of web-based digital games that are accessible regardless of the context (device, assistive tools available, situation, etc.) in which they are being used. In this work we describe the general architecture, as well as some specific examples of accessibility adaptation plugins already available.

1 Introduction

Rich Internet Applications (RIAs) and interactive content are gaining importance in modern web to enrich the navigation experience. In particular, digital games are increasingly being used in the web, not only for leisure but also for 'serious applications' like education [8], health [4], advertising [11] and even as an alternative to Captchas [1]. The drawback is that RIAs create new issues from an accessibility perspective. The problem grows for digital games where interaction cycles are extremely short and feedback is usually provided on multiple channels. Although the problem has been identified, and research is being conducted on how to address it [17], the fact is that the current level of accessibility of digital games is still rudimentary.

The limited accessibility of digital games is not motivated by a single reason. An apparent lack of awareness of game developers and the cost overhead that accessibility adds to any game development project are surely among the most relevant. A proposed approach to address these issues, at least partially, is to integrate accessibility into game development software [14], instead of focusing on ad hoc solutions for each particular title. On the one hand, this increases the visibility of accessibility

© Springer International Publishing Switzerland 2014
A. De Gloria (Ed.): GALA 2013, LNCS 8605, pp. 107–115, 2014.
DOI: 10.1007/978-3-319-12157-4_9

among developers, as it translates the problem to a language they are familiar with. On the other hand, it allows reusing previous efforts across different game development projects, resulting in significant savings and cost reductions.

When games are deployed in the web there are also further technical challenges that are difficult to address. Web content can be used (by definition) in different contexts and deployed on multiple platforms, which adds uncertainty to what technologies or assistive tools would be available. Besides, web content must be conformant to standards to ensure interoperability.

In this paper we present our ongoing development efforts in the eAdventure 2.0 game engine and how it is being designed and implemented to accommodate accessibility from its very inception. Once development is complete, game authors will be able to make accessible games more easily and automatically deploy them on the Web using HTML5 and WebGL. Most of the solutions proposed could also be applied to other types of RIAs and interactive contents.

This paper is structured as follows: Sect. 2 provides a short overview of the state-of-the-art in digital game and RIA accessibility. Section 3 introduces the eAdventure platform: what is it, what prototypes have been already developed to explore accessibility in games, and why a new version is being developed based on Web technologies. Section 4 describes the technical design rationale to introduce accessibility in the eAdventure 2.0 game engine, with Sect. 5 providing examples on how the architecture presented allows adapting the games for two specific user profiles. Finally Sect. 6 wraps up our contribution and outlines future lines of research.

2 Background

Web accessibility has traditionally focused on granting equal opportunities of access to the vast majority of the content and applications that populate the Internet, which used to be rather static and not highly interactive. Interest on making RIAs accessible is more recent. This unbalanced distribution of efforts is reflected on current status of web accessibility standards. While the Web Content Accessibility Guidelines (WCAG), which deal with static content, are a mature and stable technical standard, its counterpart for RIAs, the Accessible Rich Internet Applications (WAI-ARIA) specification, is still a draft.

Concurrently the gaming field is gradually starting to explore how to increase accessibility of digital games, not necessarily focusing on the Web [17]. The first accessibility guidelines specifically targeted to digital games were proposed by the Special Interest Group on accessibility of the International Game Developers association [5] on 2005. These guidelines provided a compendium of good practices grouped by types of disability and exemplified through case studies of games that included features to support accessibility that were available at the time. Since then, the state-of-the-art on game accessibility recommendations has been pushed forward not only by IGDA but also by other advocators and dedicated institutions [2]. However, the field is not mature enough to produce an official standard or technical recommendation similar to W3C specifications, lacking of reference tools and appropriate conformance levels.

In the academia, research initiatives on digital games have also emerged [17, 18]. Some of these initiatives have focused on the production of games that could be enjoyed by players with and without disabilities alike, while others have focused on the special needs of players with disabilities only [12]. Other experiences have focused on making popular games accessible, instead of developing an accessible game from scratch [3].

Comparatively, very few cases have explored how game technologies and development software can support accessibility. For example, in [10] a Game Accessibility Framework is introduced from a conceptual perspective. Moreover, the additional requirements of Web games remain as an open issue.

3 eAdventure

eAdventure (formerly <e-Adventure>) is an open source, high-level game authoring tool [6]. Unlike more complex tools (e.g. Unity [16]) it targets low-profile and user-generated games that could be used in different contexts, especially 'serious applications' and education. The types of games that can be produced with eAdventure are limited to 2D point-and-click games and conversational adventures. This genre is typically considered more appropriate for educational settings (and more accessibility-friendly) due to the focus on exploration and reflection as opposed to time pressure or fast-paced action [7].

3.1 Versions 1.X and 2.0

eAdventure has been in development since 2005, being v1.5 the latest version available. On 2011 it was reaching its end of life. It is built on Java, which is rapidly becoming an obsolete technology for Web clients due to the need of installing browser plug-ins and recent security holes found in Java Applets. This presents a problem in online education (a.k.a. e-learning) environments, where everything lives on the web. For that reason, we started the development of a new eAdventure game engine from scratch (v2.0). The main aim in the development of eAdventure 2.0 is to provide an extensible and multiplatform engine to supports game deployment as HTML 5 (using WebGL) Web Applications. As HTML 5 cannot be fully deployed in some devices yet (e.g. computers with old browsers or some smartphones and tablets), the eAdventure 2.0 also has native support for specific platforms (e.g. Android devices).

Both branches of the eAdventure engine currently coexist. The internal architecture is completely different in both cases. The former one is referred to as version 1.X (stable but rapidly becoming obsolete) while the new one (unstable) is referred to as version 2.0.

3.2 Previous Work on Accessibility

Previous work has already explored the introduction of accessibility in the eAdventure platform using version 1.X. In [13] the development and integration of accessibility modules for adapting the game interface dynamically is described. Three user profiles were considered: (a) screen reader users (blind); (b) speech recognition users (limited mobility in hands) and (c) users that need high contrast settings (low or limited vision). Different alternatives for users requiring screen readers were further explored in a subsequent experiment [15]. The experience gathered on these previous research activities has been used to design the core set accessibility features that will be supported by eAdventure 2.0 out-of-the-box.

4   Implementation Proposed

The basic architecture of the new version of the eAdventure engine (2.0) was described in a previous publication, which can be consulted for further details [9]. In this paper we focus on how accessibility fits within this architecture.

4.1   Engine Architecture

The 2.0 engine is modular, multiplatform and extensible. It is built upon an API that supplies functionality (e.g. access to the data model and art resources, etc.) for all basic processes of the application (e.g. rendering, collision detection, etc.) to all internal components (see Fig. 1), and enables cross-component communication. All the platform-independent functionality of the Engine API is implemented by the Engine Core, the main controller of the application. This way most of the code of the engine is implemented only once. Platform-dependent components provide implementations for the rest of the Engine API (e.g. image rendering, video reproduction, input/output, etc.).

The eAdventure data model (the description of the game) is constituted by EAdElements. An EAdElement holds no computation logic, just a piece of the description of the game or one of its components. This includes characters, items or game scenarios, but also effects triggered in the game in response to user's interactions. These effects can produce feedback for the user. For example, eAdventure 2.0 supplies effects to display formatted text on the screen, or to play a sound track. At runtime, the game engine reads the EAdElements from a XML file and translates them to GameObjects, which are the minimal game functional units, that can be manipulated.

eAdventure 2.0 uses the concept of plug-ins to support functionality and platform extension. An eAdventure plug-in is a set of classes and interfaces extending and using the Engine API. Plug-ins are programmed as independent units that are loaded at start-up. For example, plug-ins can contain extensions of existing EAdElements or GameObjects, new implementations of parts of the API, etc. A configuration file defines the plug-ins that the game engine must load at start-up.

The implementation(s) of all the parts of the Engine Core and API (e.g. EAdElements, Game Objects, Plug-ins, Core functionality, Platform-dependent components) are completely separated from the interfaces that define them. The interfaces are bound to the code components (i.e. classes) dynamically at start-up, using a technique called dependency injection (Google Guice is used for this purpose). This structure enhances the flexibility and adaptability of the engine, as the behavior of any component can be replaced dynamically (e.g. to better suit the needs of the user).

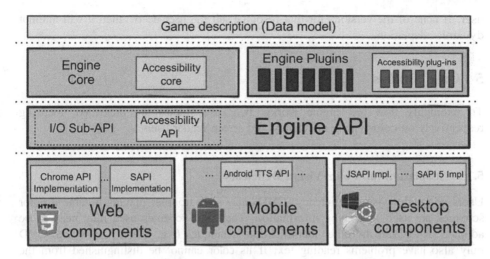

Fig. 1. Architecture of the eAdventure 2.0 engine

4.2 Accessibility Support

Accessibility is present in different components of the game architecture, including: an Accessibility API (part of the main Engine API); an Accessibility Core, responsible for implementing part of the Accessibility API and also for setting up accessibility features at start-up; Accessibility Plug-ins, a set of engine extensions to deal with particular functionalities; and Platform-dependent accessibility Components that implement parts of the Accessibility API that handle inputs and outputs, like speech recognition or text-to-speech (TTS).

Most of the code that deals with accessibility is implemented either as Accessibility Plug-ins or Platform-dependent Components. The Accessibility Plug-ins (a specific type of eAdventure plug-ins) allow changing the behavior of any component or element of the game engine. For example, a plug-in could adapt how the visual elements are rendered, or the complexity of the text or other pieces of game content. Platform-dependent Accessibility Components are designed to allow interoperability with external components by connecting the engine's I/O modules to different platform-dependent implementations of the Accessibility API (e.g. Android or HTML5). In this manner the game engine can take advantage of technologies or support tools that the user may already have installed (e.g. the JAWS screen reader, Mac Voice Over system, etc.). This favors using well-tested and implemented aiding technologies, and also allows the applications to be lighter and speed up loading times.

In the process of setting up a game for a particular user, some game content (e.g. images and text) may need to be adapted. Occasionally the content can be adapted dynamically (e.g. apply a filter to the image) but sometimes it is necessary that the engine is fed with alternative versions of these resources. For that reason, game content is highly decoupled and encapsulated. Using a namespace convention, different versions of the text scripts and images are organized in folders. When a resource is loaded in the game, the engine fetches the best version available for the characteristics of the user. If none of the versions for that resource suit the user needs, then it will attempt dynamic adaptation.

5 Case Studies

To exemplify how the engine works, two case studies are presented, focusing respectively on color vision deficiency and screen reader users.

5.1 Adaptation for Color Vision Deficiency

Users with color vision deficiency (CVD) may have troubles playing a game if color schemes are used to convey information. The color schemes used may need to be adapted or replaced by other identification techniques (e.g. icons). Users with CVD may also have problems reading text if its color cannot be distinguished from the background.

These problems are solved using the dependency injection technique. GameObjects that are responsible for visual elements of the scenes are created using an alternative version that alters the rendering code. For example, at runtime, the GameObject used to control and render a game scenario (interface GOScene) is bound to an alternative implementation (e.g. class GOSceneCVDImpl) that overrides the draw() method making interactive elements more distinguishable. Similarly, the GameObject that represents effects for showing text in the game (interface GOTextEffect) is bound to a different implementation (class GOTextEffectCVDImpl) that draws the text on a clear background using a high-contrast color scheme.

5.2 Adaptation for Screen Reader Users

The most important needs of screen reader users are (1) avoiding the mouse as input device (they can use a keyboard) and (2) providing non-visual feedback (i.e. audio-based). While the first issue poses no significant challenge from a technological per-spective, the second is a more complex issue. Dealing with non-visual feedback will typically require using text-to-speech technologies (a full voiced game may be too expensive). Web-based TTS are cumbersome as no reference API or implementation is has been adopted and implemented for the HTML5 specification.

In the case of eAdventure, a TTS API was defined (as part of the Accessibility API) to abstract all this complexity. At start-up the Accessibility Core inspects the context where the game has been launched, gathers information about the guest operative system and platform, and starts a discovery process to investigate potential TTS engines and other assistive tools installed. Considering this information, the available implementations of the TTS API that were packaged with the game are analyzed, discarding those that are not applicable in the current context. Available options are prioritized and iterated through, trying to set-up the best alternative for the user (Fig. 2).

Fig. 2. On the left, the original game screenshot. On the right, adapted version for CVD. Two adaptations are performed: (1) chemicals are identified with numbers instead of colors; (2) green-blue text color scheme, which may be hard to read, is replaced by a high-contrast alternative (Color figure online).

For example, suppose the game is launched in the Chrome Web browser on a Windows Machine (XP or above) and the Accessibility Core discovers, through a browser plug-in, that a screen reader (e.g. JAWS) is installed. It will first try to load an implementation of the TTS that connects to the screen reader, so that the voice used will be familiar to the player. If the process fails, it would try to take advantage of the TTS API Google Chrome browser provides. Next it would try to connect to Microsoft's Speech API (SAPI) provided by the OS, through another browser plug-in. Should all these alternatives fail, then the TTS feature would be disabled, as the game engine does not include a built-in TTS engine.

At start-up the Accessibility Core will also load alternative implementations of the GameObjects that show text on the screen, in a similar way as described in Sect. 5.1. When these accessible objects are rendered, they also invoke the TTS API. In this manner, each piece of text that is displayed on the screen is also played back using the TTS API (if available). Other GameObject effects are also adapted to enhance the audio feedback that is conveyed to the user. For example, when the player enters in a new scene, the game engine will generate a textual description of the scene and reproduce it using the TTS API.

6   Conclusions and Future Work

With the increasing presence of digital games on the web on one hand, and the need for ubiquitous access to content in the other, making accessible games is becoming even harder, as new technological problems are added (e.g. how to deal with text-to-speech technologies and screen readers on different platforms). The introduction of accessibility features could be facilitate by providing game development software that supports the production of games that can be delivered through the web on computers and also on other platforms, like mobile devices.

It can be assumed that HTML5 will eventually make Web games run on every single Internet-enabled device. However, the standard has not fully been debugged and adopted in several platforms, like smartphones and tablets. Thus it is still necessary to provide a native version of the games for some platforms.

In this paper we have presented the eAdventure 2.0 architecture that will allow development of accessible 2D serious games meeting these criteria. The architecture was designed with extensibility and flexibility as key drivers. The main advantage of this approach is that eAdventure 2.0 would easily support extensions to accommodate more types of disabilities and/or new platforms.

This work has only addressed the technical problems related to game accessibility. However, making a game that is enjoyable for players with different types of profiles requires more than having a technology that supports it (e.g. game authors also need to integrate players' special needs into the game design).

The features here presented are currently on a prototype state. We are currently working to reach a more stable status. The next steps will be development and evaluation of accessible games using the eAdventure 2.0 game engine.

Acknowledgements. The Spanish Ministry of Science (TIN2010-21735-C02-02), the European Commission (519332-LLP-1-2011-1-PT-KA3-KA3NW, 519023-LLP-1-2011-1-UK-KA3-KA3MP, FP7-ICT-2009-5-258169), the Complutense University (GR35/10-A-921340) and the Regional Government of Madrid (eMadrid Network - S2009/TIC-1650) have partially supported this work.

References

1. A Gaming Replacement for Those Annoying CAPTCHAs (2013). http://readwrite.com/2012/05/03/a-gaming-replacement-for-those-annoying-captchas. Accessed 13 Feb 2013
2. A straightforward reference for inclusive game design (2012). http://www.gameaccessibilityguidelines.com/
3. Allman, T., et al.: Rock Vibe: Rock Band® computer games for people with no or limited vision. In: Proceedings of the 11th International ACM SIGACCESS Conference on Computers and Accessibility, pp. 51–58 (2009)
4. Arnab, S., et al.: Serious Games for Healthcare: Applications and Implications. IGI Global, Hershey (2012)
5. Bierre, K., et al.: Game not over: accessibility issues in video games. In: 11th International Conference on Human-Computer Interaction (HCII'05) (2005)
6. eAdventure website: http://e-adventure.e-ucm.es
7. Garris, R., et al.: Games, motivation and learning: a research and practice model. Simul. Gaming **33**(4), 441–467 (2002)
8. Johnson, L., et al.: NMC Horizon Report: 2013 Higher Education Edition (2013)
9. Marchiori, E.J., Serrano, Á., Torrente, J., Martínez-Ortiz, I., Fernández-Manjón, B.: Extensible multi-platform educational game framework. In: Leung, H., Popescu, E., Cao, Y., Lau, R.W., Nejdl, W. (eds.) ICWL 2011. LNCS, vol. 7048, pp. 21–30. Springer, Heidelberg (2011)
10. Ossmann, R., Archambault, D., Miesenberger, K.: Accessibility issues in game-like interfaces. In: Miesenberger, K., Klaus, J., Zagler, W.L., Karshmer, A.I. (eds.) ICCHP 2008. LNCS, vol. 5105, pp. 601–604. Springer, Heidelberg (2008)

11. Pempek, T.A., Calvert, S.L.: Tipping the balance: use of advergames to promote consumption of nutritious foods and beverages by low-income African American children. Arch. Pediatr. Adolesc. Med. **163**(7), 633–637 (2009)
12. Sánchez, J., Espinoza, M.: Audio haptic videogaming for navigation skills in learners who are blind. In: Proceedings of the 13th International SIGACCESS Conference on Accessibility (ASSETS), pp. 227–228 (2011)
13. Torrente, J., et al.: Implementing accessibility in educational videogames with <e-Adventure>. In: First ACM International Workshop on Multimedia Technologies for Distance Learning - MTDL '09, Beijing, China, pp. 55–67 (2009)
14. Torrente, J., et al.: Introducing accessibility features in an educational game authoring tool: the experience. In: 11th IEEE International Conference on Advanced Learning Technologies ICALT 2011, pp. 341–343 (2011)
15. Torrente, J., et al.: Preliminary evaluation of three eyes-free interfaces for point-and-click computer games. In: 14th International ACM SIGACCESS Conference on Computers and Accessibility (ASSETS), pp. 265–266 (2012)
16. Unity 3D website: http://unity3d.com/. Accessed 15 Feb 2013
17. Westin, T., Bierre, K., Gramenos, D., Hinn, M.: Advances in game accessibility from 2005 to 2010. In: Stephanidis, C. (ed.) Universal Access in HCI, Part II, HCII 2011. LNCS, vol. 6766, pp. 400–409. Springer, Heidelberg (2011)
18. Yuan, B., et al.: Game accessibility: a survey. Univ. Access Inf. Soc. **10**(1), 81–100 (2011)

FILTWAM and Voice Emotion Recognition

Kiavash Bahreini(✉), Rob Nadolski, and Wim Westera

Centre for Learning Sciences and Technologies (CELSTEC), Open University
Netherlands, Valkenburgerweg 177, 6419 AT Heerlen, The Netherlands
{kiavash.bahreini, rob.nadolski, wim.westera}@ou.nl

Abstract. This paper introduces the voice emotion recognition part of our framework for improving learning through webcams and microphones (FILT-WAM). This framework enables multimodal emotion recognition of learners during game-based learning. The main goal of this study is to validate the use of microphone data for a real-time and adequate interpretation of vocal expressions into emotional states were the software is calibrated with end users. FILTWAM already incorporates a valid face emotion recognition module and is extended with a voice emotion recognition module. This extension aims to provide relevant and timely feedback based upon learner's vocal intonations. The feedback is expected to enhance learner's awareness of his or her own behavior. Six test persons received the same computer-based tasks in which they were requested to mimic specific vocal expressions. Each test person mimicked 82 emotions, which led to a dataset of 492 emotions. All sessions were recorded on video. An overall accuracy of our software based on the requested emotions and the recognized emotions is a pretty good 74.6 % for the emotions happy and neutral emotions; but will be improved for the lower values of an extended set of emotions. In contrast with existing software our solution allows to continuously and unobtrusively monitor learners' intonations and convert these intonations into emotional states. This paves the way for enhancing the quality and efficacy of game-based learning by including the learner's emotional states, and links these to pedagogical scaffolding.

Keywords: Game-based learning · Human-computer interaction · Multimodal emotion recognition · Real-time voice emotion recognition · Microphone

1 Introduction

During the last decade, several new technologies have been adopted by e-learning specialists for enhancing the effectiveness, efficiency and attractiveness of e-learning [1–3]. Nowadays, learners are often used to the web-based delivery of e-learning content and Web 2.0 affordances when communicating, working and learning together with their peers in distributed (a)synchronous settings [4, 5].

Our research aims for online game-based learning of communication skills. Game-based learning has several advantages: (1) it is a didactical approach that seems to be in-line with the learners' interests [6], (2) it is very popular nowadays [6], (3) it seems very fruitful to people [7], (4) can be very effective for skills training (see e.g., [8]), and (5) motivating [9]. This approach focusses on learning instead of entertainment, can be

© Springer International Publishing Switzerland 2014
A. De Gloria (Ed.): GALA 2013, LNCS 8605, pp. 116–129, 2014.
DOI: 10.1007/978-3-319-12157-4_10

quite informal and offers a lot of possibilities to the learners based on learners' input (audio and video). We expect that using technology, affective computing tool, and a pure web-based training system might be insufficient to encourage people to improve their communication skills as the training of such skills needs a lot of recurrent practice. For this purpose, FILTWAM will be deployed with a game-based didactical approach and integrated with EMERGO. EMERGO is a methodology and toolkit for the development and delivery of serious games [10].

FILTWAM uses webcams and microphones to interpret the emotional state of people during their interactions with a game-based learning environment for triggering timely feedback based upon learner's facial expressions and verbalizations. It is meant for discerning the following emotions: sadness, anger, disgust, fear, surprise, happiness, and neutral. It basically offers software with a human-machine interface for the real time interpretation of emotion that can be applied in game-based learning (i.e., affective computing tool). The proof of concept study reported here is a follow up of our previous study [11] and aims to extend our software for multi-modal emotion recognition with a voice emotion recognition part. We will only investigate the opportunities of a microphone for gathering affective user data in an online game-based learning context. An affective computing tool is the development of a system, which is able to recognize, interpret, and simulate human emotions. Our affective computing tool is built upon existing research [12–18]. Linking two modalities (face expression and voice intonation) into a single system for affective computing analysis is not new and has been studied before [19–24]. A recent review study by [25] shows that the accuracy of detecting one or more basic emotions is greatly improved when both visual and audio information are used in classification, leading to accuracy levels between 72 % to 85 %.

It is commonly acknowledged that emotions are an important factor in any learning process, since it influences information processing, memory and performance [26]. Also, feedback based on emotional states may enhance the learners' awareness of their own behavior. This seems relevant for communication skills training. Hence, automated emotion detection as explained in this paper may compensate for the limited number of trainers that are available for online training of communication skills in compare to face-to-face situations [27]. Interacting with digital learning environments is important for the learners; however recent developments of input devices (such as microphones) for interacting with these environments are still underexploited. Such devices not only offer opportunities for more natural interactions with the online game-based learning applications, but also offer ways of gathering affective user data during learning.

There is a growing body of studies on online and automatic voice emotion recognition systems [28–30]. In one well-known study [28] the researchers have presented a framework for classifier creation for both offline and real-time voice emotion recognition with a specific interface for German speakers. They allowed creating a dataset for joy, satisfaction, anger, and frustration emotions in the context of a training procedure for non-expert users. They received a huge range of accuracy from 24 % to 74 % for their offline speaker dependent classification approach among 29 users. They reported that this big variation is according to the uncontrolled audio recording situation in which all the recordings prepared by the users at home. They finally reported that the recognition accuracy using the naïve Bayes (NB) classifier in machine learning approach was 41 % for 10 native German speakers.

One study in real-time signal processing and recognition [29] presented a dedicated framework to support a tool for developing the social signal interpretation (SSI). The researchers introduced flexible software architecture to manage audio and video signals in both offline and online tasks. They also showed how their easy-to-use graphical user interface will allow unskilled users to easily access to data recording and classification modules. From this research we realized that it is obvious that greatest recognition software are based upon machine learning approaches and algorithms and therefore these software require a substantial amount of data for dataset training.

Another study in automatic emotion recognition by the speech signal [30] showed how to recognize emotions specifically for spoken utterances. The researchers categorized these utterances levels into two areas: semantic and signal. Semantic level comprises the spoken phrases, which are able to transfer clear reference. Signal level encompasses features, such as pitch, energy, and spectral distortions. They reported the overall accuracy 86.5 % for semantic fusion of semantic and signal characteristics of their dataset for seven emotions, such as irritation, joy, anger, fear, disgust, sad, and neutral. They also mentioned that semantic features will not detect all emotions acceptably; however they will support fusion recognition effectively.

From these studies it becomes clear that there are several unsolved issues and a real breakthrough in online and automatic voice emotion recognition systems that have not yet been achieved. We plan to deal with more emotions and increase accuracy in our real-time voice emotion recognition system. In this paper we propose (1) an unobtrusive approach with (2) an objective method that can be verified by researchers, (3) which requires inexpensive and ubiquitous equipment (microphone), and (4) which offers interactive software. Our software uses a microphone and provides the real time conversion of detected vocal intonations into emotional states. Our approach can be applied in any online game-based learning setting that requires additional ways of gathering affective data from the user during learning.

To characterize the novelty of our work, we propose the multimodal framework, which in real-time transforms data from behavioral observations into emotional states. Furthermore, this is applied in educational settings, more precise for training purposes. To our knowledge, these approaches have not yet been integrated in any other frameworks. In this paper, Sect. 2 introduces the FILTWAM framework and its voice emotion recognition part. The method for the proof of concept study of the developed software is described in Sect. 3. Results and discussion are presented in Sect. 4. Section 5 explains the conclusion of this proof of concept study.

2 The FILTWAM Framework

The FILTWAM framework encompasses five functional layers and a number of sub-components within the layers. The five layers are introduced as the: (1) Learner, (2) Device, (3) Network, (4) Application, and (5) Data. Figure 1 illustrates the framework.

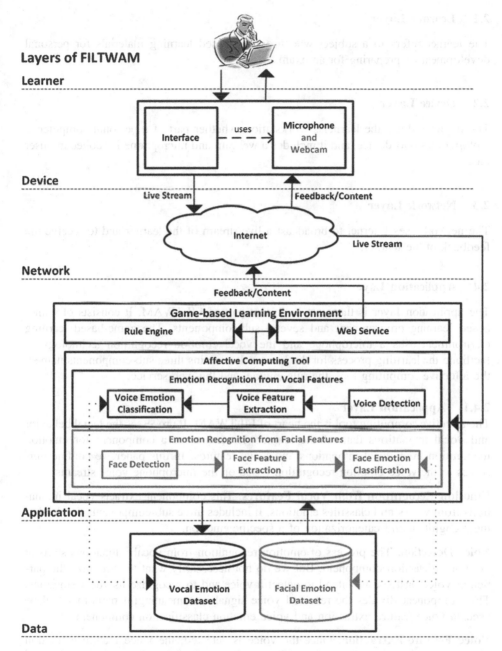

Fig. 1. The FILTWAM framework for voice emotion recognition in an online game-based environment (the face emotion recognition sub-components have been reported in our previous study [31] and are grayed consequently).

2.1   Learner Layer

The learner refers to a subject who uses web-based learning materials for personal development or preparing for an exam.

2.2   Device Layer

The device reflects the learner's workstation, whether part of a personal computer, a laptop, or a smart device, and it includes a webcam and microphone for collecting user data.

2.3   Network Layer

The network uses Internet to broadcast a live stream of the learner and to receive the feedback of the learner.

2.4   Application Layer

The application layer is the most important part of FILTWAM. It consists of game-based learning environment and several sub-components. The game-based learning environment uses a microphone and the vocal emotion recognition technology to facilitate the learning process for the learner. It contains three sub-components named: the affective computing tool, the rule engine, and the web service.

2.4.1   Application Layer

The affective computing tool is the heart of FILTWAM. It processes the facial behavior and vocal intonations data of the learner. It consists of a component for emotion recognition from vocal intonations and facial features. In this paper we confine ourselves to the voice emotion recognition based on the microphone voice streams.

Emotion Recognition from Vocal Features. This component extracts vocal intonations from voices and classifies emotions. It includes three sub-components that lead to the recognition and categorization of a specific emotion.

Voice Detection. The process of emotion recognition from vocal intonations starts at the voice detection component. But we do not necessarily want to recognize the particular voice; instead we intend to detect a voice and to recognize its vocal emotions. This component divides the received voice signal into meaningful parts that will be used in voice feature extraction and voice emotion classification components.

Voice Feature Extraction. Once the voice is detected, the voice feature extraction component extracts a sufficient set of features from voice of the learner. These features are considered as the significant features of the learner's voice and can be automatically extracted.

Voice Emotion Classification. We adhere to a well-known emotion classification approach that has been introduced by Ekman and has often been used over the past thirty years which focuses on classifying the six basic emotions: sadness, anger, disgust, fear, happiness, surprise (Ekman and Friesen, 1978). However this approach introduced for facial coding systems, but our voice emotion classification component supports classification of these six basic emotions plus the neutral emotion for vocal intonations. This component analyses voice stream and can extract a millisecond feature of each voice stream for its analysis. Currently, we use the naïve Bayes (NB) classifier classification algorithm in FILTWAM. The NB classifier is very fast and appropriate for real-time emotion recognition. Our voice emotion recognition software supports speaker independent recognition approach, which is a general recognition system and therefore its accuracy is lower than the speaker dependent recognition approach that has been reported in [28].

2.4.2   Rule Engine

The rule engine component manages didactical rules and triggers the relevant rules for providing feedback as well as tuned training content to the learner via the device. The game-based learning environment component complies with a specific rule-based didactical approach for the training of the learners. In the future we may possibly use the rule engine of EMERGO, which is a game-based toolkit for delivery of multimedia cases.

2.4.3   Web Service

The web service component transmits the feedback and training content to the learner. At this stage, the learner can receive a feedback based on his/her vocal emotions.

2.5   Data Layer

The data layer is the physical storage of the emotions. It encompasses the vocal emotion dataset, which reflects the intelligent capital of the system. Its records provide a statistical reference for emotion detection.

3   Method and Proof of Concept

Our hypothesis is that data gathered via microphone can be reliably used to unobtrusively infer learners' emotional states. Such emotional states' measurements would allow for the provision of useful feedback during online game-based training of communication skills or any other adaptive or personalized interventions that would enhance the quality and efficacy of e-learning.

3.1   Participants

An e-mail was sent out to employees from the Centre for Learning Sciences and Technologies (CELSTEC) at the Open University Netherlands to recruit the participants for this proof of concept study. The e-mail mentioned the estimated time investment for enrolling in the proof of concept study. Six participants, all employees from CELSTEC

(3 male, 3 female; age $M = 43, SD = 9$), volunteered to participate in this proof of concept study. By signing an agreement form, the participants allowed us to capture their facial expressions and voice intonations, and to use their data for the proof of concept study. The participants were invited to test the voice emotion recognition module of the affective computing software and watch their face emotions through the face emotion recognition module of the affective computing software; no specific background knowledge was requested. They were told that participation within the proof of concept study might help them to become more aware of their emotions while they were communicating through a microphone and a webcam in the affective computing software.

3.2 Design

Four consecutive tasks were given to the participants. Participants were asked to expose seven basic voice expressions (happy, sad, surprise, fear, disgust, angry, and neutral). Totally, eighty-two voice expressions were requested for all four tasks together. The participants were requested to mimic all the eighty-two emotions once. At the moment, we offer very limited learner support (just a straight forward simple feedback (name of the recognized emotion and the prediction accuracy amount)) to inform the learner whether our current prototype of the affective computing software detects the same 'emotion' as the participant was asked to 'mimic'. For the validation of the software, it is important to know whether its detection is correct. For the learners it is important that they can trust that the feedback is correct.

In the first task participants were asked to speak aloud and use the voice emotion that was shown on the face of the person that was on the image to them. There were 14 images presented subsequently through PowerPoint slides; the participant paced the slides. Each image illustrated a single emotion. All seven basic face expressions were two times present with the following order: happy, sad, surprise, fear, disgust, angry, neutral, happy, sad, et cetera. In the second task, participants were requested to speak aloud the seven basic expressions twice: first, through slides that each presented the keyword of the requested emotion and second, through slides that each presented the keyword and the picture of the requested voice emotion with the following order: angry, disgust, fear, happy, neutral, sad, surprise. For the first and second tasks, they could improvise and use their own texts. The third task presented 17 slides with the text transcript (both sender and receiver) taken from a good-news conversation. The text transcript also included instructions which voice expression should accompany the current text-slide. Here, participants were requested to read and speak aloud the sender text of the 'slides' from the transcript and deliver the accompanying voice expression. The forth task with 37 slides was similar to task 3, but in this case the text transcript was taken from a bad-news conversation. The transcripts and instructions for tasks 3 and 4 were taken from an existing OUNL training course [32] and a communication book [33].

3.3 Test Environment

All tasks were performed on a single Mac machine. The Mac screen was separated in three panels, top-left, top-right, and bottom. The participants could watch their facial expressions in the face emotion recognition module of the affective computing software at the top-left panel, they could watch their analyzed voice expressions in the voice emotion recognition module of the affective computing software at the top-right panel, while they were performing the tasks using a PowerPoint file in the bottom panel. An integrated webcam with a microphone and a 1080HD external camera were used to capture and record the emotions of the participants as well as their actions on the computer screen. The affective computing software including the face emotion recognition module and the voice emotion recognition module used the webcam with the microphone to capture and recognize the participants' emotions, while Silverback usability testing software version 2.0 used the external camera to capture and record the complete experimental session. Figure 2 demonstrates an output of both modules of the software and an experimental session for Task 4.

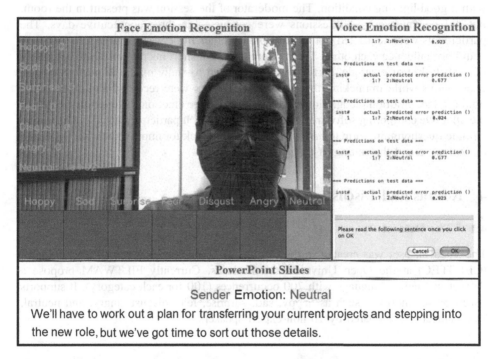

Fig. 2. The main researcher in task 4, the affective computing software including the face emotion recognition module (top-left) and the voice emotion recognition module (top-right), and the PowerPoint slide (bottom) during the experimental session.

3.4   Measurement Instruments

A self-developed online questionnaire was used to collect participants' opinions when carrying out the requested tasks. All opinions were collected using items on a 7- point scale format with possible scores: (1) completely disagree, (2) disagree, (3) mildly disagree, (4) neither disagree nor agree, (5) mildly agree, (6) agree, and (7) completely agree. Participants' opinions were gathered for: (1) perceived difficulty to mimic the requested emotions in the given tasks, (2) perceived feedback of the given feedback to mimic the emotions in the given tasks, (3) perceived instructiveness of the instructions for the given tasks, (4) perceived attractiveness of the given tasks, and (5) perceived concentration on the given tasks. Participants were also asked to report their self-assurance on (1) being able to mimic the requested emotions in the given tasks and (2) their acting skills on a similar 7-point Likert scale.

3.5   Procedure

Each participant signed the agreement form before his or her session of the proof of concept study was started. They individually performed all four tasks in a single session of about 45 minutes. The session was conducted in a completely silent room with a good lighting condition. The moderator of the session was present in the room, but did not intervene. All sessions were conducted in three consecutive days. The participants were requested not to talk to each other in between sessions so that they could not influence each other. The moderator gave a short instruction at the beginning of each task. For example, participants were asked to show mild and not too intense expressions while mimicking the emotions. All tasks were recorded and captured by both the face emotion recognition module and the voice emotion recognition module of the affective computing software. After the session, each participant filled out an online Google questionnaire form to help us to collect feedback for improvement the tasks and the software and the setting of the study.

4   Results and Discussion

4.1   The Dataset

The vocal dataset was created in the Centre for Learning Sciences and Technologies (CELSTEC) at the Open University Netherlands. Currently FILTWAM propose a dataset in English language with 700 occurrences (100 for each category). It supports seven basic emotions, such as happy, sad, surprise, fear, disgust, angry, and neutral. The dataset was prepared by 10 non-expert speakers.

4.2   The Voice Feature Extraction and Classification

The voice emotion recognition software of the FILTWAM requires reaching to a better accuracy level when all the seven basic emotions integrate in a single dataset. The voice feature extraction and the voice emotion classification could be improved to reach to higher accuracy when an equal number of actors and actresses are recruited to train the new dataset. A combination of the voice emotion recognition module of the affective computing tool of the FILTWAM framework with the face emotion recognition module of it may help us to improve the possible recognition rates.

4.3   Validation Results of the Software

In this paper we report the validation of the voice emotion recognition module of our affective computing software, all tasks, and six basic emotions as well as neutral emotion. For the first validation results, we only selected two emotional categorize (happy and neutral) from our dataset. Table 1 shows the results of the requested emotions from participants and compares the results with recognized emotions by the voice emotion recognition module of the affective computing software.

Table 1. Validation results of the software for only happy and neutral emotions for task 1, task 2, task3, and task 4 simultaneously.

		Recognized Emotion by the Voice Emotion Recognition Software							
		Happy	Sad	Surprise	Fear	Disgust	Angry	Neutral	Total
Requested Emotion	Happy	26	----	----	----	----	----	10	36
		72.2%	----	----	----	----	----	27.8%	100%
	Neutral	74	----	----	----	----	----	250	324
		23%	----	----	----	----	----	77%	100%

Each requested emotion is separated in two rows that intersect with the recognized emotions by the voice emotion recognition software. The first row indicates the number of occurrences of the recognized emotion and the second row displays the percentage of each recognized emotion. The red numbers are the correctly classified emotions and therefore the accuracy of the voice emotion recognition module, while the black numbers are the incorrectly classified emotions. The best recognized emotion in this case is still neutral 77 % followed by happy 72.2 %. Therefore the overall accuracy is 74.6 %. In accordance with [34], we realized that the classification accuracy decreases with the number of emotional categories in our current dataset. Therefore when we inserted sad, surprise, fear, disgust, and angry to our dataset, the classification accuracy decreased (see Table 2).

The achieved overall accuracy of the software between the requested emotions and the recognized emotions assuming uniform distribution of emotions is the average of the diagonal: 22.2 % (based on Table 2). The best recognized emotion is still neutral 80.6 % followed by happy 33.3 %, sad 12.5 %, surprise 8.3 %, disgust 8.3 %, angry 8.3 %, and fear 4.2 %. Currently there are three reasons for the obtained false results: (1) the malfunctioning of the software, (2) the participants were unable to mimic the requested emotions accurately, and (3) the accuracy of the trained voice emotion dataset is less than 50 % now. We know that we are in a good track, but we are not sure yet what will be changed if we recruit several actors and actresses who are capable of mimicking the requested emotions accurately to train our dataset. There will be more investigation on these issues in our feature research and development.

Table 2. Validation results of the software for all the seven emotion for task 1, task 2, task3, and task 4 simultaneously.

		Recognized Emotion by the Voice Emotion Recognition Software							
		Happy	Sad	Surprise	Fear	Disgust	Angry	Neutral	Total
	Happy	16	3	3	1	7	0	18	48
		33.3%	6.3%	6.3%	2.1%	14.5%	0.0%	37.5%	100%
	Sad	3	3	0	0	1	0	17	24
		12.5%	12.5%	0.0%	0.0%	4.2%	0.0%	70.8%	100%
	Surprise	3	2	2	2	4	2	9	24
		12.5%	8.3%	8.3%	8.3%	16.8%	8.3%	37.5%	100%
Requested Emotion	Fear	2	3	1	1	1	1	15	24
		8.2%	12.5%	4.2%	4.2%	4.2%	4.2%	62.5%	100%
	Disgust	2	4	0	1	2	2	13	24
		8.3%	16.7%	0.0%	4.2%	8.3%	8.3%	54.2%	100%
	Angry	10	3	1	0	3	2	5	24
		41.7%	12.5%	4.2%	0.0%	12.5%	8.3%	20.8%	100%
	Neutral	21	28	0	6	0	8	261	324
		6.5%	8.5%	0.0%	1.9%	0.0%	2.5%	80.6%	100%

4.4   Summary of the Measurement Parameters

In this section we report the results of the online questionnaire designed to measure the seven parameters (difficulty, feedback, self-assurance, instructiveness, attractiveness, concentration, and acting skills) mentioned in the Sect. 3.4. The participants completed the questionnaire regarding the voice emotion recognition experimental session. Table 3 summarizes the measurement parameters that filled out by the participants through the online questionnaire investigation.

Table 3. Summary of the measurement parameters.

	Answers by the Participants							
	1	2	3	4	5	6	7	Total
Difficulty It was easy for me to mimic the requested emotions in the given tasks	----	17%	17%	9%	22%	35%	----	
Feedback The feedback did help me to mimic the emotions in the given tasks	----	8%	4%	25%	25%	38%	----	
Self-assurance I am confident that I was able to mimic the requested emotions in the given tasks	3%	3%	58%	10%	10%	16%	----	100%
Instructiveness The instructions for the given tasks were clear to me	----	----	----	----	33%	59%	8%	
Attractiveness The given tasks were interesting	----	----	----	----	73%	27%	----	
Concentration I could easily focus on the given tasks and was not distracted by other factors	----	----	----	4%	12%	50%	34%	
Acting skills I regard myself as a good actor	----	33%	17%	33%	----	17%	----	

1= Completely disagree, 2= Disagree, 3= Mildly disagree, 4= Neither disagree nor agree, 5= Mildly agree, 6= Agree, and 7= Completely agree

The observation of Table 3 shows that self-assurance parameter is less for tasks 1 and 2 as compared to the other tasks. It is easy to realize that the participants don't regard themselves as actors. The difficulty parameter contrary to our expectations doesn't show any differences and all tasks seem moderately difficult. Clear instructions and feedback parameters are moderately helpful. All the tasks were interesting for the participants to do. Finally concentration parameter indicates no distraction during performance.

5 Conclusion

We have examined a proof of concept of software for real-time voice emotion recognition that is part of our FILTWAM framework. The overall accuracy of our voice emotion recognition software based on the requested emotions and the recognized emotions for two emotions (happy and neutral) is 74.6 %. However we have lower values for an extended set of the emotions. This is in accordance with [28, 34] in which we expect low accuracy for completely normal low-intensity emotions in online recognition and decreasing the classification accuracy with the number of emotional categories. This issue requires further investigation and improvement. Participants indicated that tasks 1 and task 2 were more difficult for them than tasks 3 and 4. Tasks 1 and 2 included a bigger variety of requested emotions. In combination with questionnaire results indicating participants' low self-confidence on being a good actor, this might hint at asking professional actors for a next validation study of the software. Furthermore, the findings with the questionnaire indicate that there is some room left for improving the tasks offered to participants.

We will further investigate possibly software malfunctioning and might include more training sessions for participants to improve their skills for being able to mimic the requested emotions more accurately. The FILTWAM framework aims at real-time interpretation of emotional behavior into emotional states and can be applied in game-based learning in general and seems especially useful for communication skills game training in particular. We aim to use the validated framework for communication skills game training purposes in our further research and development. We will further integrate the face emotion recognition module and the voice emotion recognition module. The current FILTWAM framework, including the face emotion recognition software and the voice emotion recognition software, is an advanced human-computer interaction setting that can be integrated with existing game-based learning environments. For our research, FILTWAM will be integrated with the EMERGO-platform [10].

Acknowledgments. We thank our colleagues who participated in the voice emotion recognition proof of concept study. This research is sponsored by The Netherlands Laboratory for Lifelong Learning (NELLL) of the Open University of the Netherlands.

References

1. Anaraki, F.: Developing an effective and efficient elearning platform. Int. J. Comput. Internet Manag. **12**(2), 57–63 (2004)
2. Nagarajan, P., Wiselin, G.J.: Online educational system (e- learning). Int. J. u- e- Serv. Sci. Technol. **3**(4), 37–48 (2010)

3. Norman, G.: Effectiveness, efficiency, and e-learning. J. Adv. Health Sci. Educ. **13**(3), 249–251 (2008)
4. Ebner, M.: E-Learning 2.0 = e-Learning 1.0 + Web 2.0? In: The Second International Conference on Availability, Reliability and Security (ARES), pp. 1235–1239 (2007)
5. Hrastinski, S.: Asynchronous and synchronous e-learning. Educause Quarterly **31**(4), 51–55 (2008)
6. Kelle, S., Sigurðarson, S., Westera, W., Specht, M.: Game-based life-long learning. In: Magoulas, G.D. (ed.) E-Infrastructures and Technologies for Lifelong Learning: Next Generation Environments, pp. 337–349. IGI Global, Hershey (2011)
7. Connolly, T.M., Boyle, E.A., MacArthur, E., Hainey, T., Boyle, J.M.: A systematic literature review of empirical evidence on computer games and serious games. Comput. Educ. **59**(2), 661–686 (2012)
8. Reeves, B., Read, J.L.: Total Engagement: Using Games and Virtual Worlds to Change the Way People Work and Business Compete. Harvard Business Press, Boston (2009)
9. Gee, J.P.: What Video Games have to Teach us About Learning and Literacy. Palgrave Macmillan, New York (2003)
10. Nadolski, R.J., Hummel, H.G.K., Van den Brink, H.J., Hoefakker, R., Slootmaker, A., Kurvers, H., Storm, J.: EMERGO: methodology and toolkit for efficient development of serious games in higher education. Simul. Gaming **39**(3), 338–352 (2008)
11. Bahreini, K., Nadolski, R., Qi, W., Westera, W.: FILTWAM - A framework for online game-based communication skills training - using webcams and microphones for enhancing learner support. In: Felicia, P. (ed.) The 6th European Conference on Games Based Learning (ECGBL), pp. 39–48. Ireland, Cork (2012)
12. Avidan, S., Butman, M.: Blind Vision. In: Leonardis, A., Bischof, H., Pinz, A. (eds.) ECCV 2006. LNCS, vol. 3953, pp. 1–13. Springer, Heidelberg (2006)
13. Bashyal, S., Venayagamoorthy, G.K.: Recognition of facial expressions using Gabor wavelets and learning vector quantization. Eng. Appl. Artif. Intell. **21**, 1056–1064 (2008)
14. Chibelushi, C.C., Bourel, F.: Facial expression recognition: a brief tutorial overview. In: CVonline: Online in Compendium of Computer Vision, vol. 9 (2003)
15. Ekman, P., Friesen, W.V.: Facial Action Coding System: Investigator's Guide. Consulting Psychologists Press, Palo Alto (1978)
16. Kanade, T.: Picture processing system by computer complex and recognition of human faces. Ph.D. Thesis, Kyoto University, Japan (1973)
17. Li, S.Z., Jain, A.K.: Handbook of Face Recognition, 2nd edn. Springer, London (2011). ISBN: 978-0-85729-931-4
18. Petta, P., Pelachaud, C., Cowie, R.: Emotion-Oriented Systems: The Humaine Handbook. Springer, Berlin (2011)
19. Chen, L.S.: Joint processing of audio-visual information for the recognition of emotional expressions in human-computer interaction. Ph.D. Thesis, University of Illinois at Urbana-Champaign (2000)
20. Fong, T., Nourbakhsh, I., Dautenhahn, K.: A survey of socially interactive robots. Robot. Auton. Syst. **42**(3–4), 143–166 (2003)
21. Sebe, N., Cohen, I.I., Gevers, T., Huang, T.S.: Emotion recognition based on joint visual and audio cues. In: International Conference on Pattern Recognition, Hong Kong, pp. 1136–1139 (2006)
22. Song, M., Bu, J., Chen, C., Li, N.: Audio-visual based emotion recognition: A new approach. IEEE Comput. Soc. Conf. Comput. Vis. Pattern Recogn. **2**, 1020–1025 (2004)
23. Subramanian, R., Staiano, J., Kalimeri, K., Sebe, N., Pianesi, F.: Putting the Pieces Together: Multimodal Analysis of Social Attention in Meetings. ACM Multimedia, Firenze (2010)

24. Zeng, Z., Pantic, M., Roisman, G.I., Huang, T.S.: A survey of affect recognition methods: Audio, visual, and spontaneous expressions. IEEE Trans. Pattern Anal. Mach. Intell. **31**(1), 39–58 (2009)
25. Sebe, N.: Multimodal interfaces: challenges and perspectives. J. Ambient Intell. Smart Environ. **1**(1), 23–30 (2009)
26. Pekrun, R.: The impact of emotions on learning and achievement: towards a theory of cognitive/motivational mediators. J. Appl. Psychol. **41**, 359–376 (1992)
27. Hager, P.J., Hager, P., Halliday, J.: Recovering Informal Learning: Wisdom, Judgment and Community. Springer, Dordrecht (2006)
28. Vogt, T., André, E., Bee, N.: EmoVoice - A framework for online recognition of emotions from voice. In: Proceedings of Workshop on Perception and Interactive Technologies for Speech-Based Systems (2008)
29. Wagner, J., Lingenfelser, F., Andre, E.: The social signal interpretation framework (SSI) for real time signal processing and recognitions. In: Proceedings of INTERSPEECH, Florence, Italy. (2011)
30. Schuller, B., Manfred, L., Gerhard, R.: Automatic emotion recognition by the speech signal, Institute for Human-Machine-Communication, Technical University of Munich, 80290 (2002)
31. Bahreini, K., Nadolski, R., Westera, W.: FILTWAM - A framework for online affective computing in serious games. In: The 4th International Conference on Games and Virtual Worlds for Serious Applications (VS-GAMES'12), Procedia Computer Science, Genoa, Italy, vol. 15, pp. 45–52 (2012)
32. Lang, G., van der Molen, H.T.: Psychologische gespreksvoering. Open University of the Netherlands, Heerlen (2008)
33. Van der Molen, H.T., Gramsbergen-Hoogland, Y.H.: Communication in Organizations: Basic Skills and Conversation Models. Psychology Press, New York (2005). ISBN: 978-1-84169-556-3
34. Dai, K., Harriet J.F., MacAuslan, J.: Recognizing emotion in speech using neural networks. In: Telehealth and Assistive Technologies, pp. 31–38 (2008)

A Survey of Haptics in Serious Gaming

Shujie Deng, Jian Chang$^{(\boxtimes)}$, and Jian J. Zhang

National Centre for Computer Animation, The Media School,
Bournemouth University, Fern Barrow, Poole, Dorset BH12 5BB, UK
{sdeng, jchang, jzhang}@bournemouth.ac.uk

Abstract. Serious gaming often requires high level of realism for training and learning purposes. Haptic technology has been proved to be useful in many applications with an additional perception modality complementary to the audio and the vision. It provides novel user experience to enhance the immersion of virtual reality with a physical control-layer. This survey focuses on the haptic technology and its applications in serious gaming. Several categories of related applications are listed and discussed in details, primarily on haptics acts as cognitive aux and main component in serious games design. We categorize haptic devices into tactile, force feedback and hybrid ones to suit different haptic interfaces, followed by description of common haptic gadgets in gaming. Haptic modeling methods, in particular, available SDKs or libraries either for commercial or academic usage, are summarized. We also analyze the existing research difficulties and technology bottleneck with haptics and foresee the future research directions.

Keywords: Serious games · Haptic devices · Haptic modeling · Force feedback · Virtual reality

1 Introduction

Serious gaming based on videogames has achieved great success in the past 20 years. The effectiveness of learning from videogames is that it will intrigue the motivation to spend time on the tasks so to master skills, the design elements as narrative context, rules, goals, rewards, multisensory cues and interactivity can also stimulate the desire of learning [1]. Virtual simulation also helps reduce the potential hazard of dangerous tasks, solves ethical issues and saves the cost. Various training applications featuring haptics have been developed as in medical [2] and rehabilitation [3] areas.

Haptic feedback has recently become an indispensable component in serious games. It provides an additional perception modality of touch, together with vision and audio to generate a more immersive user experience. Immersive learning environment and interaction require system stability and real-time feedback for all sensory including vision, audio and touch. Integration of haptics into serious gaming has brought great challenges for both hardware and software development. This paper provides a survey of haptic application in serious gaming, and current research status of haptic hardware and modeling that are available for videogames design.

Touch perception can be divided into cutaneous and kinesthetic sensations, so haptics are correspondingly composed of two parts of perceptual feedback, tactile feedback and

© Springer International Publishing Switzerland 2014
A. De Gloria (Ed.): GALA 2013, LNCS 8605, pp. 130–144, 2014.
DOI: 10.1007/978-3-319-12157-4_11

force/torque feedback. Devices can be categorized by different feedbacks they provide. Based on the game concept and budgets estimation, a suitable device genre is selected. The specifications of devices that are normally taken into consideration include degree of freedom (DOF), degree of force feedback (DOFF), size of workspace, max force/torque, stiffness, compatibility and extensibility of software development kit (SDK) etc. Commercial oriented games usually have a priority of being economic/affordable. The low-cost solution is to embed vibrotactile actuator into game devices, such as gamepads, mobile phones, etc. However, it restricts the rendering of abundant and detailed haptic feedback into unitary vibration. Medical and pedagogic oriented applications take advantage of more expensive devices, and produce more delicate feedback.

Generally, with the learning and training purposes, the force/torque and tactile perception gained from haptics provide user with better cognition of how they have performed in the task and helps them improve their performance in a more intuitive and efficient way. Especially for tasks that rely largely on haptic feedback, merely visual feedback helps little with improving performance or even causes errors. For instance, endoscopic surgical training is extremely difficult to achieve expected results without haptic feedback [4]; applications that focus on improving motor skills are also the same. More concretely, users who are visually impaired or blind benefit mostly from auditory and haptic inputs. Haptics, as the new approach to interact with virtual environments (VEs), also benefits the game industry to enlarge their market to users who are not previously reachable [5].

The remainder of this paper is structured as follows. Section 2 reviews the applications of serious games with haptic feedback. Section 3 comprehensively introduces available haptic devices, including tactile devices, force feedback devices, hybrid devices and commercial game devices. A summary of available haptic modeling is also presented in Sect. 3. Section 4 discusses the related research challenges and future directions and Sect. 5 concludes the paper.

2 Applications

Applying haptics in serious gaming introduces an additional dimension of perception. For some applications, haptic feedback is purely for improving user experience; some applications provide real-time haptic feedback for users to evaluate their performances during the tasks to enhance training effect, where haptics acts as an auxiliary function; others use it as an alternative of vision or a substitute of motor, haptics plays a main role in these applications. For the first type, discussions about how haptics improve immersive user experience and related applications can be found in previous literature. This review focuses on the latter two types.

One thing in common among the applications reviewed is that they are built on top of virtual simulation games. As stated in [4], the advantages of virtual simulation in education include:

- Applicability to students of all range of ages and levels
- Low cost and risk of complex tasks that may require expensive equipment and dangerous procedures

- Practicality of theories integrated with math, science and technical skills
- Introduction of new methodology of problem solving
- Variety of career fields requiring skills training with high fidelity of simulation

Serious gaming concepts in virtual simulation help develop more engaging game-like application with stories, rules, scoring evaluation, rewards or collaboration tasks.

2.1   Applications with Haptics as Cognitive Aux

Training and learning tasks are processes of cognition. Our brain integrates every channel of input perception to form our own understanding of a new concept, or a new set of motor manipulation. With haptic feedback, it provides intuitive perception to achieve better understanding, because it delivers an improved cognitive process with fully accessible perception of the abstract scene or phenomena. To generate long term memory of new knowledge or motor dexterity, our brain requires repetitive practice. Serious gaming with incentive of repetitiveness has been applied in areas like science education and surgical training from long time ago.

Science Education. Chan and Black [6] investigated the mental acquisition performance based on three different formats of presentation, text only, text with static visuals, and text with haptic enabled animation game. Experiments were designed for middle school students to learn Newtonian mechanics with the three learning formats respectively. The results showed that for difficult tasks, the students who learnt using haptic animation game format outperformed the others. User learning experience was also reported to be easier and more understandable than other formats.

Haptic-featured teaching helped students obtain the abstract concept more easily. Eigenvalues and eigenvector could be seen and felt directly from the physical dynamic experiments designed in [7]. The force in molecular docking could be mapped from real microscopic world to virtual macroscopic environment [8], and haptics helped students construct mental representation of the concept, as well as binding energy and strength of interactions [9].

Surgical Training. Chui et al. presented a computer-game-like surgical training simulator using force feedback joystick, Delta haptic device, wearable motion capture device CyberGlove and haptic feedback actuator CyberGrasp in [10]. Although multiple haptic devices helped improve the accuracy of haptic feedback and visual rendering, it also easily introduced system instability and asynchronization. The expensive cost of all the devices was not suitable in real application.

A blood management game for orthopedic surgery has been developed in [11]. Besides graphic simulation, the training aid integrated game features as task-oriented time-attack scenarios. It designed four difficulty levels based on blood-loss severity. Collaboration, bonus and performance evaluation were also featured in this game. The task was to stop bleeding by conducting proper rescue procedures or the game ended with over loss of blood. A 6-DOF haptic device was applied to act as surgical tools in the VE. This application set a good example of the full process of designing a surgical training game with integration of haptic devices. It illustrated the detailed game framework, game design specifications and task flowcharts of the simulation system, with the position and functions of haptic device and haptic rendering clearly shown.

A serious game for training on laparoscopic suturing surgery has been presented in [12]. It designed and developed a first prototype for suturing game using a pair of haptic devices. More advanced virtual reality (VR) simulator (see Fig. 1) using double haptic devices has been reported in [13]. Challenges have been raised in simulation of the soft tissues with visual deformation and haptic force feedback with good accuracy.

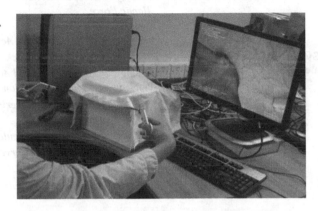

Fig. 1. VR simulator in laparoscopic rectum surgery [13]

2.2 Applications with Haptics as Main Component

Human central nervous system takes account of all sensory inputs to generate perception of the environment. One impaired modality can be compensated by other modalities. As for visually impaired users, they can hardly enjoy video games. Haptic enabled games provide them with new experience of gaming. Yuan et al. [14] talked about game accessibility in detail, and offered insights of challenges in future related research.

When the haptic perception is the impaired one, the users are in need of external stimuli to help them recover, so haptics have been widely applied in post stroke rehabilitations. The augmented force helps indicate correctness or incorrectness efficiently in the process of motor training. It also provides guidance force for skills regain.

Motor Rehabilitation. Figure 2 shows a game design conceptual model for stroke rehabilitation [15]. Training game examples have been developed based on this taxonomy. They created a VE and connected it to a haptic workbench as the design prototype. By adding new game patterns as shown italicized in Fig. 2, it could easily vary the core game and create new games for different purposes, so to personalize and customize specific rehabilitation game for all variation of training purposes. Using the same concept, a haptic immersive workbench for stroke rehabilitation games has been presented in [16].

Delbressine et al. proposed a novel playful arm-hand rehabilitation using a wearable haptic jacket supporting tilt-sensing and vibrotactile feedback with tabletop interaction [17]. The task of this game was to trap a bug, and the bug would get smaller and more difficult to catch if compensatory movement exceeded a threshold detected by the haptic vest. This design solved the problem of compensatory movements with shoulder and trunk.

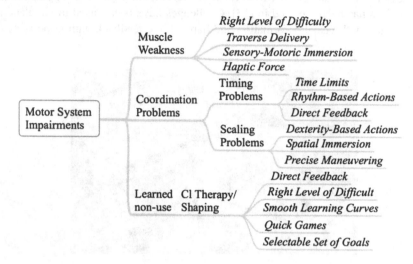

Fig. 2. A subset of the taxonomy [15]

A collaborative game "social maze" has been presented in [18]. They set up a robot-assisted rehabilitation device facilitated with haptic feedback as the central hardware component, allowing patients to train together and interact with therapist.

Haptic handwriting and games have been applied in the rehabilitation system designed in [19]. The haptic Ten Pin bowling game was combined with Novint Falcon haptic device. Handwriting is an essential skill but in a high potential to lose after stroke, since the loss of motor control will harm the complex visuo-motor coordination required by handwriting. Similarly, haptics helped children improve graphmotor skills and grip strength by haptic guidance of the trajectory path [20, 21]. A virtual soccer game was also stated in [22], for children who had walking problems to play soccer with assistance of the haptic driven gait orthosis device.

Henschke et al. presented a new approach for building appropriate serious games for children with cerebral palsy [23]. Children with cerebral palsy lack the tactile sensation, so they developed a series of haptic enabled games for this purpose. It focused on a fully accessible game design pattern for providing all available perception for impaired sensory.

Games for Visually Impaired Users. In games for blind or visually impaired users, the main outputs are audio and haptics, some with assistance of salient visual feedback. Existing literature showed satisfied gaming performance.

Yuan and Folmer designed a glove with haptic motor on the tip of each finger for blind users to play Guitar Hero [24]. It interpreted visual stimuli to haptic stimuli by mapping each button to each finger of the glove. The motor would page the user before the corresponding button that needed to be pressed. Nemec et al. [25] inspected the performance of haptic and audio based navigation in VE for visually impaired users. It showed an equal usability with tactile exploration of paper models.

3 Haptic Modeling

3.1 Haptic Device

A typical haptic device contains bidirectional haptic input and output interfaces/sensors between the device and user. Compared with visual feedback, haptic devices require much higher refresh rate ($\geq$ 1000 Hz) to achieve continuous and real-time perception [26].

Tactile Devices. Tactile Devices simulates temperature, texture, pressure, puncture, friction, roughness, shape that are perceived by cutaneous receptors under our skin. The tactile sensory is generated by actuators which can be developed in different types, mostly are electromagnetic, Shape Memory Alloy (SMA) wire, motor, pneumatic, piezoelectric, polymeric, and Electro Rheological Fluid (ERF). As stated in [27], the most popular technology is electromagnetic and the SMA wire actuation. However, each brings drawbacks in application, weight reduces the portability of electromagnetic actuated devices and low bandwidth limits the performance of SMA. A typical tactile device consists of a set of tactile elements/pins. Various spatial topologies of the pins have been proposed. Pin-matrix is most common as shown in [28–33]. Some are shown in the form of a ring [34]. The number of pins, frequency and the pin density are the main parameters concerned in design. Higher density and frequency brings smoother user experience [35]. The current focus of tactile devices research is to simplify system design and materials, to reduce the number of actuators, weight and cost to achieve equally good performance [36–38]. Non-contact tactile interfaces are emerging. An ultrasound-based tactile display using the principles of acoustic radiation pressure and hand tracking was proposed in [39]. It has achieved vibration up to 1 kHz for a volume of L51 $\times$ W26 $\times$ H19 mm^3 space.

Force Feedback Devices. The force feedback devices can be also called kinesthetic devices, which emulate motion, force, location and compliance that perceived by receptors in our muscles, tendons and joints. A detailed table of commercial force feedback hardware manufactures and devices has been given in [2]. It described the detailed specification of the most prominent devices either in commercial or research.

Similarly with tactile devices, force feedback devices also need one or multiple electromechanical transducers to generate force feedback. Common actuation types include DC motors, electromagnetic, piezoelectric, ERF, and pneumatic etc. Force feedback devices can be divided into grounded and ungrounded categories based on their portability. The popular devices such as SensAble Phantom product, Novint Falcon, Omega, Delta and Virtuose are grounded devices. Ungrounded devices such as the Immersion CyberGrasp glove and the Rutgers Master II [40] come with the shape of gloves. Others are shaped as exoskeleton arm [41, 42].

For most human perception experiment, force feedback need not be set too large (maximum force output of 2–3 N can be sufficient), but some rehabilitation exercises expect large force output and workspace.

A dilemma of force feedback devices design exists between high stiffness and low mass since higher stiffness requests larger mass of the material which is normally metal. Portability is limited by the grounded design and large weight. Better performance also associates with larger workspace and more DOF, which leads to higher price. Trade-offs between functional requirements and budget restriction can be analyzed when selecting the proper device.

Hybrid Devices. Hybrid haptic devices incorporate tactile and force feedback but also introduce design challenges from both, as well as synchronization issues and greater complexity of the hardware.

In general, the structure of a hybrid device is implemented by attaching the tactile elements on the end effector of the force feedback device. By manipulating the end effector, the tactile elements will move along with it and provide tactile feedback. An early implementation of hybrid multimodality device is designed based on a mouse [43]. It applied a solenoid pin (tactile element) resting on the mouse button providing tactile feedback for index finger and an electromagnet on the bottom of the mouse paired with an iron mouse pad that providing drag feedback. However, the mouse model is restricted by the low DOF. With force feedback devices that featured with higher than 3-DOF, a thimble with tactile element built-in is attached on the end effector. Users can insert one of their fingers into the thimble to gain both tactile and force feedback [44]. With the restriction of space and the concern of not interfering the force feedback functions, the functionalities of the tactile components on hybrid devices are relatively simpler compared to pure tactile devices. Only one actuator can be fitted into the thimble, so it can only provide single perception. Consequently, thimble design attracted lots of research attention. Kuchenbecker et al. [45] proposed a design that could detect contact location on the fingertip arc, Kuchenbecker et al. [46] had a novel design of the thimble structure for shape and surface recognition. A more complex pin-matrix tactile display component was integrated with a robotic arm WAM (Whole-Arm Manipulator) for simulation of deformable surface [47].

Haptic Devices for Entertainment and Gaming. Haptic feedback in gaming is devoted to providing immersive game experience but with more affordable price and portability for common acceptance compared with the research oriented haptic devices. More specifically, to reduce extra cost, vibration actuators have been integrated with the variety of game controllers. Distinguished by their shapes, gaming haptic devices normally appear as mice, joysticks, game pads, vest/jackets, wheels, mobile phones etc.

Microsoft's Explorer Touch Mouse and Arc Touch Mouse both provided light vibration that signals scrolling speed [48]. An optical mouse with friction feedback has been proposed in [49]. As in [43, 50], there was a magnetic iron pad underlays for energizing the mouse with electromagnet to generate 2-DOF force feedbacks.

Game pads/controllers are very common nowadays as XBOX, Wii or PlayStation dominate the game console markets. Feedbacks as rumble or vibration have become standard built-in features in these game controllers. For specific games the controller can be transformed to adapt the game environment by embedding it into extra accessories. For example, the Wii controller comes as a cuboid originally, with Wii Wheel it can be turned into a wheel for racing games, while Wii Zapper turns the controller into a snapshotting gun [51]. Joysticks can either be an individual gadget or integrated with gamepads. A haptic one provides 2-DOF force feedbacks that can mimic gear stick for controlling vehicles and planes [52].

Haptic vest/jackets are emerging gaming devices in recent years. TN Games commercialized the 3RD Space Vest [53] while Saurabh Palan et al. demonstrated a Tactile Gaming Vest (TGV) [54]. Both of them simulated the gunshot feedback by arranging tactile elements around the vest. TGV used solenoids instead of pneumatic to provide a faster experience with shorter responding time.

Haptic steering wheels were specifically for racing games or driving simulation as discussed in [55, 56]. There were also haptic chairs and seating pads incorporated into gaming.

With the development and popularization of smart phones, mobile games became graphically intense and the prevailing phone platforms also provided haptic feedback interfaces for both hardware and SDK.

Haptic devices mentioned in [2] have also been utilized in game development but not commercially viable due to their high cost. One exception would be Novint Falcon, which was originally designed for video games but also used in academic research because of its high cost-effectiveness.

3.2 Haptic Modeling

The definition of haptic modeling has been given in [57], "a series of processes to create haptic content on graphic models that are components of virtual reality, augmented reality, or mixed reality".

Various haptic modeling libraries are available as listed in Table 1. These libraries or toolkits provide programming interfaces (API) for rapid prototyping. Most of them come with not only haptic but also graphic components using either OpenGL or DirectX. Normally commercial haptic hardware will come with SDKs that are only applicable to their own devices. For example, OpenHaptics toolkit is only viable for SensAble devices that are the most popular haptic products; Virtual Hand is specifically for the CyberGlove Systems hand tracking devices. Some libraries have specifically been developed hardware independent to adapt more devices. Some provide virtual device adaptation for simulation without requiring a real device connected. Reachin API, HAPTIK and Virtual Hand have network support built in which enables haptic interaction between users. HaptX is designed for game haptics, especially Novint Falcon. The libraries will provide relatively basic haptic features, but they also offer extensibility for customized physical modeling, shape rendering, force effects, collision detection, dynamics and other third-party engines. More haptic modeling libraries are available but not widely applied as the ones listed in Table 1 [57–61].

By investigation of the available libraries, an abstract architecture of haptic modeling is shown in Fig. 3. At the lower level, the interface for different devices should be provided, or the library is customized to be hardware independent. At the top level, programming utilities are necessary, like wrappers for programming languages that are

Table 1. Common available haptic modeling libraries

Name	Devices	Languages	Network	Graphics	Opensource	Platform
OpenHaptics [62]	SensAble	C ++	No	Yes	No	Windows, Linux
CHAI 3D [63]	Hardware Independent, Virtual Device	C ++	No	Yes	Yes	Windows, Linux, Mac
H3DAPI [64]	SensAble, Novint, Force Dimension, MOOG FCS, G-Coder Systems	X3D, C ++, Python	No	Yes	Yes	Windows, Linux, Mac
Reachin API [65]	Hardware Independent	C ++, VRML, Python	Yes	Yes	No	Windows
HaptX [66]	Novint, SensAble	C ++	No	Yes	No	Windows
HAPTIK [67]	Hardware Independent (need related plugin)	C ++, Java, Matlab, Simulink	Yes	No	Yes	Windows, Linux, Mac
Virtual Hand	CyberGlove Systems, Virtual Hand	C ++	Yes	Yes	No	Windows

different with the coding language of the library itself will be provided for adaption of various development environments. Force rendering components are the core of haptic modeling libraries and it is triggered by collision detection component that will also work on graphics components. For lightweight libraries without graphics rendering, there must be extendible interfaces provided. For different purposes, the library can be tailored for specific applications. Each component comes with customization abilities for implementing user-defined functions.

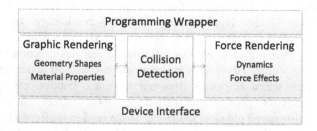

Fig. 3. General architecture of haptic modeling

4 Research Challenges

From the perspective of what we are focusing in this paper, the challenges for integration of haptics into serious gaming are similar to the challenges exist in other haptic applications. Common issues in haptic rendering has been discussed in [68].

One of the concerns attracts most attention is the computational latency of haptic rendering. The time complexity of haptic rendering algorithms increases with the more complicated scenarios, which designed to simulate Six or higher DOFs and deformable or viscous object/environment [69]. Although the computing techniques and hardware have been improved significantly these days, it is still not good enough for haptic rendering of complicated virtual environment interaction, nor are the existing physical models efficient enough to compensate computational delay [70–73]. Trade-off still exists between computational resources and real-time performance.

In terms of different game specification, different issues emerge. In training games and therapy sessions that have collaboration between experts-novices or physicians-patients, it requires local or network based haptic interactivity support for a shared virtual environment (SVE). Multiuser introduces multiple collision and mutual force impact, which means even more loaded computational task. Haptic data compression and transmission latency are additional issues brought by networks. Some efforts have been made to solve this problem [74–76].

Another major issue is the accuracy of eye-hand coordination, which is the training objective in some rehabilitation applications, for example, writing skills. Occlusion between virtual objects and real objects (hand/tool) is one of the obstacles that prevent getting a better user experience of eye-hand coordination. Techniques as chroma-key and head tracking have been applied for eliminating occlusion [77–79].

Even more sensory modalities have been integrated into VR. It is stated that in a haptic featured environment, sound generated by physical modeling and auditory synthesis techniques can highly improve fidelity [80]. The difficulty would be synchronization of sound and the impact force that caused it.

5 Conclusion

Serious games based on virtual reality share same technology basis with virtual simulation for both hardware and software development. Serious gaming introduces the entertainment and pedagogy features into virtual reality, which marks the main difference. Based on the overview given in this paper, haptics bring advantages to serious gaming in three ways: (1) introduce one more dimension of sensory modality for a more immersive game experience; (2) enhance cognitive process with one more layer of proprioception; (3) augment or compensate impaired perception system.

Challenges are confronted for both game designer and haptic engineer. Game design for education purpose requires psychological knowledge of cognition; it is necessary to figure out what cognitive process benefits from haptic modality and how the game characteristics can be applied for an optimal learning result. Haptic technology still has bottlenecks to be improved. Hardware models are mostly bulky and expensive; rendering algorithms need to be more computational effective to cope with complex VEs. It is believed that haptics in serious games will request interactivity, multimodality and portability.

References

1. Dondlinger, M.J.: Educational video game design: a review of the literature. J. Appl. Educ. Technol. **4**, 21–31 (2007)
2. Coles, T.R., Meglan, D., John, N.W.: The role of haptics in medical training simulators: a survey of the state of the art. IEEE Trans. Haptics **4**, 51–66 (2011)
3. Rego, P., Moreira, P.M., Reis, L.P.: Serious games for rehabilitation: a survey and a classification towards a taxonomy. In: 2010 5th Iberian Conference on Information Systems and Technologies (CISTI), pp. 1–6. IEEE (2010)
4. Kincaid, J.P., Westerlund, K.K.: Simulation in education and training. In: Proceedings of the 2009 Winter Simulation Conference (WSC), pp. 273–280. IEEE (2009)
5. Derryberry, A.: Serious games: online games for learning. Adobe Whitepaper, November 2007
6. Chan, M.S., Black, J.B.: Learning Newtonian mechanics with an animation game: the role of presentation format on mental model acquisition. In: Annual Meeting of the American Educational Research Association (AERA), Citeseer, San Francisco (2006)
7. Okamura, A.M., Richard, C., Cutkosky, M.R.: Feeling is believing: using a force-feedback joystick to teach dynamic systems. J. Eng. Educ. **91**, 345–350 (2002)
8. Krenek, A., Cernohorsky, M., Kabelác, Z., Ac, Z.K.: Haptic visualization of molecular model (1999)
9. Persson, P.B., Cooper, M.D., Tibell, L.A.E., Ainsworth, S., Ynnerman, A., Jonsson, B.H.: Designing and evaluating a haptic system for biomolecular education. In: Virtual Reality Conference, VR '07, pp. 171–178. IEEE (2007)
10. Chui, C.-K., Ong, J.S., Lian, Z.-Y., Wang, Z., Teo, J., Zhang, J., Yan, C.-H., Ong, S.-H., Wang, S.-C., Wong, H.-K.: Haptics in computer-mediated simulation: training in vertebroplasty surgery. Simul. Gaming **37**, 438–451 (2006)
11. Jing, Q., Yim-Pan, C., Wai-Man, P., Choi, K.-S., Pheng-Ann, H.: Learning blood management in orthopedic surgery through gameplay. IEEE Comput. Graph. Appl. **30**, 45–57 (2010)
12. De Paolis, L.T.: Serious game for laparoscopic suturing training. In: 2012 Sixth International Conference on Complex, Intelligent and Software Intensive Systems (CISIS), pp. 481–485. IEEE (2012)
13. Pan, J.J., Chang, J., Yang, X., Zhang, J.J., Qureshi, T., Howell, R., Hickish, T.: Graphic and haptic simulation system for virtual laparoscopic rectum surgery. Int. J. Med. Robot. Comput. Assist. Surg. **7**, 304–317 (2011)
14. Yuan, B., Folmer, E., Harris Jr., F.: Game accessibility: a survey. Univ. Access Inf. Soc. **10**, 81–100 (2011)
15. Goude, D., Björk, S., Rydmark, M.: Game design in virtual reality systems for stroke rehabilitation. Stud. Health Technol. Inf. **125**, 146–148 (2007)
16. Broeren, J., Sunnerhagen, K.S., Rydmark, M.: Haptic virtual rehabilitation in stroke: transferring research into clinical practice. Phys. Ther. Rev. **14**, 322–335 (2009)
17. Delbressine, F., Timmermans, A., Beursgens, L., de Jong, M., van Dam, A., Verweij, D., Janssen, M., Markopoulos, P.: Motivating arm-hand use for stroke patients by serious games. In: Conference Proceedings: Annual International Conference of the IEEE Engineering in Medicine and Biology Society, pp. 3564–3567 (2012)

18. De Weyer, T., Robert, K., Renny Octavia Hariandja, J., Alders, G., Coninx, K.: The social maze: a collaborative game to motivate MS patients for upper limb training. In: Herrlich, M., Malaka, R., Masuch, M. (eds.) ICEC 2012. LNCS, vol. 7522, pp. 476–479. Springer, Heidelberg (2012)
19. Xu, Z., Yu, H., Yan, S.: Motor rehabilitation training after stroke using haptic handwriting and games. In: Proceedings of the 4th International Convention on Rehabilitation Engineering & Assistive Technology, 31. Singapore Therapeutic, Assistive & Rehabilitative Technologies (START) Centre (2010)
20. Pernalete, N., Edwards, S., Gottipati, R., Tipple, J., Kolipakam, V., Dubey, R.V.: Eye-hand coordination assessment/therapy using a robotic haptic device. In: 9th International Conference on Rehabilitation Robotics, ICORR 2005, pp. 25–28 (2005)
21. Pernalete, N., Tang, F., Chang, S.M., Cheng, F.Y., Vetter, P., Stegemann, M., Grantner, J.: Development of an evaluation function for eye-hand coordination robotic therapy. In: 2011 IEEE International Conference on Rehabilitation Robotics (ICORR), pp. 1–6 (2011)
22. Brütsch, K., Schuler, T., Koenig, A., Zimmerli, L., Mérillat, S., Lünenburger, L., Riener, R., Jäncke, L., Meyer-Heim, A.: Influence of virtual reality soccer game on walking performance in robotic assisted gait training for children (2010)
23. Henschke, M., Hobbs, D., Wilkinson, B.: Developing serious games for children with cerebral palsy: case study and pilot trial. In: Proceedings of the 24th Australian Computer-Human Interaction Conference, pp. 212–221. ACM (2012)
24. Yuan, B., Folmer, E.: Blind hero: enabling guitar hero for the visually impaired. In: Proceedings of the 10th International ACM SIGACCESS Conference on Computers and Accessibility, pp.169–176. ACM, Halifax (2008)
25. Němec, V., Sporka, A.J., Slavik, P.: Haptic and spatial audio based navigation of visually impaired users in virtual environment using low cost devices. In: Stary, C., Stephanidis, C. (eds.) UI4ALL 2004. LNCS, vol. 3196, pp. 452–459. Springer, Heidelberg (2004)
26. Hayward, V., Astley, O.R., Cruz-Hernandez, M., Grant, D., Robles-De-La-Torre, G.: Haptic interfaces and devices. Sens. Rev. 24, 16–29 (2004)
27. Benali-Khoudja, M., Hafez, M., Alexandre, J.-M., Kheddar, A.: Tactile interfaces: a state-of-the-art survey. In: Int. Symposium on Robotics (2004)
28. Benali-Khoudja, M., Hafez, M., Kheddar, A.: VITAL: an electromagnetic integrated tactile display. Displays 28, 133–144 (2007)
29. Hasser, C., Weisenberger, J.M.: Preliminary evaluation of a shape memory alloy tactile feedback display. In: Proceedings of the ASME Winter Annual Meeting, Symposium on Haptic Interfaces for Virtual Environments and Teleoperator Systems (1993)
30. Tan, H.Z., Pentland, A.: Tactual displays for wearable computing. Pers. Technol. 1, 225–230 (1997)
31. Pawluk, D.T., Van Buskirk, C., Killebrew, J., Hsiao, S., Johnson, K.: Control and pattern specification for a high density tactile array. In: IMECE Proc. of the ASME Dyn. Sys. and Control Div., pp. 97–102 (1998)
32. Ikei, Y., Yamada, M., Fukuda, S.: A new design of haptic texture display-Texture Display2-and its preliminary evaluation. In: Proceedings of the IEEE Virtual Reality 2001, pp. 21–28. IEEE (2001)
33. Wagner, C.R., Lederman, S.J., Howe, R.D.: A tactile shape display using RC servomotors. In: Proceedings of the 10th Symposium on Haptic Interfaces for Virtual Environment and Teleoperator Systems, HAPTICS 2002, pp. 354–355. IEEE (2002)
34. Sato, K., Igarashi, E., Kimura, M.: Development of non-constrained master arm with tactile feedback device. In: Fifth International Conference on Advanced Robotics, ICAR 91, Robots in Unstructured Environments, 1991, pp. 334–338. IEEE (1991)

35. Watanabe, T., Fukui, S.: A method for controlling tactile sensation of surface roughness using ultrasonic vibration. In: Proceedings of the 1995 IEEE International Conference on Robotics and Automation 1995, pp. 1134–1139. IEEE (1995)

36. Benali-Khoudja, M., Beny, A.L., Hafez, M., Kheddar, A.: VT vector-touch: a new slip/stretch tactile display. In: Proceedings of the 2004 IEEE/RSJ International Conference on Intelligent Robots and Systems, (IROS 2004), vol. 3584, pp. 3583–3588 (2004)

37. Chinello, F., Malvezzi, M., Pacchierotti, C., Prattichizzo, D.: A three DoFs wearable tactile display for exploration and manipulation of virtual objects. In: 2012 IEEE Haptics Symposium (HAPTICS), pp. 71–76 (2012)

38. Marquardt, N., Nacenta, M.A., Young, J.E., Carpendale, S., Greenberg, S., Sharlin, E.: The Haptic Tabletop Puck: tactile feedback for interactive tabletops. In: Proceedings of the ACM International Conference on Interactive Tabletops and Surfaces, pp. 85–92. ACM, Banff (2009)

39. Hoshi, T.: Development of aerial-input and aerial-tactile-feedback system. In: 2011 IEEE World Haptics Conference (WHC), pp. 569–573 (2011)

40. Bouzit, M., Burdea, G., Popescu, G., Boian, R.: The Rutgers Master II-new design force-feedback glove. IEEE/ASME Trans. Mechatron. 7, 256–263 (2002)

41. Chen, E., Eberman, B., Marcus, B.A.: Method and Apparatus to Create a Complex Tctile Sensation. Microsoft Corporation, US (1998)

42. Frisoli, A., Rocchi, F., Marcheschi, S., Dettori, A., Salsedo, F., Bergamasco, M.: A new force-feedback arm exoskeleton for haptic interaction in virtual environments. In: First Joint Eurohaptics Conference, 2005 and Symposium on Haptic Interfaces for Virtual Environment and Teleoperator Systems, 2005. World Haptics 2005, pp. 195–201 (2005)

43. Mackenzie, I.S.: Movement characteristics using a mouse with tactile and force feedback. Int. J. Hum.-Comput. Stud. 45, 483–493 (1996)

44. Hasser, C.J., Daniels, M.W.: Tactile feedback with adaptive controller for a force-reflecting haptic display. 1. Design. In: Proceedings of the 1996 Fifteenth Southern Biomedical Engineering Conference 1996, pp. 526–529 (1996)

45. Kuchenbecker, K.J., Provancher, W.R., Niemeyer, G., Cutkosky, M.R.: Haptic display of contact location. In: Proceedings of the 12th International Symposium on Haptic Interfaces for Virtual Environment and Teleoperator Systems, HAPTICS '04, pp. 40–47 (2004)

46. Kuchenbecker, K.J., Ferguson, D., Kutzer, M., Moses, M., Okamura, A.M.: The touch thimble: providing fingertip contact feedback during point-force haptic interaction. In: Symposium on Haptic Interfaces for Virtual Environment and Teleoperator Systems, Haptics 2008, pp. 239–246 (2008)

47. Wagner, C.R., Perrin, D.P., Feller, R.L., Howe, R.D., Clatz, O., Delingette, H., Ayache, N.: Integrating tactile and force feedback with finite element models. In: Proceedings of the 2005 IEEE International Conference on Robotics and Automation, ICRA 2005, pp. 3942–3947 (2005)

48. Microsoft. http://www.microsoft.com/hardware/en-gb/touch-technology

49. Schneider, C., Mustufa, T., Okamura, A.: A magnetically-actuated friction feedback mouse. In: Proceedings of EuroHaptics 2004, Munich, Allemagne, pp. 330–337 (2004)

50. Wanjoo, P., Sehyung, P., Laehyun, K., Seungjae, S.: Haptic mouse interface actuated by an electromagnet. In: 2011 International Conference on Complex, Intelligent and Software Intensive Systems (CISIS), pp. 643–646 (2011)

51. Nintendo. http://www.nintendo.com/wii/enhance/#/accessories

52. Orozco, M., Silva, J., El Saddik, A., Petriu, E.: The role of haptics in games. In: El Saddik, A. (ed.) Haptics Rendering and Applications (2012). ISBN 978-953

53. TN Games. http://tngames.com/

54. Palan, S.: Tactile Gaming Vest (TGV) (2010). http://iroboticist.com/2010/03/26/tgv/

55. Mohellebi, H., Kheddar, A., Espie, S.: Adaptive haptic feedback steering wheel for driving simulators. IEEE Trans. Veh. Technol. **58**, 1654–1666 (2009)
56. Sungjae, H., Jung-hee, R.: The Haptic steering Wheel: vibro-tactile based navigation for the driving environment. In: 2010 8th IEEE International Conference on Pervasive Computing and Communications Workshops (PERCOM Workshops), pp. 660–665 (2010)
57. Ryu, J., Kim, H.: A Haptic Modeling System (2010)
58. Ott, R., De Perrot, V., Thalmann, D., Vexo, F.: MHaptic: a haptic manipulation library for generic virtual environments. In: International Conference on Cyberworlds, CW '07, pp. 338–345 (2007)
59. Anderson, T.G., Breckenridge, A., Davidson, G.S.: FGB: a graphical and haptic user interface for creating graphical, haptic user interfaces. Sandia National Labs., Albuquerque, NM (US); Sandia National Labs., Livermore, CA (US) (1999)
60. Yongwon, S., Beom-Chan, L., Yeongmi, K., Jong-Phil, K., Ryu, J.: K-HapticModeler™: a haptic modeling scope and basic framework. In: IEEE International Workshop on Haptic, Audio and Visual Environments and Games, HAVE 2007, pp. 136–141 (2007)
61. Eid, M., Andrews, S., Alamri, A., El Saddik, A.: HAMLAT: a HAML-based authoring tool for haptic application development. In: Ferre, M. (ed.) EuroHaptics 2008. LNCS, vol. 5024, pp. 857–866. Springer, Heidelberg (2008)
62. SensAbleTechnologies. http://www.sensable.com/documents/documents/OpenHaptics_data sheet_hi.pdf
63. Conti, F., Barbagli, F., Balaniuk, R., Halg, M., Lu, C., Morris, D., Sentis, L., Vileshin, E., Warren, J., Khatib, O.: The CHAI libraries. In: Proceedings of Eurohaptics 2003, pp. 496–500 (2003)
64. SenseGraphics. http://www.sensegraphics.com/datasheet/H3DAPI_datasheet.pdf
65. ReachinTechnologies. http://www.reachin.se/products/ReachinAPI/
66. ReachinTechnologies. http://www.haptx.com
67. De Pascale, M., Prattichizzo, D.: The haptik library: a component based architecture for uniform access to haptic devices. IEEE Rob. Autom. Mag. **14**, 64–75 (2007)
68. McLaughlin, M.L., Hespanha, J.P., Sukhatme, G.S.: Introduction to Haptics. Prentice-Hall, Upper Saddle River (2002)
69. Otaduy, M.A., Lin, M.C.: Introduction to haptic rendering. In: ACM SIGGRAPH 2005 Courses, 3. ACM, Los Angeles (2005)
70. Bathe, K.-J.: Finite Element Procedures. Prentice Hall, Englewood Cliffs (1996)
71. Teran, J., Blemker, S., Hing, V., Fedkiw, R.: Finite volume methods for the simulation of skeletal muscle. In: Proceedings of the 2003 ACM SIGGRAPH/Eurographics Symposium on Computer Animation, pp. 68–74. Eurographics Association (2003)
72. James, D.L., Pai, D.K.: Multiresolution green's function methods for interactive simulation of large-scale elastostatic objects. ACM Trans. Graph. (TOG) **22**, 47–82 (2003)
73. Chang, J., Yang, X., Pan, J.J., Li, W., Zhang, J.J.: A fast hybrid computation model for rectum deformation. Vis. Comput. **27**, 97–107 (2011)
74. Basdogan, C., Ho, C.-H., Srinivasan, M.A., Slater, M.: An experimental study on the role of touch in shared virtual environments. ACM Trans. Comput.-Hum. Interact. **7**, 443–460 (2000)
75. Kim, J., Kim, H., Tay, B.K., Muniyandi, M., Srinivasan, M.A., Jordan, J., Mortensen, J., Oliveira, M., Slater, M.: Transatlantic touch: a study of haptic collaboration over long distance. Presence: Teleoperators Virtual Environ. **13**, 328–337 (2004)
76. Liu, G., Lu, K.: Networked multiplayer cooperative interaction using decoupled motion control method in a shared virtual environment with haptic, visual and movement feedback. Computer Animation and Virtual Worlds (2012)

77. Yokokohji, Y., Hollis, R.L., Kanade, T.: What you can see is what you can feel-development of a visual/haptic interface to virtual environment. In: Proceedings of the IEEE 1996 Virtual Reality Annual International Symposium, pp. 46–53, 265. IEEE (1996)
78. Inami, M., Kawakami, N., Sekiguchi, D., Yanagida, Y., Maeda, T., Tachi, S.: Visuo-haptic display using head-mounted projector. In: Proceedings of the Virtual Reality 2000, pp. 233–240. IEEE (2000)
79. Arsenault, R., Ware, C.: Eye-hand co-ordination with force feedback. In: Proceedings of the SIGCHI Conference on Human Factors in Computing Systems, pp. 408–414. ACM (2000)
80. Avanzini, F., Crosato, P.: Haptic-auditory rendering and perception of contact stiffness. In: McGookin, D., Brewster, S. (eds.) HAID 2006. LNCS, vol. 4129, pp. 24–35. Springer, Heidelberg (2006)

An Agent Based Methodology to Design Serious Game in Social Field

Manuel Gentile(✉), Dario La Guardia, Valentina Dal Grande,
Simona Ottaviano, and Mario Allegra

Institute for Educational Technology, National Research Council of Italy,
Via U. La Malfa 153, 90146 Palermo, Italy
{manuel.gentile, dario.laguardia, valentina.dalgrande,
simona.ottaviano, mario.allegra}@itd.cnr.it

Abstract. Training and simulation games are a type of serious game that allow learners to deal with realistic scenarios, to test their behavior under controlled conditions and to increase their understanding of the simulated system/process. In these games, the educational goal changes the issues related to the simulation design. In particular, achieving right balance between realism and teaching effectiveness is an essential design criterion. The difficulties in designing this type of serious games are particularly evident in the social field. In fact, this area is characterized by a complexity that is hard to design in formal terms. Starting from recent evolutions in the field of social simulation, this paper proposes the agent paradigm as a methodological tool to guide the design of serious games in the social field. The PNPV game, designed within the framework of the European project "I can ... I cannot ... I go!" Rev. 2 (PNPV project), which aims to introduce and foster an entrepreneurial mindset among young people, is described as a case study of a serious game developed by means of the agent based approach.

1 Introduction

The effectiveness of simulation technology in education has been extensively demonstrated. According to Blikstein and Wilensky [1], simulation is an active teaching tool which is available to students and improves learner understanding of the simulated system/process.

The simulation approach finds application in the realization of serious games; serious games have had a significant effect on classroom education as well as on training programs [2].

Serious games based on the simulation approach are called training and simulation games (TSG). TSGs adopt/are based on the principles of problem-oriented learning and have been applied in a number of fields: from flight simulators to the Virtual Lab [3]. TSGs are also used in the social field where the object of study is the social process.

Creating effective and attractive learning environments is essential for motivating learners, enabling them to embark on engaging and challenging educational paths [4]. TSGs create an interactive learning environment that allows learners to deal with realistic scenarios and test their behavior under controlled conditions.

© Springer International Publishing Switzerland 2014
A. De Gloria (Ed.): GALA 2013, LNCS 8605, pp. 145–156, 2014.
DOI: 10.1007/978-3-319-12157-4_12

As pointed out by several authors [5, 6], the design of serious games is still an artisan process and no proper guidelines exist based on a validated methodological approach. Moreover, in the specific case of TSGs, the design is often driven by the simulation goal, thus shifting the emphasis from the educational aspect to the realism of the simulated system.

For this purpose, a methodology for designing and developing TSG can be applied in the social field, where the design also has to cope with the difficulties arising from the complex nature of social systems [7, 8].

The proposed method is based on recent developments in the social simulation research field and intends to adapt the agent-based design approach to design and develop a TSG in the social field.

According to Nigel [10] "human societies are complex ...the result is that it becomes impossible to analyse a society as a whole by studying he individual within it, one at time..."; moreover, in this context ensuring that the simulation environment is totally realistic may no longer be a design goal per se. Instead, achieving the right balance between realism and teaching effectiveness is an essential design criterion.

This paper describes the agent-based simulation approach in social sciences, and starting from the principles of agent-based simulation design presents the methodology used to design the serious game PNPVillage. In particular, this work also aims to clarify under which conditions the agent-based approach could be an effective solution in serious game design.

In the following section the application of agent based approach to simulate social system is described. Then, a new methodology for designing and developing TSG is proposed. Finally the experience of designing PNPVillage is reported. PNPVillage is a serious game developed within the framework of the EU-funded project "I can ... I cannot ... I go!" Rev. 2 (PNPV project) that aims to create a training model and tools for the acquisition of knowledge and entrepreneurial skills.

2   Agent Based Simulation in Social Sciences

According to Conte et al. [6], simulation is a research tool that reproduces a real system or process by means of an artificial system and provides useful and often essential insights into a large number of scientific and application sectors.

The core of simulation is the model. The models used in computer simulation are based on formal representation of the system under analysis that can be implemented in a simulation program.

In the last five years, interest in multi-agent based simulation (MABS) has grown continuously [11–13]. Multi-agent systems are software systems consisting of independent entities, called agents, each of which is able to interact with the surrounding environment according to a predetermined behaviour.

The features of the MABS model can be summarized in the following points:

- the system is built on independent entities, called agents;
- the agents can communicate with one another and with the environment;
- the agents have a proactive behavior;
- the system is intrinsically distributed.

As observed by Davidsson in [14], "MABS should not be seen as a completely new and original simulation paradigm (…) it is influenced by and partially builds upon some existing paradigms, such as, parallel and distributed discrete event simulation, object-oriented simulation, as well as dynamic micro simulation."

MABS is the right tool to analyze situations where distributed entities with an autonomous behavior are present. Moreover, the pertinence of MABS to analyze a system should be derived by determining whether that system can be suitably modeled in terms of entities and behaviors or not.

Using the MABS model, the outcome of the simulation at the macro level derives from the evolution of the interaction among the agents at the micro level, making it possible the study the emergent behavior of a system.

This characteristic highlights the close relationship between MABS and the empirical study of social science models. A large number of papers underline the importance of simulation as a tool to study social and biological systems, and numerous authors have recognized the effectiveness of MABS for the investigation of these fields [15].

In [16] Davidsson introduces a schema that facilitates understanding of the relationships among three scientific areas: Agent-Based System, Social Science and Computer Simulation (Fig. 1).

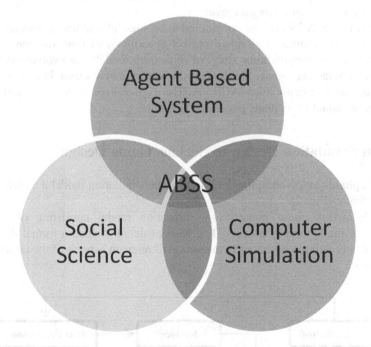

Fig. 1. The three areas constituting ABSS and their interrelationship [16]

The intersection between the Agent-Based System and Social Science concerns the study of social aspects of the agent system (norms, institutions, organizations, competitions). The intersection between Social Science and Computer Simulation focuses on the possibility of simulating social phenomena with computers using any available simulation method and model (Social Simulation - SocSim).

Agent-based social simulation (ABSS) is a specific sector of SocSim aimed to simulate and investigate social phenomena on a computer by means of agent technology.

Agent-based modeling represents an innovation with respect to traditional simulation models. While traditional approaches in general formalize the system's behavior through a set of mathematical relations, in ABSS, the behavior of complex social systems is simulated modeling the single entities and their interactions.

In other words, the system behavior is not modeled at the macro level, but emerges from the composition of the behaviors of the single entities interacting with each other and with the environment (emergent behavior). This feature avoids introducing strong assumptions a priori, such as the rationality assumption of decision-makers necessary for game theory-based models.

Moreover, in agent-based models each agent can adapt to circumstances, thus showing a sort of learning ability.

ABSS in the social sciences typically includes a large number of autonomous entities with very simple behaviors in order to allow researchers to analyze and understand how tiny modifications in the behaviors of these agents can change emergent behavior at an aggregate level.

As an example, ABSS is now considered to be a useful tool that allows researchers in the field of economics to simulate market dynamics and thus validate economic models. In fact, the computational study of economies modeled as evolving systems of autonomous interacting agents has given rise to a research sector known as Agent-based Computational Economics (ACE). ACE is a specialized area of economics of the basic complex adaptive systems paradigm [17, 18].

3   From Simulation Design to Serious Game Design

The typical phases involved in the definition of the simulation model are shown in the following figure (Fig. 2).

The abstraction phase generates a simulation model consisting of a formal description of the system or process. The level of detail of such a formal description must be suitably defined so that only the subset of relevant aspects of the target system is reproduced.

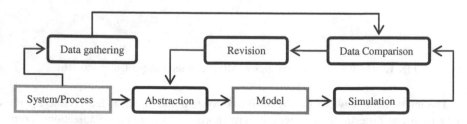

Fig. 2. Simulation model definition and validation scheme [13]

This process implies great simplification of the real world system to be analyzed and, as a consequence, it enhances the importance of correct model validation.

Models must be kept as simple as possible, provided that they are able to show valid behavior, i.e., coherent with the actual evolution of the system or process under analysis.

During the simulation phase, the behavior of the model is executed. The model generates a collection of simulated data that are to be compared with the real ones in order to adapt the model and make it closer to the target system.

The abstraction process of an ABSS involves the following steps:

- identifying the active entities (agents) of the system; agents are active since they are capable of perceptions, communications, and actions;
- specifying knowledge and behaviors of each agent; agents can correspond to both physical and logical elements, and can be permanent or transient.
- defining the subsets of system state variables to be included in the agents' private data; only the agents have the responsibility for storing and updating these data. In a MABS model, the system state is thus distributed and mainly controlled by separate agents.
- modeling the environment; the environment model also denotes the relationships among system entities and anything else needed to simulate the influence of the world surrounding the system.

Starting from the simulation design process described above, the following figure (Fig. 3) shows the design process of a TSG. First of all, the educational goals of a TSG are a key element in the abstraction process and then in the model definition. In addition, we introduce the educational step as an additional validation step.

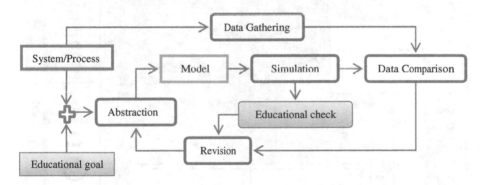

Fig. 3. Serious game model definition and validation scheme

This phase has the objective of verifying the educational effectiveness of the model from different points of view:

- allowing learners to infer the simulation model and in particular the behavior of individual agents in the system;
- validating the inferred behavioral model of each agent by means of a comparison with theoretically valid models;

- validating the emergent behavior of the system by means of a comparison with theoretically valid models at the aggregate level.

The proposed process allows the designer to check the validity of the simulation model from the point of view of realism as well as from an educational point of view, leading to the creation of an educational environment that allows learners to cope with a complex environment similar to real social systems and to acquire specific knowledge of the behavior of individual actors.

4   "I Can … I Cannot … I Go!": The PNPV Project

PNPV Village is a web-based game [19] for testing the skills of students in the management of a tourist resort (Fig. 4), and it has been developed according to the following general aims:

- to encourage competitive dynamics among students;
- to create a simulated environment resembling the real world as closely as possible, allowing students to understand the elements of complex situations;
- to promote self-monitoring, by means of indexes that summarize market trends and aid/facilitate interpretation;
- to allow students to define their strategy;
- to create a learning process by which students work initially in a simple environment and then gradually test their skills in a more complex environment.

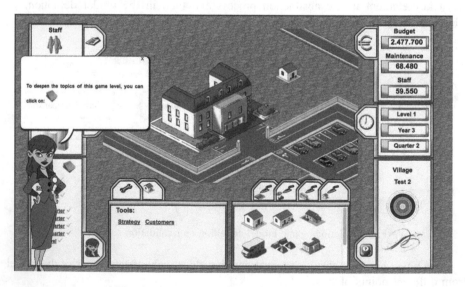

Fig. 4. A screenshot of the game user interface

The tourism market simulation in the PNPV game has been designed according to the ACE theory. In the following sections an analysis of the main phases of game design is presented.

4.1 Educational Goal

The educational goal of the game is to develop students' knowledge and skills in the management of a tourist village.

The game focuses on the following topics:

- marketing policies: market segmentation and market dynamics;
- financial and organizational management;
- social responsibility.

The market has been segmented into 5 types of customers in order to facilitate understanding of the market and to foster training in the marketing policies needed to meet customer preferences. Each type of customer is characterized by different preferences and by a different purchasing propensity, resulting in a different way of evaluating the various offers.

The segments into which the market has been divided are:

- VIP, customers with a high disposable income looking for high quality services as well as relaxation and well-being;
- Business, customers with a high disposable income who are looking for accommodation with a wide assortment of services;
- Young people, customers aged between 18 and 25 years with a low disposable income who are looking for sport and entertainment services;
- Middle Family, customers with a low disposable income who are looking for children's entertainment services
- Working Family, customers with a low disposable income who are looking for inexpensive services.

In PNPVillage several marketing tools that allow students to implement the marketing strategy of choice and position their product on the market have been included. These enable students to define: pricing policies, communication campaigns and advertising. PNPVillage also includes a series of levers that allow students to cope with the main aspects of managing a resort, such as the management of tourism infrastructure, accommodation services and staff.

4.2 Abstraction

The definition of the model started with the analysis and identification of all the actors and their interactions. This process is the result of synergistic activity between the domain expert and the multi-agent systems specialist.

The first step was to choose the structure of the market. In this case, the educational goal and the simulation goal overlapped. In fact, in order to promote competitive dynamics, all the villages operate in a single simulated market. In this way, the result obtained by a single village does not depend just on its own choices but also on those made by all the other groups. Each village competes in an environment very similar to the real world, where the success or failure of a business is determined not only by personal ability and entrepreneurial skills but also by the behavior of its competitors.

The model consists of four main groups of agents:

- Customers.
- Advertising campaign agents.
- Villages.
- Advertising brokers.

Below, a general view of the interactions between the different types of agent is presented (Fig. 5).

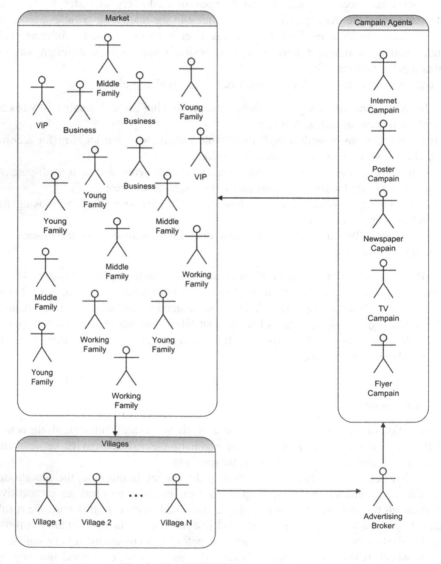

Fig. 5. The PNPVVillage agent societies

The villages are semi-autonomous agents that represent the resort. These agents are customized by the players, who can change their behavior through the decision-making levers. The main goal of the village agent is the promotion and sale of their vacation packages to the customers in the market.

The description of single agents in the model is not the main objective of this work. For a complete description of the simulation model we refer to Allegra et al. [19].

4.3 Data Comparison

The experience of the domain expert is the main element used to revise the model, including how well it corresponds to reality. Starting from the trend in the tourism market in the last few years and taking into account all the strategic and operational levers available to the players, the domain expert has provided the data used to perform the data comparison.

These data were used to verify the correctness of the model and possibly vary the characteristic behavior of the agents in the revision phase.

4.4 Educational Check and Revision

The educational check phase took place at two different times. Firstly, a group of researchers were involved in testing game activities. The goal of this step was to debug and tune the main simulation parameters.

Moreover, starting from the gaming experience the researchers were asked to infer the behavior of individual actors. The objective of this activity was to balance realism with the educational purposes of the simulation. In particular, the behavior of the single agents was made as explicit as possible to the players.

An analysis of the customer agent's behavior is given as an example. In the model, we defined a different customer agent for each market segment. The customer agent's main goal is to contract and buy holiday packages. Each agent is characterized by specific preferences that affect the contracting mechanism and evaluation of offers.

During the educational check we chose a single cycle of contracting for the customer agent. If no offer satisfied the agent's requests, he would leave the contraction phase without buying any holiday packages. The choice of a single cycle of contracting can lead to high rates of market dissatisfaction, but at the same time, it allows students to highlight the preferences of each type of customer agent; this can lead students to make informed choices guided by a more precise understanding of customer behavior.

The second phase of the education check consisted in repeating the process described above in a trial that took place in two classes of a technical institute for tourism.

The educational check was carried out during the testing phase using two types of controls: an active check and a passive check. The active check was performed by administering tests to check whether the educational content had been assimilated by the students. The passive check was performed by checking if the strategic and operational decisions taken by players of the game were consistent.

The game provides two types of decision-making levers: the strategic levers and operating levers. The strategic levers have a declarative character and represent the stated goal of the group on the basis of which the teacher has to assess the consistency of the group's operational decisions. For example, at the beginning of the game, the students have to define the customer type they intend to focus on. They can change their target customer at any level if they think that this will produce better results. Instead, the operational levers determine the results of the village.

Using the strategic levers, players set goals to be pursued through appropriate operating levers. Two main indexes have been defined, the Visibility index (VisIndex) and the Value for Money index (VfM), in order to check the consistency of the user choices; the operational levers have different influences on the VisIndex and VfM indices, depending on the type of customer.

The VisIndex measures a village's market visibility, in relation to a particular market segment. The level of a village's visibility will be calculated as a function of the investments in communication made by all the villages, for each communication channel.

The VfM is a parameter expressing the quality of the operational choices made by a single village in relation to the different types of customers. From the customer's point of view, it is the main element for evaluating and comparing the offers made by the various villages.

The following figure shows the relationship between the various levers and costs, revenues, VisIndex and VfM, which are different for each kind of customer (Fig. 6).

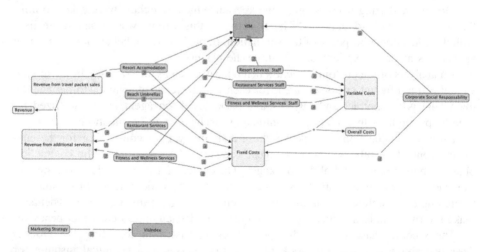

Fig. 6. The network of relationships between the levers and the game indexes

5 Conclusions

The paper proposes a new methodology for the design of training and simulation games in the social field. The proposed methodology adds new key phases to the traditional design process of a simulation, namely educational goals and educational checks.

These two phases are a key element in the design process, allowing designers to improve the educational effectiveness of the model.

As an example of an application of the proposed method, the design of the serious games PNPVillage has been described. The PNPVillage is a serious game aimed to encourage and support entrepreneurial mindset in young people and allows students to progress from a simple scenario to a more complex one with a step by step approach [19], analysing the main concepts of village management and taking decisions to improve competitiveness and results.

The adoption of the multi-agent approach in designing the PNPVillage allows the teachers:

- to control the game evolution by means of an in-process tuning of the agents behaviour;
- to simulate gradually more complex scenarios;
- to facilitate the system evolution comprehension and to improve the efficiency of the debriefing activity.

At the time the process serves the students to follow the real actions of each agent and thus to analyse the appropriateness of their decisions in the light of the developed agent models and evaluate recognize the strong points and the drawbacks of the strategies adopted.

References

1. Blikstein, P., Wilensky, U.: MaterialSim: a constructionist agent-based modeling approach to engineering education. In: Jacobson, M.J., Reimann, P. (eds.) Designs for Learning Environments of the Future: International Perspectives from the Learning Sciences, pp. 17–60. Springer, New York (2010)
2. de Freitas, S.: Using games and simulations for supporting learning. Learn. Media Technol. (Special Issue on Gaming) **31**, 343–358 (2006)
3. McDowell, P., Darken, R., Sullivan, J., Johnson, E.: Delta3D: a complete open source game and simulation engine for building military training systems. J. Defense Model. Simul.: Appl. Methodol. Technol. **3**, 143 (2006)
4. Kriz, W.C.: Creating effective learning environments and learning organizations through gaming simulation design. Simul. Gaming **34**(4), 495–511 (2003). doi:10.1177/104687 8103258201
5. Marfisi-Schottman, I., George, S., Frank, T.-B.: Tools and methods for efficiently designing serious games. In: Proceedings of the 4th European Conference on Games Based Learning, ECGBL 2010, pp. 226–234. Danish School of Education Aarhus University, Copenhagen, Denmark (2010)
6. Conte, R., Gilbert, N., Sichman, J.S.: MAS and social simulation: a suitable commitment. In: Sichman, J.S., Conte, R., Gilbert, N. (eds.) MABS 1998. LNCS (LNAI), vol. 1534, pp. 1–9. Springer, Heidelberg (1998)
7. Marne, B., Wisdom, J., Huynh-Kim-Bang, B., Labat, J.-M.: The six facets of serious game design: a methodology enhanced by our design pattern library. In: Ravenscroft, A., Lindstaedt, S., Kloos, C.D., Hernández-Leo, D. (eds.) EC-TEL 2012. LNCS, vol. 7563, pp. 208–221. Springer, Heidelberg (2012). doi:10.1007/978-3-642-33263-0_17

8. Westera, W., Nadolski, R.J., Hummel, H.G.K., Wopereis, I.G.J.H.: Serious games for higher education: a framework for reducing design complexity. J. Comput. Assist. Learn. **24**(5), 420–432 (2008). doi:10.1111/j.1365-2729.2008.00279.x

9. Cannon, H.M., Friesen, D.P.: The simplicity paradox: another look at complexity in design of simulations and experiential learning. Developments in Simulation and Experiential Learning, vol. 37 (2010). Reprinted in the Bernie Keys Library. http://ABSEL.org

10. Nigel, G.: Agent-based social simulation: dealing with complexity (2005). http://www.complexityscience.org/NoE/ABSS-dealing%20with%20complexity-1-1.pdf

11. Salamon, T.: Design of Agent-Based Model: Developing Computer Simulations for a Better Understanding of Social Processes. Bruckner Publishing, Repin, Czech Republic (2011)

12. Drogoul, A., Vanbergue, D., Meurisse, T.: Multi-agent based simulation: where are the agents ? In: Sichman, J.S., Bousquet, F., Davidsson, P. (eds.) MABS 2002. LNCS (LNAI), vol. 2581, pp. 1–15. Springer, Heidelberg (2003)

13. Gentile, M., Paolucci, M., Sacile, R.: Agent-Based Simulation. Agent-Based Manufacturing and Control Systems, pp. 119–151. CRC Press, Boca Raton (2004). doi:10.1201/9780203492666.ch4

14. Davidsson, P.: Multi agent based simulation: beyond social simulation. In: Moss, S., Davidsson, P. (eds.) MABS 2000. LNCS (LNAI), vol. 1979, pp. 97–107. Springer, Heidelberg (2001). http://dl.acm.org/citation.cfm?id=645697.665593

15. Lopez-Paredes, A., Edmonds, B., Klugl, F.: Special issue: Agent based simulation of complex social systems. Simulation **88**(1), 4–6 (2012). http://sim.sagepub.com/cgi/content/long/88/1/4

16. Davidsson, P.: Agent based social simulation: a computer science view. J. Artif. Soc. Soc. Simul. **5**(1) (2002)

17. Tesfatsion, L.: Agent-based computational economics: a constructive approach to economic theory (chapter 16). In: Tesfatsion, L., Judd, K.L. (eds.) Handbook of Computational Economics, 1st edn., vol. 2, pp. 831–880. Elsevier, Amsterdam (2006)

18. Faria, A.J.: The changing nature of business simulation/gaming research: a brief history. Simul. Gaming **32**(1), 97–110 (2001). http://sag.sagepub.com/cgi/content/long/32/1/97

19. Allegra, M., La Guardia, D., Ottaviano, S., Dal Grande, V., Gentile, M.: A serious game to promote and facilitate entrepreneurship education for young students. In: Long, C.A., Mastorakis, N.E.,Mladenov, V. (eds.) The 2013 International Conference on Education and Educational Technologies, RecentAdvances in Education and Educational Technologies, 16–19 July 2013, Rhodes (Rodos) Island, Greece (2013). ISSN: 2227-4618

Lecture Notes in Computer Science: Beyond simulators, Using F1 Games to Predict Driver Performance, Learning and Potential

Matthew Hislop, Aparajithan Sivanathan, Theodore Lim$^{(\boxtimes)}$,
James M. Ritchie, Gnanathusharan Rajendran, and Sandy Louchart

Heriot-Watt University, Edinburgh EH14 4AS, UK
{m.hislop,a.sivanathan,t.lim,j.m.ritchie,g.rajendran,
s.louchart}@hw.ac.uk

Abstract. Formula One (F1) drivers are amongst the most highly skilled drivers in the world, but not every F1 driver is destined to be a F1 World Champion. Discovering new talent or refreshing strategies are long-term investments for all competitive F1 teams. The F1 world and teams invest vast amounts in developing high-fidelity simulators; however, driving games have seldom been associated with uncovering certain natural abilities. Beyond nature and nurture to attain success at the top level, certain motor-cognitive aspects are paramount for proficiency. One method of potentially finding talent is studying the behavioral and cognitive patterns associated with learning. Here, an F1 simulation game was used to demonstrate how learning had taken place. The indicative change of interest is from cognitive to motor via more skilled autonomous driving style –a skill synonymous with expert driving and ultimately winning races. Our data show clear patterns of how this skill develops.

1 Introduction

Learning motor skills is a part of human development [1]. Our first steps and the feeling that it has "clicked" when learning to drive a car are motor skills that require visual processing, practice and dealing with a range of different scenarios. Once learnt a process becomes automated, allowing for consistently high standards of work to be achieved with far less cognitive resources than at first [2].

In F1, the stakes are very much higher compared to operating vehicles on roadways. Collisions can have a personal cost, yet when contemplating the cost/benefit of motorsport training programs an often overlooked aspect pertains to improving the performance of the driver's mind, i.e. human factors. It is one thing to engineer a fast car, but is another to have a driver who can interact between 'man and machine' to such a level as to win championships. Thus, being able to assess driver cognitive aptitude in any driver environment can greatly aid in evaluating driver ability and subsequent training programs.

Driving simulators fall into the genre of games that use a first-person and/or third-person perspective. Technically simulators are both a game and a training platform. Although driving simulators are built on a game engine, the purpose of the driving simulator as used by F1 teams is no game.

© Springer International Publishing Switzerland 2014
A. De Gloria (Ed.): GALA 2013, LNCS 8605, pp. 157–171, 2014.
DOI: 10.1007/978-3-319-12157-4_13

This paper reports the use of a driving simulator to investigate drivers' aptitude to push the vehicle to their limits and beyond. The objective focuses on how drivers build upon existing experience while gaining automatic responses and skills to handle racing situations. Mapping their experience and decision consequences in the simulator could potentially provide an insight into behavioural states and how feedback from the simulator can influence this. Thus, the simulation game can maximise the opportunity for positive outcomes and learning by addressing higher order cognitive skills.

The focus on driver ability seeks to provide a methodology to establish aptitude and learning traits of potential race champions. Grounding via behavioural data and supplemented with neurometrics (i.e. EEG trends) the wider and future aim is to develop a methodology that could be applied within the racing simulators used by F1 teams and in many other sporting fields. To show a relationship between behavioural data (performance) and learning, the hypothesis was formulated:

(A) Lap times will improve as people gain more experience, showing learning.
(B) Lap times during laps with audio distractions will improve as people gain more experience, showing learning.

2 Performance, Learning and Potential

Automation of cognitive processes (learning to drive) is a complex motor task developed after conscious cognitive training resulting in a sense of familiarity with the task at hand [3]. The Dreyfus brothers [4] take this a step further and state that there are stages between purely cognitive and purely automatic operations in which cognitive resources are increasingly freed up until purely automatic responses are generated. The Dreyfus model indicated 5 main stages of skill acquisition: Novice, Competent, Proficient, Expert, and Master. In this work the grading of the drivers follows a similar paradigm.

The *influence of external attention foci* (distractions) on performance is expected from F1 drivers. They must cope with a range of visual stimuli, altering car dynamics and the pressure of being in a competitive race environment. When all that separates the top drivers are a few hundredths of a second, the ability to be a more autonomous and consistent is crucial; essentially saving cognitive resources for other matters. Experimenting around the delayed retention of skill i.e., using skill sometime after acquiring it, has shown to be a better indicator of motor learning than measuring performance immediately following skill acquisition practice [5]. Therefore skilled drivers, who possess superior motor and cognitive autonomy while driving may respond and recover more quickly from distractions, thus exhibiting sharp reflexes and an ability to react to a changing operating environment exceptionally quickly.

3 Experimentation & Analysis Software

The F1 2011™ racing game was selected for a number of reasons but mainly due to its game engine, accurate track layout and the ability to extract telemetry data. The experiment consisted of 10 practice laps and 20 laps around the Silverstone GP track in

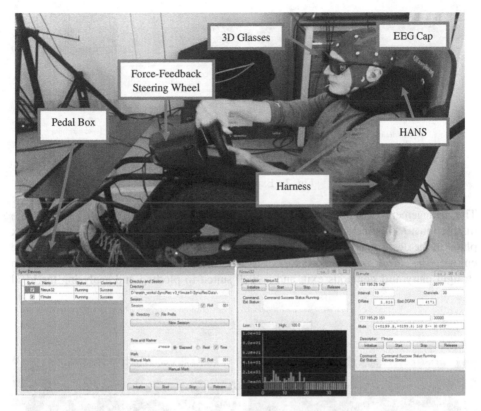

Fig. 1. Simulator recording setup and SyncRec modules [6].

Red Bull's RB7 F1 car. A stereoscopic projector provided 3D immersion and a fully adjustable racing seat along with active force-feedback steering wheel completed the setup.

Figure 1 shows the complete set up and SyncRec control interface. SyncRec [6] was used to synchronously record and fuse telemetry data with EEG data, and to control the telemetry/mute (f1mute) control panel. SyncRec was designed to handle precise synchronisation between telemetry and EEG streams. To prevent extraneous body movements that would introduce noise to the EEG recording Velcro straps were configured to represent the harness in a F1 car. A U-shape pillow emulates the head and neck safety (HANS) device and further provided constraints to extraneous head movements. Figure 1 shows the complete set up and the SyncRec control interface. The experimental protocol consisted of 4 main sections as shown in Fig. 2.

The RedBull RB7 was selected as it is the only team to have mounted their dashboard on the car chassis and not on the steering wheel. This dashboard position means that the display showing the gear setting and engine RPM is obstructed during cornering which adds to the inhibiting factor of the distraction.

Figure 3 shows a map of the Silverstone GP racetrack and the zone boundaries indicating where markers are placed within the data to locate desired data sets.

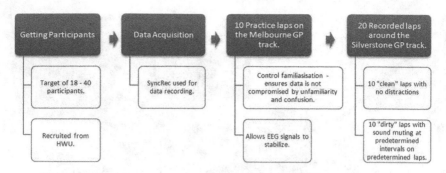

Fig. 2. Experimental method

The arrangement of lap sessions were: 13 "clean" laps (1-10, 13, 16 & 20) with no distractions; 7 "distracted" laps (11, 12, 14, 15, 17, 18 & 19) in which the muting took place in the designated zones. SynRec controlled audio suppression through the game engine. The corner of interest is Stowe for two main reasons; it is a fast corner with a straight entry and generous exit, and is well suited to plotting and analysing the ideal

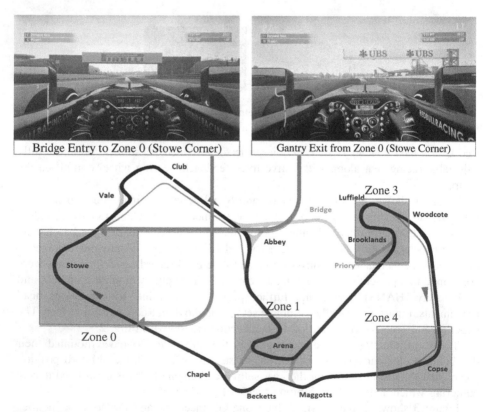

Fig. 3. Silverstone track layout indicating active mute-zones including the entry and exit markers.

racing line. SyncRec records all data continuously and automatically places markers in conjunction with the sound muting process when entering and leaving zones as depicted in Fig. 3. In order to find a specific point of interest markers are also placed within the data to align and fuse EEG, telemetry and audio omissions.

Participants were unaware which area of the track was to be scrutinised, lessening performance pressure and any excessive anticipation/expectation of a muted corner. This method removed all human error with regards to the placement of marks and the synchronous muting of the sound, which allows for data to be analysed at the exact time muting occurred.

Personal Experience	Yes	No		
Do you hold a valid UK Driving License?	☐	☐		
If no, have you ever held a UK Driving License?	☐	☐		
Do you posses a MSA or other authorised body motor sports license?	☐	☐		
If no, have you ever possessed a motor sports license?	☐	☐		
Have you every driven competitively professionally/ semi professionally?	☐	☐		
If so, please give details.				

General Experience	Never	monthly	Weekly	Daily
How often do you drive?	☐	☐	☐	☐
How often would you say you play racing simulation games (Xbox, PS3, PC etc)	☐	☐	☐	☐
Simulator Experience	Not at all	slightly	a lot	severely
Did you enjoy todays experiment?	☐	☐	☐	☐
How much did the lack of sound distract you?	☐	☐	☐	☐
Did the lack of sound affect your driving?	☐	☐	☐	☐

Grade A: Professional/Semi-Professional   Grade B: Driving AND Gaming Experience
Grade C: Driving OR Gaming Experience   Grade D: Neither Driving NOR Gaming Experience

Fig. 4. Participant demograph and driver categories.

The demographics of each driver were taken to evaluate their driving/gaming experience. Prior to experimentation this enabled them to be placed into one of the following skill categories as shown in Fig. 4.

A track boundary was obtained using data gathered from previous work [6]. Custom MatLab code was written to extrapolate, read and analyse the data from each participant's lap. A trace of the in-game dynamic racing line coordinates allowed the ideal racing line to be plotted. This enabled each participant's car position to be plotted giving an indication of how close drivers are to the ideal racing line.

3.1   Choice of Distraction

Literature indicates any distraction must interfere with the normal automated processes associated with driving [6]. Research has shown that the auditory cortex influences the brain's modelling of temporal characteristics of the auditory environment [7]. A fundamental motorsport's driving skill is deciding when to change gear. One aspect of this is listening to the pitch of the engine's revs, therefore muting the sound at given track locations was chosen as an ideal, easy to implement interrupt. Preliminary experimentation had shown that the loss of sound severely inhibited the user's ability to drive and invoked conscious thought about speed and gear selection. Any relevant driver distractor, such as rain or other cars, could have been utilised; however, the ease of embedding auditory omission into the experimental set up was a key factor here. It also provides the basis for further studies into evoked neural responses to auditory omissions.

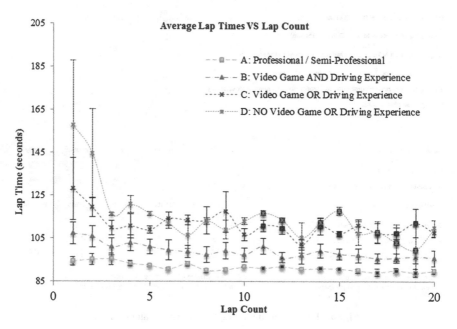

Fig. 5. Average Lap Times vs. Lap Count for each driver grade. (NB Black markers indicate distracted (audio omission) laps)

4   Results

Motorsport performance analysis must relate to data that quantifies it, namely; telemetry, lap times, car track position and deviations from the "ideal" racing line. Telemetry data was sampled at 50 Hz and recorded in binary files.

Twin-tailed paired t-tests, which allow for positive and negative change, were conducted on the data. Significance testing was also conducted in accordance with Rowntree's criteria [8] on the correlation coefficients.

Although 31 participants took part only the last 16 yielded usable telemetry data due to marker placement errors. An overview of general lap times (Fig. 5) shows the *a priori* skill classification bands plotted on the same axis. The results indicate very little overlap, proving the validity of this classification methodology. The large increase in performance over the first three laps is much more prominent for lesser skilled participants. Interestingly, the lap times tend to plateau after these three laps, indicating that introducing the distractions on lap 11 was appropriate, as participants had settled down adequately. NB: The markers are highlighted in bold to indicate laps where distractions occurred. The Lap times are shown to 3 decimal places, which is standard F1 practice.

The average lap times for all sixteen participants are shown in Fig. 6. Class A and D drivers are plotted displaying standard deviation error bars. The class B and C drivers are plotted showing started error since n>1. A large improvement in lap time is seen during the first three laps, after which it levels off. On average participants react immediately to auditory omission (distraction) and perform worse. However, they then recover and generally improve after each consecutive distracted session. The average gradient was found to be -0.53.

4.1   Driver Grade Discriminations

The average lap times for each of the driver category shown in Fig. 6. Grade 'A' represents the professional/semi-professional category and shows a strong negative correlation with an immediate worsening of lap times that improves after three laps. Average lap time improved on the first distracted lap and surprisingly worsened on the second distracted lap. The gradient was found to be -0.27.

Grade 'B' drivers displayed a strong negative correlation with an immediate improvement in lap times that levels off after three laps. On average participants immediately perform worse due to the distraction, but then quickly recover and improve on encountering the next one. This improvement was a little slower than average, with a gradient of -0.46.

Grade 'C' drivers again showed a common pattern with immediate improvement in lap times that level off after around three laps. There is also a strong negative correlation with a gradient of -0.54, slightly higher than average indicating a faster than average improvement rate. Showing another similarity, it can be seen that the distraction caused the participants' performance to immediately deteriorate nonetheless they start to recover almost immediately and a visible increase in variance is observed.

Grade 'D' posted the fastest improvement rate of all Fig. 6 clearly shows a strong negative correlation with a gradient of -1.55, almost three times the average. Again after three laps the participants seem to settle down and again the introduction of the distraction causes immediate worsening, but immediate recovery also again takes place.

4.2   Data Analysis

Observations from Fig. 6 indicates a common lap time pattern of 3 laps of rapid improvement, stabilisation to a gradual improvement, then a lesser improvement rate once distractions were introduced. Thus the analysis of the correlation coefficients can

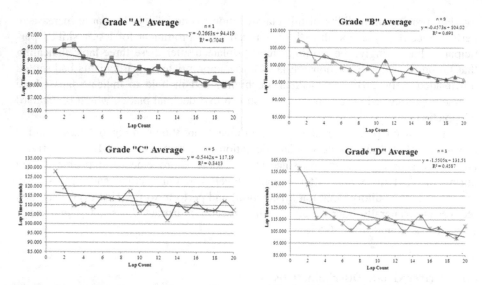

Fig. 6. Average lap time per driver grade category. Grade 'A': Professional/semi-professional drivers; Grade 'B': Driving and gaming experience; Grade 'C': Limited driving or gaming experience; Grade 'D': Neither driving nor gaming experience.

be broken down into the five observable sections: laps 1 to 3, laps 4 to 10, laps 11 to 20, and laps 1 to 20. A twin tailed t-test analysis was conducted across the lap times and yielded the following results in Table 1.

Table 1. Lap Time T-Tests

Pair	Lap Time p-Values
1 & 3	0.0062
4 & 10	0.0297
11 & 20	0.0078
1 & 10	0.0010
1 & 20	0.0002

Table 1 indicates a strong relationship between the 1st and 10th laps and the 1st and 20th laps. With a p-value of 0.0078, a factor of 10 higher than laps 1 to 10, it would appear that the distractions do reduce the rate of learning by a small degree but not enough to rule out an increasing relationship (p would have to equal 0.6+ [8]), but importantly it would appear statistically that learning still occurs. This can be clearly seen from the plots of lap time in that almost every driver category shows an improvement on the second distracted lap.

Lap time correlation coefficients found that the point of 5 % significance was −0.5, and the point of 1 % significance was −0.63. These points are shown by the dotted lines on Fig. 7:

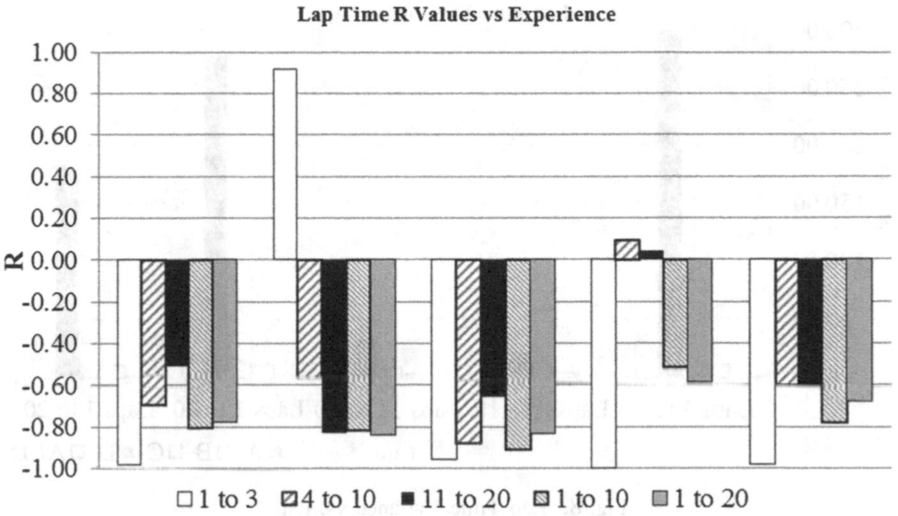

Lap Time R Values vs Experience

Fig. 7. Lap time correlation coefficients

Except for three exceptions, Fig. 7 shows that all the data is significant to the 5 % level; the results are a highly significant for 95 % of the sample population. The results also show that two thirds of the data is highly significant to the 1 % level; two thirds of the data is highly significant for 99 % of the population. For the first three laps the grade 'A' driver had a very strong correlation coefficient of –0.98.

Although lesser in degree there is still a positive correlation seen in grade 'C' categories indicating that after an initial increase in learning up to lap 3, driver performance deteriorated upon auditory omission. Reasoning as to their performance fluctuation requires further investigation. The weakness of this correlation indicates that although grade 'C' lap times worsened after lap 4, it is not statistically significant.

Figure 8 shows the variance level for each of the lap segments. As expected the more experienced drivers exhibit less variance in their lap times and are more consistent in their performance. The plot also reveals that as the experiment progresses variance decreases with each driver category. The one exception is the grade 'D' driver during the distracted laps, which could be due to very inexperienced drivers being unable to cope with the lack of sound.

5 Discussion of Results

In applying the Dreyfus paradigm, separating participants by both their driving and gaming experience provided clearer distinctions across each skill category, thus providing a valid method to classify driver skill. To better understand the correlations of performance, learning and potential, the t-tests reveal strong/very strong relationships indicating that there is a performance increase across the whole participant sample as lap count increases.

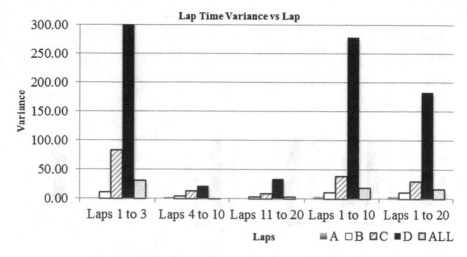

Fig. 8. Lap Time Variance vs. Lap

Although there was only one driver in the 'A' and 'D' categories, the high level of correlation coefficient significance indicates an extremely strong case to support the hypothesis that lap times have improved with experience and learning has taken place across all of the participants. The coefficient and t-test data supports that hypothesis in that as people gain more experience, they learn and improve; that is, natural ability (nature) interacts with experience (nurture).

Laps 1 to 3, with the exception of the grade 'A' driver, displayed a large decrease in lap time during the first three laps. All participants upon post-test interview indicated they only began to familiarise with the track and simulator hardware after three laps. This was verified from the average times (Fig. 6) and the statistical correlations in Fig. 7. The drivers in the lowest driver category surprisingly displayed the fastest improvement over these three laps. The data shows uniformly that the higher the skill level, the smaller the improvement. This indicates that the rate of improvement was faster for those with less experience and skill and supports the Dreyfus Model [1].

Interestingly, the grade 'A' driver immediately started to push the boundaries and actually worsened over the first few laps; this explains why the standard three-lap pattern did not apply to here. Telemetry analysis showed the participant left the track on the second and third laps, losing considerable time.

Generally, performance improvement began from laps 4 to 10. Almost all of the participants showed a strong positive correlation with significance of at least 5 % between the third and tenth lap. The exception was the 'C' grade category in which an insignificant negative correlation occurred, indicating that following the improvement seen up to lap three the drivers peaked and ceased to improve. Backed up by the t-test data there is a very strong case to support the hypothesis that learning did occur.

Laps 11 to 20 include distractions. A racing line for each lap of each driver (blue) was plotted against the ideal racing line (red) and the track boundaries (black). Fig. 9 shows the first and last lap for driver number 25. The circled area in Fig. 9(a) indicates the point where the participant left the track in lap 1. A visible improvement is seen in

Fig. 9(b). The main question here pertains to whether learning has taken place or was this due to conditioning operands as a result of repetition. Statistical analysis was conducted to provide concrete evidence that performance improvement was the result of skill acquisition/learning.

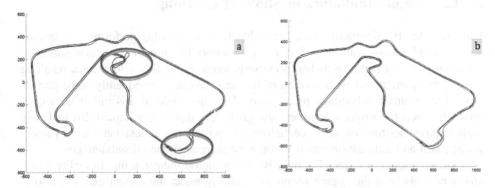

Fig. 9. Driver 25, Racing Line (a) Lap 1. (b) Lap 20.

The correlation coefficients suggest that once a distraction was introduced in the lap, 11 of the participants did not perform as well. Nonetheless the coefficients remained mostly significant to the 5 % level suggesting that they were still learning, albeit at a decreased rate. This is in keeping with the literature and shows that the distractions worked in impairing the driver's ability to drive. The higher skilled categories' lap times were not as hindered by the distractions as much as the lower categories which could indicate that skilled drivers are not affected as much by the lack of sound in a simulator since their skill allows them to drive relatively normally whilst finding solutions. Participant 20 stated that he learnt to use visual markers to help cope with the distractions and participant 26 stated that he soon adapted to the lack of sound by short shifting and using visual references. The latter also stated that the simulator environment is not 100 % realistic. In a race the sound of the engine is used by the driver as a source of information on various aspects of the car's performance such as tyre spin and subsequently tyre wear. Such variables were not modelled within this experiment. This suggests a very high level of meta-awareness; the participant was so skilled he was able to review his performance and environment whilst driving.

5.1 Variance

The variance in each of the lap sections indicate that the more experienced drivers are more consistent in their driving thus demonstrating a high level of skill as outlined in the Dreyfus Model [1]. The grade 'A' drivers' variance barely changed throughout the experiment, again showing skill. Interestingly his variance was 1607 times less than that of the grade 'D' novice driver, showing a huge difference in consistency. The plot also showed that variance decreased in every skill category as the experiment progressed, and this could be showing that as people learn, they become more consistent, again following the Dreyfus model. The clear trends also support the validity of the a priori driver classification and show that when looking for skilled drivers consistency is a key indication of ability.

6   The Use of Simulators in Showing Learning

The use of the F1 Simulator yielded valuable data for assessing performance from the standpoint of meta-cognition and learning prowess. The use of a popular simulator game meant many participants had previously raced on the Silverstone track resulting in very few participants with no idea of the track layout. Consequently some participants had an unfair advantage over others. The magnitude of this unfair advantage varies between the driver categories; the grade "A" driver (participant 26) had only been exposed to Silverstone once before, yet posted the fastest lap times. Clearly ability, skill and automation can overcome the aforementioned disadvantages.

One participant, a former Formula BMW champion indicated that in reality a race driver not only uses the engine sound to accurately select the correct gear but also to judge fuel load, tyre slippage and subsequently tyre wear. Such factors alter the breaking and turn in points for every corner on the track. All these factors were not taken into account in the simulation resulting in constant breaking and turn in points lap on lap. The lack of realism enabled participants who are skilled at the game to overcome the lack of sound by memorising these consistent breaking points, something that a real driver on a real track could not do. Future work using a real F1 simulator would allow these factors to be taken into consideration.

Figure 10 shows the relationship between the simulator game mechanics and that associated with learning. The Learning Mechanics – Game Mechanics (LM-GM) framework [9] correlates well with post-interview results and that of the cross-modal interplay of behavioural data. The mapping reveals that simulator games that pose serious content can illustrate Pavlovian associative learning. The main challenge faced by all participants is to master driving and steering a race car, and while it appears a simple task, there is a need for drivers to learn to use appropriate speeds and utilise meta-cognitive associates. Choosing a preferred option or course of action from among a set of alternatives based on observing cues about speed is required to avoid crashing.

The LM-GM also reveals the interplay between motor control, the visual system and the thought processes attributed to skills learning. Meta-cognition allocates cognitive resources for learning to cope. Here, it the basis is awareness of the surrounds and any corresponding feedback is instrumental. This is illustrated in the LM-GM mapping where the continuous cycle of cascading information from the simulated environment is immediately fed back simultaneously via visualisation and the steering control hardware. The essential learning aspect observed in this study is the relationship between the Movement (i.e. car control) and the Simulate/Response game mechanics (5 and 6 in Fig. 10). In monitoring and assessing the relationship between movement related decision-making and subsequent user responses (EEG activity, Driving/ Behavioural changes), we are able to quantify, to a certain extent, the user's ability to learn and adapt. However, since this approach correlates both concrete performance indicators (Telemetry, Racing line) and unconscious task-related indicators (EEG),

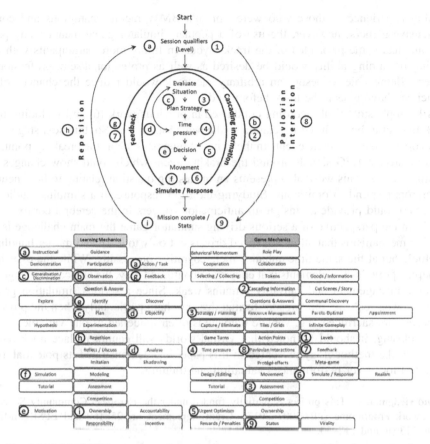

Fig. 10. LM-GM [9] mapping of simulator game mechanics and learning mechanics.

it allows for a user assessment that it not purely focused on current ability but also potential future aptitudes at conducting a task.

7 Conclusion

This paper presented a novel driver classification methodology for measuring driver performance that was valid and clearly distinguished rates of learning between different driver skill levels. A key outcome of this work was how simulators can be used to establish learning behaviour. The methodology presented is generic enough to build a foundation to further behavioural research in domains other than Formula One.

Although some assumptions have been made, the experimentation using a 3D F1 simulator game to gather behavioural correlates of learning revealed how such a game can be used to discover natural traits over the nurtured. It also provides insights to the requirements needed to implement better race driver selection and training programmes.

There are some limitations in this early work but the results are very encouraging. The participants recruited had varying skill levels, from those with no driving or gaming experience to those who were Formula BMW racing champions and comprehensive gamers; however, the use of a popular simulator game meant many participants had some prior idea of the track layout. In future more participants with no driving or gaming ability would be desired as well as professional/semi-professional drivers. Being able to design an arbitrary racetrack would reduce the chances of a participant having seen the track beforehand.

Electrophysiological recording conducted in previous work [6] and including this work has yet to be analysed in relation to the behavioural data. So, this next stage will focus on analysing discrete events in the zones of interest, such as the breaking point, to be compared to EEG signals around the braking event which could show changes as learning occurs. This work also presents an interesting question relating to how neural generators respond to omissions. Studying the EEG response to a stimulus (audio in this case) could provide an insight to anticipation triggers in the cerebral cortex.

From the perspective of a serious driving simulator game the main challenge is to provide mechanisms that allow advanced drivers not only to learn and master handling a vehicle but at the same time enhance meta-cognitive processing. While the essential gameplay provides the elements that encourage continued play, the tactical challenge of resource management and causality remains weak. Since a serious simulation game must draw on real-life, the 'arcade' format does not help particularly when the physics properties are sacrificed, e.g. vehicle damage is often modelled as one variable.

In closing, it should be noted that virtual worlds still cannot replace track days. However, the methodology presented in this paper has demonstrated its potential as a front end for driver performance evaluation and training.

Acknowledgments. This project is partially funded under the European Community Seventh Framework Programme (FP7/2007 2013), Grant Agreement nr. 258169 and EPSRC/IMRC grants 113946 and 112430.

References

1. Thelen, E.S.: A Dynamic Systems Approach to the Development of Cognition and Action. MIT Press, Cambridge (1996)
2. Schier, M.A.: Changes in EEG alpha power during simulated driving: a demonstration. Int. J. Psychophysiol. **37**(2), 155–162 (2000)
3. Shiffrin, R.M., Schneider, W.: Controlled and automatic human information processing: II. Perceptual learning, automatic attending and a general theory. Psychol. Rev. **84**(2), 127–190 (1977)
4. Dreyfus, S.E., Dreyfus, H.L.: A Five-Stage Model of the Mental Activities Involved in Directed Skill Acquisition. California University at Berkeley Operations Research Center, Berkeley (1980)
5. Kantak, S.S., Winstein, C.J.: Learning–performance distinction and memory processes for motor skills: a focused review and perspective. Behav. Brain Res. **228**(1), 219–231 (2012)
6. Sivanathan, A., Lim, T., Louchart, S., Ritchie, J.: Temporal synchronisation of data logging in racing gameplay. Procedia Comput. Sci. **15**, 103–110 (2012)
7. Raij, T., McEvoy, L., Mäkelä, J.P., Hari, R.: Human auditory cortex is activated by omissions of auditory stimuli. Brain Res. **745**(1–2), 134–143 (1997)

8. Rowntree, D.: Statistics without Tears: An Introduction for Non-Mathematicians. Penguin, London (2000)
9. Lim, T., Louchart, S., Suttie, N., Ritchie, J.M., Aylett, R.S., Stănescu, I.A., Roceanu, I., Martinez-Ortiz, I., Moreno-Ger, P.: Strategies for effective digital games development and implementation. In: Baek, Y., Whitton, N. (eds.) Cases on Digital Game-Based Learning: Methods, Models, and Strategies, pp. 168–198. IGI Global, Hershey (2012)

Paths for Cognitive Rehabilitation: From Reality to Educational Software, to Serious Games, to Reality Again

Francesco Curatelli[1(✉)], Chiara Martinengo[2],
Francesco Bellotti[1], and Riccardo Berta[1]

[1] DITEN - University of Genova, Via Opera Pia 11/A, 16145 Genova, Italy
curatelli@unige.it, {franz,berta}@elios.unige.it
[2] DIMA - University of Genova, via Dodecaneso 35, 16146 Genova, Italy
martinen@dima.unige.it

Abstract. In this paper, we propose a learning path for cognitive rehabilitation in the use of money, and of the basic activities in the economic field. Starting from the mathematical learning difficulties of kids with cognitive disabilities, we describe the educational theories and methods used, and outline a set of educational programs that we have specifically designed and implemented for cognitive rehabilitation. The achievements obtained with this learning path, presented with some case studies, make it possible the use of serious games to further strengthen the acquired theoretical and practical knowledge also in multidisciplinary contexts, and to obtain a further enhancement of the cognitive and metacognitive skills.

1 Introduction

One of the major challenges of modern society concerns the transition from integration to inclusion of people with cognitive disabilities either caused by neuromotor or other types of problems. In this context, the suitable use of Information and Communication Technologies (ICT) can foster the participation in the information society, better social relations, improved job possibilities and, in general, the active participation in the life of society and to its cultural heritage [1]. In this context, ICT can provide an essential contribution to build a *recovery path* (or *learning path*) for cognitive rehabilitation, that is a plan using educational and pedagogical theories and technologies which are suitable to develop skills that are necessary for full inclusion in society.

In particular, a major sector for the inclusion of a disabled person (for it concerns the management of important activities of daily life) is the *economic field*. With this term, we refer specifically to basic activities such as recognizing the different coins and banknotes, making payments, changing coins or banknotes with others of equal value, making purchases with rest or with discount, calculating the cost of produced goods, up to increasingly complex situations. A person with neuromotor and/or cognitive disabilities has very often significant difficulties in this field, especially in the management of the logical-mathematical meanings that are the basis of all activities in this area, but, unfortunately, the training-educational path followed by kids during school is often

A. De Gloria (Ed.): GALA 2013, LNCS 8605, pp. 172–186, 2014.
DOI: 10.1007/978-3-319-12157-4_14

unable to have a significant impact on them [2]. For this reason, among the objectives and challenges of science education there should be the identification of strategies that provide people with neuromotor or cognitive disabilities with cognitive abilities to manage this important field as early as their schooling age. This target can be pursued by means of software educational tools that have been specifically designed to implement these strategies by getting the kids involved in a suitable and effective learning path [3].

Together with these educational tools more informal learning tools can be used that emphasize the game aspects; in particular, Games-Based Learning and Serious Games (SG) refer to games whose purpose is not limited to pure entertainment and fun [4, 5] (although having fun during game playing is a major feature [6]), and for which suitable assessment methodologies have been proposed [7]. Specifically, there has been a good deal of research on the use of SGs for disability [8–10], and many research projects have been developed, e.g. [11, 12].

In our approach the use of educational tools and SGs are synergistic for a really effective learning path for cognitive difficulties. In this paper we outline how the cognitive recovery can really take place by means of a learning path in the economic field: *from reality to educational software, to serious games, to reality again.*

The starting point of this path, which is described in Sect. 2, is the first contact with the world reality in the economic field: to experience the ability to make purchases and the sequence of the needed actions, to recognize coins and banknotes according to their appearance and value, to internalize practical knowledge, such as payment methods, wallet management and internalization of the mathematical meanings. Moreover, there will be highlighted the positive aspects of this starting point and the limitations that disabled people can face.

In Sect. 3, we describe the educational and pedagogical theories and methodologies that are used in the learning path. In Sect. 4 we describe a software package of educational tools, which we have designed and implemented for the acquisition of some knowledge about the use of money and the underlying mathematical concepts. In fact, after this first contact with the world reality, a significant educational boost can be done with the use of the proposed educational software, because we have the realization, in a simulated and protected environment, of experimented situations. This makes it possible to refine the capacity of perception, attention and memory, to achieve a fuller grasp of the situation and of the meanings, and to enhance cognitive and metacognitive capacities. In Sect. 5 we outline how the learning path has been tested and validated on some students, through the results obtained in some case studies.

In Sect. 6, we describe how our educational software shares objectives and many common features with SGs in the economic field that have been specifically designed for disabled users. We compare these objectives and characteristics, highlighting how our software programs have more complex and articulated cognitive goals, which concern not only the mechanical use of the money, but also the acquisition of special mathematical meanings and the ability to respond to problematic situations. At this point, our recovery path has allowed the kids to obtain a further educational boost with the use of SGs designed for non-impaired people, such as the *Sims 3* life simulation game. This makes it possible to use the knowledge and the practical and theoretical skills so far obtained to further reinforce them also in multidisciplinary contexts, and to achieve further enhancement of the cognitive and metacognitive capacities. The experimentation we have done in this field is also a contribution to the validation of the effectiveness of SGs as educational tools for people with cognitive difficulties [13]. Closing the circle, the ultimate step and goal of the learning path involves to come back to reality again; the kids should now be able to have a conscious approach with world reality, life and work.

2   Let us Start from Reality

In our research, dedicated to the development of cognitive skills in kids with cognitive difficulties, we have dealt with cases of mild mental retardation, caused by neuromotor disabilities for cerebral palsy (*PCI*) or by metabolic pathologies, and cases of non-specific learning difficulties with no neurological damage.

In all the cases considered, we have found that the cognitive difficulties in the logical-linguistic and in the logical-mathematical fields share common features even in presence of very different cognitive problems. This observation is not at all obvious and is motivated by the fact that the *own reality* of many kids with disabilities (that is, their real life situation) has severe problems exactly in the approach with the *world reality*, i.e., with the real environment.

In fact, during the early years of life, the approach with the world reality, the formation of knowledge and cognitive development are closely linked to: the exploratory activity, the ability to move in the surrounding world and to manipulate objects, and the ability to collect information from the environment by exploring and modifying it through the their actions [14]. Since these skills can be severely affected both by motor impairment and by purely cognitive impairment, this may explain the common characteristics of cognitive difficulties in so different types of disability.

For example, in kids with PCI there may be cognitive disorders that are due to the limitations imposed by the motor impairment, especially if it is significant. However, the relationship between motor functionality and cognitive activity varies significantly during the different stages of development, and as early as during the second childhood kids may supplement the lack of motor experiences with processes of perceptual-gnosic reconstruction. So, in general the development of thought and the formation of mental representations are only partially affected by the motor impairment. On the contrary, the presence of a significant cognitive development can severely affect motor development [15].

Therefore, the presence of a cognitive deficit, whether or not associated with a motor impairment, always leads to both a reduction in the ability to interact with the external environment and to explore the world reality, and to a reduction of the ability to respond to the inputs coming from the reality itself. Consequently, the presence of a cognitive deficit slows significantly the capability of developing cognitive abilities. This is the starting condition for kids with cognitive difficulties, especially when they are significant.

As a consequence, it is essential that every kid with mild to moderate cognitive impairment be subject to a careful and precise diagnosis of his/her cognitive situation and development level of the organizational structures of thought [16]. A precise cognitive assessment of the kids, their difficulties and its potentialities may lead to the identification of suitable strategies to, at least partially, overcome the difficulties, and based on the choice of the most appropriate methodological lines. It is thus possible to start a personalized and individualized didactic path to increase the cognitive skills, done by a trained tutor at school, at home, or in an ad hoc structure. The kids who has come to our observation had been evaluated, from the cognitive point of view, by specialists (psychiatrists, psychologists, speech therapists, etc.). Their evaluations have been confirmed by us with an operative approach. In fact, the early stages of our recovery path, carried out with the pedagogical and methodological bases that will be discussed in the following sections, provide both the assessment of the cognitive level of the kid and the actual point from which to begin the learning process. The specific objectives of the didactic path must be determined on a case by case basis and continually updated during the path. For this reason, it is important that the path be articulated over a long period; in fact, every kid/young person with cognitive problems has his/her own learning times and maturation times can be very long, and certainly longer than those of non-impaired peers.

In the logical-mathematical field the cognitive difficulties and the difficulties of interaction with the outside world severely limit the possibility of acquiring the ability to analyze world reality through abstract mental models, and to formulate appropriate responses to the different problematic situations encountered in daily life, which represent one of the goal of mathematical knowledge. In particular, there are significant difficulties in making arguments that are anchored to reality, in the organization of thought, and, more specifically, in the acquisition of more conceptual achievements, such as the different meanings of the number and of the elementary operations.

In fact, the non-impaired kids start the primary school with a range of mathematical experiences, acquired in the family or in the kindergarten, which are almost exclusively based on motor or manual space-time experiences. On the contrary, in its early years of life the kids with motor, praxic and visual-spatial, or cognitive impairments have very limited experiences of this type. Hence their mathematical preschool experiences are very poor and definitely not enough to be the base for learning the concept of number in its different meanings: ordinal, cardinal, measure, value, etc. As we have clearly seen in our experience, nothing can be taken for granted and it is necessary to find specific compensatory strategies to circumvent the basic poverty in space experiences [17].

In addition, often the standard scholar learning path introduce, already during the early years, the use of numbers in abstract calculations which are completely unrelated to the meanings of the numbers. For kids with learning difficulties this can easily lead to erroneous interpretations of their cognitive situation. As we have seen in our experience, the fact that in the early school years the kids are able to perform simple calculations with numbers does not mean that they have really understood the different meanings of number and operations.

The difficulties in the logical-mathematical field are also closely linked, and greatly exacerbated, by the difficulties in the logical-linguistic field. In fact, it has been argued the fundamental role of language in the logical-mathematical field and the need to build appropriate language skills. As a result, great benefit can result from an improvement in the language skills, in particular the ability to understand the semantics of the texts and the ability to clearly and precisely express thought both orally and in writing [16].

3 The Economic Field for Recovering the Relations with the Real World and the Mathematical Meanings

As mentioned in Sect. 1, the *economic field* involves activities such as to: recognize the different coins and banknotes, make payments, make changes of coins or banknotes with others of equal value, make purchases with rest or with discount, calculate the cost of the produced goods, up to more and more complex situations. This is an area of key interest in the daily life of every person, and it is also an action area that makes it possible to really pursue the acquisition of mathematical meanings, by means of a dialectical and mutually reinforcing interaction between the operational capabilities in using money and the different meanings of the mathematical operations that underlie the real activity.

On these themes, we have developed a learning path for kids with cognitive difficulties, based on specific methodologies and on the use of software tools we have designed and implemented. Our proposed objective, which is distinctive of our approach, is not just to manage money in a mechanical way but also (to the extent that it is permitted by the cognitive difficulties) the construction and consolidation of the mathematical meanings underlying the various economic situations nature, so that these meanings become real knowledge and can be profitably used in other areas.

The approach we have followed for the recovery of cognitive difficulties is inspired by the pedagogical-instructional theories that have been developed by the research group of the Department of Mathematics (*DIMA*) at the University of Genova [18]. In particular, we use the concept of *fields of experience* [19]. The fields of experience are related to significant areas of the concrete world reality in which the kid acts. From the point of view of the learning path, they consist of the experience actually gained by the student and by the teacher, and of all the objective data that are available in the considered experience context. The use of suitable fields of experience that are embodied in reality, makes it possible to understand better the meanings of the problematic situations, and to build solving strategies by referring to already consolidated patterns of behavior, so producing a positive effect for cognitive development [20]. In the present paper we are interested in the field of experience *Coins*, which directly refers to buying experiences and, more in general, to different activities in the economic field.

Moreover, the learning path in the economic field must be accompanied by activities in other specific areas that complement the mathematical meanings. For example, activities (either on-field or simulated) in the field of experience *Calendar* are useful to build a meaningful approach to the temporal dimension, both from the psychological point of view (achievement of temporal awareness) and for its mathematical modeling [2, 17]. On the other hand, on-field or simulated activities in the field of experience *Temperature* are useful to build the measure meaning of numbers.

For the reasons already outlined in the previous section, kids with or cognitive or neuromotor disabilities have less opportunities than non-impaired peers to interact with the outside world in the economic field. For example, it is not at all easy for kids with severe motor problems to go frequently shopping at stores. Moreover, as we have seen with some of the kids we have followed, a kid with cognitive difficulties accompanying his/her mother to buy may not be able to pay due attention to the series of operations that it performs, or to remember and apply them. In addition, we have seen that often the kids deal with distrust problematic situations that are perceived as difficult, especially when previous school failures that are due to their learning difficulties have undermined their self-esteem.

According to our experience, the recovery path should start with a period of highly individualized activities, carried out with a tutor and providing a very gradual approach and, possibly, real activities in the selected field of experience. This in order to obtain, as first result, to overcome the distrust of the kids and their active cooperation. For example, it is possible to simulate buying some small real objects by using real coins. Then, when possible, it is very instructive to sometimes make real purchases in stores. This must be preceded by a phase in which the purchase is prepared (deciding what to buy and what should we do in the store, trying to know how much is the object and to understand how can we pay for it), and followed by a phase in which the person is asked to recount the various stages of the purchase.

In addition, the adoption of a gradual and individualized approach, that takes into account the difficulties of the persons and the times that are needed to learn, makes it possible to start from a low level of knowledge in a given situation, to deal after with more complex problem situations in the same situation, and to deal subsequently with even more complex situations. For example, in the economic field one can begin to deal with the simplest situations, such as to recognize the different coins/banknotes and their associated values, to compose prices to buy with exact payments (i.e., without any change). Then, one can move on to more complex situations, such as to find how much money is left in the wallet after payment, to see how much is missing in the wallet in order to buy a certain product, to make the purchase of different products, to make the purchase of more pieces of the same product, etc. In the following Section we will outline in more detail the steps of the learning process, and we will give some results of their experimental application. A more detailed description of the experimental results will be the subject of another paper.

From the point of view of the methodological choices, the learning path we have followed is based on the *method of dialogue* [21]. We have actualized it by adopting a continuous dialogue between the tutor and the pupil: in front of a problematic situation, the tutor asks the pupil to propose strategies for the solution, to justify his/her choice, and if necessary to correct the proposed strategy [16]. The method of dialogue is particularly suitable for teaching to pupils with cognitive problems. In fact, we have found that the method of dialogue is a great help for their severe difficulties in, first, forming their thoughts and, then, expressing their thoughts by means of the language.

A fundamental cornerstone of our methodology is the systematic verbalization of the dialogues, which allows the tutor to analyze the performed work and easily recognize the contribution of the pupil, so estimating with great accuracy the specific difficulties which have arisen and then adapting the learning path accordingly. Moreover, the comparison among dialogues that have been done in different periods of time makes it possible to assess the improvements achieved.

4   From Reality to Educational Software in the Economic Field

The relationship of a disabled kid/young person with reality in the economic field can be facilitated and consolidated through the use of appropriate educational software. Our learning path involves the use of a software package we have designed and implemented for the economic field: *CoLT2 (COin Learning Tool)*, *Il Cambiamonete (The Coin Exchanger)*, *Attenti al Cambio! (Watch the Exchange!)*, *Attenti al Resto! (Watch the Change!)*, *Attenti alla Spesa! (Watch your Shopping!)*, *Attenti allo Sconto! (Watch the Discount!)*. As these programs have been continuously tested on cases of different cognitive difficulties, they have been regularly updated to take into account the information acquired during the learning paths. These programs are not really SGs; however, in the next section we will see how they can be a useful basis for a conscious use of SGs designed for non-impaired users.

These programs are based on the teaching and pedagogical strategies that we have seen in the previous section and are connected to the field of experience *Coins*. For this reason, the use of these software programs is full of meanings, because they have been designed precisely to help people in consolidating the various meanings of numbers and mathematical operations that are the basis of economic transactions, even the simplest ones. For these reasons, as discussed briefly in this and in the following sections, these software programs have been much more effective than software programs that require only the mechanical and repetitive execution of exercises. The problem with the latter ones is that, with even minimal changes of the problematic situation, the user with cognitive difficulties is not able to face the new situation and provide appropriate responses. This is because the mechanical execution of operations that are not connected to real meanings does not help people to build a better inner capacity to understand and interact with the world reality.

At the base of all the programs in our package is the construction of the meaning of value of the number, which cannot be deduced from a purely set-theoretic approach and which is the foundation of a conscious use of the decimal positional system. It is well known that the tendency to count coins regardless of their value can be found in weaker non-impaired students of the first or second grade of primary school [20]. However, in situations of cognitive difficulty this situation can be recognized also later, for example in a girl who attends the sixth grade and is able to perform quite properly column additions and subtractions, but clearly without any awareness. The software package provides also a graduation of difficulty, both in content of the various programs both within each program, through the choice of the level of the game, the type of coins/banknotes to use and the type of prices.

Now let us analyze in more detail the activities proposed in each educational program. According to the gradual approach we mentioned in the previous Sect. 3, the program *CoLT2* makes it possible to address the problematic situations of the economic field starting from the simpler ones.

CoLT2 provides various activities that allow the user to recognize the different coins and banknotes and their value, to be trained in the use of the additive composition and decomposition (for making payments and purchasing more objects), to understand the different meanings of subtraction (for calculating what remains, what is missing), to consolidate the meaning of the product as repeated sum (for making multiple purchases), to manage measurement divisions (for calculating how many identical objects one can buy).

Il Cambiamonete (*The Coin Exchanger*) is inspired by the exchange machines that can be also found in school buildings when there are snacks and soft drinks vending machines that do not give change; so, it is an object the user is likely to have used (instead, it does not seem appropriate at this stage refer to the bank, which is a complex and difficult to understand system). The program address specifically the activity to change Euro coins and banknotes with others of the same value, so allowing the pupil to interiorize the value of the coins/banknotes and the teacher to evaluate the level achieved by the person. The program also promotes the skills of additive composition and decomposition, and makes it possible to recognize the result of a sum as equivalence, which is a different meaning with respect to situations in which addition is made to calculate the cumulative cost of two objects.

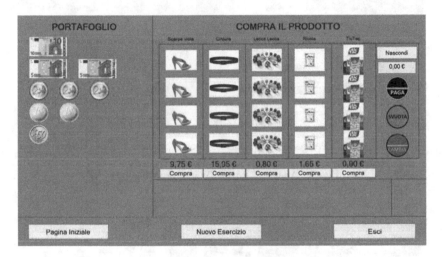

Fig. 1. Attenti al Cambio! (Watch the Exchange!).

Attenti al Cambio! (*Watch the Exchange!*) (Fig. 1) and *Attenti al Resto!* (*Watch the Change!*) (Fig. 2), are inspired by the automatic vending machines to sell products. The first program is inspired by the case in which the machine does not provide change; so, the user must pay with the exact amount, and then he/she may be constrained to exchange money before. The second program is instead inspired by the case in which the machine provides the change. In this case, the skill that is most useful and is trained is to decide if the change is correct; this skill is simpler than the calculation in advance of the same change. To this purpose, the most suitable strategy is to use additive completion, by adding the change to the actual cost and verifying that the resulting value is equal to what had been taken from the wallet.

Attenti alla Spesa! (*Watch your Shopping!*) (Fig. 3) is the two player version of *Attenti al Resto!.* The first player is the buyer and the other is the vendor. Being able to carry out two-player games is an important target of a didactic that adopt confrontation teaching [18]. Typically, people with cognitive difficulties follow at school individualized programs, which are often very different from the program followed by the rest of the class; hence they have no real chance to compare their strategies with those of their classmates. For this reason, the recovery program should include some cooperative activities with classmates whose level in the learning path is not too far, as long as this is well accepted by both students and does not generate anxiety or frustration.

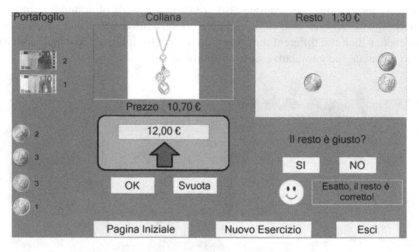

Fig. 2. Attenti al Resto! (Watch the Change!).

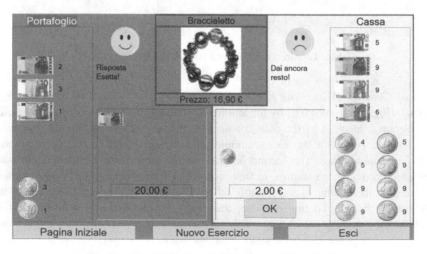

Fig. 3. Attenti alla Spesa! (Watch your Shopping!).

Attenti allo Sconto! (*Watch the Discount!*) is situated at the highest level of skills required and it should be proposed when the meanings and the operational addressed by the other programs have been actually acquired. The program can be played at two levels of increasing difficulty, with the absolute discount and with the percentage discount, respectively. In the first level it is acquired the basic discount concept and it is proposed a practical strategy which is based on the mental calculation of appropriate exchanges in order to find the discounted price. In the second level, not yet tested on the kids we are following, it is proposed an approach with the concept of percentage, which is very difficult for people with learning difficulties, with the target to interiorize the concept that underlies it, and leaving the program to perform specific calculations.

5   Case Studies and Results

The timing and the way of use of the educational software programs must be evaluated case by case, depending on the cognitive situation of the person. In this section, we will briefly present some case studies with the assessment of timing, the application of the programs and the obtained results. A more detailed presentation, which will also contain examples of the dialogue method, will be the object of a further paper. As a first observation, we can note that all the kids have perceived the enjoying aspect of the activities, so that, after having enjoyed playing a program, they explicitly asked to also try the others. In this paper we subdivide the kids followed by us into two groups: those characterized by milder cognitive difficulties and those with medium to severe cognitive difficulties.

With the kids who have milder cognitive difficulties, it has been possible to start the recovery path with a period of real activity in the field of experience *Coins*: the kids have looked at the purchases in stores made by their parents and have themselves made simple purchases. So, when the kids have started to use the programs, they already knew the coins and their value and were able to compose simple price to make purchases in stores. This approach is surely preferable when the cognitive difficulties are mild, because the use of the software after real experiences recalls already acquired minimal contents. In fact, the kids did immediately orient themselves in the use of the software, and the manipulation of the symbols in the abstract space of a program immediately recalled to them the real elements (such as coins, wallet, cash register) whom the symbols referred to. In addition, it has been possible to start the use of the programs from a non initial level, and from there to deal with more complicated situations, which the kids have been able to manage in a short time, also acquiring the understanding of the mathematical meanings.

As an example of this group we refer to the experience of M., male aged 10. When we first started using the programs *CoLT2*, *Il Cambiamonete* and *Attenti al Cambio!*, M. was able to compose and easily change prices within 30 €, without cents. We then introduced cents in the two programs, and he adapted himself to the new situation, getting a full grasp of the value meaning of the number and of the use of decimal numbers. We then moved on to use the program *Attenti al Resto!*. Initially, and despite having a quite correct perception of the problematic situation, M. did not know how to calculate the change and did not link this situation with a subtraction operation.

Using the program, which plans to make attempts and reports if they are correct or not, he has been able to reach on his own the use of the completion strategy to calculate the change. He reached more laboriously to link this strategy to the subtraction operation. We then proposed to M. to use the program *Attenti alla Spesa!* with D., male aged 13, with similar cognitive difficulties, following the strategy of the comparison that we have discussed in the previous section. M. has been able to control the actions of D. and to suggest strategies when D. was in difficulty. Hence, M. has increased his practical and theoretical knowledge, his ability to both reason about problems and control the reasoning itself, that is, his cognitive and metacognitive skills.

A different approach has been done in the case of kids with medium-severe cognitive difficulties, for which we take as example W., female aged 12. We found that W. completely lacked the value meaning of the coins, and also after some time continued to count the coins simply according to their number and not their values, although he realized that they were different in appearance. Because of her cognitive difficulties, in particular the lack of capacity of attention and concentration, she was not able to effectively interact with real situations of purchase, both when she looked at her mother purchasing, and when she was asked to purchase on her own; as the latter situation gave her anxiety she often refused even to try. In this case we have introduced quite early the use of the software programs, starting of course from the lowest initial level of *CoLT2* and *Il Cambiamonete*, obtaining as first result to improve her capacity of attention and concentration. This first result has produced better capacity of attention by W. also in the management of real situations and, gradually, a decrease of her distrust in the real life situations she faced. Instead, the times to get the first significant and, above all, lasting results were much longer; for example, it took several months to start to mature the concept of value and a conscious use of the additive composition and decomposition.

We have noted, however, that even kids with medium to severe cognitive difficulties and poor experience from real life easily recognized the real objects (coins, wallet, the items on sale, etc.) in the abstract elements of the software programs and were able to gave them their exact meanings.

6   From Educational Software to Serious Games, to Reality Again

It is worth noting that the educational software programs we have presented have many goals and characteristics in common with SGs acting within the economic field and meant for people with cognitive difficulties [11, 22], namely:

- To promote the real inclusion of persons with disabilities, preparing them to face the concrete situations of life and to enter into the world of work.
- To pursue effective training strategies to ensure the development of skills and abilities that are very similar to those gained with on-field experience.
- To use the simulation of a specific real situation to favor the possibility of facing the real situation itself with the proper tools. This is done by developing (in a simulated and protected environment) abilities, skills, specific expertise and implementation of appropriate strategies that will be used in the real world.

- To actualize *experiential learning* [23]. In fact, active learning, which consists in internalizing something that has been done in person, is much easier and more efficient than learning contents delivered during lectures, which is a passive learning. In addition, making the simulation very close to the world reality reduces the fear of facing new situations, so increasing confidence in get involved, and increases the experience in real situations.
- To have the possibility of repeating the game more and more times, with situations that are each time different and not predictable. This makes it possible to reach a full control of the problematic situation addressed and to build confidence, first in using the tool and then in addressing the real situation.
- Attention to usability, especially for users with motor impairments.
- To improve the skills of perception, attention and memory.

Some features are more specific of the SGs for cognitive disabilities, while others are more specific of the proposed educational software. Concerning the SGs, their use is attractive because of the presence, such as in commercial videogames, of 3D and graphical/movement effects, although simpler. So, the more evident recreational aspect, which is intrinsic in games, increases the motivation and involvement of the user [24, 25]. However, their cognitive objectives are often limited and then suitable for more severe cognitive disabilities.

On the other hand, for (as already said) our educational software is based on effective educational strategies, the cognitive goals can be much more complex and articulated, and can concern not only the mechanical use of the money, but also the acquisition of special mathematical meanings and the ability to respond to problematic situations. Moreover, significant improvement in metacognitive skills can be achieved [26]. Concerning the graphical aspects, even if the abstract spaces of the software programs are not a detailed depiction of the real life contexts, the kids have always oriented themselves during the use of the programs, and the manipulation of the various elements has always recalled correctly the real contexts.

As already said, both in the case of SGs aimed at users with cognitive disability and in the case of our educational software, the games recall real contents of which it is possible to have, at least partially, a direct experience. However, in the economic field there are also problematic situations in which it is not typically possible to relate directly to real experience. This is the case, for example, of the situation of buying/selling transactions in a store from the point of view of the shopkeeper. This situation requires a considerable degree of imagination and abstraction, the use of unusual meanings of addition and subtraction, and the simultaneous control of several operational steps, that is, mental operations which are problematic for people with cognitive difficulties.

However, it may be very useful to promote such acquisitions in view of future real life, at least when the cognitive situation of the kids permits it. In fact, by achieving a fuller understanding of the sale mechanisms makes it possible to pursue more complex targets, such as to calculate the production cost (starting from home production, then moving to handicraft and industrial ones), or to manage a family budget, to understand and use banking operations, etc. Finally, to improve the capacity to make abstraction and to form mental representations in more and more complex economic situations is a goal that promotes the independence of the disabled person and his/her real inclusion.

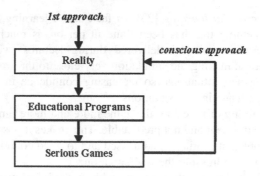

Fig. 4. The proposed learning path.

In pursuit of these objectives towards the real adult life, it is possible to plan the transition from more and more advanced educational software to real SGs, according the overall sequence of step of the learning path in the economic field so far described (*from reality to educational software, to serious games, to reality again*), which is summarized in Fig. 4.

In fact, the use of educational software, from the simplest to the most advanced ones, can be very effective in allowing even the user with cognitive difficulties to deal with the use of some types of SGs, such as the *Sims 3* life simulation game [26].

7   Conclusions and Future Research

In this paper we have presented a learning path in the economic field for cognitive rehabilitation, which adopts a constructive approach: starting from the world reality, then using the proposed educational programs, then proceeding with the use of SGs, and finally going back to the world reality.

We have described the pedagogical-didactic strategies and the software package, which are an integral part of this learning part and have been then validated with kids with cognitive disabilities. As the learning process starts from a real experience, even minimal, in the economic field, although the abstract spaces of the software program are not a detailed representation of a real-life context, the kids have been always able to immediately orient themselves in the use of the software, and the manipulation of the various abstract elements has correctly recalled the elements in the real context.

In Sect. 5 we have outlined how the application of our software programs has made it possible to obtain significant results, both in improving the cognitive function and the metacognitive capability, and in acquiring new practical and theoretical knowledge. In particular, mainly in cases with mild cognitive difficulties, there has been an increase in the ability to link thought and world reality, and the thought activity has become more and more capable to face the constraints imposed by the outside world, to manage increasingly complex situations, and to use consciously the underlying mathematical concepts. Moreover, even in cases of medium to severe cognitive difficulties, signifi-cant results have been obtained in the management of memory, both to recall past events and actions and to fix in the memory new relevant facts, and in the management of attention and concentration.

Obtaining good results in the basic activities of the economic field makes it possible, at least in some cases, to deal with more complex situations, such as to calculate costs, revenues and earnings, up to very complex ones, such as to understand and manage bank operations. These skills are very useful in adult life and are the basis of true autonomy of the disabled person and of his/her inclusion. Thus, they represent the ultimate goal of the proposed path, i.e., the return to the world reality. The learning path towards this ultimate goal can find a big boost in the use of SGs (not specific to people with disabilities). An experiment in this regard has been described in our paper [26].

Future research can concern the use of more complex SGs, involving multidisciplinary contents by kids who have completed our learning path and have reached a cognitive level that make it possible to consciously use them. In this sense, a possible serious game is *The invisible hand*, by *TiconBlu s.r.l.*, which: *"involves us in the adventure by presenting us with and making us more aware of the mechanisms which govern the world economy and the alternatives offered by the fair economy, fair trade and a critical life style"* [27]. We think that this serious game, which can yield a significant increase of knowledge in fields that can be very different from each other, could be dealt with by a person with cognitive problems, but surely only after a successful course of cognitive recovery. A further and fascinating research can be the active participation of the kids who have followed the learning path to the design and development of new educational tools or SGs.

Acknowledgments. We are highly indebted to all the kids we have followed, who are the only important subjects of the proposed learning path.

References

1. European Union: Ministerial Declaration. Conference "ICT for an inclusive society" (2006). http://ec.europa.eu/informationsociety/events/ictriga2006/doc/declarationriga.pdf
2. Martinengo, C., Curatelli, F.: Improving cognitive abilities and e-inclusion in children with cerebral palsy. In: Holzinger, A., Miesenberger, K. (eds.) USAB 2009. LNCS, vol. 5889, pp. 55–68. Springer, Heidelberg (2009)
3. Hughes, S.: Another look at task analysis. J. of Learn. Disabil. **15**, 273–275 (1982)
4. Bellotti, F., Berta, R., De Gloria, A.: Games and learning alliance (GaLA) supporting education and training through hi-tech gaming. In: Proceedings of ICALT'12, pp. 740–741 (2012)
5. Bellotti, F., Berta, R., De Gloria, A., D'Ursi, A., Fiore, V.: A serious game model for cultural heritage. ACM J. on Computing and Cultural Heritage, 5 (2012)
6. Connolly, T.M., Boyle, E.A., MacArthur, E., Hainey, T., Boyle, J.M.: A systematic literature review of empirical evidence on computer games and serious games. Comput. Educ. **59**, 661–686 (2012)
7. Bellotti, F., Kapralos, B., Lee, K., Moreno-Ger, P., Berta, R.: Assessment in and of serious games: an overview. Adv. Hum.-Comput. Interact. Article ID 136864, 1–11 (2013)
8. Grammenos, D., Savidis, A., Stephanidis, C.: Designing universally accessible games. Comput. Entertain. **7**(8), 1–29 (2009)

9. Yuan, B., Folmer, E., Harris, F.C.: Game accessibility: a survey. Univ. Access Inf. Soc. **10**, 81–100 (2011)

10. Evett, L., Ridley, A., Keating, L., Merritt, P., Shopland, N., Brown, D.J.: Designing serious games for people with disabilities game, set and match to the wii™. Int. J. Game-Based Learn. **1**, 11–19 (2011)

11. Sik Lanyi, C.S., Brown, D.J., Standen, P., Lewis, J., Butkute, V., Drozdik, D.: GOET European project of serious games for students with intellectual disability. In: Proceedings of CogInfoCom, pp. 1–6 (2011)

12. Hussaan, A.M., Sehaba, K., Mille, A.: Helping children with cognitive disabilities through serious games. In: Proceedings of ASSETS'11, pp. 251–252 (2011)

13. Girard, C., Ecalle, J., Magnan, A.: Serious games as new educational tools: how effective are they? A meta-analysis of recent studies. J. Comput. Assist. Learn. **29**, 207–219 (2013)

14. Benelli, B., D'Odorico, L., Lavorato, M.C., Simion, F.: Formation and extension of the concept in a prelinguistic child. Ital. J. Psychol. **4**, 429–448 (1977)

15. Stella, G., Zanotti, S.: Selective neuropsychological problems of learning in disability. In: Proceedings of 4th EACD Meeting (1993)

16. Martinengo, C., Curatelli, F.: Le Nuove Tecnologie per lo Sviluppo di Capacità Logico-Linguistiche in Bambini con Paralisi Cerebrale Infantile. Difficoltà di Apprendimento **16**, 171–190 (2010)

17. Martinengo, C., Curatelli, F.: Metodologie Didattiche e TIC per Favorire l'Apprendimento in Bambini con Disabilità Motoria. TD-Tecnologie Didattiche **52**, 36–42 (2011)

18. Boero, P., Douek, N., Ferrari, P.L.: Developing mastery of natural language: approach to theoretical aspects of mathematics. In: English, L.D. (ed.) Handbook of International Research in Mathematics Education, vol. 1, pp. 241–268. Lawrence Erlbaum Associates, Inc., Mahwah (2002)

19. Boero, P.: The crucial role of semantic fields in the development of problem solving skills. In: Ponte, J.P., Matos, J.F., Matos, J.M., Fernandes, D. (eds.) Mathematical Problem Solving and New Information Technologies, pp. 77–91. Springer, Berlin (1992)

20. Boero, P.: Experience fields as a tool to plan mathematics teaching from 6 to 11. In: Proceedings of II It-De Symposium on Didactics of Mathematics, vol. 39, pp. 45–62 (1994)

21. Petrovic, S., Cvetkovic, Z., Jovanovic, M.: Humanization of school according to the idea of Paulo Freire. Facta Univ. Ser. Philos. Sociol. Psychol. Hist. **11**, 33–42 (2012)

22. Sik Lanyi, C., Brown, D.J.: Design of serious games for students with intellectual disability. In: Proceedings of India HCI, pp. 151–160 (2010)

23. Kolb, D.A., Boyatzis, R.E., Mainemelis, C.: Experiential learning theory: previous research and new directions. In: Sternberg, R.J., et al. (eds.) Perspectives on Thinking, Learning, and Cognitive Styles: The Educational Psychology Series, pp. 227–247. Erlbaum, Mahwah (2001)

24. Koster, R.: A Theory of Fun for Game Design. Paraglyph Press, Phoenix (2004)

25. Denis, G., Jouvelot, P.: Motivation-driven educational game design: applying best practices to music education. In: Proceedings of ACE'05, pp. 462–465 (2005)

26. Curatelli, F., Martinengo, C.: Design criteria for educational tools to overcome mathematics learning difficulties. In: Proceedings of VS-GAMES'12, Procedia Computer Science, vol.15, pp.92–102 (2012)

27. TiconBlu s.r.l.: The Invisible Hand: a Serious Game for Fair Trade. (2011). http://www.theinvisiblehand.it

Towards an Understanding of the Relationship Between Executive Functions and Learning Outcomes from Serious Computer Games

James Boyle[1(✉)] and Elizabeth A. Boyle[2]

[1] School of Psychological Sciences and Health,
University of Strathclyde, 40 George Street, Glasgow G1 1QE, UK
j.boyle@strath.ac.uk
[2] School of Social Sciences, University of the West of Scotland,
High Street, Paisley PA1 2BE, UK

Abstract. There is accumulating evidence that playing games leads to a range of cognitive and perceptual advantages. In addition there has been speculation that digital games can support higher level thinking. In this paper we propose that viewing these gains from the perspective of executive functions can help to provide a more coherent approach to understanding the cognitive benefits of playing games. Executive functions refer to a range of higher level cognitive processes that regulate, control and manage other cognitive processes. Three models are considered: Baddeley's model of working memory [1], and two models of executive functions, that of Anderson [2], and that of Diamond [3]. The implications for serious games research and games design and for future research are considered.

1 Introduction

Systematic reviews identify a diverse range of measures of outcomes and impacts of playing serious computer games centred around knowledge acquisition, acquisition of skills, content understanding, affective and motivational outcomes and engagement [4–7]. A range of models and frameworks have been developed to support games design and the assessment and evaluation of the effectiveness of games-based learning [8–12], building upon the large data-sets made possible by the use of technology-enhanced learning analytics [13].

Underlying theoretical models include:

- cultural historical activity theory [14, 15], emphasising the mediating role of tools in learning and problem-solving;
- information processing accounts such as cognitive load theory [16];
- models of the development of self-regulated learning [17] emphasising temporal stages or 'phases' of self-regulation in learning based upon task analysis;
- knowledge space theory/competency based knowledge space theory [18, 19], which use modelling techniques to inform a conceptual understanding of assessment, adaptive tutoring and problem-solving.

© Springer International Publishing Switzerland 2014
A. De Gloria (Ed.): GALA 2013, LNCS 8605, pp. 187–199, 2014.
DOI: 10.1007/978-3-319-12157-4_15

However, it is possible to further explore the underlying cognitive processes which underpin changes in knowledge and skills acquisition and motivation associated with games-based learning and to add to our understanding of how effective learning may be supported by games [20]. In turn, such understandings may have implications for the development and design of serious digital games and for assessment and evaluation.

Serious computer game play makes demands on lower-level processes such as attention, perception, and memory as well as higher-level cognitive processes such as problem-solving, reasoning and decision making [20]. 'Executive functions' are the cognitive processes which control and coordinate these lower-level and higher-level processes and we shall consider how current theoretical models of executive functions can help us understand the outcomes of digital game play and may inform future research and games design.

2   Executive Functions

'Executive function' is an umbrella term covering a broad range of functions – some 21 according to one account [21]. Executive functions are '…responsible for the control of cognition and regulation of behaviour and thought and are intertwined with the notion of volition: the freedom to make appropriate (or inappropriate) choices from a set of possible choices' [22].

This definition highlights the complexity of executive functions, covering not only processes of attention, memory but also self-regulation of behaviour and learning, planning, goal setting, reasoning and decision-making. One of the most influential models is Baddeley's 'working memory' system [1, 23], which has a wide range of supporting evidence, including experimental studies using dual or competing task methodology, imaging studies involving fMRI scanners and clinical studies of patients with amnesia.

2.1   Working Memory

The working memory system (Fig. 1) comprises a unitary, limited capacity central executive or supervisory component which exchanges information with three passive, 'slave' systems [1, 23]:

- a phonological loop for the short-term storage of auditory data in a speech-based form and which is key to the processing of language;
- an episodic buffer which stores and 'binds' representations of a diverse range of information including verbal, visual and spatial information from working memory and other cognitive processes;
- a visuo-spatial sketchpad, a buffer for the short-term storage of spatial and visual information such as colour or shapes which comprise 'visual semantics'.

The central executive in this model is responsible for:

- controlling and coordinating the flow of information;
- accessing and retrieving information from long-term memory using retrieval strategies;

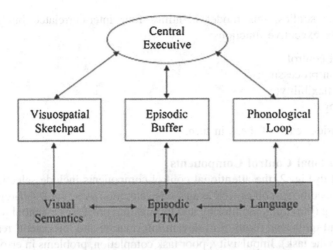

Fig. 1. Baddeley's (2007) model of working memory

- a diverse range of processes including reasoning, planning and mental arithmetic;
- control of action, planning and goal-directed behaviour.

The working memory system is widely-regarded by theorists as an executive function [2] [3]. With regard to computer gaming, the model highlights the importance of incorporating understandings of cognitive processes in games design and the development of virtual learning environments. For example, the limited capacity of the central executive and the short-term nature of storage in the phonological loop, episodic buffer and visuo-spatial sketchpad in this system highlight the importance for games designers of minimising cognitive overload, in accordance with cognitive load theory [16], and taking account of cognitive biases in problem-solving derived from the use of strategies when designing choice environments [24]. The model also emphasises the importance of individual differences in problem-solving, reasoning and visual-perceptual skills which can underpin differential performance in games-based assessment [1].

However, there are alternative theoretical accounts based upon confirmatory factor analyses and structural equation models of participants' data from cognitive tasks which have fractionated Baddeley's original concept of a unitary central executive [25, 26]. The term 'executive functions' is now widely used to subsume a broader range of cognitive processes than before [24] and we will consider two models, the Executive Control System [2], and a model recently proposed by Diamond [3] which incorporate these understandings.

2.2   Executive Control System

Anderson's executive control system model [2] (see Fig. 2) is of interest as a framework for exploring individual differences in outcomes from serious games with implications also for games design. Based upon neuropsychological data as well as factor analytic studies, this model identifies four inter-correlated but dissociable, components of executive functions:

- attentional control;
- information processing;
- cognitive flexibility;
- goal setting.

We shall consider each of these in turn.

2.2.1 Attentional Control Components

As illustrated in Fig. 2, the attentional control components include selective attention (focusing on specific stimuli as well as sustained attention over time), self-regulation and self-monitoring (initiating, monitoring and terminating processes essential for control of behaviour) and inhibition (both of irrelevant information and 'prepotent' responses not appropriate to the task). Impulsivity, poor task completion, problems in error correction and failure to respond appropriately while playing a serious game could be accounted for in terms of these components.

2.3 Information-Processing Components

The information-processing components reflect speed of response to stimuli. The components of efficiency and fluency of information-processing here could account for slow reaction times in computer games.

2.3.1 Cognitive Flexibility

Cognitive flexibility components of the model include the ability to divide attention across different sources of information and responses at the same time; working memory (as in Baddeley's model [20], a limited-capacity and time-limited active memory system with the ability to store and simultaneously process information); conceptual transfer (the transfer of a solution from one problem to another); and feedback utilisation (being able to use feedback to adapt behaviour). These components could account for poor problem-solving in games-based learning which results from continuing to employ unsuccessful strategies.

2.3.2 Goal-Setting Components

Goal-setting components include higher-order processes such as initiative, conceptual reasoning, planning, sequencing and the coordination of strategies. These components could account for poor problem-solving in digital games which would adversely affect performance.

2.4 Diamond's Model of Executive Functions

Diamond [25] identifies cognitive flexibility, working memory and inhibition as core executive functions in her model (see Fig. 3). These core processes develop during childhood and decline as we age. Higher-order executive functions of reasoning, problem solving and planning arise from the core processes.

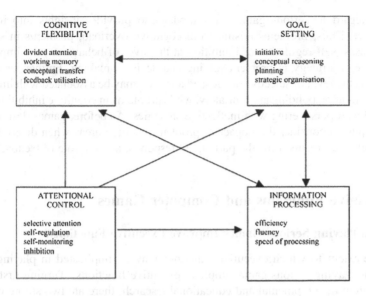

Fig. 2. Executive control system (from Anderson, 2002; p. 73)

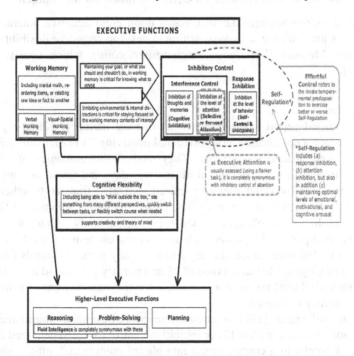

Fig. 3. Diamond's (2013, p. 152) model of executive functions

Diamond takes a wider perspective than many other theorists in this area and emphasises the relationship between executive functions and a wide range of outcomes in areas such as health, quality of life, academic and occupational achievement, and social behaviour.

With regard to serious games, this model also provides insights into individual performance. Thus, problems arising from cognitive overload, problems in switching between tasks, self-regulation or inhibition at the level of behaviour may impact upon poor choice of strategy in problem-solving and decision-making. Further, problems in inhibition at the level of selective or focused attention may be associated with impulsivity and problems in responding appropriately, while problems in cognitive inhibition may be associated with persevering with ineffective strategies. As before, games designers may find it helpful to consider the impact of problems in these areas when determining the structure of assessments, how the participant responds, and the role of feedback.

3 Executive Functions and Computer Games

3.1 Can Playing Serious Games Improve Executive Functions?

Given the extent to which executive functions may be implicated in playing serious games, can playing serious games improve executive functions? Turning firstly to the evidence from developmental and educational research, there are two strong computer games-based candidate interventions for executive functions for children:

- CogMed (http://www.cogmed.com/), based upon eight adaptive, interactive computer games and training in task-switching to develop cognitive flexibility [27–30];
- and Jungle Memory (http://www.junglememory.com/), which consists of three tasks [31].

3.1.1 Cogmed

Studies of Cogmed report improvements in working memory. Klingberg and colleagues carried out a randomised, controlled trial involving 24 participants with ADHD and controls aged around 9–10 years. They studied the outcomes of 25 days of computerised training for an average of 40 min per day, and found not only gains in scores on aspects of working memory trained, but also transfer to other working memory tasks and aspects of executive functioning, including inhibition [27].

Similarly, Holmes and colleagues' quasi-experimental study with a non-randomised control group comparing 22 pupils with low scores on tests of working memory, nonverbal and verbal intelligence, literacy and numeracy with 22 controls following 20 daily sessions of Cogmed for an average of 35 min per day [28] found improvements in verbal and nonverbal working memory scores, but in this case no transfer to measures of intelligence, literacy or numeracy.

Thorell and colleagues [29] compared the benefits of Cogmed programmes focused on spatial working memory (N = 17) or inhibition control (N = 18) delivered for 15 min each day for 5 weeks to a control group into played commercial, off-the-shelf games and a second control group who received no intervention. The results revealed that working memory training improved scores on the trained tasks and that there was evidence of transfer to non-trained working memory tasks and also to attention. Those trained on inhibition showed no benefits relative to the control groups on any of the tasks.

Finally, Nutley and colleagues [30] in a large-scale, randomised controlled trial of 101 4-year-old children receiving 15 min training on Cogmed each day for 25 days on non-verbal reasoning, working memory, combined training or a placebo found improvements in measures of fluid intelligence relative to controls for children trained in non-verbal reasoning. Participants trained in working memory showed improvement in working memory scores, but no transfer to measures of non-verbal reasoning.

3.1.2 Jungle Memory
In the case of Jungle Memory, Alloway and her colleagues [31] reported findings from a quasi-experimental study of 93 pupils aged 10–11 years with learning difficulties. 23 participants were allocated to a training group who played three Jungle Memory games targeted on working memory four times a week for 8 weeks. Their progress was compared with 32 participants allocated to an active control group, playing Jungle Memory games once per week for 8 weeks and to 39 children allocated to a passive control group, who did not play any Jungle Memory games. The results revealed that the children in the training group made significant gains in measures of both verbal and visuo-spatial working memory.

3.1.3 Studies of Games-Based Interventions with Adult Participants
There have also been studies of games-based intervention involving adult participants [32–38], with the effects of age and of transfer effects to untrained tasks of particular interest to researchers.

Buschkuel and colleagues [32] administered a computer-based training programme twice per week for 3 months to 80 year-old adults. The intervention group made significant gains in visual working memory scores compared to a control group, with evidence also of transfer to untrained tests. Dahlin and colleagues [33] provided computer-based working memory training for 5 weeks to groups of younger and older adults and observed significant gains for the training groups relative to controls on trained tasks, with the gains maintained at 18 months follow-up. There was also evidence of transfer to untrained tasks, but only for the younger age-group. However, Richmond and her colleagues [34] also provided computer-based working memory training to older adults and found evidence of transfer to untrained tasks.

Brehmer and her colleagues [35] investigated the effects of age and of transfer following 5 weeks of computerised training in spatial and verbal working memory. They compared the outcomes for 55 adults in the 20–30 years age-group with those for 45 older adults aged 60–70 years in a design that compared the training group with an active control group receiving a low level of training. They found that the more intensive adaptive training resulted in larger overall gains than for the control group, and that while both the older and the younger adults showed transfer effects to untrained tasks, that the transfer effects were greater for the young age-group. van Muijen and colleagues [36] also found that a group of 34 older adults aged between 60–77 years receiving 30 min training daily for 7 weeks on five online computer games made more improvement in measures of the executive functions of inhibition and inductive reasoning than the 20 participants of a similar age in the control group, with additional evidence of transfer untrained tasks. However, the authors add a caveat as the two groups were non-equivalent.

In contrast, McAvinue [37] failed to find any improvements in working memory in a group of older adults aged 64–79 years following a 5-week online training programme based upon Baddeley's working memory model [1]. However, there was improvement in the auditory short-term memory scores of those in the intervention group relative to the control group which were maintained at 6 months follow-up and evidence also of transfer to episodic memory.

Finally, Redick and colleagues [38] delivered 20 sessions of computer training on working memory to 23 participants aged between 18–30 years, 20 sessions of training on visual search, an active placebo control group (N = 28) and compared outcome with a no-contact group of 19 participants. The results revealed short-term improvements in trained tasks in both the working memory and placebo control, but no evidence of generalisation to more general measures of cognitive ability such as fluid intelligence.

3.2 Higher-Level Thinking and Problem-Solving

While there is substantial evidence that playing games leads to improvements in perceptual skills and working memory, there is less evidence that playing games lead to gains in higher-level thinking and problem-solving. Greenfield [39] cautioned that the visual perceptual advantages of playing games may not be matched by advances in higher-level critical thinking skills which she argues are better supported by more traditional means of learning.

A key difficulty which has to be tackled in looking at how games support 'higher-level thinking' and 'problem-solving' lies in characterizing exactly what we mean by these terms.

Authors such as Bloom [40], Piaget [41] and Resnik [42] have offered accounts of higher-level thinking which are quite different in nature. Newell and Simon's [43] early research on problem solving also identified just how difficult it is to specify generic approaches to solving problems, since the kinds of problems that people face and the strategies they use to solve them are very diverse and frequently domain specific.

Cognitive research on problem-solving has identified two generic approaches to solving problems which are widely used in education and business as a way of tackling complex problems and which are relevant to thinking about problem-solving in games. The first approach is the cyclic approach to solving problems which proposes that it is useful to view problem-solving as a cyclic process with different stages where different sub-problems are tackled at each stage. The very simple "plan, do, review" heuristic is consistent with this approach, and Kolb's [44] theory of experiential learning with the four different stages in the learning process, concrete experience, reflective observation, abstract conceptualisation and active experimentation, also reflects the cyclic nature of tackling problems. The second general approach is problem space theory, which proposes that in solving problems it is frequently useful to construct a mental representation of the problem and all possible "states" of the problem, called the problem space [43].

These two generic approaches to problem solving have been applied to problem-solving in digital games. Kiili and Ketamo [45] view the cyclic process as at the heart of problem-based learning in games. Similarly problem space theory describes the different possible states in playing a game and the different paths through a game. Spires et al. [46] examined how players explored and worked their way through the "hypothesis space" of a scientific problem solving game and found that the extent to which players did this was predictive of successful learning in the game.

However, if we want a game to support problem solving and higher level thinking we need to design the game to do this. It seems likely that in many ways games are no different from any other learning environment although they do have advantages. There is much research in education on designing effective learning environments which can guide us here [47]. For example, the CHERMUG project used cognitive tasks analysis (CTA) to design the CHERMUG games [48]. CTA aims to capture a description of the cognitive knowledge that experts use to perform complex tasks. CTA in the CHERMUG project aimed to identify the component skills, knowledge and competences required in developing a comprehensive and usable understanding of research methodology and statistics as well as difficulties that students face.

3.3   Discussion of Evidence

The studies reviewed here involving both children and adults reveal consistent short-term, specific training effects in components of working memory and in executive functions such as inhibition, with less consistent evidence for transfer and maintenance over time. Recent systematic reviews and meta-analyses confirm that this is true of interventions in this area in general, and that it is not a specific feature of computer games-based training [49–51]. There are also concerns about the designs of evaluation studies in regard to whether they incorporate a control group, and whether this is a an active control group, as well as about the duration an intensity of intervention programmes and the adequacy of the measures used and the sample size.

Computer games-based training which targets working memory and inhibition may lead to short-term improvements in executive function scores and may have beneficial near-transfer effects, but there few studies with control groups, and concerns about the duration and intensity of intervention programmes and the adequacy of the measures used [43–52]. Further research is needed to investigate the extent to which training transfers to other tasks and generalises to real-world performance and also to add to the evidence base regarding outcomes in higher-order thinking and problem-solving.

4   Conclusion

Theoretical accounts of executive functions provide a means of investigating and understanding the benefits of playing computer games. While a focus on learning outcomes grounded in pedagogy and the curriculum is of value to teachers and educators, the cognitive approach offers a level of analysis of games which may be of particular value to games researchers and designers. In this regard, Diamond's model [3] may be of interest given the level of detail of the specification of the relationship between the three core executive functions and the higher-order components. Designing games to assess specific cognitive functions such as working memory and inhibition [42] may not only develop our understanding of executive functions but also provide rehabilitative opportunities for special populations, such as children with developmental disabilities such as ADHD and adults recovering from strokes.

Areas which can be investigated include not only visual-spatial skills which are widely researched but also higher-order skills, such as problem-solving, goal-setting decision making and meta-cognition [20]. However, the frameworks also provide a theoretical rationale for controlled research studies examining the short- and long-term effects of computer games upon transferable knowledge and skill acquisition and underlying cognitive processes [53].

Acknowledgements. This work was partially supported by the Games and Learning Alliance (GaLA) - Network of Excellence for Serious Games via a grant to the second author under the European Community Seventh Framework Programme (FP7/2007 2013), Grant Agreement no. 258169.

References

1. Baddeley, A.D.: Working memory: Multiple models, multiple mechanisms. In: Roediger, H.L., Dudai, Y., Fitzpatrick, S.M. (eds.) Science of Memory: Concepts, pp. 151–153. Oxford University Press, Oxford (2007)
2. Anderson, P.J.: Assessment and development of executive function (EF) during childhood. Child Neuropsychol. **8**, 71–82 (2002)
3. Diamond, A.: Executive functions. Annu. Rev. Psychol. **2013**, 64 (2013)
4. Connolly, T.M., Boyle, E.A., MacArthur, E., Hainey, T., Boyle, J.M.: A systematic literature review of empirical evidence on computer games and serious games. Comput. Educ. **59**, 661–686 (2012)
5. Boyle, E.A., Connolly, T.M., Hainey, T., Boyle, J.M.: Engagement in digital entertainment games: A systematic review. Comput. Hum. Behav. **28**, 71–780 (2012)
6. Wouters, P., van Oostendorp, H.A.: Meta-analytic review of the role of instructional support in games-based learning. Comput. Educ. **60**, 412–425 (2013)
7. Wouters, P., van Nimwegen, C., van Oostendorp, H., van der Spek, E.D.: A meta-analysis of the cognitive and motivational effects of serious games. J. Educ. Psychol. **105**, 249–265 (2013)
8. Bayer, E.L., Mayer, T.E.: Computer-based assessment of problem-solving. Comput. Hum. Behav. **15**, 269–282 (1999)
9. Van Merriënboer, J.J.G., Kester, L.: The four-component instructional design model: Multimedia principles in environments for complex learning. In: Mayer, R.E. (ed.) The Cambridge Handbook of Multimedia Learning, pp. 71–93. Cambridge University Press, New York (2005)
10. de Freitas, S., Oliver, M.: How can exploratory learning with games and simulations within the curriculum be most effectively evaluated? Comput. Educ. **46**, 249–264 (2006)

11. Connolly, T., Stansfield, M., Hainey, T.: Towards the development of a games-based learning evaluation framework (Chapter XV, (pp. 251–253)). In: Connolly, T., Stansfield, M., Boyle, L. (eds.) Games-based learning advancements for multi-sensory human computer interfaces: Techniques and effective practices. IGI Global, Hershey (2009)
12. Mayer, I., Warmelink, H., Bekebrede, G.: Learning in a game-based virtual environment: A comparative evaluation in higher education. Eur. J. Eng. Educ. **38**, 85–106 (2013)
13. Serrano-Laguna, A., Torrente, J., Moreno-Ger, P., Fernandez-Manjon, B.: Tracing a little for big improvements: Application of learning analytics and videogames for student assessment. Procedia Comput. Sci. **15**, 203–209 (2012)
14. Vygotsky, L.: Mind in Society. Harvard University Press, Cambridge (1978)
15. Engeström, Y.: Learning by Expanding. Orienta-Konsulit, Helsinki (1987)
16. Sweller, J., Van Merriënboer, J., Paas, F.: Cognitive architecture and instructional design. Educ. Psychol. Rev. **10**, 251–296 (1998)
17. Zimmerman, B.J.: Becoming a self-regulated learner: An overview. Theory Prac. **41**, 64–70 (2002)
18. Albert, D., Lukas, J. (eds.): Knowledge Spaces: Theories, Empirical Research and Applications. Lawrence Erlbaum Associates, Mahwah (1999)
19. Reimann, P., Kickmeier-Rust, M., Albert, D.: Problem solving learning environments and assessment: A knowledge space theory approach. Comput. Educ. **64**, 183–193 (2013)
20. Boyle, E.A., Terras, M.M., Ramsay, J., Boyle, J.M.: Executive functions in digital games (Chapter 2). In: Connolly, T.M., Hainey, T., Boyle, E., Baxter, G., Moreno-Ger, P. (eds.) Psychology, Pedagogy and Assessment in Serious Games. IGI Global, Hershey (2013)
21. Baron, I.S.: Neuropsychological Evaluation of the Child. Oxord University Press, Oxford (2004)
22. Phillips, L.H.: Do "frontal tests" measure executive function? Issues of assessment and evidence of assessment and evidence from fluency tests (Chapter 9 (pp. 185–207)). In: Rabbitt, P.M.A. (ed.) Methodology of Frontal and Executive Function, p. 186. Psychology Press, Hove (1997)
23. Baddeley, A.D., Hitch, G.: Working Memory. In: Bower, G.H. (ed.) The Psychology of Learning and Motivation, vol. 2, pp. 47–89. Academic Press, New York (1974)
24. Kahneman, D., Tversky, A.: Prospect theory: An analysis of decision under risk. Econometrica **47**, 263–292 (1979)
25. Miyake, A., Friedman, N.P., Emerson, M.J., Witzki, A.H., Howerter, A., Wager, T.D.: The unity and diversity of executive functions and their contributions to complex "Frontal Lobe" tasks: a latent variable analysis. Cogn. Psychol. **41**, 49–100 (2000)
26. Baddeley, A., Della Sala, S.: Working memory and executive control. Philos. Trans. Biol. Sci. **351**, 1397–1404 (1996)
27. Klingberg, T., Fernell, E., Olesen, P.J., Johnson, M., Gustafsson, P., Dahlström, K., Gillberg, C.G., Forssberg, H., Westerberg, H.: Computerized training of working memory in children with ADHD – a randomized, controlled trial. J. Am. Acad. Child Adolesc. Psychiatry **44**, 177–186 (2005)
28. Holmes, J., Gathercole, S.E., Dunning, D.L.: Adaptive training leads to sustained enhancement of poor working memory in children. Dev. Sci. **12**, 9–15 (2009)
29. Thorell, L.B., Lindqvist, S., Bergman-Nutley, S., Bohlin, G., Klingberg, T.: Training and transfer effects of executive functions in preschool children. Dev. Sci. **12**, 106–133 (2009)
30. Nutley, S.B., Söderqvist, S., Bryde, S., Thorell, L.B., Humphreys, K., Klingberg, T.: Gains in fluid intelligence after training non-verbal reasoning in 4-year-old children: A controlled, randomized study. Dev. Sci. **14**, 591–601 (2011)
31. Alloway, T.P., Bibile, V., Lau, G.: Computerized working memory training: Can it lead to gains in cognitive skills in students? Comput. Hum. Behav. **29**, 632–638 (2013)

32. Buschkuehl, M., Jaeggi, S.M., Hutchison, S., Perrig-Chiello, P., Dapp, C., Muller, M., Perrig, W.J.: Impact of working memory training on memory performance in old–old adults. Psychol. Aging 23, 743–753 (2008)
33. Dahlin, E., Nyberg, L., Backman, L., Neely, A.: Plasticity of executive functioning in young and older adults: Immediate training gains, transfer, and long-term maintenance. Psychol. Aging 23, 720–730 (2008)
34. Richmond, L.L., Morrison, A., Chein, J., Olson, I.R.: Working memory training and transfer in older adults. Psychol. Aging 2011(26), 813–822 (2011)
35. Brehmer, Y., Westerberg, H., Bäckman, L.: Working-memory training in younger and older adults: training gains, transfer, and maintenance. Front Hum. Neurosci. 6, 63 (2012)
36. van Muijen, J., Band, G.P.H., Hommel, B.: Online games training aging brains: limited transfer to cognitive control functions. Front Hum. Neurosci. 6, 1–13 (2012)
37. McAvinue, L.P., Golemme, M., Castorina, M., Tatti, E., Pigni, F.M., Salomone, S., Brennan, S., Robertson, I.H.: An evaluation of a working memory training scheme in older adults. Front Aging Neurosci. 5, 20 (2013)
38. Redick, T.S., Shipstead, Z., Harrison, T.L., Hicks, K.L., Fried, D.E., Hambrick, D.Z., Kane, M.J., Engle, R.W.: No evidence of intelligence improvement after working memory training: A randomized, placebo-controlled study. J. Exp. Psychol. Gen. 142, 359–379 (2013)
39. Greenfield, P.M.: Technology and informal education: What is taught, what is learned. Science 323, 69–71 (2009)
40. Bloom, B.S.: Reflections on the development and use of the taxonomy in LW. In: Anderson, L.W., Sosniak, L.A. (eds.) Bloom's Taxonomy: A Forty-Year Retrospective, pp. 1–8. National Society for the Study of Education, Chicago (1994)
41. Piaget, J.: The Origin of Intelligence in the Child. Routledge & Kegan Paul, New York (1953)
42. Resnick, L.B.: Education and Learning to Think. National Academy, Washington, D.C. (1987)
43. Newell, A., Simon, H.A.: Human Problem Solving. Prentice-Hall, Carnegie-Mellon University, Englewood Cliffs, Pittsburgh (1972)
44. Kolb, D.: Experiential Learning: Experience as the Source of Learning and Development. Prentice Hall, Englewood Cliffs (1984)
45. Kiili, K., Ketamo, H.: Exploring the learning mechanism in educational games. In: Proceedings of the ITI 2007, 29th International Conference on Information Technology Interfaces, Cavtat, Croatia, 25–28 June 2007
46. Spires, H.A., Rowe, J.P., Mott, B.W., Lester, J.C.: Problem solving and game-based learning: effects of middle grade students' hypothesis testing strategies on learning outcomes. J. Educ. Comput. Res. 2011(44), 453–472 (2011)
47. de Corte, E.: Constructive, self-regulated, situated, and collaborative learning: an approach for the acquisition of adaptive competence. J. Educ. 192(2/3), 33–48 (2011)
48. Boyle, E.A., van Rosmalen, P., MacArthur, E., Connolly, T.M., Hainey, T., Johnston, B., Moreno Ger, P., Fernández Manjón, B., Kärki, A., Pennanen, T., Manea, M., Starr, K.: Cognitive task analysis (CTA) in the continuing/ higher education methods using games (CHERMUG) Project. In: 6th European Conference on Games-based Learning (ECGBL), Cork, Ireland, 4-5 October 2012
49. Melby-Lervag, M., Hulme, C.: Is working memory training effective? A meta-analytic review. Dev. Psychol. 49, 270–291 (2013)
50. Holmes, J., Gathercole, S.E., Dunning, D.L.: Poor working memory: impact and interventions. In: Holmes, J. (ed.) Advances in Child Development and Behavior, vol. 39, pp. 1–43. Academic Press, Burlington (2010)

51. Shipstead, Z.T.S., Redick, T.S., Engle, R.W.: Is working memory training effective? Psychol. Bull. **138**, 628–654 (2012)
52. Booth, J.N., Boyle, J.M., Kelly, S.W.: Do tasks make a difference? Accounting for heterogeneity of performance of children with reading difficulties on tasks of executive function: findings from a meta-analysis. Br. J. Dev. Psychol. **2010**(28), 133–176 (2010)
53. Green, C.S., Bavelier, D.: Learning, attentional control, and action video games. Curr. Biol. **22**, 197–206 (2012)

Flow Experience as a Quality Measure in Evaluating Physically Activating Serious Games

Kristian Kiili[1(✉)], Arttu Perttula[1], Sylvester Arnab[2],
and Marko Suominen[1]

[1] Tampere University of Technology, Pohjoisranta 11 a, 28101 Pori, Finland
{kristian.kiili,arttu.perttula,marko.suominen}@tut.fi
[2] Serious Games Institute, Coventry University Technology Park,
Coventry CV1 2TL, UK
SArnab@cad.coventry.ac.uk

Abstract. The measurement of the subjective playing experience is important part of the game development process. The enjoyment level that a serious game offers is a key factor in determining whether the player will be engaged in the gameplay and achieve the objectives of the game. In this paper the usefulness of flow experience in evaluating the quality of physically activating problem-solving game was studied. The aim of the paper is to explore to what extend the flow experience can facilitate the game evaluation and design process. In the study 53 junior high school students played a cooperative exergame designed to teach collaboration and communication skills. Students' playing experience was measured with a flow questionnaire and playing behavior was also observed. In general, the results indicated that the measurement of the flow experience can reveal shortages of the game and that way aid the design process. However, although the level of flow tells about the overall quality of the playing experience, the flow measurements needs to be extended with other aspects in order to be able to evaluate the implementation of the game more deeply.

1 Introduction

The measurement of the subjective playing experience is crucial part of the game development process. The ability to quantify the playing experience is important goal for both industry and academia. In general, game developers need a reliable way to measure the overall engagement level of their games and to pinpoint specific areas of the experience that need improvement [1]. Several constructs have been proposed to describe playing experience, but definitional agreement has not been achieved [2]. The most common concepts that have been linked to playing experience are engagement, involvement, immersion, presence, motivation and flow. According to Procci, Singer, Levy and Bowers [1] the concept of flow is one of the most popular constructs to describe the gaming experience. For example, several authors [3–5] have considered playing experience in terms of flow. Until now several different methods have been used to study flow experience from which self-reporting techniques have been the most common methods [6].

© Springer International Publishing Switzerland 2014
A. De Gloria (Ed.): GALA 2013, LNCS 8605, pp. 200–212, 2014.
DOI: 10.1007/978-3-319-12157-4_16

In this paper we consider the usefulness of flow experience in evaluating the quality of physically activating serious games (exergames). We report the results of the study in which the playing experience of cooperative exergame, Labyrinth Run, which involves educational objectives was measured with a flow questionnaire. In order to understand factors that affect the playing experience of Labyrinth Run we start by presenting the flow construct, design principles for educational exergames and characteristics of cooperative games. After that the details and the results of the study is presented and finally the usefulness of flow construct in evaluating the playing experience is discussed.

1.1 Flow Experience

Flow describes a state of complete absorption or engagement in an activity and refers to the optimal experience [7]. During the optimal experience, a person is in a psychological state where he or she is so involved with the goal-driven activity that nothing else seems to matter. An activity that produces such experiences is so pleasant that the person may be willing to do something for its own sake, without being concerned with what he will get out of his action. Czikszentmihalyi's [7] flow theory subsequently has been applied in several different domains including, for example sports, art, work, human–computer interactions, games and education. In the area of games it has particular value, as it maps well against the intrinsically motivating activities [3]. Theoretically, flow consists of nine dimensions [3, 7] including clear goals, challenge-skill balance, immediate feedback, sense of control, playability/action awareness merging, loss of self-consciousness, concentration, rewarding/autotelic experience and time distortion.

Goal setting is a process that, when undertaken correctly, helps to move the player toward flow. When the player is in flow the clarity of purpose occurs on a moment-by-moment basis and the player can more easily stay focused on the learning task and can respond to cues that game provides. If the goals seem too challenging or are hard to perceive the probability of experiencing flow is low. If the learning objectives are discrete from gameplay, the game may fail to produce educationally effective experiences.

Paying attention and interpreting the *feedback* that the game provides is important in evaluating whether one is on a track toward goals or not and helps in monitoring playing performance. The feedback dimension can be divided into immediate feedback and cognitive feedback. The immediate feedback keeps the player focused. If the player has to wait long before he can realize what effect his action caused, he will become distracted and loose the focus on the task. Additionally, the delayed feedback may create interpretation problems and in the worst-case even lead to misconceptions and negative learning transfer. The cognitive feedback relates to the cognitive problem solving and provides the account for learning. The cognitive feedback aims to stimulate the player to reflect on his experiences and tested solutions in order to further develop his mental models [8] and playing strategies. In other words, it focuses player's attention on information that is relevant for learning objectives.

The *playability* is included to partly replace Csikszentmihalyi's [7] *action-awareness merging* dimension, which is problematic in the learning game context. According to Csikszentmihalyi, all flow inducing activities become spontaneous and automatic, which is not desirable from a learning point of view. In contrast, the principles of experiential and constructive learning approaches give emphasis to the point that learning is an active and conscious knowledge-construction process. It is noteworthy that reflection is not always a conscious action by a player. However, only when a player consciously processes his experiences can he make active and aware decisions about his playing strategies and thereby form a constructive hypothesis to test. Thus, a distinction between activities related to solving problems or learning and controlling the game should be made. This means that controlling the game should be spontaneous and automatic, but the educational content related to a player's tasks should be consciously processed and reflected.

Generally, the aim of game design is to provide students with *challenges* that are balanced with their skill level. If the challenge is too low, a player tends to feel boredom and when the challenge is too high, a player tends to feel anxiety. Furthermore, challenges should be related to the main task so that the flow experience is possible. When both the task and the use of the artefact are complex, then the artefact and the task may detract from the player's attention. In fact, bad playability decreases the likelihood of experiencing task-based flow because the player has to sacrifice attention and other cognitive resources to the inappropriate activity. Because the information processing capacity of working memory is limited [9], all possible resources should be available for relevant information processing (the main task) rather than for the use of the game controls. Thus, the aim of the user interface design of games is to support the shift from cognitive interaction to fluent interaction. In an ideal situation, the controls of the game are transparent and allow the player to focus on higher order cognition rather than solely upon controlling tasks.

Sense of control clearly relates to the challenge-skill balance dimension. Csikszentmihalyi [7] has stated that sense of control refers to possibility rather than to actuality of the control. It can be said that a person senses when he can develop sufficient skills to reduce the margin of error close to zero, which makes the experience enjoyable. The feeling of being in control frees the player from thoughts of failure and thus the player is encouraged to perform more creatively and exploratively.

When in flow, a player is totally focused on game events and is able to forget all unpleasant things. Total concentration is one of the most powerful feelings of flow. Because flow-inducing activities require complete *concentration* of attention on the task at hand, there are no cognitive recourses left over for irrelevant information. Such concentration provides great satisfaction, which in turn leads to growth in complexity. When in flow player does not have to invest effort to keep his mind on the task.

Most of us live in the world of evaluation. During important activities such as learning, it is hard to stop thinking how others evaluate us. When a player can ignore what others think of him or her, the player has *lost self-consciousness*. The problem is that the criticism that the player may face turns his attention away from the actual task and turns too much to self, which does not facilitate the performance and playing experience. Self seems to disappear from awareness during flow and thus in flow there is no room for self-scrutiny [7]. Here the self refers to the self-esteem and thus loss of self-consciousness does not limit reflective thinking processes.

High flow feelings tend to transform player's *perception of time*. According to Csikszentmihalyi [7] during the flow experience the sense of time tends to bear little relation to the passage of time as measured by the absolute convention of a clock. Time seems to either pass really fast or the seconds may feel like minutes.

Rewarding experience refers to an activity that is done, not with the expectation of some future benefit, but simply because the doing itself is interesting and fun. Flow is so enjoyable experience that player is motivated to experience it again. In fact, Csikszentmihalyi [7] has described this autotelic experience as a end results of other dimensions that provides high motivation toward further involvement with the activity. Although winning is important in many games, flow does not depend on the final outcomes of an activity, and offers players something more than just a successful outcome. In fact, an optimal experience usually occurs when a person's body or mind is stretched to its limits in a voluntary effort to accomplish something difficult and worthwhile [7]. Such experiences are not necessarily pleasant when they occur, but they still produce enjoyment.

1.2   Design Principles for Educational Exergames

Kiili and Perttula [10] proposed the concept of educational exergames. Educational exergames combine gameplay elements from educational games (cognitively challenging games) and exergames (physically challenging games). Educational exergames are an emerging form of computer games that aim to leverage the advantages of sports and cognitive training in order to support physical, social and mental health benefits. In general, educational exergames are a new and unstudied branch of research in the era of serious games. According to Kiili and Perttula educational exergame design is hard to master because one has to understand a complex web comprised of education, sports, cognitive psychology, and technology. Thus, they have proposed a framework for designing educational exergames. The aim of the framework is to provide theoretical means to balance the amount of physical, cognitive, and sensomotoric workloads in order to optimize learning and health effects as well as to describe ways to create more engaging exertion and learning experiences mediated by the technology.

In educational exergames the body and the mind plays the central role and in the framework those are used as lenses to consider other aspects of educational exergames. When the rules, game elements and playing context are considered through exertion and learning interaction lenses several focus points that are crucial for designing educational exergames can be identified. Focus points highlight different aspects of game elements and provide conceptual guidance for design and analysis. From altogether ten focus points the Flow experience, Awareness of complexity, and Rhythm and intensity of exertion and learning are most essentials for the study reported in this paper.

Flow in Educational Exergames. The dimensions of flow experience were already discussed above, but challenge-skill balance dimension needs more clarification in educational exergame context. According to the extended dual flow model [10] Challenge-skill balance needs to be considered from both cognitive and physical perspectives. In the model the intensity-fitness balance determines the effectiveness of the exertion. If the game is too intensive, a player will fail to play the game and is unable to continue exercising. On the other hand, if the intensity is too low compared to player's fitness level, a player will enter a state of deterioration. The optimal exergaming experience can be achieved when both the psychological (cognitive) and physiological challenges are in balance and a player is in the flow zone.

Awareness of Complexity. In general, complexity can be defined as a state of the system that involves numerous elements and numerous relationships among these elements. In educational exergames the complexity is composed from several factors such as the amount of bodily controls, the amount of simultaneous players, the type and the level of learning content, the audio-visual implementation of the game, the rules of the game, and of course the relationships between these factors.

When designing educational exergames we should remember the constraints of human cognition and thus design the gameplay according to target group's skills, characteristics and knowledge. When playing educational exergames learners are challenged to extract relevant information from a game world, select corresponding parts of information and integrate all of these elements to coherent representation and at the same time track the state of the game, decide right movements to carry out, possibly communicate with other players, and interpret bodily sensations. This requires a lot from the player, because the game world changes during playing, important information may be presented only a while, and thus it needs to be kept actively in working memory in order to integrate it to earlier presented information and relate it to one's actions. This may easily impose high cognitive load in learners cognitive system and hinder learning and playing.

Rhythm and Intensity of Exertion and Learning. As the extended dual flow model argues physical and cognitive aspects of an exergame needs to be balanced. In educational exergames the balancing is even more important and challenging. The rhythm of gameplay and intensity of physical activities plays a central role in this. According to Tenenbaum [11] exercise intensity impacts the focus of attention. Thus, the integration of learning content and exergame interfaces raises new design challenges. Research on sports has shown that when the physical workload increases, attention allocation shifts from dissociation to association [12]. Association can be defined as turning the focus inward and toward bodily sensations, while dissociation is focusing outward and away from body sensations [13].

Such natural attention change disturbs processing of game elements and that way may also hider learning and problem solving. In other words, this means that during high physical workload it is hard to concentrate on problem-solving and game stimuli designed to enhance learning. In general, we can say that what higher the sum of cognitive and physical workloads is the higher the possibility to fail in the game is.

The balancing of workloads and adaptation to players characteristics is very challenging, because the cognitive and physical workloads are composed from several factors as discussed as a part of Complexity focus point. One solution to avoid cognitive or physical overload is to sequence the cognitive gameplay and physical gameplay. For example, players could first conceptually solve the puzzle and then perform the solution by controlling the game with physical movements.

1.3 Cooperative Games

Cooperation is a mode of interaction in which the actors focus on a common object and thus share the goal of the collective activity, instead of each focusing on performing their assigned actions and roles. "The important difference between coordinated and cooperative work is the common objective, which enables the participants in the distributed activity to relate to each other and make corrective adjustment to own and other's actions according to the overall objective of the collective activity" [14].

In video games, cooperative gameplay (often abbreviated also as co-op) is a feature that allows players to work together as teammates against one or more AI opponents. Playing simultaneously allows players to assist one another and create playing strategies as a team. Cooperative games are usually very motivating and external pressure or rewards are not needed. Just like in reading a book or in playing an instrument the rewards of co-op gameplay are built-in [15]. Malone and Lepper [16] have outlined different types of intrinsic motivators. Three of these motivators are group-level intrinsic motivators: competition, cooperation, and recognition. They involve interaction among people. According to Fogg [15], competition is perhaps the most powerful group-level intrinsic motivator. However, not everyone is competitive by nature, but in most situations and for most people, competition is energizing and motivating. Cooperation is another motivator, one that seems to be built into human nature. When people belong to a team, most of them cooperate. Finally, people are intrinsically motivated by recognition.

Cooperative gameplay refers also to non-zero-sum games. Situations where participants can all gain or suffer together are referred to as non-zero–sum. Thus, a country with an excess of bananas trading with another country for their excess of apples, where both benefit from the transaction, is in a non-zero–sum situation [17]. Another example is from 1970, when the three Apollo 13 astronauts were trying to figure out how to get their stranded spaceship back to earth, they were playing an utterly non-zero-sum game, because the outcome would be either equally good for all of them or equally bad [18]. Other non-zero–sum games are games in which the sum of gains and losses by the players are sometimes more or less than what they began with [17]. In zero-sum games, the fortunes of the players are inversely related. In tennis, in chess, in boxing, one contestant's gain is the other's loss. In non-zero-sum games, one player's gain needs not to be bad news for the other(s). Indeed, in highly non-zero-sum games the players' interests overlap entirely [18].

2 Method

The hypothesis of the study is that the measurement of the flow experience can reveal shortages of the game and that way aid the design process. The following subchapters describe participants, materials (the game), measures and the procedure in detail. Furthermore, it must be taken into account that in this study flow experience is measured in general level without the physical activity dimension (compare to the results of Sinclair et al. [19] presented in their study).

2.1 Participants

The study was conducted in autumn 2012 at one Finnish junior high school. The participants (N = 53) were 13–15 years old. 31 of the participants were boys and 22 were girls. 16 of the participants played games daily and others were infrequent players. Mobile phone was the most popular gaming platform among the participants. However, most of the participants used to play games also with computers and consoles. Tablets and hand consoles were used quite rarely to play games.

2.2 Materials: Labyrinth Run Game

The learning objectives of the Labyrinth Run game are: (1) teach students to work as a team, (2) teach them to take others into consideration and (3) teach them to communication skills. Labyrinth Run game (Fig. 1) is a side view platform game for 3–5 players. There are no opponents in the game, but players compete against the system as a team. The task of players' is to solve puzzle-like levels in a given time to proceed. Players must cooperate with each other to pick up a key and exit the level from a door that opens after the key is picked up. Players will be awarded points according to how quickly and how many of the players have completed the level before the time runs out. When the time runs out, the players move to the next level, regardless of how much progress has been made. The prototype version of the game has five levels.

Players move their game character by moving themselves. In their hand or pocket they have a mobile phone, which interprets the light movement into walking and sudden movement into a jump (Fig. 2). When a player walks in place, the game character walks forward on the screen. When the game character hits an obstacle, it will change the direction of walking. The game character jumps when the player jumps. There are obstacles in the game that require players to work together. Simultaneous game play allows players to assist one another by performing cooperative manoeuvres such as boosting a teammate up and over obstacles. For example, the sliding door is open only when one of the game characters is standing on the weight trigger. When a game character runs on the treadmill, elsewhere in the game is a horizontally moving platform, which can carry other game characters. One of the levels has two platforms that rise and fall like scales, depending on how many and how heavy game characters they have on. Some of the characters in the game are sturdier and weigh more.

Fig. 1. A screenshot of the Labyrinth Run game (zoomed in); one player runs on a treadmill to help another player overstep the gap with the moving platform towards the key.

Players must agree on every level what each one does. The better the cooperation works and the more accurate the choices are, the better the players get points. Labyrinth game is also a competition in a way that each player is awarded by individual points according to their performance. As mentioned previously, cooperation is necessary to solve the challenging levels. Furthermore, other players' ability to recognize players' performance; perceived activity and captured points affect the motivation.

Fig. 2. Players move their game characters by moving themselves.

A custom-made mobile client program is capable to monitor accelerometer readings in 250 ms intervals. These readings are used to determine how much a player has moved from the previous measurement. This is sent to the game in a server via a socket connection. Game interprets the information and moves the game characters accordingly. Between the game and the client is the socket server, which controls the game sessions. Upon starting the game takes a socket connection to the socket server, which starts a new session and returns the game unique QR-codes for players to join the game and to start and stop gameplay. The player takes a picture of the QR-code with the client program, which interprets the identifier from QR-code and sends it to the socket server. Client has joined the game session and from now on socket server forwards its messages to the game.

2.3 Measures

The data related to flow was gathered with an 18-item questionnaire developed by the authors. A 6-point Likert-type response format was used. The items included were derived from the GameFlow and FSS-2 questionnaires. The dimensions included were challenge, goal, feedback, playability, concentration, time distortion, rewarding experience, loss of self-consciousness, and sense of control. Each dimension was measured with a scenario-based item in order to avoid interpretation problems that have appeared in earlier studies. For example, the feedback dimension was operationalized as follows: "The game provided me such a feedback that I was aware how I was performing. I could really perceive the consequences of my actions."

2.4 Procedure

The game playing session was organized during the regular school day. First the participants were introduced to the Labyrinth game in small groups (3–5 players). In practice, participants were shown how the game is played and the idea of the game was presented. Participants played the game approximately 10–15 min depending how well the game proceeded. The playing behavior was observed and video recorded. Finally, just after the playing session participants filled in an online questionnaire (likert scale 1–6) about their playing experience. After that participants were shortly reviewed in groups.

3 Results

In this study the flow experience was measured with a questionnaire. The reliability of the used flow questionnaire indicates that the flow construct is internally quite consistent ($\alpha = .81$), which means that all nine dimensions measured the same phenomenon. The results showed (Table 1) that the flow level experienced by the players was in medium level (M = 3.46, SD = .77) and not as high as usually experienced when playing educational games [see e.g. 20]. From the Table 1 we can see that playability (M = 2.71, SD = 1.08), rewarding experience (M = 2.76, SD = 1.18), and feedback

(M = 2.80, SD = 1.21) dimensions scored the lowest. On the other hand loss of self-consciousness (M = 4.89, SD = 1.16), clear goals (M = 3.94, SD = 1.22), and concentration (M = 3.79, SD = 1.25) scored the highest.

The observations, conducted video analysis and discussions with players revealed that players had problems in figuring out how to control their game character. Although the players were informed how to control the game, they encountered problems. In fact one of playability's big dilemmas is the common gap between designers' and players' mental models. Mental model (or conceptual model) is player's explanation of how the game works. It is a simplified version of the designer's model that involves all the facts of the game. In our case player's mental model about the labyrinth game differed too much from designer's model reflected by the game, which lead to playability problems. The discussions with players revealed that the earlier playing experiences with camera based exergames like Microsoft Kinect games complicated the formation of right kind of mental model about the Labyrinth game. Almost half of the players did not understand that their posture and moving direction did not affect the behavior of their game character. Players tended to run for example to right and wondered why their character headed left in the game. This means that players assumed that their movements are mapped directly to the game world, which was not the case; (1) game character got its walking speed from player's motion intensity and the character changed direction only after collisions with walls or obstacles; (2) Game character jumped to the direction that it was facing when the player jumped, but not to direction that player jumped. In earlier studies [21] we have successfully used similar game mechanics, but the controlling was a bit different. In Diamond Hunter game the characters were moving all the time and the players controlled only the jumping. In that game users did not face any playability problems.

Table 1. Means and standard deviations of flow dimensions (N = 53).

Flow dimension	M	SD
Challenge – skill balance	3.42	1.13
Clear goals	3.94	1.22
Feedback	2.80	1.21
Playability	2.71	1.08
Sense of control	3.56	1.30
Rewarding experience	2.76	1.18
Concentration	3.79	1.25
Loss of self-consciousness	4.89	1.16
Time distortion	3.29	1.55
Flow experience (construct)	3.46	.77

The results also revealed that more frequent game players are more demanding about the implementation of the game. The radar chart (Fig. 3) shows the mean values of each flow dimension according to playing frequency. From the chart we can see that the biggest differences between daily players and infrequent players are in feedback, playability and rewarding experience dimensions. When considering the meaning of playing experience in terms of flow construct the difference was not significant $t(51) = 1.91$, $p = .06$. However, when comparing the scores in terms of playability $t(51) = 2.42$, $p = .02$, feedback $t(51) = 3.13$, $p < .001$ and rewarding experience $t(51) = 2.75$, $p < .01$ statistically significant differences were found.

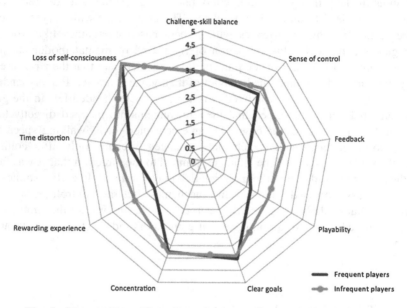

Fig. 3. Mean values of flow dimensions according to playing frequency.

The gender did not affect either the flow construct $t(51) = .50$, $p = .62$ or isolated flow dimensions. Only very small differences were found in playability, feedback and rewarding dimensions. These findings are consistent with earlier flow studies.

It was surprising that the loss of self-consciousness dimension scored the highest. In many games, especially, in exergames played publicly players tend to be shy and consider how others watch their performance. However, in this study players really loss their self-consciousness. In fact, they it seemed that the major goal of the players was not to solve the puzzle, but to learn together how to control the game characters. So, in the way, everybody had problems and they encouraged each others to test different styles to control the game. This has probably affected positively also to concentration and goal dimensions. However, we assume that the problems of the user interface reflected negatively to other flow dimensions. In fact it can be said that if some parts of the experience are too disturbing it is almost impossible to achieve deep flow state.

4 Conclusions

In this paper the usefulness of flow experience in evaluating the quality of serious games was studied. The results indicated that the measurement of the flow experience can reveal shortages of the game and that way aid the design process. For example the results of the case study showed that Labyrinth Run game did not create high flow feelings in players. In fact, the playability of the game was very low and it reflected negatively to other flow dimensions. Basically, players could not concentrate on learning objectives of the game, because they had to focus their energy to discover how to control the game characters. Based on the findings we argue that flow can be used to evaluate the overall quality of the playing experience, but it does not provide detailed information about the shortages or highlights of the game. If the aim is to study reasons why the game fails to produce a good playing experience, flow scale needs to be extended with dimensions related to game mechanics and audio-visual implementation or complementary research methods has to be used. In the future we will concentrate on developing an extended playing experience scale that takes also the game mechanics, user interface solutions, audio-visual implementation, and social aspects into account.

Acknowledgements. This work has been co-funded by the EU under the FP7, in the Games and Learning Alliance (GALA) Network of Excellence, Grant Agreement nr. 258169.

References

1. Procci, K., Singer, A.R., Levy, K.R., Bowers, C.: Measuring the flow experience of gamers: An evaluation of the DFS-2. Comput. Hum. Behav. **28**(6), 2306–2312 (2012)
2. Wirth, W., Hartmann, T., Bocking, S., Vorderer, P., Klimmt, C.: Schramm., H., Saari, T., Laarni, J., Ravaja, N., Gouveia, F. R., Biocca, F., Sacau, A., Jäncke, L., Baumgartner, T., Jäncke, P.: A process model of the formation of spatial presence experiences. Media Psychol. **9**, 493–525 (2007)
3. Kiili, K., de Freitas, S., Arnab, S., Lainema, T.: The design principles for flow experience in educational games. Procedia Comput. Sci. **15**, 78–91 (2012)
4. Cowley, A.D., Minnaar, G.: Watch out for wii shoulder. BMJ **336**, 110 (2008)
5. Sweetser, P., Wyeth, P.: GameFlow: a model for evaluating player enjoyment in games. Comput. Entertain. **3**(3), 1–24 (2005)
6. Weber, R., Tamborini, R., Westcott-Baker, A., Kantor, B.: Theorizing flow and media enjoyment as cognitive synchronization of attentional and reward networks. Commun. Theory **19**, 397–422 (2009)
7. Csikszentmihalyi, M.: Flow: The Psychology of Optimal Experience. Harper Perennial, New York (1991)
8. Ketamo, H., Kiili, K.: Conceptual change takes time: Game based learning cannot be only supplementary amusement. J. Educ. Multimed. Hypermedia **19**(4), 399–419 (2010)
9. Miller, G.: The magical number seven, plus or minus two: some limits on our capacity for processing information. Psychol. Rev. **63**, 81–97 (1956)
10. Kiili, K., Perttula, A.: A design framework for educational exergames. In: New Pedagogical Approaches in Game Enhanced Learning: Curriculum Integration, pp. 136–158. IGI Global, US (2013)

11. Tenenbaum, G.: A social-cognitive perspective of perceived exertion and exertion tolerance. In: Singer, R.N., Hausenblas, H., Janelle, C. (eds.) Handbook of Sport Psychology, pp. 810–820. Wiley, New York (2001)

12. Tenenbaumb, G., Connollya, T.C.: Attention allocation under varied workload and effort perception in rowers. Psychol. Sport Exerc. **9**(5), 704–717 (2008)

13. Scott, L.M., Scott, D., Bedic, S.P., Dowd, J.: The effect of associative and dissociative strategies on rowing ergometer performance. Sport Psychol. **13**, 57–68 (1999)

14. Bardram, J.E.: Collaboration, coordination, and computer support: an activity theoretical approach to the design of computer supported cooperative work. Ph.D. Thesis, Daimi PB-533. Aarhus University, Aarhus (1998)

15. Fogg, B.J.: Increasing persuasion through mobility. In: Fogg, B.J., Eckles, D. (eds.) Mobile Persuasion – 20 Perspectives on the Future of Behavior Change. Persuasive Technology Lab., Stanford University, CA (2007)

16. Malone, T., Lepper, M.: Making learning fun: A taxonomy of intrinsic motivation for learning. In: Snow, R.E., Farr, M.J. (eds.) Aptitude, Learning, and Instruction. Lawrence Earlbaum, Hillsdale (1987)

17. Binmore, K.: Playing for real: a text on game theory. Oxford University Press US. ISBN 978-0-19-530057-4., chapters 1 & 7, (2007)

18. Wright, R.: An Excerpt from the Introduction and Appendix I of Nonzero: The Logic of Human Destiny. Pantheon Books, New York (2000)

19. Sinclair, J., Hingston, P., Masek, M.: Considerations for the design of exergames. In: Proceedings of the 5th International Conference on Computer Graphics and Interactive Techniques in Australia and Southeast Asia, pp. 289–295 (2007)

20. Kiili, K., Lainema, T.: Power and flow experience in time-intensive business simulation game. J. Educ. Multimed. Hypermedia **19**(1), 39–57 (2010)

21. Kiili, K., Perttula, A., Tuomi, P.: Development of multiplayer exergames for physical education. IADIS Int. J. WWW/Internet **8**(1), 52–69 (2010)

SG Applications

A Business Simulation with an Agent-Based Deliberative Model of Consumer Behaviour

Márcia L. Baptista[1,2]([✉]), Carlos Martinho[1], Francisco Lima[1],
Pedro A. Santos[1], and Helmut Prendinger[2]

[1] INESC-ID/Instituto Superior Técnico, Universidade de Lisboa,
Av. Prof. Cavaco Silva, Taguspark, 2744-016 Porto Salvo, Portugal
{marcia.baptista,carlos.martinho,francisco.lima,pedro.santos}@ist.utl.pt
[2] National Institute of Informatics, 2-1-2 Hitotsubashi,
Chiyoda-ku, Tokyo 101-8430, Japan
helmut@nii.ac.jp

Abstract. Agent-based modelling, a way to simulate complex systems comprised of autonomous and interacting agents, is perhaps one of the most promising developments in experiential learning. In this paper we present a business simulation where the marketplace is modelled as an evolving system of deliberative (consumer) agents acting as utility maximizers. Concretely, we describe the deliberative-based architecture of our consumer agents and its unique properties. Additionally, we present our preliminary results which suggest participants are better able to understand the simulation when provided with the unique information of the agent-based approach.

Keywords: Beliefs Desires and Intentions (BDI) architecture · Agent based computational economics · Economic theory of consumer behaviour · Neoclassical maximization theory

1 Introduction

The problem of modelling the marketplace is perhaps the most central and unavoidable issue of a business simulation. Often, the algorithms responsible for calculating market and firm level demand have been considered the most complex and important calculations of these simulations [1]. Their importance follows from the fact that the ability of a firm to capture market share from other firms forms the essence of this kind of learning experience. Their complexity comes from the considerable number of variables involved in such algorithms, such as price, advertising and sales staff expenditures, and their intricate interaction.

Since Goosen [2] first proposed a generalized algorithm to simulate demand in business simulations, several techniques have been studied, such as the equation-based [3], interpolation-based and statistical-based [4] approach, with much effort being devoted to enhance the flexibility and validity of the proposed models.

© Springer International Publishing Switzerland 2014
A. De Gloria (Ed.): GALA 2013, LNCS 8605, pp. 215–223, 2014.
DOI: 10.1007/978-3-319-12157-4_17

A paradigm not yet extensively applied to demand modelling in business simulations [5] is the agent-based approach [6], a technique increasingly used in a broad range of social sciences, which involves the computational study of a system as a collection of autonomous interacting individual actors, the so-called agents. This paradigm presents several advantages [7] as a representational system that could help promote better demand systems for business simulations.

One major advantage of agent-based modelling is that it does not impose restrictions on the linearity, homogeneity, normality, and stationarity of its solutions. This could mean more realistic marketplace simulations and contribute to the upward trend in complexity of business simulations [8].

Agent-based models are also known for their potential to demonstrate emergent phenomena. The use of this technique could thus result in more natural descriptions of the marketplace and its individual entities, the consumers, where it would be simpler to provide more information to participants and disclose the system's structure without hindering the strategic value of the simulation game. This could in turn create more transparent [9] simulations and lead to more effective learning experiences.

Given the not yet extensively explored possibilities of agent-based modelling, we present in this paper a business simulation with an agent-based model of consumer behaviour. In the following section we review previous demand models for business simulations (Sect. 2). We then proceed to describe our consumer behaviour model (Sect. 3), prototype game (Sect. 4) and experimental findings (Sect. 5). We conclude with our final remarks (Sect. 6).

2   Background

The following approaches have been used to model demand in business simulations:

- Equation-based: mathematical functions model industry and firm demand.
- Interpolation based: an interpolation method derives the graphics of industry and firm demand functions.
- Statistical: the proportion of consumers which consume a given product is measured using purchase probability distributions.
- Agent-based: the complexity of the marketplace is captured using a bottom-up approach, modelling the behavioural rules of each consumer.

2.1   Equation-Based Models

An equation-based model consists of two functions:

1. A function of market demand (Q) calculated from the average values of demand determinants such as price (P), advertising and promotion variables (M) and product quality variables (R):

$$Q = f(P, M, R) \tag{1}$$

2. A function of firm level demand (q_i) used to calculate the weight of each firm (w_i) when allocating market share:

$$q_i = w_i Q \tag{2}$$
$$w_i = g(P_i, M_i, R_i) \tag{3}$$

The equation-based approach uses a set of equations to express the emergent relationships which occur between consumers in a marketplace.

2.2 Interpolation Approach

Goosen and Kusel [10] recognized that to try to find a single general flexible demand equation for modelling market and firm demand was an intricate task. Therefore, the authors proposed a method of implementing self-designed functions. Their proposed method had however some limitations. First, the method did not prescribe the nature of the self-designed functions. Consequently, this approach did not solve the problem of finding a flexible demand function. Furthermore, the designer had the burden of identifying all the relevant points in the modelled functional relationships. Modelling interactivity effects was also not straightforward as Gold [11] showed.

2.3 Statistical Approach

Carvalho [12] proposed another approach to model market demand. The author disagreed with the fact that previous models were mostly based on input decisions, not modelling explicitly the crucial element of a demand model: the consumer himself. Accordingly, Carvalho proposed a model of market demand based on the equimarginal principle using the gamma probability distribution to simulate the preferences of the consumers. Carvalho's model allowed a more explicit modelling of consumers given that the probability distribution parameters could be changed to reflect changes in the consumers' incomes, tastes and market dimension. However, as Gold and Pray [13] noted, it was difficult to select and modify the distribution parameter values.

2.4 Agent-Based Approach

In the general area of agent-based models of consumer behaviour, a number of models have been proposed [14–16]. These models are however, not specially as models of business simulations since their primary purpose is to explain particular economic phenomena such as the decoy effect[1] [16], or the lock-in effect[2] [14,15].

---

[1] The decoy effect can be defined as a phenomenon whereby consumers will tend to have a specific change in preference between two options when also presented with a third option which is asymmetrically dominated.

[2] The phenomenon of lock-in occurs when the consumer becomes dependent on a supplier for products and services, unable to switch to another supplier without substantial switching costs.

In contrast, we aimed to develop a demand model able to simulate simple general concepts from economics such as the law of demand, diminishing marginal returns and other phenomena such as substitution and complementary effects.

3   Model

Our proposed model of consumer behaviour[3] is based on the deliberative Beliefs, Desires and Intentions (BDI) architecture [18], perhaps the best known and most studied model of practical reasoning agents. The BDI architecture provides a simple and efficient psychological framework for modelling the behaviour of agents acting under incomplete or incorrect information in their environments. This is typically the case of consumers in the marketplace which often have to decide based on uncertain information about the prices, quality or availability of products in their surroundings. In our reasoning architecture the internal state of the consumer consists of the following elements (Fig. 1):

Beliefs represent the information the consumer holds about the current state of the world, that is, the marketplace, and its internal state. Two types of beliefs can be identified:
  – Belief in the availability of a particular product.
  – Belief that given the available budget (I) the consumer is able to purchase products.
Desires represent the goals of the consumer. For instance, the consumer can have the desire to consume an additional unit of a given product.
Intentions representing the possible courses of action. Purchase intentions are generated during the reasoning process of the consumer, each for a possible bundle of products.

The reasoning process of a consumer consists in the following steps:

Step 1 The consumer verifies if the desire to consume goods is a current goal. In the affirmative case, the reasoning process proceeds to step 2. Otherwise, the reasoning process proceeds to step 5.
Step 2 For each affordable combination of goods the consumer generates a purchase intention. This generation of intentions is supported by the current beliefs of the consumer in the availability of products at the market and its belief in his own economic capabilities.
Step 3 The consumer selects from the list of purchase intentions a preferred intention according to the maximization of an utility function. In case of identical utility values, a random factor is used to decide. The following utility function can be used to simulate the preferences of the consumer:

$$U(x_1, ..., x_n) = \sum_{j=1}^{x_1} b_1(j) + ... + \sum_{j=1}^{x_n} b_n(j) \tag{4}$$

$$x_1 p_1 + x_2 p_2 + ... + x_n p_n \leq I \tag{5}$$

---

[3] For a more detailed description of the model please refer to [17].

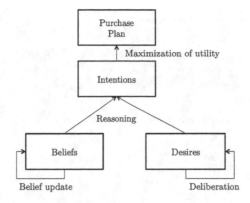

Fig. 1. The rationality elements of the BDI architecture of a consumer.

where $x_1, x_2, ..., x_n$ represent the quantities of distinct products 1, 2, ..., n which can be purchased at prices $p_1, p_2, ..., p_n$ for a consumer with a budget I.

Step 4 The consumer attempts to accomplish his preferred purchase intention as an effective purchase plan.

Step 5 The consumer updates his beliefs and desires.

4   Game

Our proposed agent-based model of consumer behaviour was implemented in a concrete business simulation to further analyse the educational possibilities of the model. The simulation game models the following entities (refer to Fig. 2):

Firms represent the participants. Each participant acts as a firm and manages a retail store where the participant can purchase and sell a number of different products to the final consumer. In each round, participants have to decide on two fundamental topics: (a) quantity of each product to purchase and (b) selling price of products at the store. The performance of firms is evaluated according to their profit.

Products represent the goods sold by firms to the final customer. Each product has an associated purchase cost and is characterized by a type and a quality measured in a scale from zero to one. The type defines the quantity in average a consumer requires of that product according to his available budget. The quality defines his preference over other products.

Consumers represent the virtual agents of the game. Each consumer decides which products to purchase and attempts to accomplish his purchase intentions. Consumers attempt to accomplish their intentions sequentially according to a random arrangement in each round of the game. The intentions of consumers to purchase a particular product from a specific firm are represented by their movement from their houses to the firm (see Fig. 3) and the

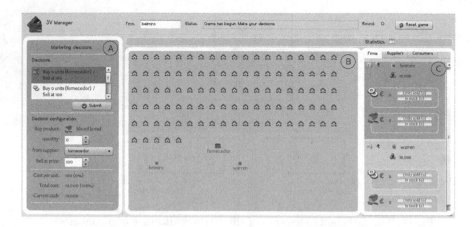

Fig. 2. Game interface: (A) panel of decisions, (B) simulation panel and (C) panel of information of firms, suppliers and consumers (Color figure online).

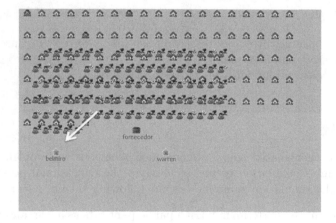

Fig. 3. Movements of consumers as displays of purchase intentions (Color figure online).

accomplishment of such intentions are expressed through graphical changes of colour (green, yellow and red representing full/partial and non accomplishment of purchase intentions respectively).

Participants are requested to submit their decisions during each round of the game which ends after all participants have submitted their decisions. After the submission of all decisions the processing of the decisions unfolds and the results are returned to the participants who can then simulate the marketplace in virtual time.

In most business simulations results are presented to participants managing firms in a static manner through the use of spreadsheets. In our game, the results of a round, are not the outcome of an equation, emerging instead from the complex interaction of several agents during a period of time. Consequently, at the end of a round participants can analyse in virtual time the animation of several indicators of performance of firms such as quantities bought, quantities sold, stock and current cash and analyse the interconnected behaviour of consumers. This execution can be rerun several times providing the participants with the possibility to revisit the simulation to acquire new learning perspectives.

5   Experimental Results

Our prototype was tested experimentally with a total of 27 volunteers, between the ages of 22 and 35 from an applied sciences background. Each participant was subject to two different exercises: exercise A where they were able to play the complete game and exercise B with same game where the participants were only provided with the final outcomes (cash, stock and quantities sold) of their decisions at the end of each round, as it is standard in business simulations. In both exercises participants played the game in pairs during five rounds. The order in which the participants performed the two exercises varied.

The results (Table 1) revealed high levels of agreement (96 %) when the participants where asked if they understood the results of the game in exercise A. However, in exercise B, the responses of the participants varied, revealing a low level of agreement, with 34 % of the respondents stating they were not able to understand the results of the game. In terms of understandability of the results, all participants rated exercise A with a higher (85.1 %) or equal (14.8 %) grade than exercise B.

A Spearman's correlation analysis showed a strong correlation ($\rho = 0.677$, $p = 0.005$) between the perceived usefulness of information and comprehension in exercise A. In exercise B, no strong correlation between these two variables was registered (Table 2).

Table 1. Results of evaluation of "I understood the results".

Classification	Exercise A	Exercise B
Agree	85 %	15 %
Somewhat agree	11 %	18 %
Neutral	4 %	33 %
Somewhat disagree	0 %	30 %
Disagree	0 %	4 %

Table 2. Results of evaluation of "The information was useful".

Classification	Exercise A	Exercise B
Agree	48 %	34 %
Somewhat agree	41 %	22 %
Neutral	11 %	22 %
Somewhat disagree	0 %	22 %
Disagree	0 %	0 %

6   Conclusion

We presented an agent-based model of consumer behaviour. The model applied concepts from artificial intelligence and was consistent with neoclassical economics. Additionally it captured the fundamental teachings of introductory economic courses and provided a natural description of economic phenomena.

A business simulation was designed with this agent-based model as its demand model. In the development of the game, we tried to create an effective interface which took advantage of the descriptive potential of the model.

Our experimental results suggest the game was more straightforward to understand due to the presence of the unique information elements provided by the agent-based model. Hence, we believe our results provide evidence that information about the consumers' final actions as well as their cognitive reasoning processes, that is, their beliefs, desires and intentions, either fulfilled or failed, can play an important role in the participants' understanding of business simulations.

References

1. Goosen, K., Jensen, R., Wells, R.: Purpose and learning benefits of simulations: a design and development perspective. Simul. Gaming 32(1), 21–39 (2001)
2. Goosen, K.R.: A generalized algorithm for designing and developing business simulations. Dev. Bus. Simul. Exp. Learn. 8, 41–47 (1981)
3. Gentry, J.W.: ABSEL: Guide to Business Gaming and Experiential Learning. Nichols/GP Publishing, East Brunswick (1990)
4. Gold, S., Pray, T.: Historical review of algorithm development for computerized business simulations. Simul. Gaming 32(1), 66–84 (2001)
5. Baptista, M.L., Martinho, C.R., Lima, F., Santos, P.A., Prendinger, H.: Applying agent-based modeling to business simulations. Dev. Bus. Simul. Exp. Learn. 41, 179–183 (2014)
6. Bonabeau, E.: Agent-based modeling: methods and techniques for simulating human systems. Proc. Natl. Acad. Sci. USA 99(Suppl. 3), 7280–7287 (2002)
7. Bankes, S.C.: Agent-based modeling: a revolution? Proc. Natl. Acad. Sci. USA 99(Suppl. 3), 7199–7200 (2002)
8. Faria, A., Hutchinson, D., Wellington, W., Gold, S.: Developments in business gaming - a review of the past 40 years. Simul. Gaming 40(4), 464–487 (2009)
9. Machuca, J.: Transparent-box business simulators: an aid to manage the complexity of organizations. Simul. Gaming 31(2), 230–239 (2000)
10. Goosen, K., Kusel, J.: An interpolation approach to developing mathematical functions for business simulations. Simul. Gaming 24(1), 76–89 (1993)
11. Gold, S.: Modeling interactive effects in mathematical functions for business simulations: a critique of Goosen and Kusel's interpolation approach. Simul. Gaming 24(1), 90–94 (1993)
12. Carvalho, G.: Modeling the law of demand in business simulators. Simul. Gaming 26(1), 60–79 (1995)
13. Gold, S., Pray, T.: The use of the gamma probability distribution: a critique of Carvalho's demand simulator. Simul. Gaming 26(1), 80–87 (1995)

14. Said, L., Bouron, T., Drogoul, A.: Agent-based interaction analysis of consumer behavior. In: Proceedings of the First International Joint Conference on Autonomous Agents and Multiagent Systems, IFAAMAS, pp. 184–190 (2002)
15. Janssen, M., Jager, W.: Simulating market dynamics: interactions between consumer psychology and social networks. Artif. Life **9**(4), 343–356 (2003)
16. Zhang, T., Zhang, D.: Agent-based simulation of consumer purchase decision-making and the decoy effect. J. Bus. Res. **60**(8), 912–922 (2007)
17. Baptista, M.L., Martinho, C.R., Lima, F., Santos, P.A., Prendinger, H.: An agent-based model of consumer behavior based on the BDI architecture and neoclassical theory. Dev. Bus. Simul. Exp. Learn. **41**, 170–178 (2014)
18. Bratman, M.: Intentions, Plans, and Practical Reason. Harvard University Press, Cambridge (1987)

Stealth Assessment of Teams in a Digital Game Environment

Igor Mayer[1(✉)], Dirk van Dierendonck[2],
Theodore van Ruijven[1], and Ivo Wenzler[1,3]

[1] TU Delft, Jaffalaan 5, 2628 BX Delft, The Netherlands
{i.s.mayer,T.W.J.vanRuijven}@tudelft.nl
[2] Rotterdam School of Management, Erasmus University, Rotterdam
The Netherlands
dvandierendonck@rsm.nl
[3] Accenture, Amsterdam, The Netherlands
ivo.wenzler@accenture.com

Abstract. There is not much research on team collaboration in digital entertainment games, nor is there much evidence for the efficacy of game-based team training or the validity of game-based team assessment. This is a shortcoming because of an increasing pervasiveness of serious games in organizational life, e.g. for operational training, management and leadership. Is it possible to establish marked relationships between psychometric constructs that measure 'team composition and performance' and 'analytics' that unobtrusively measure gameplay performance? If so, what are the implications for game-based team research and assessment? The authors conducted explorative, quasi-experimental (field) experiments with the multiplayer serious game TeamUp. One field experiment was conducted with 150 police officers as part of task-specific two-day team training. Research data were gathered through pre-game and post-game questionnaires on team constructs such as 'psychological safety' and 'team cohesion'. A large quantity of in-game data was logged to construct indicators like 'time needed to complete the task', 'speak time' and 'avoidable mistakes' to measure team performance. The conclusion of the analysis is that 'team cohesion' and 'psychological safety' correlate moderately and significantly with in-game performance indicators. Teams with an unequal individual game performance speak the most, while teams with an equally low or equally high individual performance spend significantly less time speaking. The indicative findings support the need to further develop validated analytics and game-based environments for team research and assessment.

1 Introduction

Global economic developments are emphasizing the importance of network organizations for the long-term competitiveness of organizations, where people collaborate in virtual and dispersed teams with alternative non-hierarchical forms of leadership, like distributed, shared and emergent leadership [1, 2]. Additionally, the current generation is growing up in a networked society with a ubiquitous and pervasive presence of digital games (and social media). It is therefore argued that pervasive digital (game) experiences affect the forms of collaboration with which the Net generation feels

A. De Gloria (Ed.): GALA 2013, LNCS 8605, pp. 224–235, 2014.
DOI: 10.1007/978-3-319-12157-4_18

comfortable, as team members and as team leaders [2–5]. If this is the case, we need better insight into whether and how (digital game-mediated) internal team processes are related to team performance. This is highly relevant for the (future) performance of organizations, especially when the game generation becomes entrepreneurial or reaches management levels in organizations. Against this background, we are also seeing an increasing interest in the use of serious games (SG) as alternative or complementary modes of training and assessment of individual team behavior and performance (see below for examples). If it were possible to gain insight into the relationship between team composition and team performance by observing and assessing teams or team members during digital (serious) gameplay, this would offer many new ways for the research, training and assessment of teams in a networked and digital age. So, the question is: what structural factors influence team performance in a digital game-based environment? And, perhaps even more importantly, can team performance be unobtrusively measured for research and assessment purposes?

2 Team Performance

Why do some teams perform better than others and how can we determine this (in advance)? This question has inspired a vast body of research, impossible and unnecessary to summarize here. In light of our experiments below, we limit ourselves to a brief definition of team and team performance. Cohen and Bailey (1997) define a team as "a collection of individuals who are interdependent in their tasks, who share responsibility for outcomes, who see themselves and who are seen by others as an intact social entity embedded in one or more larger social systems and who manage their relationships across organizational boundaries" (p. 241). The array of factors brought forward to explain team performance is very diverse. Psychology may focus on the combination of personality traits, team roles or leadership styles; small group research may focus on things like identity, conformity, psychological safety and cohesion; and management sciences may focus on things like team structure, size and composition, reward structures and task-related technology [6].

Team performance is notoriously difficult to assess. Most studies now agree that team performance should be treated as a multidimensional concept best to be measured in so-called performance composites as "excellent indicators of overall team effectiveness as compared to those that only assess one aspect of performance" (Mathieu et al., 2008, p. 417). Data to assess team performance can commonly be gathered at the individual, team and/or organization level. Questionnaires (tests) are common at the individual level, while surveys are most suitable at the organizational level, and observation would be needed at the team level.

3 Digital Team Games: Uses and Research

In the last decade or so, educators, trainers and assessors have become under the spell of serious games, the use of games, game technology or game principles for non-entertainment purposes [7]. The military and security sector have led the way in the use of SGs for team training and assessment, first through the exploration of the use of entertainment games like Counter Strike [8] and Call of Duty [9], followed by the development of 'serious' games like America's Army [10]. Military operational team training and assessment are increasingly conducted in SG environments like Virtual Battle Space [11]. These are used to set up specific scenarios for military training and assessment: army, air force, navy, marine, special forces, humanitarian intervention and emergency relief teams [12, 13]. Rather similar to game-based, military team training is the virtual game-based training of first responders, personnel working in hazardous environments and emergency managers [14, 15]. A number of game environments and research publications focus on medical teams [16, 17]. Outside the military, security and safety area, we mostly find leadership training as a sub-genre of business and management games. A number of SGs in this genre are worth mentioning: Virtual Leader [18], Fligby [19, 20], the Gaining Leadership Program [21] and the Leadership Game [22]. A few other serious games such as [23] are used for assessment and recruitment of new staff. There are hardly any SGs that specifically address team training and assessment in the field of non-military security and safety. One important exception is Novicraft [24]. In principle, any commercial off-the-shelf (COTS) enter-tainment game can be used for team training or assessment, as long as the game is multiplayer and team-based [25, 26]. Theories on leadership and team collaboration in multiplayer games are few and far between [27–31]. A few studies have been published on socialization, social behavior, leadership, teams and collaboration in virtual worlds (VW) like Second Life (SL), Active Worlds (AW), EVE online (EoL) and World of Warcraft (WoW) [3, 4]. There are a number of significant theories and studies on leadership, teams and collaboration in virtual, online environments [2, 32, 33]. In addition, research publications on the use of SG for psychological individual and team assessment are very scarce [34].

4   Methodological Challenges of Game-Based Assessment

The main barrier to the diffusion of SGs in organizational life is the questioned validity (e.g. predictive value), especially where matters like individual and team assessment or scientific research are concerned. However, the fundamental advantage of digital SGs for training and assessment is that data can be unobtrusively gathered, logged, saved and analyzed, for debriefing, assessment or research purposes. Stealth assessment – also referred to as non-invasive, unobtrusive, non-disturbing assessment – can poten-tially increase the learning efficacy of SGs, because much of the learning in SGs now remains rather 'implicit' and 'subjective', for instance through personal debriefings. In order to develop stealth methods and tools for game-based team training and assess-ment, knowledge and skills from the field of SGs (e.g. learning efficacy, game design and analytics) and organizational behavior (e.g. assessment, team processes and organizational development) need to be synthesized. This is largely unexplored terri-tory to which we want to contribute through experimental study. Is it possible to establish marked relationships between validated constructs that measure 'team com-position and performance' and 'analytics' that unobtrusively measure gameplay per-formance? If so, what are the implications for game-based team research and assessment? The authors are using the SG TeamUp (© TU Delft/The Barn) for a series of team training and assessment sessions while at the same time validating and studying team performance with a battery of high-quality psychometric tests. This research is leading to new scientific insights on how game players can be assessed based on their gameplay instead of self-reported tests.

5 TeamUp – The SG Research Environment

TeamUp is a high-quality multiplayer, 3D SG developed by students of TU Delft in the Netherlands who started up their own company, The Barn, around it. A demo movie can be watched at: www.seriousgaming.tudelft.nl. In the game, four players need to self-organize, communicate, collaborate and arrange teams, communication and leadership in order to solve five levels of puzzle/team challenges that require team communication and coordinated action. This may require different and alternating forms of leadership and self-organization. In the scenario, the players find themselves stranded on a deserted island with Mayan ruins. They need to get to the other end of the island to be picked up.

The game was built as a total conversion mod in UDK engine (Unreal) by an internal team of professional game designers; the graphics, user interaction and simulation models are of very high quality [35]. The game communicates with speech systems and a data logging tool.

Teams may be homogenous or heterogeneous on one or more dimensions like age, gender, nationality, game-experience, leadership, preferred team roles, etc. They may be composed at random, self-selected or assigned. The game itself can be played in a synchronous, co-located or distributed fashion. In our preferred setup, we arrange four players of a team at four sides of one or two tables – positioned in a cross – so that they face each other and can look see their own screens but not those of other players. The players can be in positioned in different rooms in a distributed fashion, using a form of distance communication like the Unreal in-game speech function or external devices. In one experiment with police officers, the players used their regular handheld devices. The players are not allowed to stand up, look at other screens, take over other players' navigation or use any forms of communication other than speech (no writing or gestures).

The game can be best experienced by playing it – and we do not want to give away too much about the challenges. The present version of the game consists of five puzzle levels.

1. Door puzzle: players need to navigate from their arrival dock to a closed door giving access to a cave. Entering the cave through the door requires coordinated action with two people needing to stand on two signs inside or outside to open the door and keep it open.
2. Tile puzzle: This level is loosely based on the well-known training game 'the Maze' [36] or 'Minefield' [37]. Four players need to find one correct path across an 8×8 tile maze. When a player steps on a wrong tile, he will fall through and one of the team members can try again.

3. Maze puzzle: One player stands high on platform where he has overview of three team members struggling to find the exit in a maze.

4. Bridge puzzle: The team needs to break up into various subgroups to solve small puzzles: a. entering a dark ruin where one team member leads with a flare and another needs to follow. One person needs to stay behind in the ruin standing on a sign. b. Two players need to use their weight and distance to balance a bridge allowing them to climb onto a platform. One person needs to stay behind on the platform to stand on a sign. If and when four avatars stand on four signs dispersed throughout the level, a bridge to the next level is lowered.

5. Pillar puzzle: team members alternate in leadership, trying to communicate and solve a series of four communication and coordinated action puzzles. Correctly solving one of the four puzzles opens a little bridge to the next puzzle where another team member becomes the leader of a similar, but more difficult, team challenge.

6   Research Setup

To date, two versions of TeamUp have been used between November 2010 and December 2012 for training and education purposes, combined with user testing and quasi-experimental data collection to give a data set of 347 respondents divided over 87 game instances of 4 players. In 2012, TeamUp was rebuilt from the ground up in UDK. Game levels 1, 3 and 4 were added. In addition, services for logging and scoring were put in place, so that the game can log any kind of game data, communicate with a scoring, assessment and visualization tool and supports services like distributed play (headsets, walkie-talkies, etc.). Version 2 of the game was played in Fall 2012 as part of a two-day training session with around 150 police officers – some of whom had a military background – in charge of Close Protection (CP) of VIPs. Situational awareness, visual cueing, sense making and distributed team communication through handheld devices or walkie-talkies are important competences for these trainees. The assessment tool was improved and adapted to suit the user group and training objectives. A small group of educational technologists (20) played the same TeamUp version 2 as part of a workshop at an international Educational Technology Convention in November 2012.

The analysis of results will focus primarily on the data in the experiment with police officers (n = 152 individuals; n = 38 teams) because this experiment has a homogenous group and real team training purposes. The game is under constant development and new team training sessions are anticipated. Moreover, the assessment instrument and digital tool are being improved.

7   Self-Reported Team Composition and Performance

We measured the following constructs for team composition by making use of pre-game and post-game questionnaires.

Table 1. Team composition constructs

No.	Name	Constructs (mean & standard deviation)	Definition	Reference
1	Competence	Personal competence	The expressed confidence in playing computer games before starting TeamUp.	[38]
2	Joy	Experienced joy	The joy expressed by the team while playing TeamUp.	
3	Pressure	Perceived pressure	The perceived pressure while playing TeamUp.	
4	Achievement	Achievement	The need to achieve while playing TeamUp.	
5	Perceived competence	Perceived competence	The perceived competence after having played TeamUp.	[38]
6	Psychological safety	Psychological safety	Psychological safety experienced in the team while playing TeamUp.	[39]
7	Cohesiveness	Team cohesiveness	The experienced cohesiveness in the team while playing TeamUp.	[40]
8	Exchange	Team exchange	The experienced exchange of information, tasks, etc., in the team while playing TeamUp.	[40]
9	Communication	Team communication	The communication in the team while playing TeamUp.	

Team scores for the above constructs were calculated as means (M) and standard deviations (σ) on the basis of the individual answers of the four players that made up each team. The calculated mean Σ (1,2,3,4)/4 gives an indication of the team's strength on the relevant item or construct. The calculated standard deviation (σ) gives an indication of the team's homogeneity/heterogeneity on the relevant construct (Table 1).

8 Observed Team Composition and Performance

We developed the following additional constructs for unobtrusively observing team performance while playing the game: time (TIME) needed to complete (puzzles 1, 2, 3, 4, 5 of) the game, the distance (DISTANCE) covered in (puzzles 1, 2, 3, 4, 5) in the game and the (avoidable) mistakes (ERROR) in puzzles 2 and 5.

Team communication was calculated as the minutes during the game that players in a team speak to each other (SPEAK TIME). When we divide this number by TOTAL PLAY TIME, we get an indication of the intensity of the communication among the team players independently of how long they take to complete it (SPEAK TIME INTENSITY) (Table 2).

Table 2. Observed team performance constructs

No.	Var. name	Construct	Definition	A1	A2	B3	B4
1	TIME TOTAL	Total game time	Time from leaving dock until all buttons pushed at end of game.		v1	v2	v2
2	TIME1	Door puzzle time	Time from leaving dock until 4th player passes through door.	–	–	v2	v2
3	TIME2	Tiles puzzle time	Time from checkpoint before door until 4th player crosses maze.	v1	v1	v2	v2
4	TIME3	Maze puzzle time	Time from finishing Tiles puzzle until all buttons beyond maze pushed.	v1	v1	v2	v2
5	TIME4	Bridge puzzle time	Time from checkpoint before initial button until bridge is lowered.	–	–	v2	v2
6	TIME5	Pillars puzzle time	Time from checkpoint until final bridge is lowered.	–	–	v2	v2
7	DISTANCE_TOTAL	Total game distance	Distance in game in meters covered by all team members combined.	–	–	v2	v2
8	DISTANCE1	Door puzzle distance	Distance covered by all team members during the Door puzzle.	–	–	v2	v2
8	DISTANCE2	Tiles puzzle distance	Distance covered by all team members during the Tile puzzle.	–	–	v2	v2
9	DISTANCE3	Maze puzzle distance	Distance covered by all team members during the Maze puzzle.	–	–	v2	v2
10	DISTANCE4	Bridge puzzle distance	Distance covered by all team members during the Bridge puzzle.	–	–	v2	v2
11	DISTANCE5	Pillars puzzle distance	Distance covered by all team members during the Pillar puzzle.	–	–	v2	v2
12	ERROR2	Tiles puzzle avoidable mistakes	Number of wrong tiles stepped on after a safe passage through the maze was known.	–	–	v2	v2
14	ERROR5	Pillar puzzle avoidable mistakes	Number of resets in Pillar puzzle.	–	–	v2	v2

Table 3. Team communication based on speak time

No.	Var. name	Construct	Definition	A1	A2	B3	B4
1	SPEAKTIME_TOTAL	Team speak time	Total time (in min.) that all members of the team were speaking to each other.	–	–	v2	–
2	SPEAKTIME_ INTENSITY	Intensity of speak time in team	SPEAKTIME_TOTAL divided by TIME_TOTAL	–	–	v2	–

9 Testing Team Composition and Performance

Figure 1 below summarizes the relatively large number of moderate to strong, significant correlations (Pearson ρ) between the team compositions constructs (M and σ) and the in-game team performance constructs. For reasons of space, we focus upon two important constructs – team cohesiveness and psychological safety – that seem dominant in their relationship with team performance constructs (Table 3).

1. Team cohesiveness is important because it has a moderate, significant, negative correlation with both total time (−0.38) and total distance (−0.37). In other words, the more cohesive teams take less time to play the game and covers a shorter distance.
2. Psychological safety is important because it has correlations with a large number of team performance constructs, including total distance (−0.37). The higher the psychological safety, the shorter the total distance covered in the game. When the four team members have a greater difference of opinion about the psychological safety in their team, they have a lower performance on nearly all performance constructs.

In short, game analytics like 'play time' and 'avoidable mistakes' can be strong indicators of 'team cohesion' and 'psychological safety'. Conversely, when a team struggles with the gameplay this puts a strain on internal cohesion and makes the team members feel less safe. If such arguments are true and can be validated in more detail through future research, an improved version of TeamUp (or other games), with validated analytics, can be used for stealth observation of such aspects as team composition and performance in order to assess a team's strength for certain tasks in the future, or to train it for these.

Another interesting observation is that the 'time' that team members speak to each other is largely influenced by the differences among the team members in terms of individual game performance (see Table 4). When team members have a more or less equally high individual performance, there may not be so many reasons to speak to each other and communication can be short, to the point and possibly even non-verbal. When all team members have an equally low individual performance, they may not know so well how to speak to each other and what about. But when one or two team members have greater insight into what needs to be done and how, while one or two other team members do not know so well, the speak time among the team members increases markedly. In short, teams with unequal individual performance levels communicate more.

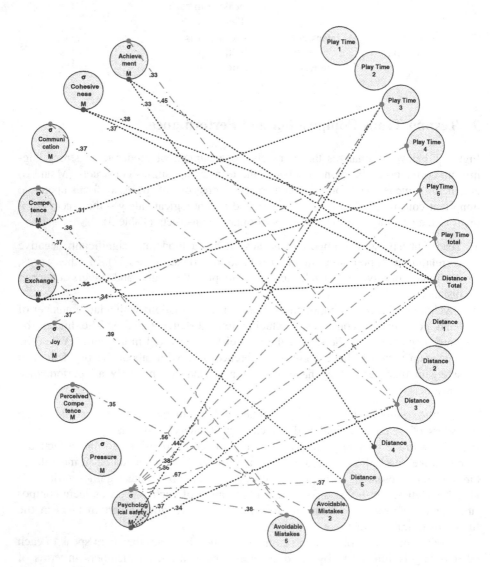

Fig. 1. Correlations between team composition and team performance

Table 4. Speak time and team performance

		R_TIME_TOTAL	R_TIME_C1	R_TIME_C2	R_TIME_C3	R_TIME_C4	R_TIME_C5	R_DISTANCE_TOTAL	R_DISTANCE_C1	R_DISTANCE_C2	R_DISTANCE_C3	R_DISTANCE_C4	R_DISTANCE_C5	R_ERRORS_C2	R_ERRORS_C5
SD_R_S PEAKTI ME	R	.41**	.15	.26	.31	.13	.52**	.12	-.20	-.10	.08	-.01	.58**	-.20	.43*
	Sig	.01	.38	.12	.07	.44	.0	.47	.25	.58	.65	.96	.0	.23	.01
	N	35	36	36	36	36	35	36	35	35	35	35	35	36	35
R_SPE AKTIM E_TOT AL	R	.79**	.22	.58**	.4*	.23	.77**	.44**	-.05	.36*	.15	.10	.51**	.03	.51**
	Sig	.0	.20	.0	.02	.17	.0	.01	.76	.03	.39	.57	.0	.87	.0
	N	35	36	36	36	36	35	36	35	35	35	35	35	36	35

10   Conclusion

The findings above indicate that team cohesiveness and psychological safety are important factors influencing team performance in the TeamUp digital game-based environment. In addition, we are able to substantiate that teams with an equal individual performance, either high or low, speak the least, while teams with an unequal individual performance speak more.

Even more important than the precise findings themselves is the fact that they support the need for further development of validated analytics and game-based environments for team research and assessment. The research and results are highly explorative and indicative. We are well aware of significant limitations. First, the experiments discussed in this paper are based on a single game that is still under construction. We have not yet compared it with some of the other digital team games discussed above and therefore cannot generalize. Research data about other serious games are not available, which implies that we would need to arrange gameplay and data collection ourselves.

Second, data were gathered during real-life game sessions, and not under experimental, lab conditions. Sometimes things went differently than expected with players, technology or questionnaires. The reason for not testing in a lab is that it is difficult to find a significant number of professionals – like police officers – to play in a lab. More importantly, we believe that the efficacy of serious games can only be proven under the conditions for which they are designed – in real-life education, training, etc.

Third, we operationalized team composition and leadership with just a few possible constructs. On the basis of the promising results, we feel that the research models and constructs should be expanded and improved. This can only be done through an iterative series of experiments.

Fourth, the data and insights in these and future experiments should feed back into the design, facilitation and debriefing of the game in order to improve its power as a real-life training and assessment tool.

Acknowledgements. The authors wish to thank several teams of TU Delft students who participated in our Serious Game Design Project course for conceiving the TeamUp game. We thank Arne Bezuijen and Bas van Nuland for merging original ideas with their own, for turning prototypes into a high-quality product and for having enough courage to start up their company, The Barn, around it. We are grateful to the players who tested TeamUp and to the Dutch police for their trust in the game.

References

1. Pearce, C.L., Conger, J.A.: Shared Leadership: Reframing the Hows and Whys of Leadership, vol. 57(3), p. 330. Sage Publications, Thousand Oaks (2003)
2. Gressick, J., Derry, S.J.: Distributed leadership in online groups. Int. J. Comput. Support. Collaborative Learn. 5(2), 211–236 (2010)
3. Malone, T.W., Cadwell, T., Scarborough, J., Roy, S.: Leadership in Games and at Work: Implications for the Enterprise of Massively Multiplayer Online Roleplaying Games. Most, pp. 1–34 (2007)
4. Siitonen, M.: Exploring the experiences concerning leadership communication in online gaming groups. In: Proceedings of the 13th International MindTrek Conference Everyday Life in the Ubiquitous Era on MindTrek 09, p. 90 (2009)
5. Yee, N.: The labor of fun: how video games blur the boundaries of work and play. Games Culture 1(1), 68–71 (2006)
6. Bettenhausen, K.L.: Five years of groups research: what we have learned and what needs to be addressed. J. Manag. 17(2), 345–381 (1991)
7. Michael, D.R., Chen, S.: Serious Games: Games that Educate, Train, and Inform. Thomson Course Technology PTR, Boston (2005)
8. Counterstrike: Global Offensive, (Webpage). http://blog.counter-strike.net/index.php/about/. Accessed 14 Feb 2013
9. Call of Duty, (Webpage). http://www.callofduty.com/blackops2. Accessed 14 Feb 2013
10. America's Army, (Webpage). http://www.americasarmy.com
11. Virtual Battle Space 2 (VBS2), (Webpage). http://products.bisimulations.com/products/vbs2/overview. Accessed 13 Feb 2013
12. Andrews, A.: Using advanced gaming technology for teaching critical thinking, problem solving, and leadership skills. In: Interactive Technologies Conference Proceedings (2007)
13. van der Hulst, A., Muller, T., Besselink, S.: Bloody serious gaming – experiences with job oriented training. In: Industry Training, no. 8169, pp. 1–11 (2008)
14. Stern, P.A., Harz, C.R.: Serious games for first responders: improving design and usage with social learning theory (Volume B). ProQuest, p. 218 (2008)
15. Harz, C.R., Stern, P.A.: Serious games for first responders: improving design and usage with social learning theory (Volume A). ProQuest, p. 212 (2008)
16. LeRoy Heinrichs, W., Youngblood, P., Harter, P.M., Dev, P.: Simulation for team training and assessment: case studies of online training with virtual worlds. World J. Surg. 32(2), 161–170 (2008)
17. Østergaard, H.T., Østergaard, D., Lippert, A.: Implementation of team training in medical education in Denmark. Qual. Saf. Health Care 13(996), i91–i95 (2004)

18. Virtual Leader, (Webpage). http://www.simulearn.net/site_flash/index.html. Accessed 12 Feb 2013
19. Csikszentmihalyi, M.: Flow: The Psychology of Optimal Experience. Harper Perennial, New York (1991)
20. Fligby, (Webpage). http://www.slideshare.net/zadvecsey/presenting-fligby-01102012v41# btnNext. Accessed 12 Feb 2013
21. The Gaining Leadership Program, (Webpage). http://www.ranj.com/content/werk/the-gaining-leadership-program. Accessed 12 Feb 2013
22. The Leadership Game, (Webpage). http://www.pixelearning.com/services-the-leadership-game.shtml. Accessed 12 Feb 2013
23. Houthoff Buruma The Game, (Webpage). http://www.ranj.com/nl/content/werk/houthoff-buruma-the-game. Accessed 20 Feb 2013
24. NoviCraft, (Webpage). http://www.teamingstream.com/. Accessed 12 Feb 2013
25. Manninen, T.: Interaction Forms and Communicative Actions in Multiplayer Games. Game Studies 3(1) (2003)
26. Manninen, T.: Virtual team interactions in networked multimedia games – Case: 'Counterstrike' – multi-player 3d action game. In: Presence (2001)
27. Lewis, S., Ellis, J.B., Kellogg, W.A.: Using virtual interactions to explore leadership and collaboration in globally distributed teams. In: Human Factors, no. Cmc, pp. 9–18 (2010)
28. Jakobsson, M.: Questing for knowledge - virtual worlds as dynamic processes of social interaction. In: Schroeder, R., Axelsson, A.-S. (eds.) Avatars at Work and Play: Collaboration and Interaction in Shared Virtual Environments, pp. 209–225. Springer, Dordrecht (2006)
29. Brown, B., Bell, M.: Play and sociability in there: some lessons from online games for collaborative virtual environments. In: Schroeder, R., Axelsson, A.-S. (eds.) Avatars at Work and Play: Collaboration and Interaction in Shared Virtual Environments, pp. 227–245. Springer, Dordrecht (2006)
30. Hamalainen, R.: Designing and evaluating collaboration in a virtual game environment for vocational learning. Comput. Educ. 50(1), 98–109 (2008)
31. Yee, N.: The psychology of massively multi-user online role-playing games: motivations, emotional investment, relationships and problematic usage. In: Schroeder, R., Axelsson, A.-S. (eds.) Avatars at Work and Play: Collaboration and Interaction in Shared Virtual Environments, pp. 187–207. Springer, Dordrecht (2006)
32. Priest, H.A., Stagl, K.C., Klein, C., Salas, E.: Virtual Teams: Creating Context for Distributed Teamwork. American Psychological Association, Washington, DC (2006)
33. Sivunen, A., Siitonen, M.: Comparing experiences on leadership in virtual teams and online multiplayer gaming clans. In: ICA 2010 Singapore, vol. 35, June 2010
34. Boyle, E.A., Hancock, F., Seeney, M., Allen, L.: The implementation of team based assessment in serious games. In: 2009 Conference in Games and Virtual Worlds for Serious Applications, pp. 28–35 (2009)
35. Bezuijen, A.: Teamplay The further development of TeamUp, a teamwork focused serious game, TU Delft (2012)
36. Sweeney, L.B., Meadows, D.L.: The Systems Thinking Playbook. Pegasus Communication, Durham (2001)
37. Thiagarajan, S.: Design your Own Games and Activities. Pfeiffer, San Francisco (2003)
38. Competence example items
39. Edmondson, A.C.: Psychological safety and learning behavior in work teams. Adm. Sci. Q. 44(2), 350 (1999)
40. Seers, A.: Team-Member Exchange Quality: A New Construct for Role-making Research (1989)

Unveiling California History Through Serious Games: Fort Ross Virtual Warehouse

Nicola Lercari[1(✉)], Michela Mortara[2], and Maurizio Forte[3]

[1] University of California Merced,
5200 North Lake Rd, Merced, CA 95343, USA
nlercari@ucmerced.edu
[2] CNR-IMATI, Via de Marini 6, 16149 Genoa, Italy
[3] Duke University, 112 East Duke Building, Durham, NC 27708, USA

Abstract. Between 1812 and 1841, Fort Ross was a Russian fur trading outpost and multi-cultural colony located in the Northern California coast. Current Fort Ross is a popular California State Historic Park visited every year by over 100,000 visitors from all over the world. In March 2011, California State Parks and the University of California Merced started the Fort Ross Virtual Warehouse project— a digital scholarship initiative aimed to enhance a pilot serious game on Fort Ross developed by California State Parks Staff in the early 2000s— with the goal to explore novel ways for archiving, disseminating, and teaching cultural and historical information. After twenty-four months of development, Fort Ross Virtual Warehouse serious game is ready to be tested in a user study with elementary school students. This paper exposes key features, design solutions and game mechanics of Fort Ross Virtual Warehouse along with preliminary assessments of the game performed as an expert evaluation by the leader of the Special Interest Group on "serious games for humanities and heritage" of the GALA Network of Excellence (www.galanoe.eu).

1 Introduction

In the last decade the joint effort of research teams, independent game companies, and cultural institutions in the development of digital-based learning tools has proved that serious games (SGs)—specifically digital games for more than just entertainment— entail novel cultural paradigms and define new ways of learning [1, 2]. One of the most noticeable outcomes of this evolving scenario is the implementation of a number of historical SGs that represent specific eras, events, or dynamics through a trans-disciplinary approach which blends together computer science, archaeology, history, geography, social sciences, and the arts. This article seeks to provide designers and scholars with a methodology to employ in historical serious games as well as generate a reflection on new tools for cultural visualization and education. For example, how can we design an effective narrative-interactive gameplay that preserves historical accuracy and allows users to have fun? How can we structure an integrated point of view on the reconstructed environment that grants embodiment, playability, and situated learning? What are the features of a serious game that enhance cultural awareness and comprehension? The opportunity to test SGs as learning tools regarding American history became an interest in March 2011 when California State Parks (CSP) and the

© Springer International Publishing Switzerland 2014
A. De Gloria (Ed.): GALA 2013, LNCS 8605, pp. 236–251, 2014.
DOI: 10.1007/978-3-319-12157-4_19

University of California Merced (UCM) started a digital scholarship initiative—the Fort Ross Virtual Warehouse (FRVW) project—with the purpose of exploring novel ways for archiving, disseminating, and teaching cultural and historical information [3]. Role-play and the employment of multimedia products and SGs are not new practices to CSP. In the early 2000s, Elizabeth Prather along with a group of CSP representatives and contractors designed and developed Virtual State Parks, a pioneering educational project that employed real-time 3D graphics, digital storytelling, and Fort Ross as the pilot setting. The goal of this groundbreaking work was to involve students, families, and parks' visitors in the virtual discovery of California history [4]. In addition, CSP has a long experience in historical re-enactment. Specifically, the Fort Ross Environmental Living Program (ELP) has involved California students, parents, and volunteers in hands-on learning activities organized by the historical interpreters at Fort Ross (FR) for years [5]. What is innovative in FRVW is our integrated approach to the creation of a virtual learning environment based on scientific data, historical narrative, and experiential learning. Our serious game (SG) complements the pedagogical goals of the ELP with a pre-visit and post-visit virtual tool. Thus FRVW aims to enhance the comprehension of historical and social dynamics as well as train pupils on the topography of FR and the location of its main points of interest (POIs). In addition, FRVW grants access to an in-game repository of primary historical sources—the Fort Ross Journal—and stimulates creative thinking through role-play, challenges, and rewards. The scientific nature of FRVW is determined by a realistic and accurate 3D environment that has been reconstructed using instrumental data—such as LiDAR and terrestrial laser scanning data—obtained through surveys of the topography and architecture of FR [6]. The representation of the cultural landscape and socio-economic activities performed in the SG has also been validated by the historians who work at Fort Ross State Historic Park (FRSHP) and manage the ELP. After a long phase of development—that spanned twenty-four months and involved researchers both at UCM and Duke University—FRVW SG is now ready to be tested. The main user study has been designed according to the Game and Learning Alliance Network of Excellence (GALA NoE) guidelines for SGs evaluations [7]. Elementary school students from ages 7 to 11 will start testing FRVW during the 2015–2016 School Year. The user study will involve teachers and students who participate to the ELP in California as well as pupils in Durham, North Carolina. The purpose of this study is to evaluate how the integration of digital tools, historical simulation, and hands-on activity can improve the understanding of history, generate cultural awareness and engage young students in novel ways of learning. At the present time, a preliminary expert evaluation has been performed on FRVW by the leader of the Special Interest Group on "serious games for humanities and heritage" of the GALA Network of Excellence, as detailed in Sect. 6.

2 Related Work

The analysis of a number of digital-based games related to cultural heritage [7] suggests that historical SGs favor a realistic simulation of the past. Our findings verify the importance of realism in digital simulation as many historical SGs have been developed as 3D realistic environments [9–13]. Some games demonstrate that 3D sceneries are able to support situated cognition in a realistic/meaningful environment whether players can interact with cultural objects in their actual context [14–16]. Virtual museum and virtual tourism SGs also tend to be as realistic and accurate as possible. These last types of SGs allow players to explore accurate reconstructions of historical buildings or manipulate precious artifacts without risk of damage [15–19]. Realism per se does not make a SG validated by historians. Previous works on digital urban history show that an accurate and effective simulation of the past must rely on virtual environments implemented through the integration of documentary and iconographic sources [20, 21]. Our inquiry on SGs indicates that role-play is another fundamental feature of educational and historical game-like virtual environments [22]. Role-play increases the empathic connection between players and their virtual alter-egos, enhancing the emotional involvement of users in the simulation. Thus, the active involvement of the player in the historical simulation improves the comprehension of the causes that generated the simulated events and amends the understanding of their consequences [11, 12, 23]. Therefore role-play is often employed in historical SGs for raising awareness about the socio-economic condition of individuals in specific historical eras [23, 24].

3 Historical Context

In the second half of the 18th century, the exploration and colonization of the North Pacific experienced an eastbound expansion of the colonial power of the Russian Empire. Since the 1760s Russian explorers and *promyshlenniki* (hunters and traders) had travelled through the Bering See and the Gulf of Alaska in search of hunting-grounds and ideal places to establish *redoubt*s (fortified outposts) [25]. In 1799 Tsar Paul I chartered the Russian American Company (RAC) with the rights to most of Alaska's natural resources, the monopoly on all foreign trade, and the management of the colonies in Russian America (Alaska). Although some RAC outposts proved to be successful and self-sufficient colonies, other *redoubt*s required to be supplied by sea from the Russian mainland with long and expensive trips that were affecting the RAC's profit [26].

In the early 1800s the company hoped to find another center for the trade of fur located in an area that could also provide supplies to other *redoubt*s in Alaska [25]. In 1808 Ivan A. Kuskov was entrusted to explore the Western Pacific coast and sailed towards *New Albion* (Northern California). He identified a promising location on a promontory near a centuries-old Kashaya-Pomo Native American village called *Mettini*. In 1812 Kuskov established a settlement at Bodega Bay and few months later the Russian colonists started building Fort Ross on the bluff nearby *Mettini* [26]. The initial period of sea otter hunting was very profitable. The population and number of buildings at Ross settlement had grown steadily until the second half of the 1820s (see Fig. 1). Soon, the outpost became a relatively peaceful multicultural colony whose population consisted of Russians—mainly RAC employees—Alaskan hunters with their families, Kashaya and Coast Miwok workers, as well as Russian-Native American Creoles [26].

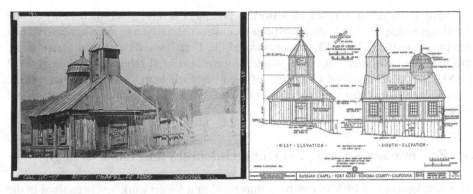

Fig. 1. Example of historical sources employed for modeling the chapel at Fort Ross - Library of Congress, Prints & Photographs Division, HABS.

The golden age of the Ross colony did not last for long. Despite the resources that the RAC employed to establish farms, orchards, and mills, agriculture at FR was never very profitable because the adverse coastal climate conditions. Furthermore, the overexploitation of the sea otter population soon compromised the fur trade. By the end of the 1830s, FR was no longer lucrative [26].

In the early 1840s Alexander G. Rotchev—the last Fort manager—was instructed to find buyers for everything that could not be removed and shipped back to Alaska, (see Fig. 2). In 1841 John A. Sutter, a Swiss pioneer and Mexican citizen, signed with Rotchev a bill of sale which transferred him the ownership of buildings, livestock, orchards, and all the non-transferable equipment located at Port Roumianzoff, the Ross settlement and the Russian American ranchos in Alta California [26]. Sutter salvaged many of the buildings and reused the materials at Sutter's Fort, an agricultural and trading colony located in the Sacramento Valley. After Sutter, the ownership of FR passed through a number of other people until the California Historical Landmarks League bought it in 1903. In the first months of 1906, FR became a California State Park, but few weeks later, a catastrophic earthquake struck Northern California and

Fig. 2. Fort Ross watercolor painting by Ilia G. Voznesenskii (1841) - from the collection of the Peter the Great Museum of Anthropology and Ethnography (Kunstkamera), Russian Academy of Sciences. Coll. n° 1142-6.

seriously damaged a number of historical buildings at FR. Since then many of the buildings inside the stockade have been reconstructed and made once again available for public visiting. In 2012, in occasion of the Fort Ross Bicentennial Celebration, the main magasin and a Russian windmill were also been rebuilt. Throughout 2012 FRSHP has been involved in a series of events and celebrations that engaged historic associations, American and Russian authorities, as well as enthusiastic visitors and students.

4 Preliminary Survey, Learning Outcomes and Game Design

The development of FRVW can be summarized in a 6-step workflow organized in the following phases: (1) *Conceptualization* (2) *Research and Data Acquisition* (3) *Game Design* (4) *Post-processing and Modeling* (5) *Game development* (6) *Beta testing and Finalization*. Our work in phase 1 has been inspired by a vast set of design guidelines, reports, and pedagogical curricula developed by CSP representatives and ELP historians [27]. Specifically the newly implemented ELP Clerk curriculum encouraged us to design the playing character (PC) Vasilii Starkovskii—the FRVW's protagonist—as a RAC apprentice clerk who arrived at Fort Ross in the first half of 1820s to get trained and then work at the RAC Warehouse [28].

The conceptualization of our SGH has been facilitated by the analysis of qualitative and quantitative data related to FRVW potential users that we received as results of a focus group and a survey conducted in 2008 by an independent research firm on behalf of CSP. The purpose of this analysis was to include the educators who participate in the ELP in the preparation of the SG. Specifically, the focus group involved 14 instructors of different ethnicities who have been teaching 3th, 4th, and 5th grade courses in Northern California for a period of 3–10 years. Prior to the beginning of FRVW design, the members of the focus group participated to a collective interview in which they could express opinions, suggestions, and concern about the potential usage of the SG with their students. However, CSP desired to draw conclusions about a larger number of teachers. Therefore the contractor organized a survey that involved a net target population of 127 teachers. The quantitative study was implemented in the form of a questionnaire which was sent via mail to the participants. A total of 47 completed questionnaires were returned determining a response rate of 37 per cent. The surveyors objectively defined this number as relatively small but reported that the results were interesting and potentially useful [29]. This preliminary analysis addressed relevant topics such as whether the FRVW initiative would have been of interest for the educators, whether their classroom could support the usage of the SG, what timing was fitting best the educational goals, what content they would find useful, and what technological facilities were accessible to the students (see Fig. 3).

The results emphasized the teachers' enthusiasm about using FRVW—especially before the visit to FRSHP—in a formal education environment. The ideal game session length was expressed in a period between two and four hours with the possibility to re-play the game for a shorter time. In terms of computer support the survey underlined that all the students have computer access and that the schools provide a fast internet connection with an average speed between 1 to 3 MB/s.

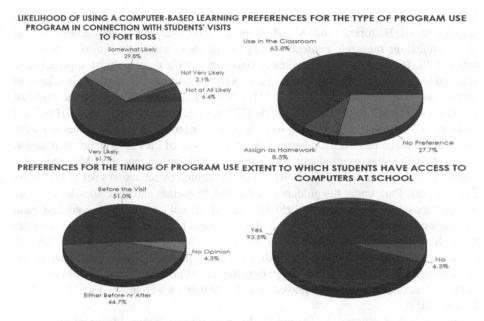

**LIKELIHOOD OF USING A COMPUTER-BASED
PROGRAM IN CONNECTION WITH STUDENTS' VISITS
TO FORT ROSS**

Somewhat Likely
29.8%

Not Very Likely
2.1%

Not at All Likely
6.4%

Very Likely
61.7%

LEARNING PREFERENCES FOR THE TYPE OF PROGRAM USE

Use in the Classroom
63.8%

No Preference
27.7%

Assign as Homework
8.5%

PREFERENCES FOR THE TIMING OF PROGRAM USE

Before the Visit
51.0%

No Opinion
4.3%

Either Before or After
44.7%

**EXTENT TO WHICH STUDENTS HAVE ACCESS TO
COMPUTERS AT SCHOOL**

Yes
93.5%

No
6.5%

Fig. 3. Graphs visualizing results from the 2008 survey conducted among ELP teachers

The educators' feedback also expressed preference for game content such as California geography, historical role-play on cultures of Fort Ross, factors behind the establishment of the Ross colony, interaction with Spanish and Mexican California [29]. Becoming acquainted with the voice and opinion of the teachers who will use FRVW with the students taking part to the ELP, as well as learning from their concerns and suggestions helped us answer the following methodological questions: what is the best learning environment for a SG on FR? Should FRVW be a pre-visit or post visit tool? How long should a game session be? Is it more effective to develop a stand-alone or a team gameplay?

As previously mentioned, the target audience of FRVW is made of students that participate in the ELP or other pupils with an interest in the History of California and the North Pacific colonization. Therefore we found essential to involve a number of FRHP historians, CSP staff, and ELP leaders directly in the Research and Data acquisition phase of development as well as in the Design phase and Finalization and Beta Testing phase as primary players. All these stakeholders collaborated with the UC Merced team to include in FRVW a specific learning process that could boost historical interpretation and culture awareness in elementary school students. Feedback from teachers and pupils participating in the ELP has been also taken into consideration during this second phase of development to calibrate the game on the specific needs of the end users. In order to imbue FRVW with a larger pedagogical value, we also decided to analyse content standards and regulations for K-5 education (from Kindergarten to 5th grade) which comply with the ELP's mission as well as with the guidelines adopted by the California State Board of Education (CSBE) in 1998 as a foundation of the state of California's education system [30]. The learning outcomes we designed in phase 2 are inspired by the Grade K-5 and Grade 6-8 CSBE standards.

More precisely CSBE's learning paradigm identifies 3 main categories associated to acquisition of Historical and Social Sciences analytical skills: *chronological and spatial thinking*; *research, evidence, and point of view;* and lastly *historical interpretation* [30]. Previous works specifically underline that a constructivist approach and situated learning are best practices in the implementation of educational SGs related to history and cultural heritage [13, 16, 31]. Although some critics exist to the minimal guidance associated to this learning style [32], we decided to design our SGH using a task-based, constructivist approach to pedagogy. It needs to be reported that we were confident to make this decision because the primary use of FRVW is as pre-visit tool to be used in the classroom under the direct supervision of teachers. Moreover, the learning process enabled by our SGH is complemented by an actual visit to Fort Ross State Historic Park under the guidance of the Park historians and educators. In addition, our previous experience in the field of cultural virtual environments and historical simulation persuaded us to design a digital-based learning tool meant to educate through the synthesis of scientifically accurate cultural data and to inform through engaging interactive activity [33]. Findings and results from phase 1 and 2 persuaded us to design FRVW as a digital role-play game meant primarily for a formal education environment that could also be played from home using a web browser and Unity Web Player plugin.

In Table 1, Columns A, B, and C describe three different historical and social sciences analytical skills to be acquired by the user of FRVW. Each skill can be developed independently from one another through the achievement of 4 different learning outcomes characterized by incremental levels of complexity as described in Rows 1, 2, 3, and 4. In order to allow users to achieve such learning goals, we designed FRVW as a series of experiential activities that generates understanding of the geographical and cultural information enclosed in FR virtual cultural landscape. Thus, in FRVW the exploration of the scenario is the place where users can negotiate chronological and spatial thinking skills as well as historical interpretation competences. A constructivist approach allowed us to determine that the comprehension of the FR historical context is built up from the experience of the landscape and the completion of engaging tasks and learning activities.

To foster the situated learning aspect of the game and allow users to achieve the learning goals expressed in Table 1 Column C, we also decided to include in the game an interactive catalogue of primary and secondary historical sources. This features—named Fort Ross Journal—is a pivotal element in the formal education phase of the user experience. While immersed in the digital simulation of FR historical buildings or while walking through the virtual Kashaya village, or the Russian cemetery, students and teachers can access together an in-game catalogue of validated cultural and historical sources through the Fort Ross Journal feature.

5 Game Mechanics and Reward System

FRVW has been developed using the game development ecosystem Unity 3D as a modular game in which narrative gameplay (Challenge Mode) is separate from explore gameplay (Explore Mode). In both modalities, users interact with the environment and

Table 1. Skills to be acquired and learning outcomes to be achieved in Fort Ross virtual warehouse

	Skill A - chronological & spatial thinking	Skill B - research – evidence – POV	Skill C - historical interpretation
Learning outcome – Lev.1	Place people and events related to FR history in a chrono-logical sequence and within a spatial context	Differentiate between primary and secondary sources on Fort Ross history	Summarize the key events of Fort Ross era and explain their historical contexts
Learning outcome – Lev.2	Explain how past and current FR are different, identify similarities, differences, permanence and change that reflect California history and geography	Pose relevant questions about FR history and cultures in regards to events, documents, oral histories, letters, diaries, artifacts, maps, artworks, and architecture	Identify the human and physical characteristics of the Ross colony and explain how those features form its unique character
Learning outcome – Lev.3	Develop map skills, determine the absolute locations of places and interpret symbolic representations on a map of FR colony	Distinguish fact from fiction by comparing documentary sources on historical figures and events with fictionalized characters and events	Identify and interpret the multiple causes and effects of historical events that occurred at Fort Ross
Learning outcome – Lev.4	Assess the advantage/disadvantage of the location of specific places at FR (e.g., proximity to the harbor) and understand how geographic significance can change over time	Distinguish fact from opinion in historical narratives and stories about the Ross settlement and Russian colonization of North Pacific	Conduct cost-benefit analyses of the business of the Russian American Company and Russian colonization of North Pacific

historical characters through the Player Character (PC) Vasilii Starkovskii, a young Russian man who lived at Fort Ross and worked in the Fur Warehouse in the 1820s (see Fig. 4).

- *Challenge Mode* (CM) consists of a narrative-interactive gameplay which engages the player in a 1.5 h. training quest on Fort Ross history, economy, and cultures. Along the story line the protagonist Vasilii needs to accomplish a number of tasks to become a qualified RAC clerk. CM is based on 5 interactive challenges based on clerk's training tasks (e.g. doing inventory, trading items, calculating the warehouse daily balance, etc.) and related text-based quizzes to verify the acquired knowledge and skills. Moreover, CM gameplay is enriched by 7 sub-tasks that stimulate

Fig. 4. Game menu screen (left); view of the Russian windmill and map feature (center); view of Vasilii interacting with a Native American NPC at the Kashaya village (right)

the player to explore specific locations in the scenario through the usage of the Mini-Map feature. In CM user meets 11 historically accurate Non Player Characters (NPCs) and interact with them through a text-based dialog interface. The edutainment value of CM is reinforced by 4 in-engine cutscenes—specifically in-game cinematics generated in real-time by the game engine—that provide further information about the historical context and grant a better identification of the players in the player character and narrative. In Challenge Mode, cutscene 1 and 2 also provide high quality cinematic opening and closing to enhance immersion in the narrative. CM also presents an Inventory feature, used to organize collected objects, and an Event Notifier feature which helps users to keep track of the assigned tasks and sub-tasks with notifications and memos (see Fig. 5).

- *Explore Mode* (EM) consists of a free-roam navigation of the FR colony that allows players to acquire spatial knowledge at their own pace without any scripted interaction. The usage of EM is mostly useful in a formal environment where tutors and students can use FRVW together. This is especially relevant for what concerns in-context browsing of historical sources stored in the Fort Ross Journal. To avoid a potential drop of interest—caused by its non-structured navigation—EM includes a Timer feature which limits the gameplay to 20 min per session and compels the

Fig. 5. Inventory screen (left), interaction with NPC and event notifier feature in CM (center); detail of the badge clipboard (right)

students to play FRVW repeatedly. EM differs from CM also for what concerns the interaction with NPCs. EM dialog presents the users more detailed information about the historical characters represented by the NPCs, but do not have narrative components. The Map feature is also used in EM to promote spatial learning of FR environment.

- *Reward System*. FRVW's pedagogy is based on the exploration of the reconstructed cultural landscape and on the completion of training tasks. Players are motivated to learn through a scaffolded learning system based on tasks, performance assessment, and learning incentives. Specifically, in CM the clerk supervisor (NPC Mr. Khlebnikov) evaluates the player's performance and delivers to Vasilii up to 5 competence badges as rewards for the accomplished tasks. Moreover, 2 cutscenes can be unlocked by the player as bonus features. Challenges 1 (Inventory) and 3 (Trade) are meant to stimulate the player to explore the Fur Warehouse and the Ross colony with the purpose to find, collect, and trade specific items used in the Environmental Living Program. When an item is collected, a pop-up inventory window explains pupils the artifact's features. Challenge 1 and 3 are completed when the amount of items required in the prompt is reached. Upon completion the player receives a badge from Mr. Khlebnikov. Our design associates the progression of the game to a successful completion of challenge 1 and 3. In this way we make sure that all the students receive at least 2 badges throughout the game and do not feel they are following behind. The completion of Challenges 2 (Language), 4 (Culture), and 5 (Ruble) does not entail an automatic delivery of competence badges. Such challenges are characterized by text-based multiple choice quizzes that allow the game to assess knowledge learned in previous tasks. At the end of each quiz, the player's performance is assessed through an automated evaluation script that recognizes the correct answer and assigns a score. In case of a top score, NPC Mr. Khlebnikov delivers to the player a competence badge for each successful challenge. When the score is not satisfying the player is urged to work harder and concentrate more on the learning tasks. This design produces a positive competition between players while stimulates them to replay the game in order to reach a higher score and earn all the badges. When all of the 5 challenges are completed the player is prompted to visit the Fort Commandant's house where he is congratulated by the NPC Karl Von Schmidt. There the player also receives a Diploma of Completion that makes him a fully qualified clerk. Such Diploma—customized with the player's name and earned badges—can be saved in the player's local computer. Then the game suggests pupils to print the Diploma and bring it with them when visiting Fort Ross State Historic Park to receive freebies and congratulations from the park's staff.

6   Preliminary Game Evaluations

As previously discussed, an extensive user study of FRVW will take place in the School Year 2015–2016. However, this paper delivers a preliminary evaluation of FRVW based on the SG description template formulated by the GALA NoE [7]. The preliminary evaluation of Fort Ross Virtual Warehouse aims to describe the principles and elements to be used in the design of the actual user study. This preliminary work is based on a set of criteria that have been currently employed in the creation of the GALA repository of serious game descriptions. Currently, GALA NoE collaboratively tested and described more than 40 serious games with the aim to generate a publicly available on-line serious game catalog. The GALA NoE template provides a general description of the SG (e.g. year of release, target user, learning curve, effective learning time) and covers technological aspects of SG design and development (e.g. platform, game engine, user interface, game mechanics, algorithms, compliance to standards and interoperability); it also describes SG as a learning environment (e.g. if and how the game provides feedback, supports motivation, allows gradual learning/scaffolding, facilitates self-assessment, invites to active learning) and defines the context of use according to the design goals (e.g. if the setting is formal or informal, which are the role of the students and of the teachers, the learning goals and expected outcomes). Furthermore, the GALA NoE template provides an application-oriented analysis based on the following parameters: *effectiveness, efficiency, usability, diffusion, feedback and assessment support, exploitability, reusability in different contexts, motivation*, and *engagement*. Each of these parameters was assigned a value from 1 to 5, where 1 is the lowest and 5 is the highest. The following evaluation of FRVW has been performed with a medium/high level of confidence by the leader of the Special Interest Group on "serious games for humanities and heritage" of the GALA Network of Excellence—an expert on serious games studies who was neither involved in the design of our SGH nor collaborated with the development team. The goal of this section is to provide an informed analysis of FRVW explicitly oriented on the impact of the SGH on its end users (e.g. students and teachers, or visitors and cultural mediators in a park or museum). These preliminary observations will be used as a reference in the design of the user study to be performed with elementary school students and teachers during the School Year 2015–16 with the goal to verify the effectiveness of FRVW as an educational tool.

- *Effectiveness* (efficiency in meeting the learning goals). The following considerations focus on the context of use of the game as a pre-visit application: Score: 5/5 (Excellent). The SG seeks to introduce the FR environment to the students prior their visit to the park and to communicate historical and daily life events related to FR history. To accomplish these goals, the SG is designed as a role-play game in which the player acts as an apprentice clerk and executes daily duties. In order to make progress in the narrative, the player has to interact with objects (e.g. doing inventory of items at the warehouse) or trade with other characters (e.g. Native Americans basket waivers or Alaskan hunters). Before a new task is assigned, players are invited to explore new locations and become acquainted with the environment. In FRVW there is no facility to teleport to other POIs therefore walking through the various locations might be overwhelming. This action, though, is a successful way of having the players become familiar with FR and surrounding areas. This SGH has the potential to reach high effectiveness when it is complemented by the actual visit to the park.

- *Efficiency* (how time and resources are managed to reach the learning goals). Score: 4/5 (Good). Scaffolded learning is well supported and the employed non-mediated learning strategies are a successful way to allow users to gain spatial knowledge of the FR environment.
- *Usability* (level of easiness of use). Score: 2/5 (Needs Improvement). Player interacts with the SG by navigating the environment, collecting objects, speaking with NPCs, and accessing additional resources via user interface (e.g. journal, map, and inventory). In FRVW automatic triggering and point-and-click make interaction very simple. Selection of objects needs refinement, though, when objects are very close to player. FRVW features a WASD keyboard-based and "mouse-look" mouse-based movement control. The navigation can be challenging because the camera zooms in and out and orbits 360 degrees. This camera design allows for a better point of view on the environment, but can cause an initial discomfort in non-expert users. In addition, some usability issues are due to narrow indoor passages that make the navigation of some buildings inconvenient. The camera also needs refinement because it goes through solid objects (e.g. walls and roofs) when player leaves a building or is very close to external walls. However, these known issues are due to the current implementation and do not derive from the game design.
- *Diffusion* (the level of circulation of the game). Score: N/A. FRVW has not been officially released yet. However, we expect a wide diffusion of the game since it is sponsored by California State Parks and it will be used in the schools that participate to the ELP. Moreover, the FRSHP is also considering an on line deployment of the game following a pay-per-play model with a minimum subscription fee of about 1 USD.
- *Feedback and assessment support* (capability of the game to provide performance assessment and feedback to the players). Score: 4/5 (Good). Activity assessment and feedback are provided during the challenges via the Event Notifier or the text-based dialogues with NPCs. Furthermore, a final performance assessment is provided in the Diploma of Completion which displays a badge symbol for any successfully completed challenge.
- *Exploitability* (learning curve, applicability to an actual learning context, role of teachers and students, need of special hardware/software, timing, etc.). Score: 5/5 (Excellent). The game has been developed for a formal education context and may entail online learning. In FRVW the learning curve is low, the interaction mechanism is simple, and pupils can start playing immediately after the initial cutscenes introduce the environment and the game goals. In this SG there is no need for special equipment. The whole session is expected to last about 1 hour and a half so that the game can perfectly fit the school schedule. Particularly noticeable is the FR Journal feature that provides teachers with useful materials for lesson and test planning as well as offers students rich and validated historical sources.
- *Reusability* (capability of the game to be used in different contexts). Score: 5/5 (Excellent). The primary context of usage is the classroom in which the teacher acts as a mediator. However, the game is self-explanatory and provides extensive information through the Help feature, dialogues with NPCs, and inventory resources. Thus, FRVW can be also played by everyone in a private context (e.g. at home or on the web).

- *Motivation* (capability in motivating players to learn). Score: 4/5 (Good). The game is effective in motivating players to learn FR history. This goal is achieved through a role-play mechanism. Narrative assigns the player a specific role within the Fort Ross community. The identification with Vasilii Starkovskii triggers interests in the daily activities of the Ross colony. This feature provides pupils with an insight on the tough life of the early pioneers in America and makes them reflect on how past and present diverge. Furthermore, the game is designed as a pre-visit tool which precedes an actual trip to FRSHP and generates positive expectations and pre-visit knowledge. This seems to be a successful choice because pupils will arrive to FR with their interests already triggered and most likely they will be more eager to acquire first-hand knowledge about the site.
- *Engagement* (capability of engaging users in the gameplay). Score: 3/5 (Average). The narrative of the SG is good as well as the embodiment in the main character. The level of immersion in the game might be improved, especially refining the navigation and limiting the amount of text in the interaction with NPCs. Too much text is likely to interrupt the narrative flow, especially with a young audience. Voice recordings or text-to-speech technique could help to improve the dialog system or make it easier for young users to follow the narrative.

7 Conclusions

The diffusion of SGs and other computer-based scholarly practices in schools, museums, parks, and other cultural institutions can be interpreted as the result of a new trend in contemporary pedagogy which promotes the integration of formal and informal education paradigms, learning-by-doing, digital simulation, narrative-interactive activities, and collaboration between learners.

Our experience in the design and implementation of Fort Ross Virtual Warehouse convinced us to value SGs as suitable tools for teaching history, archaeology, and a variety of humanities-related topics to 21st-century students. Prensky underlines that today's pupils feel an increasing urgency to learn skills and knowledge that are immediately applicable in the real world. This need of immediacy brings students to pay more attention to what is real and practical and not just relevant [33].

The learner-centered paradigm that we used in FRVW promotes a learning-by-doing approach to education. Our method transforms historical serious games in non-mediated learning environments able to communicate validated historical knowledge to an audience of young digital natives as wells as to stimulate cultural awareness about the different constituencies of today's American society. In this paper we have demonstrated that FRVW game is a digital learning tool able to engage the players in a historically accurate training experience developed through role-play, interaction between different cultures, spatial discovery of cultural landscapes, and first-hand access to historical sources. The identification and embodiment of the player in the protagonist Vasilii Starkovskii increases the sense of presence in the historical context. This brings students to ask new questions about events occurred in the 1800s and eventually produces a better cultural awareness of the consequences of the colonization of North America. To promote inclusiveness, the original design of FRVW included 5 player characters/profiles (a Russian clerk, a male Alaskan hunter, a female Native American cook, a Russian Militia, and a Spanish priest) to represent all the ethnicities and genders that interacted in the Ross colony. Due to budget constraints, the current version of FRVW could not include all of these story lines and PCs and was limited to the clerk narrative. Future developments of FRVW include the possibility to improve the SG as follows: implement new player characters and learning activities; reinforce the text-based interaction through text-to-speech technologies; enhance the navigation of buildings and camera controller; redesign the Fort Ross Journal and Help features using web links, hypertext, and multimedia technologies. The upcoming user study will bring new insight on the pedagogical paradigm we employed in FRVW. The data gathered with California students— involved in the Environmental Living Program— will be compared with game analytics and post-game session data collected using FRVW in formal educational sessions. The game evaluations will present to the scientific community qualitative and quantitative data on the value of pre-visit and post visit tools for museums and historical sites. Future assessments will also provide feedback on the usage of SGs in formal educational environments side by side with traditional pedagogical activities.

Acknowledgements. The Fort Ross Virtual Warehouse serious game is a new, enhanced version of Virtual State Parks, a pilot project designed and developed by Elizabeth Prather with the support of Robin Joy Welman and California State Parks representatives and contractors in the early 2000s. The design and implementation of Fort Ross Virtual Warehouse is the result of an interagency agreement between California State Parks and the University of California Merced (Contract: C0221001: Fort Ross Virtual Warehouse Project). Fort Ross Virtual Warehouse was finalized between 2012 and 2013 by a team from the University of California Merced and Duke University. Special thanks are due to Elizabeth Prather, Robin Joy Wellman, California State Parks Staff, the game developer Joe Schultz, the Kunstkamera Museum of San Petersburg, the graphics artist Paul Davey–Mattahan, and the musician Andrei Krylov. Michela Mortara has taken part in the preliminary evaluations of the Fort Ross Virtual Warehouse thanks to the support of the EU NoE "GALA: Games and Learning Alliance", contract n. 258169, FP7-ICT-2009.4.2.

References

1. Prensky, M.: Digital Game-Based Learning, pp. 1–19. McGraw-Hill, New York (2001)
2. Zyda, M.: From visual simulation to virtual reality to games. IEEE Comput. **38**(9), 25–32 (2005). IEEE
3. Forte, M., Lercari, N., Onsurez, L., Issavi, J., Prather, E.: The Fort Ross virtual warehouse project: a serious game for research and education. In: Proceedings of the 18th International Conference on Virtual System and Multimedia (VSMM 2012), pp. 315–322. IEEE (2012)
4. Handler Miller, C.: Digital Storytelling. A Creator's Guide to Interactive Entertainment, pp. 144–148. Focal Press, Burlington (2004)
5. Environmental Living Program. Fort Ross Historic State Park. http://www.fortrossstatepark.org/elp.htm. Internet (May 17, 2013)

6. Lercari, N., Forte M., Onsurez L., Schultz J.: Multimodal reconstruction of landscape in serious games for heritage: An insight on the creation of Fort Ross Virtual Warehouse serious game. In: Proceedings of the Digital Heritage International Congress (Digital Heritage 2013), vol. 2, pp. 231–238, 28 Oct 2013
7. Luccini, A.M., Mortara, M., Catalano, C.E., Romero, M.: D3.2 – Second SG Thematic Field Report – Annex 5 – Humanities and Heritage Field Rep. Restricted Deliverable, The GALA Project (FP7/2007-2013 grant agreement n° 258169) (2013)
8. Mortara, M., Catalano, C.E., Bellotti, F., Fiucci, G., Houry-Panchetti, M., Petridis, P.: Learning cultural heritage by serious games. J. Cult. Heritage, 15(3), 318–325 (2014)
9. Christopoulos, D., Mavridis, P., Andreadis, A., Karigiannis, J.N.: Using virtual environments to tell the story: the battle of Thermopylae. In: Proceedings of 3rd International Conference on Games and Virtual Worlds for Serious Applications (VS-GAMES) (2011)
10. Christopoulos, D., Gaitatzes, A.: Multimodal interfaces for educational virtual environments. In: 13th Panhellenic Conference on Informatics 2009, PCI'09, pp. 197–201. IEEE (2009)
11. Gaitatzes, A., Christopoulos, D., Papaioannou, G.: The ancient olympic games: being part of the experience. In: Proceedings of 5th International Symposium on Virtual Reality, Archaelogy and Intelligent Cultural Heritage (VAST 2004). Eurographics, pp. 1–10 (2004)
12. Doulamis, A., Liarokapis, F., Petridis, P., Miaoulis, G.: Serious games for cultural applications. In: Plemenos, D., Miaoulis, G. (eds.) Intelligent Computer Graphics 2011. SCI, vol. 374, pp. 97–115. Springer, Heidelberg (2012)
13. Remembering 7th street - http://7thstreet.org. Internet (27 May 2013)
14. Frochauer, J., Seidel, I., Gartner, M., Berger, H., Merkl, D.: Design and evaluation of a serious game for immersive cultural training. In: Proceedings of the 16th International Conference on Virtual Systems and Multimedia (VSMM 2010), pp. 253–260. IEEE (2010)
15. Froschauer, J., Arends, M., Goldfarb, D., Merkl, D.: Towards an online multiplayer serious game providing a joyful experience in learning art history. In: Proceedings of the 3rd International Conference on Games and Virtual Worlds for Serious Applications (VS-GAMES) (2011)
16. Froschauer, J., Merkl, D., Arends, M., Goldfarb, D.: Art history concepts at play with ThIATRO. ACM J. Comput. Cult. Herit. 2013 Spec. issue on serious games for cultural heritage, vol. 6-2. ACM, New York (2013)
17. Minett, L., Gavin, C.: The middleton mystery: an adventure at Belsay hall: interpreting heritage through the design and development of a computer game. In: Proceedings of Electronic Visualisation and the Arts (EVA 2008), London (2008)
18. Bellotti, F., Berta, R., De Gloria, A., Cardona, S.: An architectural approach to efficient 3D urban modeling. Comput. Graph. 35-5, 1001–1012 (2011)
19. De Paolis, L.T., Aloisio, G., Celentano, M.G., Oliva, L., Vecchio, P.: MediaEvo project: a serious game for the edutainment. In: Proceedings of 3rd International Conference on Computer Research and Development (ICCRD 2011), vol. 4, pp. 524–529 (2001)
20. Lercari, N.: An open source appoach to cultural heritage: Nu.M.E. project and the virtual reconstruction of Bologna. In: Forte, M. (ed.) Cyber-Archaeology, pp. 125–133. BAR, Archaeopress, Oxford (2010)
21. Lercari, N.: Nuove Forme di Comunicazione per Nu.M.E. (2010). In: Bocchi, F., Smurra, R., (eds.): La Storia della Città per il Museo Virtuale di Bologna. Un decennio di Ricerche nel Dottorato di Storia e Informatica, pp. 217–225. Bononia University Press, Bologna (2010)
22. Forte, M., Lercari, N., Galeazzi, F., Borra, D.: Metaverse communities and archaeology: the case of Teramo. In: Proceedings of EuroMed 2010—Digital Heritage—Short papers, pp. 79–84. Archeolingua, Budapest (2011)

23. Francis, R.: Revolution: learning about history through situated role-play in a virtual environment. In: Proceedings of the American Educational Research Association Conference (2006)
24. Playing History – The Plague. www.playinghistory.eu. Internet (27 May 2013)
25. Chevigny, H.: Russian America: The Great Alaskan Venture, 1741-1867, pp. 43–160. Binford & Mort, Portland (1992)
26. Essig, E.O., Ogden, A., Dufour, C.J.: Fort Ross: California Outpost of Russian Alaska, 1812-1841, pp. 1–71. The Limestone Press, Fairbanks (1991)
27. Fort Ross Virtual Warehouse Project. Guideline 1- Design Document and Specifications for Preliminary Storyboard Layout. California State Parks, pp. 1–20 (2008)
28. Fort Ross Environmental Living Program. Clerks Curriculum. Guideline Document. California State Parks (2008)
29. Franz, J.D.: Fort Ross Environmental Living Program: Survey of Participating Teachers, pp. 5–45. California State Parks and JD Franz Research (2008)
30. History–Social Science Content Standards for California Public Schools, Kindergarten Through Grade Twelve, pp. 1–23. CDE Press, Sacramento, CA (Reposted 23 June 2009)
31. Loscos, C., et al.: The CREATE project: mixed reality for design, education, and cultural heritage with a constructivist approach. In: Proceedings of the 2003 IEEE and ACM International Symposium on Mixed and Augmented Reality (ISMAR 2003), pp. 282–283. IEEE and ACM (2003)
32. Kirschner, P.A., Sweller, J., Clark, R.E.: Why minimal guidance during instruction does not work: an analysis of the failure of constructivist, discovery, problem-based, experiential, and inquiry-based teaching. Educ. Psychol. 41(2), 75–86 (2006)
33. Lercari, N., Toffalori, E., Spigarolo, M., Onsurez, L.: Virtual heritage in the cloud: new perspectives for the virtual museum of Bologna. In: Proceedings of 11th International Symposium on Virtual Reality, Archaeology and Cultural Heritage (VAST 2011). Eurographics, pp. 153–160 (2011)
34. Prensky, M.: Teaching Digital Natives: Partnering for Real Learning, pp. 9–31. Corwin, Thousand Oaks (2010)

Entrepreneurship Competence Assessment Through a Game Based Learning MOOC

Mireia Usart[1(✉)] and Margarida Romero[1,2]

[1] ESADE, Universitat Ramon Llull, 08034 Barcelona, Spain
{mireia.usart,margarida.romero}@esade.edu
[2] Université Laval, Québec, QC G1V 0A6, Canada

Abstract. Massive Open Online Courses (MOOC) are becoming a game changer in the field of Higher Education and lifelong learning. However, the MOOC pedagogical model is almost exclusively a reproduction of the lecture-oriented approach. We introduce a Game-Based Learning approach in a MOOC that aims to encourage entrepreneurship through the use of Serious Games (SG). In this study, we analyse the entrepreneurship skills developed in a Game-Based Learning MOOC (GBL MOOC) according to five assessed activities developed during the course: presentation and participation in a general debate; an entrepreneurial aptitude test; the Metavals SG; the Hot Shot Business SG; and a final questionnaire. The results of the final questionnaire show a good perception of the utility of the GBL MOOC for entrepreneurship studies, and an acceptable overall degree of satisfaction with the use of SGs during the MOOC.

1 The MOOC Opportunities for Lifelong Learning

Massive Open Online Courses (MOOC) have been gaining popularity as an educational model since the first courses were organised in 2008 [1]. MOOCs enable anyone to engage in virtual educational environments and have the potential to provide education on a global scale. Nevertheless, there is still a long way to go before these environments become comparable to other online and in-class university courses, especially in terms of evaluation, personalisation, and certification [2]. Furthermore, students in MOOCs report a high drop-out rate, usually only seven or eight per cent of learners completing courses [3], or tend to leave the course in a few weeks if they are not motivated or interested in the content, due to their life's time constraints.

MOOCs have considerable potential to enable the massive development of knowledge and skills among those adult learners who show enough motivation, self-regulation, and cognitive quality time to engage and succeed in online courses. However, the current MOOC teaching model has mostly reproduced the lecture-oriented approach with very low ratios of teachers per participant. Game Based Learning (GBL) is an active learning methodology that aims to place students at the centre of the learning process. The combination of GBL with MOOC models could therefore enable an increase in engagement rates for MOOCs, together with a more active role for students. In this paper, we propose improving MOOCs by adding a gamification process at two levels: firstly, integrating SGs in the MOOC structure; secondly, introducing competition among students to encourage engagement in the MOOC.

© Springer International Publishing Switzerland 2014
A. De Gloria (Ed.): GALA 2013, LNCS 8605, pp. 252–264, 2014.
DOI: 10.1007/978-3-319-12157-4_20

In this paper, we introduce a GBL approach to the Introduction to Entrepreneurship (IE) MOOC, developed in the context of the Erasmus FP7 Project 'Stimulating Entrepreneurship through Serious Games'. The IE MOOC aims to promote entrepreneurship competence among the adult Catalan population through the use of SG and gamification of the MOOC together in order to help learners engage in the course and reduce the drop-out rates reported. The LORE (www.LORE.com) platform is used to support the design and delivery of the course, focusing on the social interactions of the participants and the course activities. The IE MOOC integrates the use of two SGs, the MetaVals game [4] covering the field of introductory finance, and Hot Shot Business (HSB) [5] which simulates running a small or medium enterprise (SME). This paper focuses on the assessment of entrepreneurship skills in the IE MOOC, and a study of the relations between the entrepreneurship profiles and learner experience in terms of active participation in the discussion space and results of the MetaVals and HSB SGs.

2 Entrepreneurship Competence

Almost all educational stakeholders agree on defining entrepreneurship as an important objective for the 21st century education, but there is no agreement on its characterisation as a skill. While some authors consider entrepreneurship as a competence in itself, other authors consider that entrepreneurship is a set of competencies. Among the authors who defend entrepreneurship as a single competence, Berglann, Moen, Roed and Skogstrom [6, p. 180] accept that there is no consensus on the definition of entrepreneurship; however, these authors accept that entrepreneurs face risks associated with owning a firm. May [7] defines entrepreneurship competence as 'the process of bringing something new into being'. Bygrave and Hofer [8], in the context of business literature, defend a popular view of the entrepreneur as someone who 'perceives an opportunity, and creates an organization to pursue it'.

There are also researchers who describe entrepreneurial competence as a multidimensional construct. Lathi [9] affirms that entrepreneurial competence is the synthesis of knowledge, skills, aptitudes, and personal qualities for the performance of specific professional tasks. Schmitt-Rodermund [10] used measures for leadership, curiosity, and entrepreneurial skills to form a latent indicator of entrepreneurial competence. Researchers focused on entrepreneurship as a set of traits and skills that coincide in some of the competencies an entrepreneur must show, such as creativity and flexibility [11, 12].

Gibb [13] defines entrepreneurship as a set of behaviours, attributes, and skills that enable individuals and groups to create, change, innovate, and cope with high levels of uncertainty and complexity in all aspects of their lives. These competencies can be taught and must be taken into account when designing courses. According to Lazear [12], entrepreneurs need not be expert in any single skill, but must be sufficiently good at a wide variety of skills to make sure that a business does not fail.

In this study, we rely on the existing approach that defines competence as 'a series of desirable attributes including appropriate kinds of knowledge, skills, abilities, and aptitudes' [14] and the definition of entrepreneurship of Bygrave and Hofer [8] as a person who 'perceives an opportunity, and creates an organisation to pursue it'. We also rely on Rae's work [15], who considered entrepreneurship as a contextual process of becoming an entrepreneur, in which the entrepreneur is permanently learning and developing in relation to himself/herself and his/her environment. Based on these approaches, we define entrepreneurship competence as the set of attributes, aptitudes, skills, and abilities needed to act in an entrepreneurial way and so create a context and organisation that generates value.

In the following sections, we will explain how the gamification process and the implementation of SGs in the IE MOOC could help in the training and evaluation of the various entrepreneurship aptitudes, social abilities in terms of participation and pro-activity, and also the skills and abilities such as flexibility, innovation and risk-taking.

3 The IE MOOC Pedagogical Plan

The main objectives of the IE MOOC are to encourage entrepreneurialism, involve participants in a MOOC, and encourage the sharing of knowledge and competition among course participants. The course was designed following an asynchronous learning model, where students manage their own learning time and the pace of their activities – with the only restriction of the time boundaries set by the availability of the MOOC (from May to June 2013). The use of SGs in the course also enabled facilitators to grade student activity [16]. Finally, course facilitators decided to implement a gamification approach in the MOOC to incentivise participation and competition [17] during the course.

To reach the objectives, the IE MOOC was defined as a free online course divided in four topics and guided by two facilitators. These topics aimed to give an overview of basic entrepreneurship skills and tips in the fields of finance and marketing from a basic starting point where participants present their entrepreneurship profile until the final virtual construction of an SME. The first topic was focused on the presentation of each participant and their entrepreneur profile. This topic included a mandatory activity, a presentation in the LORE discussion zone. There were complementary tasks, such as questions on articles and discussions on various videos on entrepreneurship. This topic aimed to help students interact and learn about the LORE platform and the goals of the course. The second topic was focused on the entrepreneur profile. Students had to complete the entrepreneurial aptitude test (TAI) [18] and could also participate in an open discussion on entrepreneurship aptitudes. The third topic focused on financial aspects of entrepreneurship, such as an understanding of basic accounts and financial plans. This topic included the MetaVals SG as a mandatory activity, and facilitators gave different links for further information. Finally, Topic 4 of the course aimed to guide students through the planning and growth of an SME. Among the different games that could help students in the creation of an SME, the facilitators chose Hot Shot Business (HSB) due to its learning time (less than 30 min), its contents on basic entrepreneurship such as marketing and finance, and also because it could be played freely online. SGs used in this course, and in particular, HSB, can be seen as competences-based learning as they are realistic, provide coaching, and are inviting to learn. The authenticity of tasks in these educational setting (types of problems, constraints, information and materials) can lead to better entrepreneurship competence training [19].

In summary, students who aim to pass the course had to complete four mandatory activities and a final satisfaction questionnaire. The pedagogical design and the results of these activities will be further explained in the next sections.

3.1 Gamification of the IE MOOC Assessment

The IE MOOC was designed with a Game Based Learning (GBL) approach to encourage entrepreneurship education from an active learning methodology. The IE MOOC includes two serious games as two of the four learning activities to be developed through the course. From this perspective, the IE MOOC has a GBL approach. In addition, the participation process of the course has been gamified, including all the learning activities. Gamification does not require the use of games, or GBL activities, but the introduction of game design elements in the course. Gamification is defined by Deterding, Dixon, Khaled and Nacke [17] as 'the use of game design elements in non-game contexts'. Following Fishman and Deterding [20], gamification is the art of using game design principles to create a gameful framework for learning and teaching that is not only focussed on scorings and rankings. Gamification, used as a tool for assessment, aims to promote both competition and collaboration among participants [21, 22] and therefore, when applied to entrepreneurship courses, it can be useful for practicing these competencies, added to the training of other entrepreneurial skills such risk management [19]. In the IE MOOC, the scores for the participants are calculated based on the following activities:

(1) Participation: number of contributions to the discussion space.
(2) Completion of the Entrepreneurial Aptitude Test – TAI®.
(3) Total score on the Metavals Serious Game.
(4) Projected net balance in the entrepreneurship game Hot Shot Business.

Participants in the IE MOOC must obtain at least 20 points to pass the course, distributed as follows: 4 points for their presentation as part of Topic 1, and 4 points for completing the TAI; 6 points for playing MetaVals, and 6 more points for playing at least three virtual weeks of HSB. However, as a part of the gamification of the course, a maximum of 50 points could be obtained if participants earn the 30 extra points offered in each of the topics (see Table 1).

3.2 The Use of SG in the IE MOOC

In the present case study, the course can be classified as a GBL MOOC because, apart from the gamification aspect, focused on the evaluation process or assessment of the MOOC, two SGs have also been implemented as part of the pedagogical plan [23]. MetaVals and HSB were chosen to help students safely practice key skills and competences [24] related to the concepts in Topics 3 and 4. Facilitators aimed to show students real applications of the materials and discuss these through active, competences-based learning. The aim was to facilitate SGs where participants could demonstrate, in a practical manner, the competences acquired during their study of the materials.

Table 1. Gamification rules for IE MOOC.

IE MOOC game rules	Description of the game rules
+ 3 points for the person who first answers a post/exercise/etc + 2 points for the second answerer, +1 point to the third −1 point for the last three people to answer (Max. 12 points per participant)	The aim of this scoring is to promote social interaction during the course and minimise procrastination, thus help participants manage their time
+1 point per topic for students who post doubts or share relevant information in the MOOC (Max. 6 points per participant)	Encourage knowledge-sharing among participants and allows students to show their creativity and proactive skills
+ 2 points per topic for participants resolving a doubt or answering a point on a previous message + 3 points if the answer is supported by one or more significant references from the field (Max. 12 points per participant)	Encourages significant knowledge sharing among participants and trains in the skill of risk-taking, as students are invited to answer questions even if they are unsure of the answer

MetaVals game in IE MOOC. MetaVals is a computer-based SG designed by the learning innovation team in ESADE and the SME Ouak [25] in the context of the FP7 Network of Excellence Games and Learning Alliance (GaLA). It is a sorting game where students play in dyads with a virtual peer against the rest of the class. The aim of MetaVals, in the context of the course in Topic 3, is to enable students to practice basic financial concepts such as assets and liabilities. A welcome screen asks players to introduce their age and knowledge of finance. A second screen follows with information about the virtual peer. This key data can help players in the correction and discussion phases (e.g., a virtual peer with a low level of understanding on finance may give wrong answers). After general instructions are given by a virtual guide, the player starts playing individually by classifying six items as assets or liabilities (e.g., 'computer software', or 'bank loan'); after this first phase, six other items appear, but now the player has access to his virtual peer's answers. After this correction phase, a final discussion phase starts; and the player has to decide if the 12 items were correctly classified; the winning pair will have the highest number of correct answers in the quickest time.

HotShotBusiness in IE MOOC. HSB is a web-based, free simulation game designed to teach basic business concepts and encourage entrepreneurship [4]. In the context of MOOC, this SG was implemented as part of Topic 4 to practice the skills and contents concerning entrepreneurship that were presented in the MOOC. This final activity helps students start an SME with the guidance of two virtual characters. Course facilitators prepared a guide for the game to help students understand the concepts before starting the game. These concepts were related to investment, marketing, product and incomes. Students could access the game and play without time restrictions, but facilitators recommended spending at least 45 min or completing six weeks of the SME simulation game. Results of the HSB are not directly accessible to the course facilitators; to obtain the results for each participant, the HSB activity requires the participants to make a screenshot of the balance obtained at the end of each of the three first weeks of running their SME in the HSB game. The screenshots must be posted by each student in the course discussion zone in order to be shared with other participants and be available for feedback by course facilitators.

The decision of implementing both gamification and SGs in the course was mostly due to the need to assure students' participation and active engagement through motivation. There are students that prefer competition, (e.g., business men and adult workers in a competitive ambient). Nevertheless, this could be a necessary but not sufficient condition for engaging enough students. SGs can also be a practical manner to check knowledge acquisition and foster participation. Furthermore, the SGs had previously been implemented in the context of the first year eSG project, without the gamification process; and the researchers aimed to analyze the inclusion of this second ingredient.

4 Assessment of the Entrepreneurship Profile Using the TAI in the IE MOOC

Lazear [12] observed that entrepreneurs need not be expert in any single skill, but must be sufficiently good at a wide variety of skills to make sure that the business does not fail; that is, entrepreneurs must be multi-skilled. Among the various tests for measuring entrepreneurship, we can differentiate among those that measure entrepreneurial intentions or motivation, entrepreneurial behaviour, entrepreneurial styles, and entrepreneurial profile. We focus on the latter, as we aim to study entrepreneurial competences. There are various instruments that measure the profiles of entrepreneurs, some of which are focused on academic entrepreneurs, such Academic Entrepreneurship Questionnaire (AEQ), developed by Brennan, Wall and McGowan [26]; or research-based entrepreneurs. We aim to study entrepreneurship in general, and for this reason we selected the Entrepreneurial Aptitude Test (TAI) – which analyses eight factors and consists of 75 statements.

4.1 The TAI Test for Profiling the IE MOOC Participants

The entrepreneurial aptitude test (TAI) is an instrument that can be used to define aptitude for an entrepreneurial profile [20]. TAI describes entrepreneurial potential with regard to eight factors: goal orientation; leadership; adaptability; need for achievement; need for self-empowerment; innovation; flexibility, and autonomy. The TAI has acceptable metric characteristics and sufficient criteria reliability; as well as presenting significant correlations with career development and entrepreneurial jobs. The TAI has also been used in other courses of the second year of the Erasmus Project 'Stimulating Entrepreneurship through Serious Games' (eSG).

5 Methodology

A total of 76 Catalan adults registered using the public application form for IE MOOC (available in a Google Site). Of these, 45 students accessed the LORE course within the first two weeks, 30 completed the TAI, and finally, 13 completed the four mandatory activities of the course. The 30 active participants during the two weeks of the course were 15 women and 15 men, with an average age of (M = 31.8, SD = 8.7).

The IE MOOC was placed in the open platform LORE (www.lore.com), a web-based Virtual Learning Environment (VLE) that enables 'ICT non-experts' to create a MOOC. LORE looks like a social network and aims to help participants easily interact through this VLE. Topic 1 of the course, entitled 'presentation and discussion', took place in the discussion zone of LORE. Topic 2 was the completion of the TAI, which was accessed through the VLE but placed in a Google form. Access to the two web-based SGs was also achieved via LORE, and participants could interact in the same place. All the materials used in the MOOC were placed in the LORE library zone, and participants could access their profiles in the participants' zone. The design of the MOOC allowed facilitators and researchers to centralise interaction data and trace gamification scores in one environment.

6 Results

In this section, results of the TAI and the SGs are presented – as well as the gamification data for the IE MOOC. Taking this information into account, results are discussed in relation to the scorings of the SGs (MetaVals and HSB) in the context of the IE MOOC, and the global score of the gamification process.

6.1 TAI Results

A total of 30 participants in the IE MOOC completed the TAI. Results were divided into four groups (based on quartiles and media measures). These groups are named in relation to their degree of entrepreneurial aptitude as low, low-medium, medium-high, and high. That is, students in the first group have, on average, little aptitude to become or succeed as entrepreneurs. A detail of the results can be seen in Table 2:

Table 2. Entrepreneurial aptitude scores of IE MOOC participants based on TAI.

	F1*		F2		F3		F4		F5		F6		F7		F8	
	M	SD	M	SD	M	SD	M	SD	M	SD	M	SD	M	SD	M	SD
Total	3.13	0.50	3.14	0.60	3.35	0.50	3.04	0.50	2.65	0.50	3.58	0.50	3.88	0.70	2.84	0.60
Low	2.71	0.23	2.69	0.62	3.21	0.69	2.98	0.41	2.58	0.46	3.33	0.40	3.56	0.82	2.35	0.72
Low-Medium	3.27	0.42	3.11	0.29	3.43	0.46	2.69	0.51	2.33	0.54	3.29	0.56	3.86	0.48	2.95	0.33
Medium-High	3.29	0.50	3.19	0.65	3.33	0.59	3.14	0.59	2.81	0.52	3.81	0.55	3.62	0.65	2.85	0.64
High	3.52	0.50	3.90	0.41	3.42	0.59	3.65	0.65	3.00	0.47	4.12	0.44	4.50	0.38	3.42	0.43

*F1: goal orientation; F2: leadership; F3: adaptability; F4: need for achievement; F5: need for self-empowerment; F6: innovation; F7: flexibility; F8: autonomy.

Results for each factor indicate that students in the IE MOOC score higher in Factors 6 and 7, that is, participants show, on average, high levels of flexibility and innovation. The lowest factors are Factor 5 and 8. Students in the MOOC have less need for self-empowerment and autonomy.

6.2 SG Results

From all students accessing the game (N = 18), 16 completed the three phases of the SG (89 %), and all the students completed the pre-test on finance. Furthermore, 12 of the participants (67 %) also completed the Zimbardo Time Perspective Inventory (ZTPI), a 56-item, 5-point Likert-scale questionnaire that provides a temporal perspective profile of the participant. Results from the pre-test, ZTPI, and MetaVals phases can be accessed in Table 3.

Table 3. MetaVals and students' TP results in the IE MOOC.

Pre-test*		Score phase 1		Time 1 (s.)		Phase2 score		Time 2		Phase3 score		Time 3	
M	SD	M	SD	M	SD	M	SD	M	SD	M	SD	M	SD
2.62	0.5	4.00	1.5	66.5	49.7	4.71	0.9	35.1	24.8	4.12	2.2	46.9	18.4

Age		Past Negative		Past Positive		Present Fatalist		Present Hedonist		Future	
M	SD	M	SD	M	SD	M	SD	M	SD	M	SD
28.2	6.34	2.95	0.66	3.22	0.33	2.73	0.51	3.4	0.61	4.0	0.43

*Results from the pre-test are scored out of 3; phases of the game score a maximum of 6 points (1 for each item to classify)

Results show that all students playing the MetaVals SG had an acceptable level of financial awareness before gameplay; therefore, high-scoring results in the game are expected. From the scorings of the three phases (see Table 3) we can confirm the assumption. Time spent in the game was, on average, less than expected in the design. This could be due to the fact that participants were, on average, future-oriented with a high score for present hedonism; and so preferred to play fast in order to end the game and move on to the remaining activities so they could win the final gamified competition.

If we take a look in detail at assets and liabilities, there are four items that have a high rate of wrong answers from participants: bank deposits and shareholders (outstanding disbursements) were wrongly classified as liabilities instead of assets; and reserves (voluntary or legal) were incorrectly classified as assets. The decrease in time and increase in scoring of phase 2 could be due to the fact that students play against a virtual peer that could be helping them in this second stage of the game (as it is only a correction stage); but hampering their results in the third phase (as they have to reach a consensus). Significant results on time issues should be studied in further detail.

A total of 13 students played the HSB game; four of whom reached the third week of virtual play, and a total of 9 participants finished the 6-week gameplay. The HSB weekly challenges were: week 1 – the simulation begins with a focus on responding to customer needs; week 2 – players see how pricing decisions affect a business; week 3 – the importance of marketing is illustrated; week 4 – the difference between marketing a business and marketing a product or service is shown; week 5 – competition is introduced into the marketplace; and week 6 – learning from the previous five weeks of gameplay is applied. Detailed results can be seen in Table 4:

Table 4. Weekly HSB challenges.

	Week 3								Week 6	
	Rent		Marketing		Loan		Projected net		Final balance	
Group	M	SD	M	SD	M	SD	M	SD	M	SD
Low	1029.25	1305.08	78.13	79.55	110.82	313.25	4975.25	5107.37	45.13	46.33
Low-medium	1437.16	924.14	66.14	50.00	0	0	3210.14	3025.70	29.12	27.45
Medium-high	1132.38	428.00	28.35	10.71	110.82	313.25	2168.38	819.57	19.67	7.43
High	1108.42	515.63	89.86	57.00	0	0	3074.19	2824.75	27.89	25.62

The goal set by the game designers [4] is that players should earn $2,000 in six virtual weeks. As shown in Table 4, all students in the MOOC who played HSB had a better result for the week 6 final balance than the objective set by the designers. Low and low-medium profile entrepreneurs showed the highest final balance results. To analyse student performance in HSB in relation to entrepreneurial skills, data from the third and fifth weeks was studied. Two players asked for a bank loan – one of whom belonged to the medium-high profile entrepreneur group. This can be related to the fact that entrepreneurs are not risk adverse, that is, they prefer financing their start-ups themselves. Furthermore, when looking at the marketing expenses, we can observe that high profile entrepreneurs (M = 89.86; SD = 57.00) spent more marketing than the lower profiles (M = 78.13; SD = 79.55). Finally, we note that the high profile group also spent more time marketing than the other groups.

6.3   Gamification Results

Students in general did not actively participate in the discussion zone during the MOOC, apart from the mandatory activity, where 67 % of the participants performed their task. Among the 12 players, the average score for the 30 possible extra points for the gamification aspect of the MOOC was very low (M = 1.5; SD = 2.9). In the mandatory exercises, where students could have obtained a total score of 30 points, the average was M = 12.6 (SD = 7.2). This can be seen clearly by examining how many participants completed all the activities (N = 13), which is less than 50 % of the total of students who started the course and completed the TAI (N = 30). Finally, among the six students (2 men, 4 women; M = 29.8 years old, SD = 9.5) who scored highly in the course, 50 % could be considered as high-level entrepreneurs according to the TAI results. Furthermore, a student who scored as a low-level entrepreneur was among the winners because she obtained the highest results in the two SGs. On average, winners showed high TAI factors for: flexibility (M = 4.3, SD = 0.5); leadership (M = 3.4, SD = 0.6); need for achievement (M = 3.2, SD = 0.8) and innovation (M = 3.8, SD = 0.7).

Finally, looking at the relation of TAI scores in the IE MOOC with the scorings in the SGs and gamification, we can observe (see Table 5) that students rated as medium-high entrepreneurs scored lower in both SGs and active participation (measured as posts in the discussion space) than the rest of the groups. Furthermore, high aptitude entrepreneurs were the group that scored highest in MetaVals, and participated the most in discussions. Nevertheless, these participants did not succeed in being the best in HSB, where low profile entrepreneurs seem to be better candidates for starting an SME.

Table 5. Scores in SGs and discussion zone for each entrepreneurship group according to TAI.

	TAI Score		Age		Score MetaVals		Score HSB		Discussion space	
Entrepreneurship Group	M	SD	M	SD	M	SD	M	SD	M	SD
Low	86.38	8.53	27.50	4.34	40.97	36.48	40.04	49.04	1.13	0.99
Low-medium	101.57	1.51	43.50	5.54	41.27	40.55	24.97	24.90	2.71	2.06
Medium-high	108.86	15.4	32.29	7.89	20.63	35.39	7.43	19.67	0.71	0.76
High	124.00	7.96	27.00	5.26	47.22	40.06	25.62	27.89	3.00	3.30

7 Discussion

This study presents the design and implementation of an MOOC focused on entre-preneurship. In particular, the aim of the course was to share knowledge on basic entrepreneurial concepts among Catalan adult entrepreneurs. Following Kuratko [27], the core objective of entrepreneurship education must include: skill-building courses on negotiation, leadership, new product development, creative thinking, and exposure to technological innovation. In the IE MOOC, we provide training for these skills; spe-cifically, negotiation and creative thinking in the discussion zone of LORE, in SGs, and incentivised by a gamification process, and designed for leadership skills. According to Lazear [12], entrepreneurs need not be expert in any single skill, but must be suffi-ciently good at a wide variety of skills to make sure that the business does not fail. The inclusion of two SGs has helped participants in the development of different skills such new product development (HSB) and negotiation (MetaVals). The fact that the course was totally developed online could help participants adjust to technological innovation. Facilitators and other participants guide students with doubts (on the platform or the different activities) through the discussion zone. As Guetl and Picker affirm [28], MOOCs can support the exchange of knowledge and ideas – and building a social network and gaining specific expertise are the most important steps before starting a business. In our case study, the low participation rates in the discussion zone could be limiting this exchange of knowledge; nevertheless, the most active profiles showed a high level of engagement and also contacted each other in a Facebook group.

The TAI showed a high degree of flexibility among participants and this has helped facilitators guide the course. Driessen and Zwart [29] believe that entrepreneurial skills such as market awareness, creativity, and flexibility must be taken into account when creating the entrepreneurship course. Moreover, Leadbeater and Goss [11] argue that flexibility is one of the most important skills for entrepreneurs. From the analysis of the results of the TAI scores combined with the scores in the SGs and gamification, we can affirm that students rated as medium-high profile entrepreneurs scored lower in both SGs and active participation than the rest of the groups. This could be due to the fact that lower profiles made a greater effort to improve their initial level and were challenged by the activities. Furthermore, high aptitude entrepreneurs were the group that scored highest in MetaVals and participated the most in discussions – this could be due to their competitive nature and leadership qualities.

Finally, low profile entrepreneurs seem to be better at HSB. This may be because these individuals with these profiles are more eager to learn how to run a SME; and while higher profiles may have more aptitudes it is possible that these aptitudes are unrelated to finance, marketing or clients. Following Gibb [13], entrepreneurial competence must also be measured as knowledge on these issues – and not only skills. Entrepreneurs in the IE MOOC who played HSB obtained a better result for the week 6 final balance than the objective set by the designers – and this can again be related to entrepreneurial competence: students are competitive, they show greater flexibility, adaptability, and are not averse to risk, as they prefer financing with their own funds rather than borrowing from a bank.

Despite the limited sample size, some lessons can be learnt from this case study for an open course for entrepreneurs. The high completion rate in the IE MOOC indicates that implementing gamification in a MOOC may encourage the participation of entrepreneurs, independently of their entrepreneurial aptitudes. The combination of SGs as student-centred activities with the gamification approach could be an engaging context for adult students. Further studies with larger samples and various profiles should be conducted to examine the significance of these results.

Acknowledgements. This study has been developed in the context of the Network of Excellence Games and Learning Alliance (GaLA) and the Erasmus Project "Stimulating Entrepreneurship through Serious Games" (eSG) funded from the European Community's Seventh Framework Programme (FP7/2007-2013).

References

1. Mallon, M.E.: MOOCs. Public Serv. Q. **9**(1), 46–53 (2013)
2. Cooper, S., Sahami, M.: Reflections on Stanford's MOOCs. Commun. ACM **56**(2), 28 (2013)
3. Little, B.: You MOOC, iMOOC. Train. J.**5**, 19–22 (2013)
4. Padrós, A., Romero, M., Usart, M.: Developing serious Games: Form Face-to-Face to a Computer-based Modality, vol. 25. E-learning papers (2011)
5. Everett, J.: Building a business simulation for kids. Comput. Entertainment **1**(1), 1–18 (2003)
6. Berglann, H., Moen, E., Roed, K., Skogstrom, J.F.: Entrepreneurship: Origins and returns. Labour Econ. **18**, 180–193 (2011)
7. May, R.: The Courage to Create, p. 37. Norton, New York (1975)
8. Bygrave, W.D., Hofer, C.W.: Theorizing about entrepreneurship. Entrepreneurship Theor. Pract. (p. 14) **16**(2), 13–22 (1991)

9. Lathi, R.K.: Identifying and integrating individual level and organizational level core competencies. J. Bus. Psychol. **14**(1), 59–75 (1999)
10. Schmitt-Rodermund, E.: Pathways to successful entrepreneurship: parenting, personality, early entrepreneurial competence, and interests. J. Vocat. Behav. **65**(3), 498–518 (2004)
11. Leadbeater, C., Goss, S.: Civic Entrepreneurship. Demos and Public Management Foundation, London (1998)
12. Lazear, E.: Balanced skills and entrepreneurship. Am. Econ. Rev. Pap. Proc. **94**, 208–211 (2004)
13. Gibb, A.: The future of entrepreneurship education – determining the basis for coherent policy and practice? In: Kyrö, P., Carrier, C. (eds.) The Dynamics of Learning Entrepreneurship in a Cross-Cultural University Context. Research Centre for Vocational and Professional Education, University of Tampere, Tampere (1995)
14. Gonczi, A., Hager, P.: The competency model. In: Peterson, P., Baker, E., McGaw, B. (eds.) International Encyclopedia of Education, pp. 403–410. Elsevier, Oxford (2010)
15. Rae, D.: Understanding entrepreneurial learning: a question of how? Int. J. Entrepreneurial Behav. Res. **6**(3), 145–159 (2000)
16. Sadigh, D., Seshia, S.A., Gupta, M.: Automating exercise generation: a step towards seeting the MOOC challenge for embedded systems. In: Workshop on Embedded Systems Education (WESE), Tampere, Finland. ACM (2012)
17. Deterding, S., Dixon, D., Khaled, R., Nacke, L.: From game design elements to gamefulness: defining gamification. In: Proceedings of the 15th International Academic MindTrek Conference: Envisioning Future Media Environments (p. 9), pp. 9–15. ACM (2011)
18. Cubico, S., Bortolani, E., Favretto, G., Sartori, R.: Describing the entrepreneurial profile: the entrepreneurial aptitude test (TAI). Int. J. Entrepreneurship Small Bus. **11**(4), 424–435 (2012)
19. Nab, J., Pilot, A., Brinkkemper, S., Berge, H.T.: Authentic competence-based learning in university education in entrepreneurship. Int. J. Entrepreneurship Small Bus. **9**(1), 20–35 (2010)
20. Fishman, B.J., Deterding, S.: Beyond Badges & Points: Gameful Assessment Systems for Engagement in Formal Education, University of Wisconsin, Wisconsin, Madison (2013)
21. Sheldon, L.: The Multiplayer Classroom: Designing Coursework as a Game. Cengage Learning, Boston (2011)
22. Romero, M., Usart, M., Ott, M., Earp, J.: Learning through playing for or against each other? promoting collaborative learning in digital game based learning. In: ECIS 2012 Proceedings, Paper 93. http://aisel.aisnet.org/ecis2012/93, ISBN: 9788488971548
23. Romero, M.: Game Based Learning MOOC. Promoting Entrepreneurship Education. Elearning papers, no. 33, pp. 1–5 (2013)
24. Mawdesley, M., Long, G., Al-Jibouri, S., Scott, D.: The enhancement of simulation based learning exercises through formalised reflection, focus groups and group presentation. Comput. Educ. **56**(1), 44–52 (2011)
25. Romero, M., Usart, M., Todeschini, T.: A serious game for individual and cooperative learning activities, serious game classification (2011). http://serious.gameclassification.com/EN/games/18150-MetaVals/index.html
26. Brennan, M., Wall, A., McGowan, P.: Academic entrepreneurship: Assessing preferences in nascent entrepreneurs. J. Small Bus. Enterp. Dev. **12**(3), 307–322 (2005)
27. Kuratko, D.F.: The emergence of entrepreneurship education: development, trends, and challenges. Entrepreneurship Theor. Pract. **29**(5), 577–598 (2005)

28. Guetl, C., Pirker, J.: Implementation and evaluation of a collaborative learning, training and networking environment for start-up entrepreneurs in virtual 3D worlds. School of Information Systems, Curtin University (2011)
29. Driessen, M.P., Zwart, P.S.: The role of the entrepreneur in small business success: the entrepreneurship scan. Working paper, University of Groningen (1999)

Evaluation of "Cultural Awareness –
Afghanistan Pre-deployment": A User Study

Alessandra Tesei[1(✉)], Alessandra Barbieri[1],
Ion Roceanu[2], and Daniel Beligan[2]

[1] NATO-STO CMRE, Viale S. Bartolomeo 400, 19126 La Spezia, Italy
{tesei,barbieri}@cmre.nato.int
[2] Carol I National Defence University, 68-72 Panduri Street,
Bucharest, Romania
{iroceanu,daniel.beligan}@adlunap.ro

Abstract. Attention to *human factor* in conducting any type of military operations is an objective of utmost importance in the context of troop training within NATO. To this purpose, a number of serious games were sponsored by NATO and the Ministries of Defence (MoDs) of various nations, addressing different aspects of cultural awareness in approaching human beings during a mission. A significant example is "Cultural Awareness–Afghanistan Pre-deployment", a serious game distributed by UK MoD and widely adopted in Defence Schools to support pre-deployment training of troops in Afghanistan. In the context of GALA, the European Network of Excellence on Serious Games, the Romanian National Defence University and NATO-STO CMRE conducted a user study focused on the learning impact of this serious game. The study was first run in parallel on different typologies of players in order to get different perspectives of evaluation; respective results were then merged and compared to achieve a more complete view, and, hence a better understanding of the advantages and limitations of this type of learning tool.

1 Introduction

Awareness of the importance of *human factor* in conducting military/security operations has strongly increased within NATO in the latest years. The revolution in military affairs, dating from the end of the Cold War, and the technology breakthroughs achieved in a number of different fields, dramatically changed the way NATO considers the role of the human operator in military activities. This is particularly true when military staff is involved in complex socio-technical systems, with their difficult multi-language, multisystem and multicultural contexts, in uncertain and ambiguous environmental and conflictual situations. It is considered that new approaches to military situations, with a focus on human factor, mostly benefit multinational operations and - in particular - Operations Other Than War (OOTW) [1].

Part of the effort of NATO ACT and MoDs of various NATO Nations consists in sponsoring and, in some cases, contributing to develop serious games [2], seen as *learning environments* addressing various aspects of cultural awareness and human

© Springer International Publishing Switzerland 2014
A. De Gloria (Ed.): GALA 2013, LNCS 8605, pp. 265–275, 2014.
DOI: 10.1007/978-3-319-12157-4_21

behavior correctness during various kinds of security missions (e.g., against terrorism, illegal trade of weapons, etc.).

One of selected best practices of game-based training application on this topic is "Cultural Awareness Training - Afghanistan" [3] a serious game sponsored and distributed by UK MoD and widely adopted in Defense Schools to support pre-deployment training of troops in Afghanistan within International Security Assistance Force (ISAF). ISAF's main objective in Afghanistan is to conduct security and stability operations throughout the country together with the Afghan National Security Forces (ANSF). The "Cultural Awareness Training - Afghanistan" game provides a self-paced training environment that generates and develops the cultural competency of trainees, helping them to perform successfully in civil-military operations based on relevant cultural information. Serious Games, unlike entertainment games, necessitates the implementation of specific educational and technical requirements related to peda-gogical constructs, learners' assessment and standardization [4, 5]. To this aim MAN has carried out the implementation of the "Cultural Awareness Training - Afghanistan" on the ILIAS (Integrated Learning, Information and Work Cooperation System) platform of the "Carol I" National University of Defense in Romania [6]. ILIAS is an open source web-based Learning Management System (LMS) which supports learning content management (including SCORM 2004 compliance) and tools for collaboration, communication, evaluation and assessment.

In the context of GALA, the European Network of Excellence on Serious Games [7], the Romanian National Defense University and NATO CMRE conducted a user study particularly focused on the learning impact of this game. Thanks to the interoperability feature implemented by MAN, the user group study could be conducted remotely, in parallel on different kinds of user groups (soldier trainees at MAN, and civilian/military staff at CMRE) in order to get different perspectives in the game test and evaluation. Responses were then statistically analyzed and compared, in order to achieve a more complete and wider view.

This work aims at describing how the user studies were conducted and at presenting and discussing the feedback received by the users through a post-briefing questionnaire.

2   "Cultural Awareness – Afghanistan Pre-deployment" Serious Game

"Cultural Awareness - Afghanistan" is part of a pre-deployment course, the main objectives of which are to train troops (a) to familiarize with the specificities of a mission (in terms of techniques, tactics and risks); (b) to familiarize with the geography of the area; and, above all, (c) to learn the best approach to keep with local people. It was developed in 2007 by LINE Communication, the UK corporate which works very close with the UK MoD for training and education programme. LINE worked with the MoD in identifying authentic scenarios the troops could face, possible cultural factors that could influence them and ways in which service personnel could react. Culture is a subjective issue and our opportunity was to raise awareness and facilitate a behavioural shift rather than teach individual elements of Afghan culture. The course needed to be adaptable; it needed to be available as a pre-deployment desktop resource for classroom based training and for commanders to use with their troops in any environment once deployment had taken place.

In this context the "Cultural Awareness" serious game is intended to help the users to develop and reinforce skills in identifying relevant cultural information, generating decision criteria and selecting alternatives. The skills which can be achieved through the game mainly consist in:

- basic knowledge of Afghan culture, and, more importantly,
- capability of making the best decisions in various scenarios and situations, by using available resources.

The game consists on a first introduction (aimed at providing with background information on Afghanistan geography, population and culture), followed by a set of game scenarios where the players can verify and improve the cultural awareness achieved in the first part.

It integrates audio and visual assistance able to provide the user with useful information and, hence, support feedback and performance assessment. The development concept revolves around adaptable decision-making scenarios and real-time assessment of actions. The student can choose among different scenarios and his/her performance is assessed along the game by showing escalated/decreased state of conflict, depending on his/her personal choices and answers.

It is clear that the first target users for which the game has been conceived belong to military personnel who will perform missions in Afghanistan theatre of operation. However, such training can be extremely useful also for those civilians who have to participate to humanitarian missions with administrative, logistic, or support tasks. Indeed, some of the scenarios included in the game address such kinds of applications.

The major characteristics of the game as a learning environment follow.

- The primary purpose of the game is to help players learn something real about the reality of battlefield, not simply to entertain them.
- In the military field, learning the games rules (which means to accomplish the training task) can be the difference between being dead or alive, to survive and carry out the mission on the battlefield.
- Players are *autonomous*. They need to be free to make decisions. Only a very short pre-briefing on how to access the game through the web and to use the game's man-machine interface is provided at the beginning.
- There are different game scenarios classified according to various types of missions. The scenarios propose possible situations, and solutions to the problems encountered can be found among the theoretical inputs provided in an introduction. The difficulty level increases from scenario to scenario: they need to apply, evaluate or adapt the knowledge/experience background provided in the introduction, depending on the difficulty level of the specific problem [8, 9]. This means that in

the most complicated cases the user cannot directly find the solution in his background knowledge, but needs to associate various factors and, hence, extrapolate/adapt the solution from the whole fund of cultural awareness gradually achieved during the game.

- Users can repeat an action as many times as they want, until awareness is complete.
- Users have the possibility to access available resources (pop-up windows with information in the form of text) while playing, if they have doubts or do not remember some knowledge element.
- The scenarios, situations and tests are presented through a combination of photos, text, and videos with interview to military experts.
- A game characteristic is immediate feedback. Feedback motivates and stimulates action, even when it is negative. Players see the consequences of their actions and receive an instant response if they acted well or not.
- Assessment is given during the game by displaying both the correct answers/solutions, and a conflict indicator:

  - feedback is provided via virtual human presence embedded in the game (videos with short interviews or statements by military personnel actually involved in operations and with profound, direct experience on the field);
  - if the player fails, the culture risk indicator clearly indicates this, and a video explains the related risk.

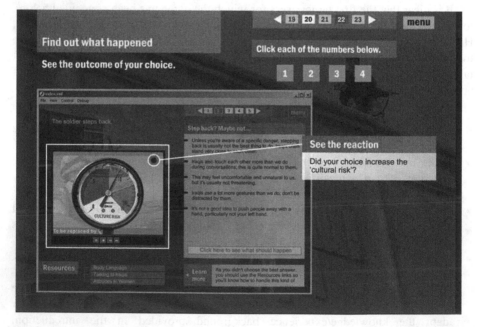

Fig. 1. Snapshot of "Cultural Awareness Training - Afghanistan" game. The cultural risk indicator.

3 Organization of User Studies of "Cultural Awareness – Afghanistan" at MAN and at CMRE

The study was first conducted in parallel on different typologies of players (soldier trainees at MAN; and volunteer players - civilian and military staff - at CMRE). The results of respective analyses were then fused and compared.

3.1 Characteristics of the User Groups

More than 600 MAN users played the game and 60 of them answered the post-briefing questionnaire. They are Romanian students at the National Defense University and other military personnel which will perform missions in Afghanistan.

They are highly *goal-oriented*. This SG is part of their pre-deployment training course, and they usually know what goal they want to attain. Their motivation is high, as players are totally aware that acquired knowledge is crucial for their future missions and will be applied on the field in near future.

Further, they know that learning objectives have to be achieved through their own effort, in order to be of real value to them.

At CMRE 40 users were involved. They are volunteers belonging to the staff. Most of them are civilian Staff, although some military staff volunteered to participate in the test, and the majority of participant are of Italian nationality. Non-Italian participants are nationals of a diversified sample of NATO nations. A They do not expect to apply what learnt immediately to real life. However, they are deeply aware of the problem and might be involved in operations on the field.

In general, they have various degrees of familiarity with military operations from different perspectives. Only a limited number of users (three people) have got first-hand experience on the field.

As an average they have medium experience as video-game players, very low/no experience as serious-game users. Most of them have mid to high technical expertise in modeling & simulation or computing (Fig. 1)

Some information can be retrieved from the data shown in Fig. 2 on the profile of the MAN and CMRE players as a whole group.

3.2 Criteria of Assessment of Game Learning Impact Through User Groups

The procedure for the evaluation of the game through user groups was defined as follows:

(1) Provide users with a quick pre-briefing (only instructions on how to access the game and to use its man-machine interface) either in a classroom or via email.
(2) Let users play on their own.

(3) Ask users to fill an on-line post-briefing questionnaire. Excluding some initial profiling questions aimed at drawing the layer profile and basic knowledge on the topic, all the questions are focused on assessment of the game impact as a learning tool. Most questions expect multiple answers; only a limited number allow open answers.

(4) Collect all local answers (separately at MAN and CMRE) and make local (marginal) statistical analysis.

Share answers between MAN and CMRE, and subsequently compare and merge results. The following subsection presents a summary of most significant results of the global statistical analysis of answers.

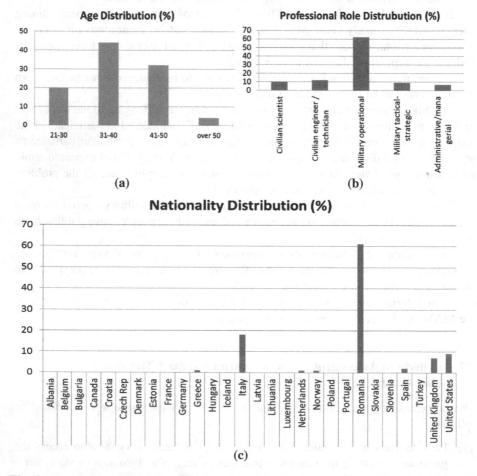

Fig. 2. Description of players' profile, in terms of (a) histograms of age, (b) professional role and (c) nationality (in percentage, over 100 users among CMRE and MAN).

3.3   Statistical Analysis of Evaluation Results

A statistical analysis of the most interesting and significant results of the game evaluation through user groups is presented in this paragraph.

One of the preliminary issues investigated was on previous training experience (through briefings, reading, etc.) on this topic. The great majority of CMRE users had not received any other type of training before, while about one half of MAN users had.

All users believe the information contained in the game correspond to real life situations.

Another important aspect investigated is time scale assessment of learning curve (i.e., time needed to understand how to play the game – excluding the time to go through the introductory briefing) and effective learning time (i.e., total amount of time needed to achieve the game learning objectives – again excluding the time taken to go through the introductory briefing) experienced by a user. As summarized in Fig. 3, answer statistics show that on average the game is extremely intuitive ad easy to use. The effective learning time is also extremely low: this suggests that the game allows an effective use of time and favours quick knowledge transfer.

A number of game characteristics determining its usefulness as a learning tool are then addressed in the questionnaire (see Fig. 4). Attention is particulalry focused on usability, level of immersion and engagement, motivation capability, but also on interactivity level and assessment tools provided.

Again, the game is considered on average very easy to use (which confirms previous results on average duration of learning curve), and very helpful in achieving learning objectives. Level of interactivity is medium, although information resources provided on demand are considered highly valuable. An important result is that the assessment tools provided in the game are very much appreciated; this is a feature of major importance for a serious game devoted to education and training.

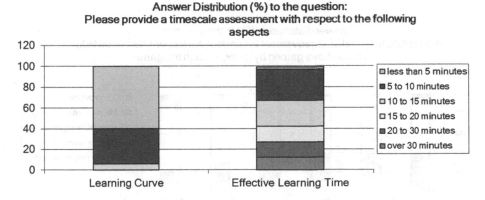

Fig. 3. Users' responses on duration of their own learning curve and effective learning time (in percentage, over 100 users).

Two sets of questions refer to the kind of learning goals users believe to have achieved by completing the game(cognitive learning goals, according to the revised Bloom's taxonomy [8, 9], as well as soft skills). As presented in Fig. 5, users believe to have improved their knowledge at each of the revised Bloom's taxonomy level, up to the top one, i.e., the adapting/creating level. It is particularly interesting that users get this awareness at the end of their game session; in fact an increasing difficulty level, leading the player to pass from mere remembering and understanding to analyzing, is implemented on purpose in the different game scenarios. As expected, evaluation and adaptation/creation learning goals are not considered to be deeply addressed by the game as the lower levels are; this is perfectly coherent with the game goals (Fig. 6).

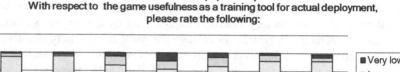
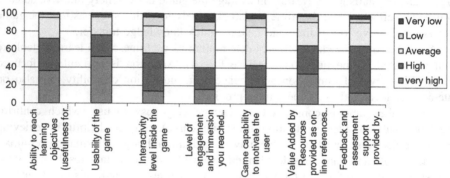

Fig. 4. Users' responses on a set of game features related to its usefulness as a training tool (in percentage, over 100 users).

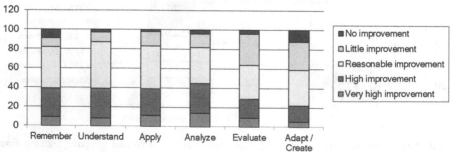

Fig. 5. Users' responses on cognitive learning goals (in percentage, over 100 users), according to the revised Bloom's taxonomy [8, 9].

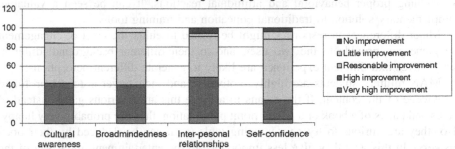

Fig. 6. Users' responses on selected soft-skill learning goals (in percentage, over 100 users).

The same enthusiastic feedback is expressed at average in the case of soft skills: again most of users state to have experienced an improvement (from reasonable to high) in the psychological skills selected.

4   Discussion

A summary follows of most significant feedbacks/responses at the two sites. Some responses are common to the two user groups:

- Great majority of participants at both sites consider this game very useful.
- All considers the topic and content very interesting.
- Most participants believe that the game enables a good knowledge transfer, quicker than other more traditional means (such as books or slides).

At MAN the most interesting results are:

- Most of participants at both sites consider that this game is *very well made*.
- Most believe that the game represents a real support in terms of theoretical training for future deployment.
- Most users state that they were curious to try/test new learning tools.
- Most players state:

    – the interface is very friendly and contains catching audio-visual materials;
    – the content is attractive, with detailed features which enable a good fixation of knowledge.

At CMRE the view is partly different.

- Most judge its man-machine/graphical interface too static, basic and obsolete.
- About one half of them considers the game boring and not immersive at all, and suggests to significantly improve its graphical interface to make it more appealing.
- Feedback and assessment are considered appropriate and successful.

The evaluation is generally very positive, and the SG seems to be well received as a new and modern way for assimilating appropriate knowledge with the purpose of determining proper behavioral and attitudinal reactions. It can be seen a valuable, complementary solution to traditional education and training tools.

Major differences in responses might be related to either the level of engagement the game can provide to the two user, and to their different background: different perspectives and different experience are likely to generate different perceptions.

MAN military students are highly motivated, and their target is to get profound knowledge of the content. If the means to achieve this are a serious game instead of pages and pages of a book or a power point presentation, they are probably very happy; also, they are curious to try new learning tools (as it can be deduced by their open answers). In this way they give less importance to the entertainment/fun aspect of the serious game, usually related to 3D sophisticated and realistic animations and high level of interactivity.

CMRE users seem to have more expectations in terms of technology and entertainment than a strong will of achieving learning goals. Although they are interested in the topic, and wish to achieve some knowledge, they look at (and much weight) the fun aspect of the game as well. Hence, many consider the serious game boring and not efficient enough; these users are generally video-game experts, hence for them using arrows and mouse, possible at the same time, as in a typical 3D, technologically advanced game, is not a barrier. However, they tend to underestimate that the simplicity of its user interface and the low-mid interactivity level very much decrease the game learning curve, and make the game extremely user-friendly for any kind of user, from neophyte to video-game expert.

In conclusion, the richness of information and realism provided through video segments with *interviews to people* really operating in the field seems to be a very clever and successful expedient to:

(1) make the players feel to get in touch with something real and useful for a future deployment,
(2) make users more confident on what they are learning,
(3) contribute to make their effective learning time short.

The *simplicity and lack of refinement of its graphical interface* annoys the most "technological" users, but allows to achieve a very smooth, almost instantaneous learning curve *for all users*, independently from their background as video game players. So, the simplicity of the user interface and of the game engine very much increases the game *usability*. Too refined 3D graphics (implying a certain ability with mouse and keyboard to move in the scenarios and interact with the virtual environment) may be seen as a barrier by non-expert users.

Furthermore, the success and generally positive feedback obtained from this user study applied to "Cultural Awareness – Afghanistan Pre-deployment" seems to suggest the following consideration. After all, the level of fidelity and refinement of the virtual reality created by a game of the latest generation (i.e., generally characterized by refined 3D graphics and sophisticated game engines) is certainly important for the effectiveness of a game, but more important is the *content*, the learning goals selected, the motivation that is transferred to the user. If the content and the information to transfer are too limited, and are not able to convince to be real, a nice 3D graphics does not help. This is particularly valid when the learning objectives are mainly of *cognitive kind*.

This is an important *lesson learnt*: very simple games, but providing clear learning objectives and real-life references, may be very successful even nowadays, even in a field such as security, where very high-tech solutions and extremely refined (but often quite complicated) tools are often pushed and advertised as fundamental features.

Acknowledgments. The authors wish to thank all players who kindly participated and contributed to this user study. This work was partially funded by the ECFP7 GALA Network of Excellence on Serious Games.

References

1. RTO Meeting Proceedings 77: Human Factors in the 21st Century, Paris (2001)
2. http://www.act.nato.int/qboarders-ahoyq-wins-peoples-choice-award-at-iitsec-2010
3. http://www.line.co.uk/wp-content/uploads/2009/11/LINE_mod_ca-afghan3.pdf
4. Breuer, J., Bente, G.: Why so serious? On the relation of serious games and learning. Eludamos. J. Comput. Game Cult. **4**(1), 7–24 (2010)
5. Tang, S., Hanneghan, M., El-Rhalibi, A.: Pedagogy elements, components and structures for serious games authoring environment. In: Proceedings of 5th International Game Design and Technology Workshop (GDTW), Liverpool (2007)
6. Ştefan, A., Roceanu, I., Beligan, D., Tesei, A., Barbieri, A.: Standards in practice: a serious game perspective. In: The 9th International Scientific Conference E-Learning and Software for Education, Bucharest (2013). doi:10.12753/2066-026X-13-120
7. http://www.galanoe.eu
8. Anderson, L.W., Krathwohl, D. (eds.): A Taxonomy for Learning, Teaching and Assessing: A Revision of Bloom's Taxonomy of Educational Objectives. Longman, New York (2001)
9. Krathwohl, D.R.: Revising Bloom's taxonomy. Theory Pract. **41**(4), 212–218 (2002)

Evaluating the Effectiveness of Serious Games for Cultural Awareness: The Icura User Study

Michela Mortara[1(✉)], Chiara Eva Catalano[1], Giusy Fiucci[2], and Michael Derntl[3]

[1] CNR IMATI-Ge, Via de Marini 6, 16149 Genoa, Italy
{michela.mortara,chiara.catalano}@ge.imati.cnr.it
[2] ORT-France, 16, villa d'Eylau, 75116 Paris, France
giusy.fiucci@ort.asso.fr
[3] Advanced Community Information Systems (ACIS),
RWTH Aachen University, Informatik 5, Ahornstr. 55, 52056 Aachen, Germany
derntl@dbis.rwth-aachen.de

Abstract. There is an increasing awareness about the potential of serious games for education and training in many disciplines. However, research still witnesses a lack of methodologies, guidelines and best practices on how to develop effective serious games and how to integrate them in the actual learning and training processes. This process of integration heavily depends on providing and spreading evidence of the effectiveness of serious games This paper reports a user study to evaluate the effectiveness of *Icura*, a serious game about Japanese culture and etiquette. The evaluation methodology extends the set of instruments used in previous studies by evaluating the effects of the game on raising awareness, by avoiding the selective attention bias and by assessing the medium-term retention. With this research we aim to provide a handy toolkit for evaluating the effectiveness a serious games for cultural awareness and heritage.

1 Introduction

There is an increasing awareness about the potential of serious games (SGs) for education and training in many disciplines such as healthcare, military/defense, politics, corporate applications and industry. However, much has still to be done to integrate serious games in the actual learning and training processes. Such integration heavily depends on revealing, providing and spreading evidence of their effectiveness, which is one of the main goals of the European network of excellence GALA [1]: the project explores different application domains in several special interest groups, including humanities and heritage [2].

Cultural content is very diverse: on the one side, there is the physical, or "tangible" cultural heritage such as historic sites and buildings, monuments, documents, works of art, machines, and even the natural environment which represents the setting where a society exists (or existed) and which influences its evolution and customs. On the other side, there are many further factors which deeply characterize a culture and have a non-physical nature, namely the "intangible" cultural heritage.[1] These factors include social

---

[1] http://www.unesco.org/culture/ich/doc/src/01851-EN.pdf

© Springer International Publishing Switzerland 2014
A. De Gloria (Ed.): GALA 2013, LNCS 8605, pp. 276–289, 2014.
DOI: 10.1007/978-3-319-12157-4_22

values and traditions, customs and practices, philosophical values and religious beliefs, artistic expression, language, folklore and rules of behavior in a society, without forgetting the influence of past events on that society. Intangible heritage is particularly difficult to preserve, and we believe serious games have the potential to maintain and communicate effectively especially this immaterial legacy. In fact, they are able to recreate accurately not only a physical setting but rather provide a comprehensive experience including spoken language, traditional music, and aesthetic elements.

An extensive and up-to-date survey on the serious games proposition in the cultural sector is given in [3], which highlights the educational objectives of games, analyzes the complex relations between genre, context of use, technological solutions and learning effectiveness, and finally identifies and discusses the most significant challenges in the design and adoption of educational games in cultural heritage. Above all, the main lack is a formal and methodological assessment of the effectiveness of serious games as learning tools with respect to other traditional means. In fact, the most common approach to analyze the effectiveness of SGs in the humanities and heritage field (but not limited to this domain) is a simple test after the game session (e.g. Playing History [4]) or the comparison of pre and post test results to measure learning effects. The latter approach has been used in a former evaluation of *Icura* [5], Travel in Europe [6], ThIATRO [7, 8] to give a few examples. In some cases, users are split into a group of people who actually play the game (experiential group), and a control group, who learns the same educational content by other means, typically an oral presentation. Users are randomly assigned to avoid allocation biases. This approach allows not only to estimate the game efficacy per se, but also to compare the game learning impact with other traditional teaching methods. Concerning the content of the tests, they typically include direct questions related to the learning content provided by the game.

An interesting issue related to the pre- and post-tests is the so called "selective attention" phenomenon: in the case of *Icura*, the authors in [5] argue that since the pre- and post-tests comprise the same twelve questions, it is possible that "the player may remember those questions and, wittingly or unwittingly, pay more attention to find the correct answers during gameplay". They suggest to change the question ordering or to design a pre-test which comprises several questions that are not actually answered during the game.

The game evaluations often also cover the aspect of user satisfaction, with a set of questions in the post-test focused on the game usability and the user engagement and fun, whereas a deeper analysis of user experience emerge only in those few cases where particular I/O devices are involved (for instance, [9]).

The post-test is always done straight after the experience. According to [10] "games have the power to create this kind of long-term knowledge by connecting the learning content with meaningful actions". However, none of the state-of-the-art serious games evaluated the impact on long-term knowledge.

The educational objectives clearly affect the set-up of a proper evaluation methodology. Specifically, games for humanities and heritage often aim at impact the affective sphere of players beyond communicating knowledge but comprehensive studies including the affective impact are still lacking; the specific impact with respect to different levels of cognitive and affective gain (e.g. following Bloom's taxonomy [11]) should be devised starting from the specific educational goals of serious games.

In the perspective of a complete assessment, this paper contributes with a practical user study: we selected *Icura* as an interesting representative of serious games for cultural awareness, and based our study on the assumptions mentioned above, trying to overcome some limitations of the original evaluation. In the next section, we briefly describe the game features, while major details can be found in [5, 10]. In Sect. 3, the experimental setting is described, while Sect. 4 discusses the experimental results. Finally, Sect. 5 concludes the paper.

2 About *Icura*

Icura is an adventure game released in 2010 by the Electronic Commerce group at Vienna University of Technology. The player embodies an Austrian tourist arriving in Japan for the first time. He has been in contact with his Japanese host through the couch-surfing network and he is supposed to stay at his house. Unfortunately, he did not manage to get his precise address and after his arrival has to find out where exactly his host lives. He has got only a print-out of his e-mail with a few information about the Japanese culture, and then the player has to find his host accomplishing several sub-tasks.

The game takes place in a 3D virtual world representing a fictive isle in Japan. The environment is realistic, as buildings, temples, aesthetic styles and natural landscape are Japanese-style, and a soft traditional music plays in the background. Playing the game and exploring the environment, the player learns about Japanese culture and etiquette, which can either raise cultural interest or support a real pre-trip planning. To make a few examples, the player has to learn about *tsutsumi*, the art of gift-wrapping; to manage the right salutation for each kind of person; or to follow the adequate behavior in a syncretic temple.

From the technological point of view, the game was developed using the Torque Game Engine Advanced, an open source system offering support to the creation of 3D models, graphics, sound and light effects for games and simulations. It runs on Windows with no special system requirements. It is single player with no social mechanisms; the learning curve is quick and the player is typically operative in less than 5 minutes. The effective learning time for a first-time player is typically less than one hour. The player engagement is maintained by eye-catching graphics, clear sub-goals, the final score sheet, and the Information Agent (IA), a kind of virtual tutor who provides information, hints and feedback avoiding the player to get stuck in the game. The target audience of the game is the general public, there are no knowledge pre-requisites to playing the game.

From the pedagogical point of view, the adventure genre and the 3D setting are suitable for implementing the constructivist and the learning-by-doing models: the 3D immersive environment represents a tangible learning context where the player can actively build his/her own knowledge through exploration, manipulation and interaction. The learning content is organized into small units related to sub-tasks, from simple to complex. In order to fulfill tasks the player has to interact with non-player characters (NPCs), gaining new knowledge and applying it to solve puzzles and advance in the game. Some subtasks require to combine objects or use objects in the scene (e.g. use the steam from a teapot to take a sticker off a wallet).

The game is complemented by a pre- and a post-test: 12 multiple choice quiz questions about Japanese culture are asked before and after the game session. The entry test is a measure to determine the player's level of preliminary knowledge but does not serve to personalize automatically subsequent gameplay. After the session, the player receives a final score and a short summary displaying the wrong answers from the post-test and the time taken to complete the game. Both the final summary and the feedback provided by the Information Agent during the game follow the reflection principle: Sheng et al. [12] point out the importance of including an opportunity for the players to stop and think about what they are learning.

A first evaluation of the game effectiveness and of the user satisfaction with the game have been reported by the developers themselves in [5]. *Icura* has been evaluated at Vienna University of Technology involving 20 people aged between 21 and 43 years, mostly expert gamers. The evaluation was carried out in five steps: a pre-questionnaire collecting demographic data and user proficiency with computer games; the pre-test assessing the starting level of knowledge about Japanese culture; the game session; the post-test with the same questions as the pre-test to assess improvement of knowledge about Japanese culture; a post-questionnaire to determine the overall satisfaction with the game. They found that, on average, 5.05 correct answers were given in the pre-test against an average of 10 in the post-test, concluding that *Icura* successfully communicates information about Japanese culture and etiquette.

3 Experimental Setting

In the present study we aimed to go beyond the previously existing evaluation with respect to three issues. First, we wanted to address a higher number and higher diversity of study participants and avoid the selective attention bias. Second, we wanted to evaluate to what extent *Icura* is capable of transmitting higher level knowledge rather than just information and to actually raise interest in Japanese culture at affective level. Finally, we also mention preliminary results about the assessment of medium-term retention.

3.1 Target Population

In order to increase the number of *Icura* players, we took advantage of the GALA network to attract a wider group of participants. However, since the game is designed for the public at large, we also paid attention to include players beyond the university context, but who can identify themselves with the main character (i.e., a young man travelling by couch-surfing). We were able to attract 61 volunteer players to participate in this evaluation study: 27 from CNR-IMATI Genova, 17 from RWTH Aachen University, and 17 from ORT FRANCE, Paris. One person did not complete the tasks assigned.

3.2　Design of the Evaluation Procedure

As the developers of *Icura* pointed out in [5], the pre- and post-tests included the same questions, and they tried to counteract the selective attention bias by presenting them in a different order in the post-test, which was useful to some extent but could not completely exclude a bias. As an alternative, they also suggested including many irrelevant questions in the pre-test (questions which will not get an answer in the game) so that the player is unable to focus his/her attention on searching for specific answers [10]. Instead, our strategy was to use different questions in the pre-test. Therefore, new pre-test questions were designed just to identify each participant's average knowledge of the Japanese culture and have the same complexity of those of the post-test. We are aware of losing the chance of directly comparing the correct answers from the pre- and post-tests; however, a relevant increase has been already proved by [5]. We argue that this approach is reasonable because our aim was not just assessing a quantitative measure of the increase of knowledge but also to evaluate whether higher-order knowledge was transferred and whether the game was successful in raising awareness about the Japanese culture.

To achieve this aim, we defined questions with respect to the expected educational goals with reference to the different levels of the Bloom's taxonomy [11], which is a classification of learning objectives organized into three "domains": Cognitive, Affective, and Psychomotor. Each domain includes different ordered knowledge and skills levels. The learning objectives of *Icura* can be recognized in the Cognitive and Affective domains. The levels in the Cognitive domain are: Remembering, Understanding, Applying, Analyzing, Synthesizing and Evaluating. Accordingly, the expected learning outcomes are that the learner simply remembers data, or understands information, or, at higher levels, is able to apply the new knowledge, decomposes concepts to understand their structure and relations, builds a structure or pattern from diverse elements and eventually makes judgments about the value of ideas or materials. Categories in the Affective domain are: Receiving phenomena, Responding to phenomena, Valuing, Organizing and Internalizing values. Students reflect such levels of affection when: they show interest in the topic being taught; actively participate and show motivation; attach values to the educational messages, organize these values solving conflicts among contrasting ones into a unique value system; and finally internalize these values, behaving accordingly.

We matched the educational objectives of the game against the Bloom's taxonomy and investigated proper ways to assess the learning impact with respect to the specific levels of cognitive/affective gain each objective refers to. In Table 1 an excerpt of our approach is shown. In collaboration with the game developers, we mapped each intended learning goal with a set of expected outcomes, each one related to a specific level in the Bloom's taxonomy. The assessment of each expected learning outcome is made accordingly: multiple choices questions for outcomes related to Cognitive/Remembering level; open answers about outcomes related to higher Cognitive levels; observation during the whole session, interviews and open answers for outcomes related to the Affective domain.

Table 1. Educational objectives of *Icura* matched against Bloom's taxonomy.

Learning goal	Type of learning	Expected learning outcome	How to assess
Learn about the Japanese culture and etiquette	Cognitive (Remembering)	The learner remembers the Japanese word for "gift-wrapping"	*Multiple-choice (MC) Question: Who or what is "Tsutsumi"?*
		The learner remembers the Japanese word for say "hello"	*MC Question: How do you say "Hello" in Japanese?*
		The learner recalls the most popular religions in Japan	*MC Question: Which religions are prevalent in Japan?*
	Cognitive (Understanding)	The learner understands that saying "no" is impolite	*MC Question: What do you have to keep in mind when talking to a Japanese man or woman?*
		The learner understands that keep off shoes is a sign of respect	*MC Question: When you are invited as a guest in Japan, what do you have to keep in mind?*
	Cognitive (Applying)	The learner is able to use the correct salutation	*Accomplishment of the game task and MC Question: You are going to talk to a senior person named Shotaro and you want to show high respect for him. Which salutation is best to choose in this situation?*
	Cognitive (Analyzing)	The learner is able to identify the main characteristics of the Japanese culture	*Open Answer (OA) Question: How would you describe in 3 adjectives the Japanese culture?*
	Cognitive (Synthesizing)	The learner is able to generalize and deduce new facts about the Japanese culture	*OA Question: What can you deduce from the facts you learnt in the game about the Japanese culture?*
	Cognitive (Evaluating)	The learner is able to compare the Japanese culture against his own	*OA Question: How would you compare the Japanese culture to the Western?*
Raise awareness about the Japanese culture	Affective (Responding to phenomena)	The learner shows new interest towards the principles of the Japanese culture and behavior, he is willing to respond and take the questionnaire, and even to find out more by himself	*Observation during the experience; Likert question: The game is able to motivate the user on the learning topic; OA Question: Did the game increase your interest towards Japan/Japanese culture? Would you read more about Japan? Would you visit it?*

(Continued)

Table 1. *(Continued)*

Learning goal	Type of learning	Expected learning outcome	How to assess
	Affective (Valuing)	The learner identifies positive (or negative) aspects in the Japanese culture and behavior (with respect to our own culture)	*OA Questions (if the respondent spontaneously assign positive/negative connotation): How would you describe in 3 adjectives the Japanese culture? What can you deduce from the facts you learnt in the game about the Japanese culture? How would you compare the Japanese culture to the Western?*
	Affective (Internalizing values)	He changes his mind about japan, and maybe now he wants to apply some behavior in his own life or he would like to visit Japan.	*OA Question in the long-term post-test: Did you take any concrete action to explore further the Japanese culture? If so, which?*

3.3 Assessment of Medium-Term Retention

The authors in [5] identified the lack of evaluation of long-term retention as the major open issue in their work. The evaluation took place right after the game session, while they expressed the wish to repeat the test after one year or later.

For the sake of this paper we repeated the post-test questionnaire after 6 months approximately since the game session, leading to a medium-term analysis of retention. We did not send out the post-test as it was but rather added new open questions to assess whether the game has really influenced the players' perception of Japan and whether they actually put in practice what they previously declared to (e.g., whether they have recommended the game to a friend, or whether they have looked for more information about Japan). We were able to collect 16 answers so far.

4 Experiment

Different evaluation sessions were conducted in Genova, Paris and Aachen in the period from December 2012 to April 2013. When all players had the game installed on their computers, the instructor briefly introduced the game controls, i.e. how to move the player character, what actions the mouse clicks perform, and similar hints that do not reveal anything about the objective or solution to the game. Players played on their own or in couples, depending on the number of the available computers. In the following, we report about the demographics of the participants and we summarize the results coming from the different phases of the experiment: the multiple-choice questionnaires before and after the gaming session (pre- and post-tests), the questionnaire with Likert scaling about game analysis, and the open questions about the affective impact of the game.

4.1 Demographics

In total 61 volunteers participated in the evaluation sessions. The participant sample consisted in 24 university students (39 %), 11 teachers (18 %), 15 researchers (25 %) and 11 individuals with other profiles (18 %), ageing from 21 to 67 (mean = 32,8). 19 players were female (31 %) and 42 were male. About their gaming expertise, 15 % declared not to play any digital games; 54 % consider themselves casual gamers; 26 % play games regularly and only 5 % are hard-core gamers.

The mean level of familiarity with Japanese culture was rated at 1.88 on a Likert scale from 1 (poor) to 5 (excellent), indicating rather poor familiarity on average. The level of interest in Japanese culture was rated slightly higher (mean = 2.95) on the same scale. Two participants were Japanese.

4.2 Pre and Post Tests

Considering the 60 users who completed both pre- and post-tests, we can report an average of 7.36 out of 13 correct answers in the pre-test and 10.81 out of 13 on the post-test, with an average increase in the number of correct answers from the pre- to the post-test of 3.63 (see the histogram in Fig. 1). However, such data cannot reasonably be directly correlated to learning gain since the questions in the two tests were different.

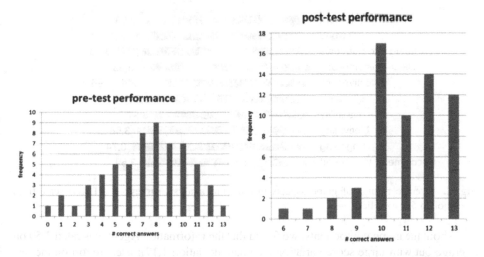

Fig. 1. Pre-test and Post-test performance

As expected, there was a positive correlation between the ratings of familiarity with Japanese culture and the number of correct items scored in pre-game test. However we note how the higher increase was achieved by students with the lowest previous knowledge or interest in Japan: 15 players answered correctly to less than 6 out of 13 questions in the pre-test (average of 3.6 correct answers). In the post-test, those users reached an average of 9.73 correct answers (average increase of 6.13). No participant scored worse in the post-test than in the pre-test. In the light of the rather moderate interest in Japanese culture as obtained in the pre-game survey, this is an encouraging result. Therefore, we can confidently support conclusions in [5, 10] about *Icura*'s educational potential.

Observing the participants during the game sessions, the instructors noticed high interest and motivation, the participants remained very focused even in those cases when they played in pairs and evidently had fun: some mentioned that it was fun because of the resemblance of the experience with "Monkey Island" (cited in the game dialogues). They were also motivated on the learning topic: for instance, students asked to know the correct answers to the pre-test.

4.3   Game Analysis Survey

The game analysis survey administered after the playing session focused on two aspects (see also Fig. 2): first, the factors that, according to the players, contributed most to determine the learning impact ("Rate how much you feel the following components helped you learning the educational content of the game"); second, the evaluation on a five point scale of the dimensions: effectiveness, efficacy, usability, ability of the game to motivate on the learning topic, and engagement. Finally, we asked if the respondent would recommend the game to a friend.

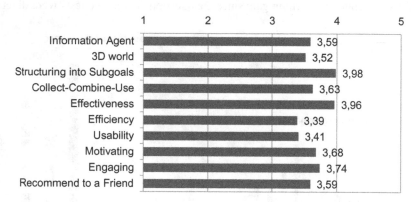

Fig. 2. Average ratings of game aspects in the game analysis survey on a Likert scale from 1 = poor to 5 = excellent.

About the game components, we found that the Information Agent was rated 3,59 on average but with large score variation (standard deviation 1,17): users report on the one side that it is helpful in avoiding deadlocks, on the other side it interrupts the flow and the text was very small. The comments provided with the rating indicate that many participants "did not pay much attention" or felt that the instructions by the agent were not clear.

The structuring of goals into sub goals was rated most helpful (mean = 3,98), and appreciated the collect-combine-use mechanism of interaction with objects (mean = 3,62) to solve quests – they were aware they effectively learnt from that mechanism. However, carrying out the combine operation by selecting one object and then right-clicking on the other one was considered cumbersome (this is reflected in a low score in usability).

Feedback about the 3D world and the usability were highly diverse (mean = 3,51 and 3,40, respectively, standard deviation = 0,96 for both), evidently depending on users' level of expertise with playing digital games. Mid-core and expert gamers rated the 3D world very positively (e.g. "it looks nice" and "immersive and authentic"). They felt the game was quite basic with simple rules, easy and with low cognitive load. They found the tasks very easy and suggested to have a longer version, adding tasks not strictly related to educational content and including reward videos which could give more insights on the Japanese culture. Many would have preferred to listen to dialogues (and not just to read them) in order to understand the right pronunciation of Japanese terms. Interestingly, some would appreciate the serious game as a massive multiplayer online experience, which would foster a wider diffusion, and some others wish increased realism through replicas of real geographic locations.

The overall feeling of the participants who seldom play digital games (including the majority of teachers participating in the Paris session) was that the 3D did not facilitate the learning since movements were difficult. They suggested a 2D setting instead, "maybe a point and click type 2D game would even be more suitable for the learning purpose". Some teachers suggested to add more content and to have more learning objectives.

All the profiles however found not intuitive the combine action. Overall, they noticed a good balance between learning and fun and they enjoyed the game.

The effectiveness of the game to reach the learning objectives was rated very positively with the highest average rating of 3,96 and lowest standard deviation (0,82). Participants responded that the game helped them learn about Japanese culture and some Japanese words through the dialogues and interaction with the game; they became aware of the main information a person should know when first going to Japan and acquired some cultural and language skills through the game.

The efficiency was rated lower at 3.38. In the post-game survey many participants noted that the game would be improved if there were more "useful information" during the gameplay, and having "more hints" available. Some explicitly mentioned the walking around as a major source of frustration since the "walking distances [...] unnecessarily increase the time spent" with the game. During the gaming session it was evident to the instructors that many participants had troubles with understanding the game instructions and controlling the interactions in the collect-combine actions, for example, "how to wrap the present". Not surprisingly then, the usability was also rated moderately with a mean of 3.40. The motivating aspect, that is, the game capability of raising interest in the learning topic was rated fairly with an average of 3.67 as well as and the level of engagement in the gameplay (3,74). Only 9 participants would not recommend the game to a friend. Finally, as evident from Fig. 3, players mainly regard

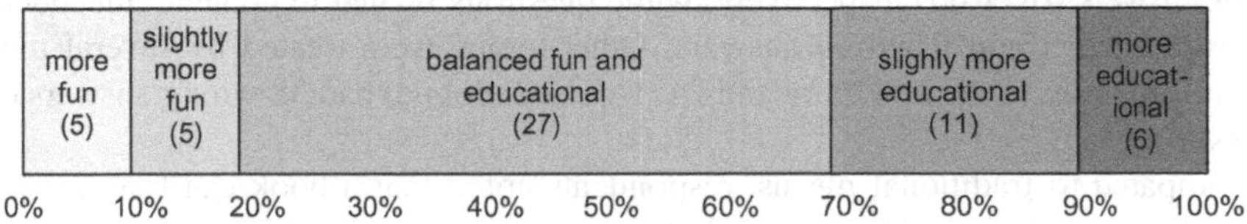

more fun (5)	slightly more fun (5)	balanced fun and educational (27)	slighly more educational (11)	more educat-ional (6)

0%   10%   20%   30%   40%   50%   60%   70%   80%   90%   100%

Fig. 3. Perception of balance between fun and education in the game

Icura as well balanced between education and fun, with 17 participants leaning more towards educational and 10 participants leaning more towards fun.

4.4 Higher-Level Knowledge Assessment

From the perspective of Bloom's taxonomy, the responses to open-ended questions eventually show that the players were able not only to remember and apply new knowledge by solving the required tasks, but could also analyze and synthesize concepts about the Japanese culture: they describe it as "traditional, polite, formal" and from what they learnt in the game they deduce "it is a culture based upon respect", "ceremonial", "it is based on deeply established traditions and people are willing to preserve them". At Evaluation level, they were able to compare Japanese and western traditions that are perceived as definitely different and more flexible: "the Japanese culture seems to me more balanced and calm, while the western is more future-oriented and dynamic". At Affective level, the game reinforced the idea of a real visit in those already fascinated by Japan (one actually spent holidays in Japan after the session), while did not impact those with low interest; however, all were able to attach values to the Japanese behaviour they were exposed to ("the Japanese culture always pays attention to the preservation of the past and of traditions, while the western risks to lose the precious lessons from the previous generations"). We can conclude that *Icura* effectively stimulates higher-level knowledge and has impact at the affective level.

4.5 Discussion

Generally, the level of satisfaction is related to the ability of the players in games: casual/mid-core gamers appreciated *Icura* more than non-gamers, who had to concentrate on the 3D environment and interaction first, and hard-core gamers, who found the game to be too simple.

From the conducted analysis we also get some evidence about what is the most effective mechanisms to trigger learning. In *Icura* learning is facilitated by one or more of these modalities: through information given by the Information Agent; through information given within dialogues with NPCs; through information given by textual resources in the inventory; and through educational content embedded as sub-tasks. Coupling each multiple-choice question in the post-test with the modalities the corresponding information is conveyed in the game and looking at the number of correct answers for each question, we can conclude that the Information Agent was actually the least effective means, while facts related to sub-tasks were highly successful. In fact, five questions about data given just by the Information Agent got 13, 24, 11, 31 and 4 wrong answers (over 60) respectively, while questions related to content embedded as sub-tasks rated 2 and 0 wrong answers. Other topics were treated by several means (e.g., information in the inventory and IA, IA and dialogue) had 38 wrong answers over 6 questions.

Compared to traditional means, respondents noted that a book can transmit more information in a direct, quicker way, but the game lets you experience things in a fun way, and this aspect may make the difference in the long-term retention ("it is so fun it is impossible to forget"); interestingly, they noted that engagement makes the game the perfect tool when the learning/training has to be repeated over time. Teachers involved in the Paris session generally agreed that the game is better and more visual compared to other traditional educational tools like books and videos. They were also homogenous in thinking that the game has to be complemented with traditional education in a blended learning approach. An idea of complementing the game was also to invite some Japanese descendant into the classroom.

Concerning the medium-term retention, from the limited feedback we collected so far, we can observe that the average number of correct answers for those people only slightly decreased (from 11,5 to 10.18). Individually, three people did not change their scores and two people even increased their correct answers, while the other eleven respondents got a lower score than in the post-test. The question causing most errors was "how to say 'yes' and 'no' in Japanese" (11 errors over 16 respondents), a notion transmitted in the game by the Information Agent only. Questions about topics addressed both by the Information Agent and within dialogues witness a decrease of 3–4 correct answers. The two questions having no decrease in score are related to tasks in the game (the right behavior when entering a temple or paying a visit to a private house). Our impression is that a game can considered comparable with traditional means when transmitting textual information, while it reaches its full potential when exploits the interaction capabilities proper of this medium.

Concerning their change of attitude, 10 respondents over 16 declared the game did increase their interest in Japan, and of those, 3 did concrete actions due to the game play (i.e., they looked for more information about Japan on their own). Almost everyone declared to have recommended the game to a friend.

5   Conclusion

In this paper, we presented a user study of a serious game belonging to the cultural awareness category where we gave a more extensive evaluation of the learning impact with respect to the state-of-the-art. The evaluation methodology was extended in multiple ways: we involved more players; we designed a slightly different experimental setting to overcome the selective attention bias and to assess both cognitive and affective gain; and we tackled the question of assessing medium-term effects and retention. Currently, the collection of medium-term data is ongoing; however, preliminary results are encouraging.

In the challenging perspective of conceiving formal methods to assess the learning impact of serious games, we have shown evidence of the limitations of using just pre- and post-game questionnaires; a complete analysis of game effectiveness for topics related to cultural awareness has to include the evaluation of higher level knowledge and impact at affective level, since those cognitive levels are the most peculiar ones of such applications. In fact, the main goal of *Icura* was to inform about the Japanese culture to stimulate curiosity and even a visit in the country.

Moreover, the outcome of our evaluation proved experimentally that the vantage point of serious games with respect to traditional learning means is the direct interaction of the learner/player with the learning material. It appears evident, and confirmed also by the explicit players' opinion, that game mechanics play a crucial role: the educational objectives should be embedded as game tasks and not simply transmitted by textual information. To understand deeply the relation between specific design choices and learning effectiveness ad hoc games have to be deployed, where different features can be turned on and off to be tested with a randomized control trial.

Finally, in the perspective of the learning evaluation, we believe that it is key to identify all the educational goals unambiguously from the early stages of the game design, both the specific target knowledge and the intangible values such as raising awareness and supporting motivation. This will drive, not only the suitable game mechanics to transmit the different levels of knowledge to the players, but also the definition of the data to be collected, of the proper analysis tools and consequently of the suitable learning metrics for the following phases of the game evaluation.

Acknowledgments. This research was supported by the European Commission in the Seventh Framework Programme Network of Excellence "GALA: Games and Learning Alliance" (http://galanoe.eu), contract no. 258169, FP7-ICT-2009.4.2. The authors thank Dieter Merkl for his support and Josef Froschauer for his collaboration in classifying *Icura*'s educational objectives and all the participants to this user study.

References

1. EU NoE GALA – Games and Learning Alliance - contract n. 258169, FP7-ICT-2009.4.2. www.galanoe.eu
2. Mortara, M., Bellotti, F., Berta, R., Catalano, C.E., Fiucci, G., Houry-Panchetti, M., Petridis, P.: Serious games for cultural heritage: the GaLA activities. In: VAST 2011: International Symposium on Virtual Reality, Archaeology and Intelligent Cultural Heritage. Prato (FI), Short and Project Papers, pp. 69–72, October 2011
3. Mortara, M., Catalano, C.E., Bellotti, F., Fiucci, G., Houry-Panchetti, M., Petridis, P.: Learning cultural heritage by serious games. Elsevier J. Cult. Heritage. doi:10.1016/j.culher. 2013.04.004 (in press)
4. Playing History website. http://www.playinghistory.eu/front
5. Frochauer, J., Seidel, I., Gartner, M., Berger, H., Merkl, D.: Design and evaluation of a serious game for immersive cultural training. In: 16th International Conference on Virtual Systems and Multimedia (VSMM), pp. 253–260 (2010)
6. Bellotti, F., Berta, R., De Gloria, A., D'Ursi, A., Fiore, V.: A serious game model for cultural heritage. ACM J. Comput. Cult. Herit. **5**, 4 (2012)
7. Froschauer, J., Merkl, D., Arends, M., Goldfarb, D.: Art history concepts at play with ThIATRO. ACM J. Comput. Cult. Herit. **6**(2) (2013) (to appear)
8. Froschauer, J., Arends, M., Goldfarb, D., Merkl, D.: Towards an online multiplayer serious game providing a joyful experience in learning art history. In: Third International Conference on Games and Virtual Worlds for Serious Applications (VS-GAMES) (2011)
9. Seidl, M., Judmaier, P., Baker, F., Egger, U., Jax, N., Weis, C., Grubinger, M., Seid, G.: Multi-touch rocks: playing with tangible virtual heritage in the museum - first user tests. In: VAST 2011: International Symposium on Virtual Reality, Archaeology and Intelligent Cultural Heritage. Prato (FI), Short and Project Papers, pp. 73–76, October 2011
10. Froschauer, J.: Serious Heritage Games: Playful Approaches to Address Cultural Heritage. Ph.D. Dissertation, Faculty of Informatics, Wien University of Technology, May 2012

11. Bloom, B.S., Engelhart, M.D., Furst, E.J., Hill, W.H., Krathwohl, D.R.: Taxonomy of educational objectives: the classification of educational goals. Handbook I. Cognitive Domain, Longmans, Green, New York (1956)
12. Sheng, S., Magnien, B., Kumaraguru, P., Acquisti, A., Cranor, L.F., Hong, J., Nunge, E.: Anti-phishing phil: the design and evaluation of a game that teaches people not to fall for phish. In: 3rd Symposium on Usable Privacy and Security (SOUPS '07), pp. 88–99. ACM, New York (2007)

Beyond Gambling Temptations:
An Experimental Design Project to Detoxify Players from Irresistible Illusions of Gambling

Annamaria Andrea Vitali$^{(\boxtimes)}$, Margherita Pillan, and Pietro Righi Riva

Politecnico di Milano, Via Durando 38/A, Milan, Italy
{annamariaandrea.vitali,margherita.pillan,
pietro.righi}@polimi.it

Abstract. Last years have seen an increase diffusion of gambling in Italy: Italian population in 2011 spent around 80 million of euros playing games of chance [1], in spite of economic crisis. The increasing offer of gambling is partly tied to the increasing number of pathological gamblers. This paper aims to apply a design perspective - usually common in game design researches - on gambling interactive experience, understanding how games of chance are structured and how they are related to cognitive errors and superstitions that occur both in frequent or infrequent gamblers. As a first theoretical result we outlined an initial rhetoric framework of gambling, connecting cognitive errors and superstitions to the design and interactive attributes of games of chance, and supported by former researches in the field. Secondly, we suggested an experimental application of our approach suitable for further researches: a set of digital interactive artifacts, as serious games, providing meaningful gambling experiences and intended to lead players towards a new consciousness about their approach to games of chance.

Keywords: Gambling · Pathological gambling · Meaningful play · Play rhetoric · Interaction design · Games of chance

1 Introduction: Research Process and Objectives

The word gambling defines all that games in which players bet money on uncertain event they can't control, as for example roulette, dice, slot machine, et cetera. Games of chance fall under Caillois' category of *alea*. With this term Caillois designated "all games that are based on a decision independent of the player, an outcome over which he has no control, and in which winning is the result of fate rather that triumphing over an adversary" [2]. In gambling players are all at the same levels: none can prevail over other players for his skills or abilities, as instead it happens for skill games.

Despite this clear definition, according to existing literature in the field [3], gamblers believe it is possible to find strategies, rules and indicators to foresee the result of a draw even if it relies on chance: gamblers play as they are playing a skill game. This inappropriate approach to gambling is due to the fact that games of chance are designed to hide chance and the independence of bets, as stated by Ladouceur [4]: players are induced by games features to believe they can increase their skills

© Springer International Publishing Switzerland 2014
A. De Gloria (Ed.): GALA 2013, LNCS 8605, pp. 290–303, 2014.
DOI: 10.1007/978-3-319-12157-4_23

continuing gambling. When this perception prevails over any other emotions, pathological behavior may arise in vulnerable player, the pathological gambling, defined in DSM-IV [5] as a persistent and recurrent maladaptive gambling behavior, characterized by several symptoms: gamblers are preoccupied with gambling and think a way to find money to gamble, desire to plan future venture, need to gamble with increasing amounts of money in order to achieve the desired excitement and escape from real problems.

For this reasons, cognitive therapies aim to understand and fix how the pathological players perceive events that occur during a gamble session that means to understand and fix players' perceptions and interpretation of chance.

The objective of this paper is to address the existent psychological researches on gambling by a design approach inherited from game design field. Firstly, the research provides a new gambling definition explaining how gambling can be interpreted from a design point of view and how it affects gamblers' psychology and cognitions. Then we propose a categorization of play and game attributes of games of chance – the gambling rhetoric model – connecting gamblers' cognitive errors to specific design attributes of games (with the support of former gambling researches in psychology field [6–9]). This first theoretical outcome supports the idea that gamblers' approach to gambling results from an interactive learning process while playing: it means that interactive playful and gambling experiences may be used as serious games suitably designed according to the gambling rhetoric model to fix player's approach to gambling. As a result, we propose an experimental application of theoretical outcomes, a set of digital prototypes for meaningful interactive experiences supposing that it might be possible to prevent the beginning of pathological gambling increasing players' awareness of their inappropriate approach to games of chance.

2   Reframing Gambling Experience: A Design Approach

Players' perception and cognition about gambling reveals wrong approaches to games of chance. Players are immerse in intense perceptive experiences that depend on game features and play contexts: rules and mechanics, graphic features, sounds and rhythms of actions contribute to cognitive errors and illusions that could end up in pathological behaviors. This approach is widely supported in several research papers by Griffiths and Parke: they stated that there are structural characteristics in gambling, "that facilitate the acquisition, development, and/or maintenance of gambling behavior irrespective of the individual's psychological, physiological, or socioeconomic status" [9] (p. 212). For this reason "by identifying and understanding how games are structured (i.e. game design and associated feature) we are really try to unravel what makes some games problematic for vulnerable players, what makes them playable or fun for social players and therefore, what makes it engaging and commercially successful" (ibd., p. 213).

Referring to these psychological researches, we propose a design-driven gambling definition based on a specific interpretation of play experience (Sect. 2.1): the aim is to provide a design approach to gambling explaining how it is suitably designed to affect gamblers' perceptions and emotions during a gambling session.

2.1   Related Theories: Play as Interaction, Sense Making and Persuasion

Game design literature provides a number of definitions of play and game, and it's interesting to notice how we can define gambling through some key points derived from those definitions [e.g. 10–12].

First of all gambling is a *system of rules*, designed to seem tougher than it actually is. It is an *engaging activity* against chance, as gamblers *believe to have control* over outcomes they can't foresee. And last, gamblers are *emotionally involved* with the experience and the result of a gambling session, as they strongly believe to have the power to influence the outcomes.

For our purpose, it is interesting to stress the engaging and immersive characteristics of gambling experience, which we can explain starting from Pichlmair's [13] definition of playing games. If playing games means experiencing an interactive process between players, setting, rules and game representations [13], by interacting with game representation, players are immerse in interactive and emotional experiences: as consequence they create meaning, because the interactive process between games and the players can be interpreted as a sense making process. Referring to Dewey's Theory of Inquiry [14], in fact, interaction is an essential part of human cognitive processes because every action, decision, and behavior is resulted from iterative interactions with world representations: interactions are a "making-sense process" that generates meanings. Consequently, games as interactive and inquiry process on game representation, as any other cognitive process, enable *meaningful play* experiences [10]. Moreover the meaningful play resulting from interaction within game representations, rules and players, helps establishing players' ideas, thoughts, and emotions. These perspectives, according to the definition of game design as *design of choice* [10], fit designers with an important role: they can influence player choices, expectations and emotions, by defining interactions and feedback between the player and the system. By this way we can explain the connection between playing game as interaction, learning process and the rhetoric power of design and interactive features in games, and then in games of chance too.

2.2   A New Definition of Gambling

Assuming last definitions of play as interaction, we reframed gambling experience from a design driven perspective: gambling is an interactive and emotional experience, an inquiry process between gamblers, rules and representation of chance in real world. The player through his choices – placing bets - has an active role and expresses his illusory beliefs to control the outcomes of the game. While playing gambling, the feedback and the difference between the actual results of a draw and player's desired outcomes contribute to the onset of emotions, illusions and cognitive errors affecting players' next choices. Gambling is interaction, because player's choices depend on previous outcomes received from game system; and it is also sense making process, because gambler believes to have an active role on casual events due to expertise acquired continuing gambling and mental models derived from past experiences (Fig. 1).

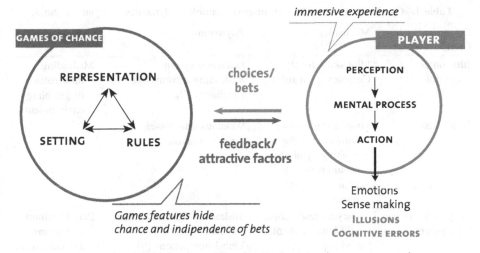

Fig. 1. A new definition of gambling: interactive experience representations

3   Mapping Gambling Experience: The Gambling Rhetoric Model

Defining gambling as a sense making process resulting from interpretation of signs of games confirms that games of chance are artifacts suitably designed to induce a specific cognitive interpretation of gambling phenomena, inducing behaviors through interactions. Consequently it's possible to define a framework - we called *gambling rhetoric*[1] *model* – mapping signs and design attributes of gambling, according to three main categories: 1) *mechanics* [15], the rules of a game and all actions allowed to the players; 2) *playworld elements* [12], all the narrative elements of games, as visual and sound features; 3) *context factors*, rhetoric components of play environment.

Every component of these categories is put in relationship with the three main gamblers' cognitive errors we took into consideration - near miss [16], suspension of judgment [6] and illusion of control [17] - that we defined gamblers' *dynamics* [15] – players' "run-time behavior" while playing according to mechanics and input/feedback game system. In the next paragraphs we are going to explain how different rhetoric attributes are related to each one of gamblers' dynamics, supported by former gambling studies (Table 1).

---

[1] In this research the term rhetoric refers to play rhetoric - the use of play activities and playful interactions to communicate meaning forming emotions and behaviors [12].

Table 1. Gambling Rhetoric Model, mapping gamblers' dynamics and game features.

Dynamics/ Cognitive errors	Mechanics	Playworld	Context
Illusion of control	Idiot skills [6, 9] Complexity of rules	Reference system Misleading information Familiarity [9]	Misleading information in gambling environment
Near Miss	To find symbols or numbers similar to winning symbols or numbers Waiting for draw results	Winnings and losses representation	
Suspension of judgment	Money representation Credit balance display Speed [9]	Misleading light and sound effects Verbal interactions [9]	Play Proximity and intrinsic association [8]

3.1 Illusion of Control

Langer defined illusion of control as "an expectancy of a personal success probability inappropriately higher than the objective probability would warrant" [17] (p. 311). Moreover, a number of play and game definitions [10, 12] defines play as an engaging activity in which the players believe to effect – and then control - the outcomes of the game. This is not what really happens in games of chance, for their intrinsic nature, but it is what it seems to gamblers – that is the illusion of control -, and this is enough to ensure gamblers' emotional involvement: they strongly believe that their reasoned choice will increase win probability. In fact, as stated by Griffiths "in some chance settings, those conditions which involved factors of choice (e.g. being able to choose your own lottery ticket), familiarity (e.g. having a favorite fruit machine), involvement (e.g. being able to throw your own dice in a game of craps) and/or competition, stimulate the illusion of control to produce skill orientations" [7] (p. 352). From this point of view, most of the players experience illusion of control every time they decide to place a bet.

According to some observation made in gambling environment and former researches, from a design perspective in games of chance illusion of control is affected by those *mechanics* and interactions that Griffiths defined as *idiot or pseudo skills* [6, 9], all those useless interactions between gamblers and games interfaces: press the hold button in slot machine to stop a reel, press the start button, choosing a number at the lottery, choosing the bet size, choosing different bet strategy at roulette game. Gamblers do all these actions after a deep reasoning process ignoring that however they can't affect the randomness of a draw. Idiot skills may be considered a consequence of an apparent *complexity of rules*: specific rules, supposed magical strategies (for example the wide number of bet types or mathematical strategies at roulette game) induce the player to think that a deep knowledge and expertise are required to achieve the best results.

Also *playworld* attributes, contribute to illusion of control hiding randomness and the independence of bet. In many games of chance the *game reference system,* for example the games based on numbers draws, has a strong influence on players' choices, because they will choose their bets according to favorite numbers, birthday dates, or previous draws results. Some games, moreover, are suited with a report of last sessions results *(misleading information)*: this makes the players think that there is a relationship between future draws session and paste one, but it is not true. Another example is games naming, as it happens for scratch cards: even if the mechanics of scratch cards are always the same, there are a lot of different types of this fortune tickets named and designed in different way, according to the different themes they want to recall. More the playworld recalled is known by players, more they will believe to have control on game results thanks to their previous *familiarity* [9] with game reference system.

In the end, there are some aspects in *contexts* of play influencing gamblers' perception of control. We are referring for example to the presence of recent winnings announcements, or bet suggestions in lottery offices. They are *misleading information* as players believe that choosing a place is better than another one to increase win probability.

3.2   Near Miss

Near miss phenomena was described by Reid as "a special kind of failure to reach a goal, one that comes close to being successful. [...] In such cases, the occurrence of a near miss may be taken as an encouraging sign, confirming the player's strategy and raising hopes for future success" [16] (p. 32), and more "At a more behavioristic level it is conceivable that a near miss may to some extent have the same kind of conditioning effect on behavior as a success" (ibd., p. 34). For this reason, even if they are in losing conditions, players will continue to play. The near miss is strictly connected to the games objective and *mechanics* and players' expectations: players have to *guess a number* or the right symbols match on slot machine reels, or find winning numbers on scratch card. The mechanics are always the same: players' emotions grow while *waiting for the draw results*, while the ball jumps from one slot of the wheel to another, the reels of slot machine stop one after other, or numbers on scratch card are uncovered by players' hands. In most cases, the player has the perception to be closest to the win, but in the end it doesn't happen. However gamblers' perception of a closest huge win is so strong that they will continue to bet. Near miss dynamic is supported also by *playworld* attributes *(winning and losses representation)*: in slot machine for example win and defeat are not strongly differentiated by each other, as similar sounds and lights effects are employed in both the situations. This is why near wins could be perceived as real wins instead.

3.3   Suspension of Judgment

The last cognitive error is suspension of judgment about money expenditure. Gamblers often continue to play even if they are in financial losing conditions, because they do not really realize how much money they have spent before to reach a winning. According to Griffiths, suspension of judgments is due to all those "structural characteristics, which temporarily disrupt the gambler's financial value system e.g. betting with chips instead of money at the roulette table where money's true value can be disguised or seen as fun money" [6] (p. 115). We call the *mechanic* affecting this dynamic *money representation* and it is employed to shift gamblers' attention on entertainment experience instead of money expenditure, for example when fiches or casino smart cards are used instead of money, gamblers play online gambling trough virtual account, winnings are paid as paper tickets that player can re-bet instantly. Another mechanic connected to suspension of judgment is the *credit balance display* in slot machine or online gambling. Although real time credit counter is usually employed, a more detailed total bet counter separated from a total win counter could be more useful to improve gamblers' responsibility. All these features then, must be related to *speed* of play [9]: fast plays decrease gamblers' attention to money expenditure, due to the lack of time for reasoning.

Playworld attributes like *misleading sounds, lights and visual effects*, cooperate in setting up the immersive and interactive experience of gambling. Games theme and style are often apparently simple and uninteresting, as simple and trivial as to seem the money bet by players. Colorful and funny written words and dialogues (*verbal interaction* [9]), invite players to play again and again like if money lost were not a real/serious issue. The same effect is achievable through some *context attributes*, as the *proximity play or intrinsic association* [8]: gambling offer outside casino is often associated to other daily activities, for example the presence of lottery pools office in shopping center, the possibility to buy scratch card at supermarket, slot machine located in bar and pub. These strategies offer people more opportunity to play gambling, as it is placed at the same level of other stuff such as drink a coffee with colleagues or buy food at supermarket, et cetera. By this way, the players undervalue the importance of money spent playing gambling.

4   Experimental Applications: The Design of Meaningful Gambling Experiences

The gambling rhetoric model and the new gambling definition provided, confirmed from a design perspective that gamblers' perceptions and cognitive errors while playing, are affected by games of chance design: in vulnerable players this may set the beginning of pathological gambling. What type of solution can we provide as designer? The questions are: is it possible to change gamblers experience of gambling? Is it possible, through game play, improve users' awareness about their cognitive errors to prevent the beginning of pathological behaviors? In this part of the paper, we propose an initial application of the theoretical approach toward the design of interactive and digital gambling experiences, as serious games, suitably designed according to the gambling rhetoric model to fix player's approach to gambling [18]. These meaningful games are intended to lead players towards a new consciousness about gambling illusions, deconstructing games of chance. The aim of the projects is to use these artifacts like a playful prevention: if games of chance affect gamblers' cognitive approach, then by the same way, we can change that approach through interaction and meaningful play experiences. This idea is supported firstly by the fact that as we have seen in previous paragraphs interaction is a sense making process, secondly because we decided to use gambling "language" to design products for gamblers: by this way the prototypes should be more attractive for our target users, the gamblers. For each prototype realized with Unity [19] and available to play here [20], we choose an existing game of chance (roulette and slot machine) and one of the main cognitive dynamic related to the game. Then we defined the message we want to communicate and the appropriate interactive grammars and interfaces suitably designed to convey the desired interactive experience. The concepts of the prototypes were previously presented as a poster during the Praxis and Poetics - Research Through Design Conference (3rd – 5th September 2013, Newcastle). In the next paragraphs each prototypes will be explained through the gambling rhetoric model.

4.1 Fast Roulette

Fast Roulette prototype intends to explain one of the most important fundamentals of gambling: house always wins in the end. The interactive grammar we designed is based on a fast simulation of one thousand draws that shows aspects of roulette game that usually are not undoing the emotions that occur every time players are waiting for the results. Players are invited to place their bets, and then to see draw by draw what would happen to their money through a line graph that displays real time credit balance and a set of counters. At the end of the fast simulation apart from the fact that player won or lost, the line graph displays all the losing events that preceded the end of simulation: probably in real world player would have stopped play before for lack of money. According to our rhetoric framework, this artifact deals with the cognitive error of suspension of judgment, here interpreted as lack of player's awareness about money expenditure. If usually, as in many other games of chance, there are no possibilities to keep track of money bet or won, in fast roulette winnings and losses are clearly showed to the player revisiting the rhetoric power of money visualization and credit balance display: during the fast simulation, three counters and a line graph show actual player's credit, the total amount of money bet and money won (Table 2, Figs. 2 and 3).

Table 2. Fast Roulette: dynamics and rhetoric features explained.

Dynamic/Cognitive errors	Rhetoric features	Message
Suspension of judgment	*Mechanics:* Money visualization Credit balance display	House always wins

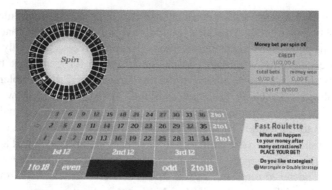

Fig. 2. Fast Roulette, starting interface.

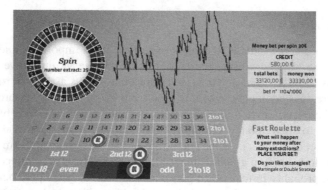

Fig. 3. Fast Roulette, end of simulation: line graph display player's credit balance.

4.2 Invisible Roulette

Favorite numbers, birthday dates, and statistical study of past drawn usually affect gamblers' choices [21]: gamblers believe that a deep knowledge of rules and playworld elements of a game, will lead them to a certain win. These beliefs are tied to the apparent complexity of games of change rules hiding the randomness of gambling. For example, the first time you play at a roulette table you have the impression that a deep knowledge of all the different types of bets (inside bets, outside bets, straight, split, corner, column bets, dozen bets, black or red, odd or even et cetera) is required to have

Table 3. Invisible Roulette: dynamics and rhetoric features explained.

Dynamics/Cognitive errors	Rhetoric features	Message
Illusion of control	*Mechanics:* Complexity of rules *Playworld:* Reference system	Numbers have not memory

more chance to win. Invisible roulette explains illusion of control resulting from the rhetoric power of complexity of rules and game reference system (playworld rhetoric), by the gradual elimination of signs from game interfaces, questioning the player how he will decide his next bet: starting from a classic roulette game interface, at the end of our interactive experience the player will face a blank roulette, without colors or numbers on the table and on the wheel. The players will be forced to place random bet, because there will be no more signs and reference components affecting their reasoning: the ball will drop in one slot instead of another, apart from the number or the color over it. The wheel and table interfaces change draw after draw and players are asked to reason on their next choice: What if each slot is numbered? What if there are no numbers and colors? We provide the players four levels to play with four different interfaces (Table 3, Figs. 4, 5, 6 and 7).

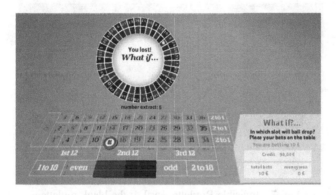

Fig. 4. Invisible Roulette, level 1: classic roulette table.

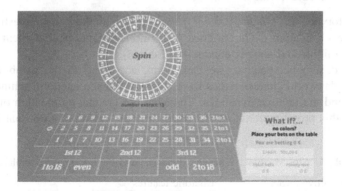

Fig. 5. Invisible Roulette, level 2: roulette without colors.

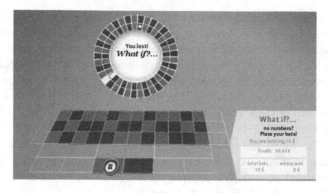

Fig. 6. Invisible Roulette, level 3: roulette with unconventional colors and without number

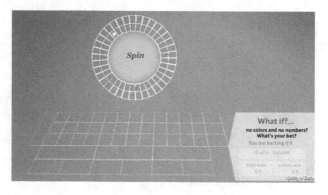

Fig. 7. Invisible Roulette, level 4: the blank roulette

4.3   Slot Machine: What if?

The last prototype, *Slot Machine: What if?* aims to explain how the interestingness of a slot machine - a random event enriched with emotional and entertainment appeal - is partly tied to lights and sounds effects [6] (Table 4).

From a design perspective, we can affirm, according to the gambling rhetoric model, that playworld characteristics have a great influence on slot machine gambling experience and the relative dynamics. Therefore the gradual elimination of playworld elements in this prototype reduces slot machine at its essential: an instant lottery.

Table 4. Slot Machine: What if?: dynamics and rhetoric features explained

Dynamics/Cognitive errors	Rhetoric features	Message
Illusion of control	*Playworld:* Reference system	
Near Miss	*Playworld:* Winnings and losses representation	
Suspension of Judgment	*Playworld:* Misleading lights and sounds effects	

The interactive experience is divided into five levels: lights and sound effects are turned on or off one after the other to provide the players different play experiences. The aim is to underline how the game would be boring without unusable and misleading special effects and when sounds and lights are employed only in win conditions: as a result the rhetorical framework of this prototype may be employed to effect all the three cognitive dynamics described in this paper. If we use light and sound effects only in win conditions, we could help the player to pay more attention to money expenditure, instead that use them to reinforce suspension of judgment. Moreover, also near miss is affected: lights and sounds in slot machine are employed to represent wins and losses, but the playworld of slot machine gambling is so rich and chaotic that it is quite difficult to recognize a successful bet, from an unsuccessful one, especially in case of near miss. If we do not use lights and sounds except in real win conditions, instead, we would help the players to understand that losing is more common than winning. In the end, illusion of control is enlightened in the last level of our prototype, where symbols on reels - as part of slot machine "misleading playworld" - are deleted: the players usually believe that symbols appear on reels according to a precise sequence that if learned, could allow them to foresee if the next symbols match, is a winning one or not. But, as slot machine is an instant lottery, it is not possible, so, to make players aware of it, a play experience without symbols and reference system was supposed (Figs. 8 and 9).

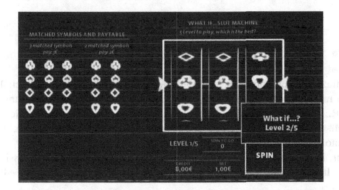

Fig. 8. Slot Machine, level 1: lights and sound are turned on.

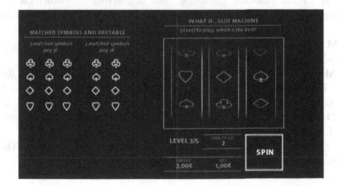

Fig. 9. Slot Machine, level 3: lights and sound are turned of.

5 Conclusion

The experimental part of this research, proposed a solution to the beginning of pathological gambling, in a playful way: serious digital and interactive gambling experiences to explain how games of chance are structured, and how every players could be affected by intense emotions, perception and cognitive errors or illusions. The project is based on previous psychological researches and adopted the cognitive therapies approach, revisited through game design. Cognitive therapies in fact explain gamblers' approach to gambling, but they also aim to help pathological gamblers in setting up new interpretations of gambling and chance: we supposed that it is achievable with the support of interactive meaningful games that involve directly the players inviting them to doubt of their beliefs about the possibility to foresee and control outcomes of a gambling session. Future researches could firstly evaluate the use of prototypes, testing and verifying their effectiveness in creating new meaning and awareness in gamblers.

Other researches must expand and refine the gambling rhetoric model connecting psychological researches and finding to design field. Moreover other experiments may apply the experimental approach we used for roulette and slot machine to every other game of chance, supposing the design of other interactive grammars based on the gambling rhetoric model.

References

1. Amministrazione Autonoma dei Monopoli di Stato (aams), Giochi pubblici: 18,4 miliardi di euro la raccolta netta nel 2011, Press release 16 February 2012. www.aams.it
2. Caillois, R.: Man, Play, and Games, p. 17. University of Illinois Press, Chicago (2001)
3. Croce, M., Zerbetto, R.: Il gioco e l'azzardo. Il fenomeno, la clinica, le possibilità d'intervento. 3rd ed. Franco Angeli (2001)
4. Ladouceur, R., Sylvain, C., Boutin, C., Doucet, C.: Il gioco d'azzardo eccessivo, vincere il gambling. Italian ed. by Carlevaro, T., Capitanucci, D. Centro scientifico editore, Torino (2005)
5. DSM-IV. Manuale Diagnostico e Statistico dei Disturbi Mentali. 3rd edn. Elsevier Masson, Milano (1995)
6. Griffiths, M.: Fruit machine gambling: the importance of structural characteristics. J. Gambling Stud. 9(2), 101–120 (1993). Kluwer Academic Publishers-Human Sciences Press
7. Griffiths, M.: The Role of cognitive bias and skill in fruit machine gambling. Br. J. Psychol. 85(3), 351–369 (1994)
8. Griffiths, M., Parke, J.: The environmental psychology of gambling. In: Reith, G. (ed.) Gambling: Who Wins? Who Loses?, pp. 277–292. Prometheus Books, New York (2003)
9. Parke, J., Griffiths, M.: The role of structural characteristics in gambling. In: Smith, G., Hodgins, D., Williams, R. (eds.) Research and Measurement Issues in Gambling Studies, pp. 211–243. Elsevier, New York (2007)
10. Salen, E., Zimmerman, E.: Rules of Play, Game Design Fundamentals. The MIT Press Cambridge, Massauchusetts (2003)

11. Juul, J.: Half-real: video games between real rules and fictional worlds. The MIT Press, Cambridge (2005)
12. Frasca, G.: Play the message, Play, Game and videogame Rhetoric. Ph.D. Dissertation, IT University of Copenhagen, Denmark (2007)
13. Pichlmair, M.: Designing for emotions, arguments for an emphasis on affect design. Ph.D Dissertation, Vienna University of Technology (2004)
14. Dewey, J.: Logic: The Theory of Inquiry. H. Holt & Company, New York (1938) (cited in Pichlmair, M.: Designing for emotions, arguments for an emphasis on affect design. Ph.D Dissertation, Vienna University of Technology (2004))
15. Hunicke, R., LeBlanc, M., Zubek, R.: MDA: a formal approach to game design and game research. In: Challenges in Games AI Workshop, Nineteenth National Conference on Artificial Intelligence, San Jose (2004)
16. Reid, R.L.: The psychology of the near miss. J. Gambl. Behav. **2**(1), 32–39 (1986). Springer, Kluwer Academic Publishers-Human Sciences Press
17. Langer, E.J.: The Illusion of control. J. Pers. Soc. Psychol. **32**(2), 311–328 (1975)
18. Vitali, A.: Magic Interactions? Game Design to Counterattack Gambling Irresistible Illusions. Poster presented at Praxis and Poetics - Research Trough Design Conference, Newcastle, 3–5 September 2013
19. Unity Game Engine, www.unity3d.com
20. Magic interactions? Game Design to counterattack gambling irresistible illusions, Prototypes website. http://andreavitalidesign.it/magicinteraction
21. Everitt, B.S.: Le leggi del caso. Guida alla probabilità e al rischio. UTET SpA, Torino (2008)

Player-Specific Conflict Handling Ontology

Charline Hondrou$^{(\boxtimes)}$, Eleni Tsalapati, Amaryllis Raouzaiou,
Kostas Karpouzis, and Stefanos Kollias

Image, Video and Multimedia Systems Lab, School of Electrical
and Computer Engineering, National Technical University of Athens,
Iroon Politechniou 9, 15780 Athens, Greece
{charline, etsalap, araouz}@image.ntua.gr,
{kkarpou, stefanos}@cs.ntua.gr

Abstract. This paper presents an ontology that leads the player of a serious game - regarding conflict handling - to the educative experience from which they will benefit the most. It provides a clearly defined tree of axioms that maps the player's visually manifested affective cues and emotional stimuli from the serious game to conflict handling styles and proposes interventions. The importance of this ontology lies in the fact that it promotes natural interaction (non-invasive methods) and at the same time makes the game as player-specific as it can be for its educational goal. It is an ontology that can be adapted to different educational theories and serve various educational purposes.

Keywords: Serious game · Ontology · Conflict · Emotion analysis

1 Introduction

Concern about violence in schools has been increasing, and, correspondingly, conflict handling and resolution as well as peer mediation training programs have been proliferating [1]. Very popular tools in this process are Serious Games (whose primary purpose is other than pure entertainment). According to [2], the purpose of game-based learning/serious games is to leverage the power of computer games to captivate and engage end-users for a specific goal, such as to develop new knowledge and skills. A conflict handling game creates an artificial social environment in which the children are presented with different options when it comes to dealing with a conflict. It is very important to bear in mind that conflict is not necessarily bad. This point has been very effectively made by developmental psychologists who work with children who have changing responses to conflict as they grow older [3]. The type of game indicated in the ontology described in this paper encourages an integrative way of dealing with a conflict (Sect. 2.1).

The digital game industry has lately realized an important shift towards Natural Interaction (NI). The keyboard and mouse are not necessary anymore, non-verbal behavioral cues are the new – natural – means of interaction. Research work in the fields of psychology and cognitive science related to non-verbal behavior and communication point out the importance of qualitative, expressive characteristics of body motion, posture, gestures and general human action during an interactive session [5, 6].

© Springer International Publishing Switzerland 2014
A. De Gloria (Ed.): GALA 2013, LNCS 8605, pp. 304–315, 2014.
DOI: 10.1007/978-3-319-12157-4_24

In the ontology presented in this paper visual information is used, providing important cues about conflict progress and possible subsequent reactions of the player. Affective analysis of the player is used in the abovementioned game in order to detect their emotional state during conflict. Conflict provokes different reactions from the participants according to their character and expressiveness ("To recognize that we are in conflict is to acknowledge that we have been triggered emotionally" [4]).

The relations between different concepts in the conflict handling and game playing domain, as well as the player's affective behavior, are represented in an ontology in a multidisciplinary way. Researchers and developers in the fields of affective computing and conflict management/resolution will benefit from this, since it will offer access to relations and concepts from different sources.

Within the context of computer and information science, an ontology defines a set of representational primitives that model a domain of knowledge or discourse [7]. Thus, ontologies can capture a shared understanding of this domain and at the same time provide a formal and machine manipulable model for it. According to Oberle [31], ontologies can be classified according to purpose, specificity and expressiveness. In this context "purpose" ranges from application ontologies to reference ontologies (which are mostly used for terminological reasons). "Specificity" refers to foundational, core and domain ontologies, with the last being low on generality, and being more specific - and deeper - when describing a particular domain. The "expressiveness" of the ontologies distinguishes lightweight from heavyweight ones. Gruninger [32] describes the benefits of ontologies in three classes. The first class refers to their interoperability. Ontologies are both human readable and machine processable enabling communication between systems, between humans, and between humans and systems. The second class refers to their ability to enable computational inference (in the sense that they derive implicit facts to enhance traditional browsing and retrieval technology [33]). The third class refers to their reuse and organization of knowledge. Within this framework, ontologies are not only an efficient method for representing a domain, which in this case is the conflict handling game, but also a method for performing automated reasoning tasks to extract any required implicit knowledge.

In this paper we chose to develop a core, lightweight ontology around the axis of a serious game so that we established a tree of clear axioms as a generic guide. That way, the users can focus on the concepts involved in the ontology and be creative with the implementation of the individual parts. In terms of representing the conflict domain, this ontology maps visually manifested affective cues and emotional stimuli from the serious game to conflict handling styles, and proposes interventions. As a result, it can be used by game developers to design and implement their own conflict management scenarios or design non-player characters that illustrate prototypical behavior and respond to specific events in the game environment. The ontology can also be extended to utilize information from player models or emerging information about the player (e.g. by questionnaires or interviews before playing the game) which can help define the player's status or conflict handling style before the game experience. Thus, adaptation of the game narrative or procedural generation [34] of conflict scenarios can be employed to present a truly personalized player experience and maximize the serious game's learning potential.

2 The Player

2.1 Conflict Handling Mode

In [8] the five modes of handling conflict are presented. These modes are described as: forcing, withdrawing, smoothing, compromising and problem solving. This scheme was reinterpreted in [9] by considering the intentions of a party in the following way: cooperativeness and assertiveness. The former describes attempts to satisfy the concerns of others, while the latter describes attempts to satisfy one's own concerns. The values of these dimensions combined describe the modes of behavior: competition, collaboration, compromise, avoidance and accommodation [10]. The competition mode suggests that one party places their interests before those of another party, and thus adheres to their own solution in solving the conflict. The collaboration mode suggests that solutions which are optimal for both parties are adopted. The compromise mode is employed when solutions that are acceptable for both parties are adopted. The avoidance mode occurs when a party displays passive behavior and shows no interest in conflict resolution. Finally, the accommodation mode occurs when one party allows the other to control the situation.

References [11, 12] differentiate the styles on two basic dimensions: concern for self and concern for others. The first dimension explains the degree (high or low) to which a person wants to satisfy the concerns of others [13] (Fig. 1). For each of these styles, the interpretation in a game environment is mentioned.

- Dominating: high concern for self and low concern for others (win/lose).
- Avoiding: low concern for self and others. Removing themselves from the conflict, resulting in no solution (lose/lose).
- Obliging: low concern for self and high concern for others. Willing to let the other person have their way, giving in and giving up (lose/win).
- Compromising: intermediate in concern for self and others. It may be appropriate when the goals of the conflicting parties are mutually exclusive (lose/lose).

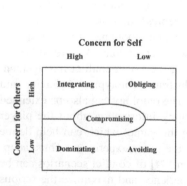

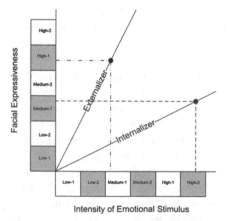

Fig. 1. Conflict handling models by Rahim M.A. [13]

Fig. 2. Correlation of facial expressiveness and emotional stimulus

- Integrating: high concern for self and others. Awareness of both sides in a conflict, solving a conflict through working together. It is associated with problem solving which may lead to creative solutions (win/win).

2.2 Conflict Handling Models: Cultural Aspects

The Face Negotiation Theory was proposed in [14] in order to understand how different cultures throughout the world respond to conflict. According to this theory, our self-image, or face, is at risk in conflict and our culture is attached to the way we deal with this issue and communicate. There are many different strategies and factors affecting how cultures manage identity [15]. In [14] it is argued that in collectivist cultures, the face of the group is more important than any individual face in that group. In individualist cultures, the face of the individual is more important than the face of the group. People from collectivistic cultures usually adopt the avoiding or integrating conflict styles because the "mutual" face or the face of the group is the top concern. People from an individualistic culture adopt a dominating conflict style because their main concern is maintaining self face because they have a "face" independent from that of the group. The Face Negotiation Theory is proposed as a useful tool in order to expand the ontology analyzed in this paper. With further analysis, the theory could replace the conflict management questionnaire mentioned in Sect. 4, used to characterize the player, or enhance it.

2.3 Facial Expressive Response Amplification

According to [16] all strong emotions result in some degree of activation of the organism (i.e., principle of stimulus dynamism) but there are individual differences in the gain operating on the expressive and sympathetic facial response channels of individuals. Focusing on the facial expressive response, the individuals can be categorized as externalizers when their somatic nervous system is characterized by high gain and as internalizers when it is characterized by low gain.

3 Facial Expression

Psychologists have examined a broader set of emotions, but very few of the studies provide results which can be exploited in computer graphics and machine vision fields. Many studies [17–21] suggest that one of the main characteristics of emotion is - among others - activation (also defined as arousal, expressiveness etc.). This is the characteristic we analyze in this ontology. We specify how "expressive" the player is (the quantity of facial movement they have) without defining the valence (positive or negative evaluation of the emotion). We could say that the player's emotional state is simply rated in terms of the associated activation level, i.e., the strength of the person's disposition to take some action rather than none. Facial analysis includes a number of processing steps which attempt to detect or track the face and to locate characteristic facial regions on it such as eyes, mouth and nose. The following step is to extract and follow the movement of facial features, such as characteristic points in these regions, or model facial gestures using anatomic information about the face [22, 23]. Although the Facial Animation Parameters (FAPs) provide all the necessary elements for MPEG-4 compatible animation, we cannot use them for the analysis of expressions from video scenes, due to the absence of a clear quantitative definition framework. In order to measure FAPs in real image sequences, we have to define a mapping between them and the movement of specific Facial Definition Parameters (FDPs), i.e. Feature Points (FPs), which correspond to salient points on the human face. A detailed description of the analysis procedure can be found in [24]. The measurement of FAPs requires the availability of a frame where the player's expression is found to be neutral. This frame will be called the neutral frame and is manually selected or interactively provided to the system. For every facial feature (eyes, eyebrows, nose, mouth), a mask is extracted. The final feature masks are used to extract 19 FPs; FPs obtained from each frame are compared to FPs obtained from the neutral frame to estimate facial deformations and produce the FAPs. These deformations are used to define how expressive the player is, since large deformations characterize expressive players.

3.1   Facial Expressiveness and Emotional Stimulus

The facial expressiveness as a function of the intensity of an emotional stimulus is described for two individuals in [16]. As can be seen in the graph of Fig. 2, which is based on [16], the function for the individual A who is characterized as an internalizer is different from the individual B who is considered to be an externalizer. It can be seen from this graph that the threshold on the axis of facial expressiveness over which an intense emotional stimulus is revealed for an internalizer is lower than the equivalent threshold for an externalizer.

4   Conceptual Model

In this ontology the Facial Expressiveness of a player at the moment of a game event leading to conflict, as well as their Facial Expressive Response Amplification (Sect. 2.3), is used to determine the Intensity of the Emotional Stimulus. Once this is accomplished, the Player's Conflict Mode (Sect. 2.1) is taken into consideration in order to present the appropriate Educative Intervention. The term "Educative Intervention" will be used throughout this paper as a term that involves several types of intervention – that can take the form of a transition to a different game environment, a pop-up window, the introduction of an NPC, the teacher's intervention etc. - aiming to guide the player towards an integrative way of dealing with conflicts in a social environment. The Facial Expressiveness and Facial Expressive Response Amplification data is acquired from questionnaires that are given to the player prior to the game (examples can be found in [25, 26]). Thus, the player's Conflict Handling Mode will be characterized as dominating, avoiding, obliging, compromising or integrating whereas they will be characterized as an externalizer or internalizer in regard to their Facial Expressive Response Amplification. The Facial Expressiveness of the player is derived from the video recording of them playing the game while being faced with a game event leading to conflict. Such a game event generates a conflict of interests between two players and occurs when the actions of one person attempting to reach his or her goals prevent, block or interfere with the actions of another person attempting to reach his or her own goals [27]. The video is then processed by the facial analysis software in order to determine the levels of Facial Expressiveness.

The ontology takes into consideration whether the player is an externalizer or an internalizer in order to determine which of the two graphs in Fig. 2 characterizes the individual, as well as the intensity of the facial expression. Using the graph mentioned above, the intensity of the emotional stimulus can be determined (Fig. 4). The user of this ontology can determine the threshold over which the intensity of the emotional stimulus is high enough to require the introduction of the Educative Intervention. In this paper the level "Medium-2" is considered to be this threshold. Note that, as described in Sect. 3.1, the threshold in the axis of Facial Expressiveness over which an intense emotional stimulus is revealed for an internalizer is lower than the equivalent threshold for an externalizer.

No action will be taken by the game in the following cases:

1. There is no intense emotional stimulus.
2. The player's conflict mode is already Integrative.

In all other cases the Educative Intervention will be implemented aiming towards an integrative resolution of the upcoming conflict. The Intervention will be adapted to the player i.e. it will be dictated by the player's conflict mode (Figs. 5, 6, and 7). The type of Intervention (pop-up window, NPC, etc.) will be determined by the ontology users.

The complete graph of the ontology can be seen in Fig. 3.

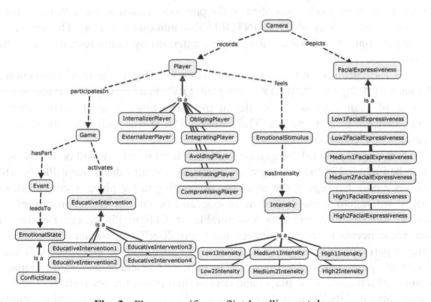

Fig. 3. Player specific conflict handling ontology

Fig. 4. Description of the concept Medium1 Intensity

Fig. 5. Description of the concept Educative Intervention

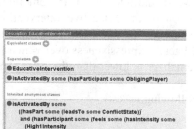

Fig. 6. Description of the concept Educative Intervention1

Fig. 7. Description of the concept Educative Intervention3

5   The Ontology

In this work, the Player Specific Conflict Handling Ontology (PSCHO) is developed, based on the generic model described in the previous section along with the ontology engineering methodology –METHONTOLOGY– introduced in [28]. The objective is to develop an ontology flexible enough to be extended by future researchers for their purposes.

For the formalization of the conceptual model described in the previous section the Web Ontology Language (OWL) was adopted. OWL is a language for producing web ontologies of high expressivity while, at the same time, is machine readable and enables extension by third parties. The ontology PSCH was built using the free, open source ontology editor Protégé [29].

The first step is to build the glossary of terms from which we will derive the set of terms to be included in the ontology. Our glossary contains the concept Player which constitutes a core concept of the ontology. According to the player's conflict modes, and since we regard these modes as unique and permanent characteristics of each player, we introduce the concepts AvoidingPlayer, ObligingPlayer, etc. For the same reasons the concepts ExternalizerPlayer and InternalizerPlayer are also introduced. As the player participates in a game it is necessary to introduce the concept Game to represent any game played by a player. The concept Camera is also used to represent the camera which records the player and depicts their Facial Expressiveness. The Facial Expressiveness and its levels as they are specified in Fig. 2 are represented respectively with the concepts FacialExpressiveness, Low1FacialExpressiveness, Low2FacialEx-pressiveness etc. Also, during the game the player feels an emotional stimulus which has a specific grade of intensity. Hence, the concepts EmotionalStimulus, Intensity and its respective levels Low1Intensity, Low2Intensity etc., are required to describe the domain of interest. As was described in the previous section, the camera records the player while they are faced with a game event leading to conflict. Therefore, we assume that an Event which is part of a Game leads to an EmotionalState and at the same time a ConflictState is an EmotionalState. Finally the Educative Interventions are represented with the concept EducativeIntervention and, for the purposes of our ontology, are categorized in four types: EducativeIntervention1, EducativeIntervention2, Educa-tiveIntervention3, EducativeIntervention4 (the number of types of Intervention is arbitrary here, it is to be determined by the user of the ontology).

According to METHONTOLOGY the second step in the ontology development is to build concept taxonomies to define the concept hierarchy. The hierarchy is depicted in the graph of the Fig. 3 for brevity. The binary relationships between the concepts of the taxonomy are also depicted in the same graph. Although it could not be clearly depicted in the diagram, most of the relationships have a respective inverse one. For instance, the relation "activates" (domain: Game, range: EducativeIntervention) has an inverse relation defined as isActivatedBy whose domain is the EducativeIntervention and whose range is the Game. The set of relations between the concepts of the ontology are demonstrated in the Table 1.

The ontology is completed with a set of terminological axioms that capture addi-tional knowledge about the domain. In particular, new axioms are required to define the various levels of intensity: Low1Intensity, Low2Intensity etc., based on the plot of Fig. 2. For instance, as is demonstrated in Fig. 4, the concept Medium1Intensity can be defined as: (a) the intensityOf some emotional stimulus that isFeltBy some External-izerPlayer who is being recorded by some camera that depicts High1FacialExpres-siveness, or (b) the intensityOf some emotional stimulus that isFeltBy some InternalizerPlayer who is being recorded by some camera that depicts Low2Facial-Expressiveness. Hence, if there is an internalizer or externalizer player for whom the camera records respectively Low-2 or High-1 Facial Expressiveness, then the intensity of the emotional stimulus will be defined as Medium-2. The rest of the levels of intensity are defined in a similar way.

For the purpose of our study it is also necessary to describe every Educative Intervention that appears in the ontology. As was described in the Conceptual Model section, when the intensity of the emotional stimulus exceeds a particular threshold an Educative Intervention is activated. In this ontology we assume that the threshold is any value that belongs to the range of Medium-2 intensity. Hence, we introduce a new axiom that describes the concept EducativeIntervention. This axiom is formally dem-onstrated in Fig. 5 and expresses that the EducativeIntervention isActivatedBy some game that hasPart an event that leadsTo some ConflictState and hasParticipant some player that feels some emotional stimulus that hasIntensity of: Medium2Intensity, High1Intensity or High2Intensity. Each one of the four Educative Interventions is activated according to the conflict mode that describes the player. For instance, as it is shown in Fig. 6, if the participant is a DominatingPlayer then EducativeIntervention1 is activated. Furthermore, as it is shown in Fig. 7 if the participant is an ObligingPlayer then EducativeIntervention3 is activated.

Table 1. Binary relation table of PSCH ontology

Relation	Domain	Range	Inverse Relation
activates	Game	EducativeIntervention	isActivatedBy
depicts	Camera	FacialExpressiveness	isDepictedBy
Feels	Player	EmotionalStimulus	isFeltBy
hasIntensity	EmotionalStimulus	Intensity	isIntensityOf
hasPart	Game	Event	isPartOf
hasParticipant	Game	Player	isParticipantOf
leadsTo	Event	EmotionalState	–
Records	Camera	Player	isRecordedBy

6 Case Example

In this section a case study is presented in order to show the process of applying the Player-Specific Conflict Handling Ontology in a real-life situation. The terms used below, which are also part of the ontology, are accompanied by the relevant section in which they are explained and to which the reader can refer if needed. It is important to mention that the ontology provides a structure with solid rules that will ensure the outcome that we need. Having said that, each individual component such as the questionnaires used, the facial analysis software, the educational game etc., can differ according to the ontology user's needs. The same applies for establishing thresholds.

Andrew is a 12-year old boy that has been having problems at school such as being alienated by the other students and ultimately being on his own quite often. More specifically all disagreements with other students result in him being alone in the school yard. After observing this for a few weeks, his teacher gives him two questionnaires to answer. The Berkeley Expressivity Questionnaire, proposed by Gross J.J. and John O.P. [26] gives Andrew a score of 2 in terms of expressivity (on a scale of 1 to 7). With this score he is characterized as an "Internalizer" in terms of Facial Expressive Response Amplification (Sect. 2.3). The Conflict Management Styles Quiz, developed by Reginald Adkins [25], characterizes the student as having an "Avoiding" style of Conflict Handling (Sect. 2.1).

The student is now going to have a month of educational game-playing sessions in order to learn how to deal with potential conflicts in an integrative way (Sect. 2.1). The computer game has a series of events leading to conflict (Sect. 4). During these events Andrew's facial features are analyzed by a Facial Analysis software developed by [30] and the degree of his Facial Expressiveness (Sect. 3) is measured. This measurement is the equivalent of Medium-1 as it is depicted in Fig. 2. Because Andrew is an Internalizer, the graph of Fig. 2 reveals that the Intensity of the Emotional Stimulus (Sect. 3.1) that he is experiencing while playing the game is at the level of High-2.

The designer of the specific game has determined that the threshold over which the Intensity of the Stimulus is considered to be too high is Medium-2. Any measurement over this threshold is an alert for the game to take an action. This action is that Andrew will now find himself in a new level where he will be part of a team of NPCs. He will have the chance to observe the Avoiding NPC being alienated from the group activities, and the Integrating NPCs working together towards solving the conflicts with the opposite team. Finally he will be asked to follow the example of the Integrating NPCs and we hope he enjoys the results!

7 Conclusion – Future Work

In this paper the ability of ontologies to perform automated reasoning tasks to generate any required knowledge, was used in order to create a serious game for conflict handling that implements player-adapted educative interventions. The ontology presented allows for its users to implement the educative interventions they think are more appropriate and helpful according to the players, the environment in which the game is played and the game itself.

Further work can be done towards multimodality, adding more inputs to the analysis software. These could be the player's voice or gestures, since the technology is already being used in commercial tools such as Microsoft Kinect, Nintendo Wii etc. Another input could be the biological signals which would add more accuracy to the detection of the stimulus' intensity. This is even more feasible at present, while maintaining the natural interaction aspect of the ontology as much as possible, since non intrusive, wireless EEG, HR, BP, SC sensors are widely available.

Acknowledgements. This research was co-financed by the FP7 ICT project SIREN (project no: 258453) and by the European Union (European Social Fund ESF) and Greek national funds through the Operational Program "Education and Lifelong Learning" of the National Strategic Reference Framework (NSRF) Research Funding Program: "THALES. Investing in knowledge society through the European Social Fund".

References

1. Johnson, D.W., Johnson, R.T.: Conflict resolution and peer mediation programs in elementary and secondary schools: a review of the research. Rev. Educ. Res. **66**(4), 459–506 (1996)
2. Corti, K.: Games-based learning; a serious business application. Inf. Pixel Learn. **34**(6), 1–20 (2006)
3. Laursen, B., Hafen, C.A.: Future directions in the study of close relationships: conflict is bad (except when it's not). Soc. Dev. **19**(4), 858–872 (2010)
4. Jones, T.S.: Emotional communication in conflict. In: Eadie, W.F., Nelson, P.E. (eds.) The Language of Conflict and Resolution, pp. 81–104. Sage, Thousand Oaks (2001)
5. Wang, N., Marsella, S.C.: Introducing EVG: an emotion evoking game. In: Gratch, J., Young, M., Aylett, R.S., Ballin, D., Olivier, P. (eds.) IVA 2006. LNCS (LNAI), vol. 4133, pp. 282–291. Springer, Heidelberg (2006)
6. Kaiser, S., Wehrle, T., Schmidt, S.: Emotional episodes, facial expressions, and reported feelings in human-computer interactions (1998)

7. Gruber, T.: Ontology. In: Liu, L., Özsu, M.T. (eds.) Encyclopedia of Database Systems, pp. 1963–1965. Springer, New York (2009)
8. Blake, R., Mouton, J.: The managerial grid: the key to leadership excellence. Gulf Publishing Company, Houston (1964)
9. Thomas, K.W.: Conflict and Conflict Management. Rand McNally College Pub. Co., Chicago (1976)
10. Thomas, K.W.: Conflict and conflict management: reflections and update. J. Organ. Behav. 13(3), 265–274 (2006)
11. Rahim, A., Thomas, V.B.: Managing organizational conflict: a model for diagnosis and intervention. Psychol. Rep. 44(3c), 1323–1344 (1979)
12. Rahim, M.A.: A measure of styles of handling interpersonal conflict. Acad. Manag. J. 26(2), 368–376 (1983)
13. Rahim, M.A., Garrett, J.E., Buntzman, G.F.: Ethics of managing interpersonal conflict in organizations. J. Bus. Ethics 11(5), 423–432 (1992)
14. Ting-Toomey, S.: A face negotiation theory. In: Kim, Y., Gudykunst, W. (eds.) Theory and Intercultural Communication, pp. 47–92. Sage, Beverly Hills (1988)
15. Khaledm, R., Ingram, G.: Tales from the front lines of a large-scale serious game project. In: CHI 2012, pp. 69–78 (2012)
16. Cacioppo, J.T., Uchino, B.N., Crites, S.L., Snydersmith, M.A., Smith, G., Berntson, G.G., Lang, P.J., et al.: Relationship between facial expressiveness and sympathetic activation in emotion: a critical review, with emphasis on modeling underlying mechanisms and individual differences. J. Pers. Soc. Psychol. 62(1), 110–128 (1992)
17. Mehrabian, A.: Pleasure-arousal-dominance: a general framework for describing and measuring individual differences in temperament. Curr. Psychol. 14(4), 261–292 (1996)
18. Russell, J.A.: A circumplex model of affect. J. Pers. Soc. Psychol. 39(6), 1161–1178 (1980)
19. Schlosberg, H.: Three dimensions of emotion. Psychol. Rev. 61(2), 81 (1954)
20. Whissell, C.: The dictionary of affect in language. Emot. Theor. Res. Exper. 4(113–131), 94 (1989)
21. Russell, J.A., Lewicka, M., Niit, T.: A cross-cultural study of a circumplex model of affect. J. Pers. Soc. Psychol. 57(5), 848–856 (1989)
22. Karpouzis, K., Caridakis, G., Kessous, L., Amir, N., Raouzaiou, A., Malatesta, L., Kollias, S.D.: Modeling naturalistic affective states via facial, vocal, and bodily expressions recognition. In: Huang, T.S., Nijholt, A., Pantic, M., Pentland, A. (eds.) ICMI/IJCAI Workshops 2007. LNCS (LNAI), vol. 4451, pp. 91–112. Springer, Heidelberg (2007)
23. Caridakis, G., Raouzaiou, A., Bevacqua, E., Mancini, M., Karpouzis, K., Malatesta, L., Pelachaud, C.: Virtual agent multimodal mimicry of humans. Lang. Res. Eval. 41(3–4), 367–388 (2007)
24. Caridakis, G., Tzouveli, P., Malatesta, L., Raouzaiou, A., Karpouzis, K., Kollias, S.: Affective e-learning system: analysis of learners state. In: Tzanavari, A., Tsapatsoulis, N. (eds.) Affective, Interactive, and Cognitive Methods for E-Learning Design: Creating an Optimal Education Experience, p. 275. IGI Global, Hershey (2009)
25. Conflict Management Styles Quiz. http://www.ncsu.edu/grad/preparing-future-leaders/docs/conflict-management-styles-quiz.pdf
26. Gross, J., John, O., Richards, J.: Berkeley expressivity questionnaire. Psychology 72, 435–448 (2000)
27. Deutsch, M.: The Resolution of Conflict: Constructive and Destructive Processes. Yale University Press, New Haven (1977)

28. Corcho, Ó., Fernández-López, M., Gómez-Pérez, A., López-Cima, A.: Building legal ontologies with METHONTOLOGY and WebODE. In: Benjamins, V., Casanovas, P., Breuker, J., Gangemi, A. (eds.) Law and the Semantic Web. LNCS (LNAI), vol. 3369, pp. 142–157. Springer, Heidelberg (2005)

29. Knublauch, H., Fergerson, R.W., Noy, N.F., Musen, M.A.: The protégé OWL plugin: an open development environment for semantic web applications. In: McIlraith, S.A., Plexousakis, D., van Harmelen, F. (eds.) ISWC 2004. LNCS, vol. 3298, pp. 229–243. Springer, Heidelberg (2004)

30. Asteriadis, S., Karpouzis, K., Kollias, S.: Feature extraction and selection for inferring user engagement in an HCI environment. In: Jacko, J.A. (ed.) HCI International 2009, Part I. LNCS, vol. 5610, pp. 22–29. Springer, Heidelberg (2009)

31. Oberle, D.: Semantic Management of Middleware. The Semantic Web and Beyond, vol. 1. Springer, New York (2006)

32. Gruninger, M., Lee, J.: Introduction – ontology: different ways of representing the same concept. Commun. ACM **45**(2), 39–41 (2002)

33. Bürger, T., Simperl, E.: Measuring the benefits of ontologies. In: Meersman, R., Tari, Z., Herrero, P. (eds.) OTM-WS 2008. LNCS, vol. 5333, pp. 584–594. Springer, Heidelberg (2008)

34. Yannakakis, G.N., Togelius, J.: Experience-driven procedural content generation. IEEE Trans. Affect. Comput. **2**(3), 147–161 (2011)

Doing Useful Work Using Games

Kam Star[1,2](✉)

[1] Serious Games Institute, Coventry University,
Cheetah Road, Coventry CV1 2TL, UK
[2] PlayGen Ltd, 42-46 Princelet Street, London E1 5LP, UK
kam@playgen.com

Abstract. Games that are fun to play may also be used to carry out useful activity, for example in solving scientific problems. In this paper we review four so called games with purpose, games whose primarily objective for the designers are for carrying out tasks that would be difficult for automated algorithms as well as a game as a learning tool with the ability to generate useful metadata as a side benefit. Design elements which have demonstrated contribution to the effectiveness of the games are highlighted. Additionally an objective method for evaluating the performance of the games are discussed.

1 Introduction

Calculations that are easy for humans but hard for algorithms.

According to researcher at the Entertainment Software Association, by the age of 21 the average American spends the equivalent of five years of working a full time job 40 h a week playing computer games. The constructive channelling of human brainpower through computer games may potentially be an untapped source of intellectual capacity. Arvidsson and Sandvik [1] argue that playing games may be regarded as a kind of unpaid immaterial labour, implying players' creativity and general intellect may be utilised for the benefit of the game designer's intent.

Some trivial tasks which are easily solved by people can challenge the most sophisticated algorithms and artificial intelligence. Computer games which utilise human intelligence in order to carry out useful tasks otherwise difficult for algorithms to perform are described as 'games with a purpose' or **GWAP** by Von Ahn and Dabbish [20].

For the purpose of this paper the following four games have been examined:

- **ESP game** aka Google Image Labeler, which provides meaningful tags for images on the Web, a task which is almost impossible to achieve using computer-vision algorithms.
- **Foldit.** A biochemical discovery game. Designed to make it possible for non-experts to make useful contribution to the scientific domain of protein folding.
- **CityLights.** A music metadata validation game.
- **Spectral game** a game that involves matching molecules to their spectra graph.

Scientific discovery games or **SDG** as described by Cooper et al. [3] are a type of GWAP that are concerned with harnessing the enormous collective problem-solving

© Springer International Publishing Switzerland 2014
A. De Gloria (Ed.): GALA 2013, LNCS 8605, pp. 316–323, 2014.
DOI: 10.1007/978-3-319-12157-4_25

potential of the game playing population, but who are not familiar with the specific scientific domain.

SDGs are about using human problem solving ability to solve computationally difficult scientific problems. They provide game like mechanisms for non-expert players to help solve these problems. Foldit fits perfectly within this description. Crowdsourcing the discovery of protein's natural shapes.

The Spectral game is also arguably an SDG. Although its creators see it more as a Serious Game. It's aims is to leverage open data and crowdsourcing for education. The game involves matching molecules to various forms of interactive spectra graphs. Interpretation of spectra is an essential skill for organic chemists and many students struggle to grasp the nuances of various spectroscopy techniques. It was created by bringing together Open Source spectral data, a spectrum viewing tool and a workflow that combined these within a gaming framework.

CityLights is a GWAP and has many similarities with ESP although its aims is to validate the accuracy of existing metadata associated with a song, such as mood, quality, time and place to listen to the song. It was designed to use player competition and music exploration as its principle fun aspects.

2 Elements for Success

This section examines some of the critical design elements relating to the success of each of the games as described by the authors of the related papers. The frameworks formulating each approach to developing the various games are also identified and briefly discussed.

Von Ahn and Dabbish argue that the critical ingredient for a successful GWAP lie in persuading enough human-hours to be spent playing the games with a probabilistic guarantee that the game's output is correct [20]. They also present three frameworks for designing and deploying GWAPs, covering basic rules and winning condition that lead to optimum outcomes - that is holding the player's interest whilst compelling them to perform the intended computation. The three types of game have been described are:

A. Output-agreement Games: Where two players are given the same input and must produce the same output. For example input is an image and the output would be a matching keyword as in ESP.
B. Inversion-problem games: Where one player is the "describer" and the other player the "guesser". To win the guesser must give the same output that was given to the describer.
C. Input-agreement games: Where two players are instructed to produce output describing their input, then determine whether they have been given the same input.

Tversky and Kahneman demonstrate that the way in which a choice is framed, that is the words and phrases used to describe the choice to the decision maker, has a direct relation to its propensity to persuade [19].

It can be argued that one of the ingredients of success of these games is in the way the game frames the computational task to the player. For instance In the Output-agreement game, rather than asking players to describe what they see, players are asked to "think like the other player", and to describe what the other player may be thinking.

Research confirms humans along with other social animals are wired to be emphatic [4]. In essence people are wired to be able to think like others. The Decety and Philips argue that this ability to think like others is an innate human motivation requiring a multitude of cognitive mechanisms. They further report that the degree with which the subject is successful in completing the cycle of empathy displays a strong link with reward mechanisms within the brain. Therefore thinking liking other players may be described as a rewarding social engagement mechanism which would help to increase fun and enjoyment from a game.

Games such as charades and the 2012 game app "Draw Something!" a game where the players play in pairs to guess what the other is drawing. Bought by Zynga for $200M a mere 6 weeks after it was developed, rely on this type of mechanism [21].

The Inversion-problem game is designed in a way to collect facts as a side effect of playing - i.e. the player is never asked to "enter facts about milk" rather the task is framed as "enter facts about milk that will help the other person guess its milk" - the subtle difference between the two approaches means a mundane computational task is transformed from a task about entering the player's knowledge to a task about emphatic thinking.

In order to increase player enjoyment some additional elements can be incorporated into the Inversion-problem game. These included transparency and alternation. Transparency allows the describer to give small hits to the guesser, making the process much more interactive. Whilst alternation meant that after each round the players swap roles. Creating variety and fully involving both players.

In order to discourage players from random guesses the scoring in input-agreement games strongly penalise incorrect guesses. Rather than de-motivating the player by punishing them with negative points, the point system can be designed to increase points for streaks of correct answers.

The design process for each of the games seems to have been entirely different. With the Foldit team being the only one that included game designers. Foldit brought together biochemistry, game design, art and computer science - in an interactive, multi-disciplinary and iterative approach to design. Where the design was continually evolved in response to gameplay traces, player feedback and expert analysis.

The development of Foldit is ongoing, and according to the authors of the game, the game is constantly being updated. Playtesting is used as a way of uncovering what element of the game are fun and which can be most confusing and difficult to understand. One form of play testing carried out by the team is 'think-alouds' these have players play through the levels and say out loud what they are thinking [14]. This helps to decipher what works well and what could be adjusted to make the gameplay more fun.

Foldit is essentially a 3D jigsaw puzzle, a simulation tool for shaping proteins framed within a context of a game with challenges and competition. It was developed to show that human's innate spatial reasoning can make it possible for non-experts to make useful contributions to the field of protein shape problems [3]. In Foldit the solution for the problem is unknown, therefore the game could not be designed with a specific solution in mind. Rather the game must provide the tools needed to assemble the solution, in a similar way as lego provides the building blocks to create anything the player desires. These types of game can be described as open-ended simulation games or sandbox games [17].

According to wikipedia, the definition of sandbox games encompasses a large variety of different types of games, from non-linear entertainment games to virtual worlds and simulation games. Sweetser defines sandbox games as simulations, except for the somewhat loose definitions of tasks, challenges, and completion [18].

Squire identifies the use of sandbox games for their capacity to recruit diverse interests, provide an engaging interface for creative problem solving, and enable players to carry out productive acts [17]. Therefore the use of this type of sandbox framework for a GWAP appears to be well suited to situations where creative problem solving is required. By providing the building blocks and defining the interaction behaviours that mimic the real-world constraints of the problem within the game, the players may be able to discover previously unknown scientific solutions [3].

3 Exploring Mechanisms for Player Engagement

The central tenet of GWAPs is player enjoyment while carrying out the computational task, as such players are not directly instructed to solve the computational problem - rather to think like the other player. Other features incorporated in GWAP are taken from challenges outline by Malone [11, 12] - these include timed response, score keeping, player skill level, high score lists and randomness.

Timed response is an effective motivator since motivational theory posits that goals that are both well-specified and challenging lead to higher levels of effort than goals that are too vague or easy to accomplish [9].

The Foldit game uses timed response by having scientists post problems to the server, these puzzles are usually available for a week, before a winner is announced. Similarly on the ESP and Spectra Game time response is used to motivate players for their input.

Player Skill Levels is also used by the ESP and Foldit game. Here players are shown their current skill level and the number of points needed to reach the next level. The ESP game has provided a tremendous amount of data to support the effectiveness of player skill level ranking as it relates to engagement. Data from 200K players indicates that 42 % of scores fall within a few points of a rank cut-off. Given that the point intervals for ranking within ESP occupy less than 2 % of the possible cumulative scores, the data strongly suggests that many players continue playing just to reach a new rank. The data provided does not indicated whether after levelling up to a new rank and logging off, the players came back to improve their ranking. Goh et al. [7] argue that displaying the players' skill level to other players is a contributor in replayability of image tagging games.

Scoring in SDGs must direct players toward the solution by encouraging them to explore the solution space. For this Foldit used a competition form where player's goal is to do better than other players. Although players can also collaborate as teams - all players are ranked against each other in terms of their effectiveness in a highscore list.

Highscore lists within EPS were divided into multi-levels, from the last hour to day to all time, varying in difficulty and providing strong, positive motivation for extended play. Particularly useful for those who are competitive.

The authors of CityLights assert that by giving points even for actions not connected with their purpose players will return in the future [6]. They call this "proper scoring" and assert that player enjoyment is provided by highscore lists, however these assertions are not shared by other researchers in this area such as Deterding et al., who argue that for scoring to count, it must be meaningful [5]. This suggests that meaningless scoring for actions that are not related to the skills within the game or as part of a feedback loop is unlikely to be an effective mechanisms for the purpose of replayability.

The gaming elements within the Spectral Game included increasing difficulty as the player progressed through the game by an ever increasing complexity of the spectra. It also included a timed element of finding the right answer before a countdown expires. Players were given their performance relative to recent and top players. Players can also associate themselves with groups which could help in direct score comparison amongst members through the highscore lists.

The output in GWAPs must be accurate and the development team used a variety of techniques including random matching, player testing and repetition - until a certain number of consistent outcomes had been achieved. Von Ahn and Dabbish additionally used paid participants and independent raters to evaluate the quality of the output produced in the game to ensure it meets the required standards [20].

In order for a relatively complex game to be better received by players, the players must be introduced to the components of the game in a step by step manner [15] - within SDGs the gameplay, visualisations, interactions and evaluation methods all require some training - carried out as part of introductory levels to the game.

Accurate visualisation is one of the key aspects of an SDG [3]. The visualisation must sufficiently reflect and illuminate the natural rules of the system. In Foldit this meant showing the fundamental properties of proteins. The visualisations must also manage and hide the complexity of the system such that players are not immediately overwhelmed - this was achieved by hiding all but the most critical aspects of the puzzle as the player progressed. Visualisations must also be approachable by players rather than baffle them, for this the Foldit team used a cartoonish look, and enabled players to customize their view as they become more experienced with the system.

Interactions within SDGs must respect the constraints of the system, that is the possible solutions must be plausible within the scientific domain. Interactions must also be sufficient to explore the solution space; it must be possible to achieve the correct output from the given input. Within Foldit this was achieved by running puzzles where the solution was visible as a guide, this demonstrated that it was possible to achieve the correct output with the interactions given to the player.

In a successful GWAP the interactions should be intuitive and fun - within Foldit this concept is brought to life as 'touchability'. The ability to interact with the protein as though you could actually touch it, push it, pull it and shake it. The difference between a GWAP and a general online game (or website) whose aim is to capture screen-time, is in the formers' ability for useful work to be carried out as a by-product of play, whilst the latter is often only concerned with play for fun or in the case of a website, potentially devoid of the play as an engagement mechanism.

4 Evaluating Success

GWAPs can be evaluated in terms of their efficiency and expected contribution. Von Ahn and Dabbish define the method of measuring the performance of this type of game as; the average number of problem instances solved per human hour, multiplied by the average amount of overall time an individual will play the game [20].

For instance if during one hour of playing the game an average player carries out 100 tasks and the average lifetime playability of the game per player is 2 h. The expected contribution per player (CPP) is a score of 200. This CPP score represents an objective measure which can be used to compare and assess the effectiveness of variety of a GWAPs around a specific topic. Since CPP is not concerned with the number of players, rather the expected output from each individual playing the game, the task of marketing and dissemination can be ignored. A game with a higher CPP score is more valuable.

In order to evaluate whether Foldit was capable of being used to find tangible solutions, the solutions were entered into a protein structure prediction methods competition. The results found by players compared favourably to other methods used including automated systems. Cooper et al. concluded that the game has been designed in such a way that players can use it to solve the specific biochemical problems [3].

Evaluation of CityLight was carried out by comparison of the outcomes to a priori created by experts. Since only 78 players took part and 50 % of the tags did not receive sufficient evaluation. According to Dulavcka and Bieliková 66 % (n = 1300) of the tags were evaluated correctly. However in considering the vast number of tags which were not evaluated the game is less than 33 % (n = 78) accurate in identifying the correct tags, with a failure rate of over 67 % (n = 78) [6].

Dulavcka and Bieliková assert that the common problem with most existing GWAPs is a cold-start which causes an insufficient number of players from engaging with the game [6]. However CityLights attracted less than 80 players, compared to all other GWAPs reviewed which many thousands or hundreds of thousands of players. This supports the hypothesis that the cold-start is potentially not the common problem, rather the lack of fun and interest as identified by Von Ahn and Dabbish [20].

The key feature of the CityLight game was to show tags that had strong support or not so good support. However since tags are displayed to the player grouped together the value of the validation approach is limited because a correct tag may be mixed in a group with incorrect tags and the player would have no choice but to label the entire group incorrect.

Although the definition of the Spectral Game is more fitting with a Serious Game because of its primary goal as an educational tool rather than a human computation output. The authors have noted one of the critical side benefits of the game has been the examination of the open data and reporting of potential issues with it. Since players can flag incorrect spectra and leave comments associated with it for the curators of the open data. This has resulted in the deletion, reassociation and correction of certain spectra from the database through the crowd effort.

The methods of objective evaluation described by Von Ahn and Dabbish was unique amongst all the paper reviewed and deserves to be adopted by others as a scientific approach to measuring the effectiveness of a GWAP and improvement in game design [20].

5 Other Related Work

Using people to solve discrete tasks that computers find difficult to accomplish automatically is not new - Amazon's Mechanical Turk (AMT) is a platform within which individuals carry out small tasks for small sums of money. The tasks are knows as HITs (Human Intelligence Tasks), and include activities such as choosing the best among several photographs of a storefront, writing product descriptions, or identifying performers on music CDs.

The difference between AMT and GWAPs are in the lack of financial incentives insofar as people willingly perform HITs in GWAPs without a need for monetary remuneration.

The Open Mind Initiative is a worldwide research programme aimed at teaching computer programs commonsense facts - whilst OMI shares many of the elements of GWAPs, the difference in the way that GWAPs are designed to be enjoyable.

6 Conclusion

The papers reviewed here make a compelling case in the argument for the use of games as a method of carrying out useful computational work by players. The studies examined suggest that is it possible to carry out useful work as a side benefit of playing these games. Moreover that this is a type of work that could be paid for, being carried out for free by the players. In effect free immaterial labour in return for fun.

Some of the traits making GWAPs successful were identified as: Framing, competition, timed-response, transparency, alternation, streak-scoring, high-scores, step-by-step introduction, increasing difficulty and appropriate visualisation and manipulation tools within the game.

As a method of objectively measuring the effectiveness of various GWAPs, a CPP (Calculations Per Player) score has been identified. CPP represents the total number of calculations a single player will on average perform during a lifetime play of a particular game.

Further research into the traits and design elements that contribute positively to the success of GWAPs, building on the work reviewed here, could perhaps yield a 'best practice' or guidelines for designers and developers of this type of serious game.

References

1. Arvidsson, A., Sandvik, K.: Gameplay as design: uses of computer players' immaterial labour. Northern Lights: Film Media Stud. Yearb. 5, 89–104 (2007)
2. Bradley, J.C., Lancashire, R.J., Lang, A.S.I.D., Williams, A.J.: The Spectral Game: leveraging Open Data and crowdsourcing for education. J. Cheminform. 1, 1–10 (2009)
3. Cooper, S., Treuille, A., Barbero, J., Leaver-Fay, A., Tuite, K., Khatib, F., Snyder, A.C., Beenen, M., Salesin, D., Baker, D.: The challenge of designing scientific discovery games. In: Proceedings of the Fifth International Conference on the Foundations of Digital Games, pp. 40–47 (2010)

4. Decety, J., Jackson, P.L.: The functional architecture of human empathy. Behav. Cogn. Neurosci. Rev. **3**, 71–100 (2004)
5. Deterding, S., Dixon, D., Khaled, R., Nacke, L.: From game design elements to gamefulness: defining gamification. In: Proceedings of the 15th International Academic MindTrek Conference: Envisioning Future Media Environments, pp. 9–15 (2011)
6. Dulačka, P., Bieliková, M.: Validation of music metadata via game with a purpose. In: Proceedings of the 8th International Conference on Semantic Systems, pp. 177–180 (2012)
7. Goh, D.H.L., Ang, R.P., Lee, C.S., Chua, A.Y.K.: Fight or unite: investigating game genres for image tagging. J. Am. Soc. Inform. Sci. Technol. **62**, 1311–1324 (2011)
8. Jesse Schell: When games invade real life | Video on TED.com
9. Locke, E.A., Frederick, E., Lee, C., Bobko, P.: Effect of self-efficacy, goals, and task strategies on task performance. J. Appl. Psychol. **69**, 241 (1984)
10. Locke, E.A., Latham, G.P.: A Theory of Goal Setting & Task Performance. Prentice-Hall Inc, Englewood Cliffs (1990)
11. Malone, T.W.: What makes things fun to learn? Heuristics for designing instructional computer games (1980)
12. Malone, T.W.: Heuristics for designing enjoyable user interfaces: lessons from computer games. In: Proceedings of the 1982 Conference on Human Factors in Computing Systems, pp. 63–68 (1982)
13. Open world. Wikipedia, the free encyclopedia (2012)
14. Ramey, J., Boren, T., Cuddihy, E., Dumas, J., Guan, Z., Van den Haak, M.J., De Jong, M.D.T.: Does think aloud work?: how do we know? In: CHI'06 Extended Abstracts on Human Factors in Computing Systems, pp. 45–48 (2006)
15. Salen, K., Zimmerman, E.: Rules of Play: Game Design Fundamentals. MIT Press, Cambridge (2003)
16. Shneiderman, B.: Designing for fun: how can we design user interfaces to be more fun? Interactions **11**, 48–50 (2004)
17. Squire, K.: Open-ended video games: a model for developing learning for the interactive age. In: Salen, K. (ed.) The John D. and Catherine T. MacArthur Foundation Series on Digital Media and Learning, pp. 167–198. MIT Press, Cambridge (2007)
18. Sweetser, P.: Emergence in games (2008)
19. Tversky, A., Kahneman, D.: The framing of decisions and the psychology of choice. Science **211**, 453–458 (1981)
20. Von Ahn, L., Dabbish, L.: Designing games with a purpose. Commun. ACM **51**, 58–67 (2008)
21. Yarow, J.: Here's Why $200 Million Is Cheap for Draw Something [WWW Document]. Business Insider. http://articles.businessinsider.com/2012-03-21/tech/31218846_1_zynga-revenue-rate Accessed 1 Jan 13)

Workshop

Acquiring 21st Century Skills: Gaining Insight into the Design and Applicability of a Serious Game with 4C-ID

Peter van Rosmalen[1]([⊠]), Elizabeth A. Boyle[2], Rob Nadolski[1],
John van der Baaren[1], Baltasar Fernández-Manjón[3],
Ewan MacArthur[2], Tiina Pennanen[4], Madalina Manea[5],
and Kam Star[6]

[1] Open University of the Netherlands, Heerlen, The Netherlands
peter.vanrosmalen@ou.nl
[2] University of the West of Scotland, Paisley, UK
[3] Universidad Complutense de Madrid, Madrid, Spain
[4] Satakunta University of Applied Sciences, Pori, Finland
[5] University of Medicine and Pharmacy of Craiova, Craiova, Romania
[6] PLAYGEN, London, UK

Abstract. Despite the growth of interest in serious games, there is little systematic guidance on how to assure a game fits the instruction required. Game design frameworks are still under development and do not help to articulate the educational merits of a game to a teacher nor fit with their background. In this paper we discuss the results of a GaLA workshop which examined how a widely applied instructional design model, 4C-ID, can ease the uptake of serious games by offering teachers a model fitting their background to assess games on the applicability for their learning contexts. The paper will introduce the 4C-ID model and its use in the CHERMUG project with the design of mini-games for research methods and statistics. Next, we will discuss how workshop participants used the 4C-ID model to evaluate two games on their applicability for a given learning context. The participants indicated that the approach can support teachers in deciding if and how to use a given serious game.

1 Introduction

Despite the growth of interest in serious games, there is still little systematic guidance concerning which kind of game is better for which purpose and how to assure a game fits the instruction required. The complexity of the field is clearly illustrated by, for instance, Connolly et al. [1] who in a recent review study classify games on genre, subject discipline and intended outcome. As a result, for developers the design and development of a game and for instructors the selection and application of a game can be quite an experimental process.

Design and development. Only recently, there exist a number of frameworks which attempt to integrate the knowledge and experience with regard to education, games and

© Springer International Publishing Switzerland 2014
A. De Gloria (Ed.): GALA 2013, LNCS 8605, pp. 327–334, 2014.
DOI: 10.1007/978-3-319-12157-4_26

software [e.g. 2–4]. These frameworks are important tools to assist in the design of serious games. However, they are as yet not fully matured nor investigated as, indirectly, shown in the limited evidence on the effectiveness of serious games and the apparent difficulty in assessing the educational merits of serious games [1]. Moreover, these frameworks do not necessarily fit with the background of teachers.

Selection and Application. With the advent of social media it is widely accepted that teachers and learners are not only consumers but also may have an active role in sharing and co-creating content, debating and sharing opinions [5]. Social media such as social networks, online videos and wikis are not merely used to connect or entertain but also support informal learning [6] by enabling learners to ask questions, to debate and to share opinions and materials with other learners. Paradoxically, one strand of technology enhanced learning, i.e. game-based learning, aligns slightly with this development. Games, while there to experience, explore and collaborate, are almost exclusively designed by professionals, and because of their manifold appearances, difficult to value or comprehend. Generally teachers have insufficient knowledge about games and their beneficial usage in classrooms [7]. Educational games are considered fundamentally different from prevalent instructional paradigms [8]. Williamson [9] reports an urgent need for the training of teachers both at the initial training stage and the stages of continuous professional development, to pursue a better understanding of how to use games in their class-rooms as well as understanding the implications of games as cultural forms of young people's lives. The general impression is that games require complex technologies and that games are difficult to organise and to embed in a curriculum [10]. The latter is of importance since the use of ICT and games, in particular, only tends to be successful if it closely fits with the existing teaching practice [11].

A way to support the game design and to support the application of a game would be to build upon a proven framework which integrates a sound instructional foundation, fits with teachers' experiences and fits sufficiently with existing game principles. Huang and Johnson [12] propose using the 4C-ID model [13]. Key elements of this approach are authentic tasks, task classes, variation and increasing complexity in task classes, the distinction between supportive and procedural information and the proposed practice to automation of selected part-tasks. The overall design focus is on the integration and coordination of different levels of learning tasks and as such fits very well with existing game design practice. Recent studies [14, 15] confirmed the applicability of the model for game design and their embedding in education. Additionally, at a small scale 4C-ID was successfully applied by teachers for reviewing serious games and discussing how they could be used from their perspective in an educational setting [16, 17].

In the next section we will introduce the CHERMUG games and how 4C-ID influenced their design. We will conclude with a description of how the two games have been trialled following a set of questions derived from the 4C-ID model and summarise the participants' findings.

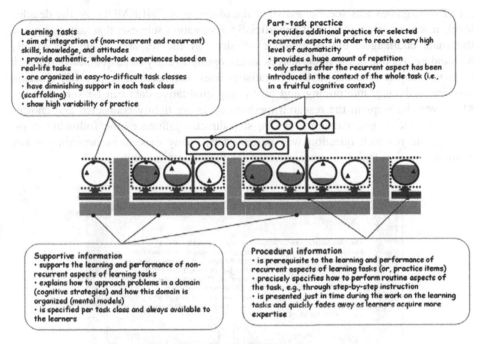

Learning tasks
• aim at integration of (non-recurrent and recurrent) skills, knowledge, and attitudes
• provide authentic, whole-task experiences based on real-life tasks
• are organized in easy-to-difficult task classes
• have diminishing support in each task class (scaffolding)
• show high variability of practice

Part-task practice
• provides additional practice for selected recurrent aspects in order to reach a very high level of automaticity
• provides a huge amount of repetition
• only starts after the recurrent aspect has been introduced in the context of the whole task (i.e., in a fruitful cognitive context)

Supportive information
• supports the learning and performance of non-recurrent aspects of learning tasks
• explains how to approach problems in a domain (cognitive strategies) and how this domain is organized (mental models)
• is specified per task class and always available to the learners

Procedural information
• is prerequisite to the learning and performance of recurrent aspects of learning tasks (or, practice items)
• precisely specifies how to perform routine aspects of the task, e.g., through step-by-step instruction
• is presented just in time during the work on the learning tasks and quickly fades away as learners acquire more expertise

Fig. 1. The four component instructional design model [13].

2 CHERMUG Game Based Learning Design: Cognitive Task Analysis and 4C-ID

The CHERMUG project (www.chermug.eu) aimed to develop a digital game to support students in learning about research methods and statistics. Acquiring expertise in this area poses significant challenges for many students.

Our first step in developing a game was to identify the skills and competences required. A technique which has been developed to help analyse the higher level cognitive functioning required in tackling complex tasks is Cognitive Task Analysis (CTA). CTA is defined as "the extension of traditional task analysis techniques to yield information about the knowledge, thought processes and goal structures that underlie observable task performance" [18]. Cognitive task analyses have been used for a number of different purposes including the development of training and fit very well with the 4C-ID model since it can yield detailed information on the skills and competence required, how they decompose and are interconnected and stepwise should be learnt.

The CTA was based on a set of 13 interviews with experts selected for their knowledge of and involvement with teaching research methods and statistics [19] and resulted in a number of findings important for the design of the game. At the global level the research cycle (research question, data collection, data analysis, discussion & conclusion) presented in the briefing sheet was generally accepted by staff as providing a useful framework for presenting research methods to students. Moreover, designing a set of mini-games was seen as assisting the adoption of CHERMUG. At the detailed level, it was widely agreed that superficially observation suggests that statistics cause the main challenges, but in practice all steps in the research cycle are equally demanding. As one of the interviewees stated, opting to carry out a qualitative research methods project in order to avoid statistics does not necessarily pay off, since in practice analysing, interpreting and abstracting qualitative data can be very difficult. Moreover, the steps in the research methods cycle are tightly connected and choices made or lack of understanding at one step directly influences the following steps. Finally, the research question was perceived by many experts as providing a key challenge in developing a coherent approach to research methods.

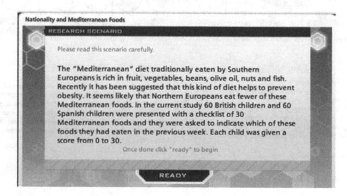

Fig. 2. The research scenario of one of the games.

The findings of the CTA were used in the design applying 4C-ID in the following way [20]. A set of mini-games was designed each based on an authentic and complete task (see Fig. 2 for an example of the research scenario of one of the games) distributed over three task classes, one with 3 games for qualitative research and two task classes on quantitative research (Table 1). Each of the task classes contained tasks with variation and increasing complexity. The supportive information is expected to be offered in advance in the class room or in an e-learning environment. Procedural information is

Table 1. The CHERMUG mini-games divided by their task classes and topics

Task class (Topic)/Level			
	Qualitative	Quantitative (Chi-square)	Quantitative (T-test)
Level 1	Main differences between qual. & quant. Analysis	Gender & reward	Nationality & Mediterranean food
Level 2	Simulating a quantitative research study	Exercise program & drop-out	Gender & protein consumption
Level 3	Writing to a journal	Media consumption & obesity	Type of diet & weight loss
Level 4		Skipping meals & obesity	
Level 5		Nationality & body image	

implicit through the rigorous structure chosen for the games. Finally, a set of use cases [21] and best practices [22] was prepared to describe the possible use of the games within different settings. The examples chosen should be transparent for teachers and ease the use of the games in their curricula.

3 Workshop Program and Results

Workshop Setup. The workshop started with two presentations (1) an explanation of the 4C-ID model and (2) an introduction to the CHERMUG project. The participants were asked to briefly study the 4C-ID model (http://chermug-workshop.wikispaces.com/) and answer the following set of questions (Fig. 1) for the anticipated overall learning design in which the games would be used *and* for the games themselves, i.e.:

1. Learning tasks, i.e. the extent to which:
   - the game uses whole learning tasks;
   - the game uses a variety of tasks i.e. stressing different elements or examples;
   - the game uses task classes i.e. offering both simple and (more) complex examples;

2. Supportive information i.e. the extent to which:
   - the game uses supportive information;

3. Procedural information, i.e. the extent to which:
   - the game uses procedural information;

4. Part-task practice, i.e. the extent to which:
   - the game uses part-task-practice.

   Next, the participants were asked to play a CHERMUG game (www.playgen.com/chermug) about research methods and statistics and Enercities (http://www.enercities.eu) a game about building a sustainable city each for around 15–20 min. They received the following assignment "Assume you are a teacher who wants to assess possible use of the game, i.e. look at the game and 'guess' which learning tasks can be supported/achieved by the game and/or additional materials". Each of the games was followed by a questionnaire with questions that helped to classify serious game characteristics (based on the GaLA serious game evaluation form) and questions to assess if and how the game could be used in the given situation. Additionally, the questionnaire asked how the game was perceived in general and how useful the questionnaire was to help evaluating the applicability of a game and to determine any additional learning materials or activities needed. Finally, the workshop was closed with an open discussion of the experiences of the participants.

   Participants and Results. Twelve persons participated in the workshop. All were experienced users, i.e. had average to good experience with using games in education. The participants worked in pairs (with exception of two) and completed one review round (the two CHERMUG games); the second game was played but not reviewed due to time limitations. The results were as follows.

First of all, the games were positively appreciated on various aspects including effectiveness, efficiency, usability and motivation. Moreover, it revealed that the participants agreed that the game design was based on whole learning tasks. The majority also agreed that the games made used of variability of practice from one to the next game ("different research methods are well introduced"). Questions how to use the games within the lesson practice with regard to variability and more tasks were clear but - in the discussion - the participants mentioned that they did miss the required teaching expertise in this domain to be able to come up with suggestions. With regard to procedural and supportive information the players were guided implicitly by the used scenario structure ("implicit by the scenario structure"), detailed explanations were only given if mistakes were made ("explanations are only given when something goes wrong"). The questions what additional procedural and supportive information should be added in the lessons were clear but again due to lack of domain knowledge difficult to answer ("yes, I can imagine there is a lot of additional (introductory) material").

Finally, with regard to use of the 4C-ID model and the questions derived from it, most participants did positively appreciate the way the questions could help them to evaluate the applicability of games for their use. Critical remarks were focussed on the wordings of some questions which were sometimes ambiguous or required a better introduction to the model.

4   Conclusion

The key elements of the 4C-ID instructional design model i.e. authentic tasks, the distinction between supportive and procedural information and the proposed practice to automation of selected part-tasks fits well with game practice. The participants in the workshop could relatively easily reflect upon the games played with the help of the questions despite the challenge to play a game in a domain where they had limited familiarity. Equally important, the approach proposed helped to reflect beyond the game to the actual lesson plan in which games will be used and assisted in thinking about the design and the activities required to make best use of the games. The 4C-ID, though actually intended for curricula design, did give guidance on how to assess serious games and their usage.

Obviously given the size of the experiment (only two games, the limited time and number of participants) it is not possible to draw any firm conclusion as yet. Nevertheless, we do believe that the positive response to the model together with the research behind the model and the literature discussed, related to the use of the model for serious game design, warrant further research.

Acknowledgments.   The work described in this paper was partially supported by the European Community under the Lifelong Learning Programme project CHERMUG nr. 519023-LLP-1-2011-1-UK-KA3-KA3MP. The paper does not represent the opinion of the European Community, and the European Community is not responsible for any use that might be made of its content.

References

1. Connolly, T.M., Boyle, E.A., MacArthur, E., Hainey, T., Boyle, J.: A systematic literature review of empirical evidence on computer games and serious games. Comput. Educ. **59**(2), 661–686 (2012)
2. Harteveld, C.: Triadic Game Design: Balancing Reality, Meaning and Play. Springer, London (2011)
3. De Freitas, S., Rebolledo-Mendez, G., Liarokapis, F., Magoulas, G., Poulovassilis, A.: Learning as immersive experiences: using the four dimensional framework for designing and evaluating immersive learning experiences in a virtual world. Br. J. Educ. Technol. **41**(1), 69–85 (2010)
4. Pernin, J., Michau, F., Mandran, N., Mariais, C.: ScenLRPG, a board game for the collaborative design of Gbl scenarios: qualitative analysis of an experiment. In: Proceedings of the 6th European Conference on Games Based Learning, Cork, Ireland, 4–5 October 2012, pp. 384–392 (2012)
5. Silius, K., Miilumäki, T., Huhtamäki, J., Tebest, T., Meriläinen, J., Pohjolainen, S.: Students' motivations for social media enhanced studying and learning. Knowl. Manage. E-Learn. Int. J. **2**(1), 51 (2010)
6. Sloep, P.B., Van der Klink, M., Brouns, F., Van Bruggen, J., Didderen, W. (eds.): Leernetwerken; Kennisdeling, kennisontwikkeling en de leerprocessen. Houten, Nederland, Bohn, Stafleu, Van Loghum (2011)
7. NFER: Teacher Voice Omnibus Survey. (2009). http://www.nfer.ac.uk/nfer/what-we-offer/teacher-voice/PDFs/futurelab.pdf. Accessed 24 August 2012
8. FAS: Harnessing the Power of Video Games for Learning. Summit of educational games. Washington DC, Federation of American Scientists. (2006) http://www.fas.org/gamesummit/Resources/Summit%20on%20Educational%20Games.pdf
9. Williamson, B.: Computer games, schools, and young people. a report for educators on using games for learning. Futurelab: Bristol. (2009). http://archive.futurelab.org.uk/resources/documents/project_reports/becta/Games_and_Learning_educators_report.pdf. Accessed
10. Klopfler, E., Osterweil, S., Salen, K.: Moving learning games forward; obstacles, opportunities and openness. MIT - The Education Arcade, Boston, MA (2009). Accessed 15 September 2011
11. Vier in Balans Monitor 2012 (2012) http://www.kennisnet.nl/fileadmin/contentelementen/kennisnet/Over.kennisnet/vier-in-balans-2012.pdf. Accessed 5 December 2012
12. Huang, W.D., Johnson, T.: Instructional game design using cognitive load theory. In: Ferdig, R. (ed.) Handbook of Research on Effective Electronic Gaming in Education, Hershey, PA, Information Science, pp. 1143–1165 (2009) doi:10.4018/978-1-59904-808-6.ch066
13. Van Merriënboer, J.J.G., Kirschner, P.A.: Ten Steps to Complex Learning, 2nd edn. Routledge, New York (2012)
14. Lukosch, H., Van Bussel, R., Meijer, S.: A game design framework for vocational education. Int. J. Soc. Hum. Sci. **6**(1), 453–457 (2012)
15. Enfield, J.: Designing an educational game with ten steps to complex learning. Doctoral Dissertation (2012)
16. Van der Baaren, J., Nadolski, R., Van Rosmalen, P.: Serious games: wat kun je er mee in het hoger onderwijs? In: Workshop EHON Conference, 7 June 2012, Heerlen, The Netherlands (2012)

17. Nadolski, R.J.: 4C-ID voor educatieve games? Evalueren van bestaande educatieve games via het 4C-ID model. Presentation Masterclass 'Hoe maak je een eenvoudige serious game?' 12 March 2013, Heerlen, The Netherlands (2013)
18. Chipman, S.E., Schraagen, J.M.C., Shalin, V.L.: Introduction to cognitive task analysis. In: Schraagen, J.M.C., Chipman, S.E., Shalin, V.L. (eds.) Cognitive Task Analysis. Lawrence Erlbaum Associates, Mahwah (2000)
19. Boyle, E., Van Rosmalen, P., MacArthur, E., Connolly, T., Hainey, T., et al.: Cognitive task analysis (CTA) in the continuing/ higher education methods using games (CHERMUG) project. In: Proceedings of the 6th European Conference on Games Based Learning, Cork, Ireland, 4–5 October 2012, pp. 63–71 (2012)
20. Van Rosmalen, P., Boyle, E.A., Van der Baaren, J., Kärki, A.I., Del Blanco Aguado, A.: A case study on the design and development of mini-games for research methods and statistics. EAI Endorsed Trans. Game Based Learn. **14**(3): e5 (2014)
21. Kärki, A., Pennanen, T., Isberg, S.: CHERMUG Deliverable 24: Use Case Scenarios (2014)
22. Kärki, A., Pennanen, T., Isberg, S.: CHERMUG Deliverable 23: Best Practice Case Studies (2014)

Posters

An Instructional Approach for Developing Serious Games

Félix Buendía-García[1(✉)], Sol García-Martínez[2],
Eva Mª Navarrete-Ibañez[3], and Mª Jesús Cervelló-Donderis[3]

[1] Universitat Politécnica de Valencia, Camino de Vera s/n,
46022 Valencia, Spain
fbuendia@disca.upv.es
[2] Evoluciona - Proyectos Web, S.L, Valencia, Spain
sol.garcia@e-red.es
[3] Servicio de Formación Diputación de Valencia, 46002 Valencia, Spain
{eva.navarrete,mjesus.cervello}@dival.es

Abstract. Serious games are currently present in almost every educational context. The current work deals with the design and development of serious games based on an instructional approach to train transferable skills in public administration settings. This approach can be a valuable way of supporting instructors when they are designing games for public employees in lifelong learning processes by means of metaphors or similar mechanisms close to their working experience. Such design process is also based on modeling mechanisms in order to formally represent the game components. The proposed approach is complemented with the use of a development tool to elaborate this type of game by mixing traditional design steps with an instructional strategy to provide structured learning bites in training settings. Several game prototypes have been developed to test this approach in the context of courses for public employees. The obtained outcomes reveal the wider possibilities of serious games as educational resources, as well as the use of game achievements to evaluate the acquisition of transferable skills.

1 Introduction

The game-based learning paradigm is now present in almost every educational context, spreading the concept of gamification [1] and serious games. Multiple initiatives have been launched dealing with how serious games can support formal education in schools [2] and higher education [3]. There are also examples applied to training settings although these games are usually oriented towards specific professional areas such as medical [4] or military scenarios [5]. The success of serious games can be generally linked to the phenomenon of the net or gamer generation whose members are currently studying in our schools and universities. In the case of training settings, the role of serious games has to be adapted to adult users who are not used to playing in this way and have tight time restraints. Traditionally, this role has been focused on simulators and other immersive techniques addressed to training for specific tasks [6]. However, the need to incorporate new social and transferable skills for lifelong learners gives

© Springer International Publishing Switzerland 2014
A. De Gloria (Ed.): GALA 2013, LNCS 8605, pp. 337–348, 2014.
DOI: 10.1007/978-3-319-12157-4_27

serious games a wider spectrum within the context of a knowledge society in a state of continuous change.

This paper deals with the development of serious games oriented towards training transferable skills in public administration. These organizations are ever more concerned about the call for new training strategies. Serious games offer an excellent opportunity to promote active learning among staff who have to cope with changes in their job assignments and responsibilities. They also provide a way to teaching alternative skills outside their usual routines. The current work proposes serious games as a way of involving public workers in their training process while taking into account their time restrictions. The aim is to produce small learning bites that get the interest of workers with tight schedules and limitations in acquiring the relevant skills. This idea is linked to the principle that "in adult education small is beautiful" [7]. The serious games proposed are based on mechanisms close to the users' experience, using metaphors or similar elements, and adapted to their level of expertise. Such games can be considered as learning resources addressed to achieving specific skills but introducing motivating factors to uptake generic job competencies.

This instructional approach has to be supported by mechanisms that facilitate rigorous and systematic game development. Several types of framework have been proposed for formally representing and developing different types of games. Some of these proposals incorporate formal instructional issues, for example, well-established learning theories [8] or try to reduce game design complexity in higher education [9]. PIMI [10] proposes another formal framework to assist in the design and development of serious games through an iterative process. However, few of these frameworks focus on serious games for learning professional capabilities [11] and they usually need to be adapted to teach transferable skills. Training settings have traditionally been supported by simulations and immersive worlds as basic techniques to meet learning requirements in these settings. These techniques have succeeded when specific goals or skills are required, for example, in adaptive training systems [12]. In the case of more generic or transferable skills, the use of metaphors can provide an appropriate mechanism to acquire these skills. These metaphors can be linked to users' seamless experiences during their formal education such as reading books or answering quizzes, but also in their professional and daily activities. The selected metaphors should not interfere with the training activities and should become a transparent item in the process, in order to encourage the acquisition of transferable skills. In the context of the current work, several game samples have been developed with the purpose of checking the adequacy of the proposed approach in lifelong learning areas and addressing the generic skills considered useful for public administration employees. These samples are mainly concerned with learning experiences in a government organization known as *DiVal* (Diputació de Valencia) but they can easily be transferred to other professional settings such as universities or hospitals. This development has been supported by the use of a tool called *EAdventure* [13] which allows game designers to rapidly generate small prototypes that can be tested by instructors who are not necessarily expert in game-based learning disciplines.

The remainder of the paper is organized as follows. The second section describes the approach used to develop game prototypes for training transferable skills. The third section reports on the development of games that apply the approach in the context of a specific public organization and are tested under usability issues. Finally, Sect. 4 provides the main conclusions and suggests future lines of research.

2 Instructional Game Approach

The proposal for developing small games in public administration settings is based on a strategy that combines traditional steps in the design of games with an instructional approach to integrate game learning requirements. The design and development of computer games have been widely addressed by authors such as Crawford [14] or Pederson [15] who provide game designers with different perspectives for designing such products. However, the choice of the right method is difficult due to the diversity of game features and aims, particularly, in a learning context. In this work, an instructional game approach is presented based on the importance of a structured and systematic development process combined with the use of techniques to quickly produce adaptable games. The current proposal also allows an instructional designer to actively collaborate in creating the game by fitting the play elements to the required learning goals or taking advantage of game outcomes to assess the user's progress. There are several stages that compose the global approach, which are close to the instructional steps proposed in the ADDIE model [16]. Such stages address issues such as: (i) the conceptual definition of the experience that arises out of the game; (ii) the design of the game components; (iii) the implementation of the game prototype; and (iv) the evaluation of the developed product. Instructional issues are transversal to the game development in the sense that it is considered as an educational resource used in a specific training context to enable generic or specific skills. The stages involved in this process are described in the next sections.

2.1 Conceptual Definition

The first stage is the conceptual definition, which gives a general description of the experience associated with the target game and represents an abstract outlook of the game purpose and its main features and needs. This perspective comprises several issues, such as a title for the game, its learning goals or the game training focus. This conceptual definition agrees with the holistic view that is part of the framework proposed by Bjork & Holopainen [17] considering the game as an undividable experience. This view provides an important meeting point for instructors and game designers. The key issue can be centered on the question "Why should learners play?" instead of "Why do players play?" thus establishing the instructional focus of the game [18]. In the current context, game experiences are related to professional settings that require specific knowledge items or practice abilities, but these experiences can also be extended to more generic skills. For example, the core game conception can promote a systematic search habit or encourage teamwork responsibilities. Learning goals thus have to be carefully defined and connected with well-known taxonomies as well as with those game actions that permit the required goals to be achieved and with the associated training skills.

Table 1 shows a list of Bloom competencies which can be related to transferable skills in a public administration context. For example, a knowledge-based goal can be associated with recalling information on safety protocols in a *Risk Management* course. The skills represented can be linked to game actions such as "identify critical objects" in a safety scenario or "explore systematically" this scenario. This basic definition enables a game conception that can be adapted to fit specific learning contents and activities in further steps.

Table 1. Learning goals and their relationships with game actions

Goals	Skills	Game actions
Knowledge	Learners can recall information about safety protocols and public hiring procedures	Identify or collect critical game objects
Comprehension	Learner can explain legal topics and understand organizational conditions and conflicts	Select game descriptions or follow narrative paths
Application	Learners can solve problems, assign public job responsibilities, apply technical specifications and assist citizens	Choose game options or launch character conversations
Analysis	Learners can determine public or social responsibilities, explore roles and assign tasks to team members	Assign role functions or configure game activities
Synthesis	Learners can build or prepare a plan/project	Review game outcomes
Evaluation	Learners can make judgments about managing a project or a plan scheduling	Answer relevant questions or select game options

2.2 Game Design

The game design deals with the different views that complement the description of the game from its core conception in the previous stage. In the framework proposed by Bjork & Holopainen [17] the structural view describes "the basic parts of the game manipulated by the players and the system" while the dynamic view allows the designer to specify "the flow of the game" through player actions, character conversations or state changes. Schell [19] divides game elements into four basic categories: mechanics, story, aesthetics and technology and other categories can be proposed to classify these elements such as characters, items, objects or mechanisms [18]. Whatever the model selected, the main question is how to match these structural and dynamic components to the instructional issues required by the game. In this context, it is important to choose an appropriate visual scenario that involves the user in the learning process, for example, using a metaphor close to his experience. It is also crucial to describe game actions that promote certain training objectives, e.g. collecting objects or assigning roles to game characters. Some of these actions are displayed in Table 1 and include their relationship to Bloom competencies in a public administration context.

All these steps are present in the design of other instructional products. For example, a lesson presentation or a screencast recording are designed according certain aesthetic criteria and different roles and functions can be assigned to project activities in a course. Games introduce a leisure factor, which adds an extra motivation in the learning or training process [20] but they can be considered as a complementary resource within the overall system. This accumulation of game components leads designers to deploy methods and techniques that help them to elaborate a game model before implementing it. Such modelling process can take advantage of elements and notations that represent the game in a systematic and formal way. The visual game components can be represented by sketches or storyboards, and, scripts or state charts can be used to model the dynamic game behaviour [18]. The dynamic component is perhaps the most difficult part to model in an educational product. Some notations that combine the modelling of both technical and instructional issues can be useful in this context [21, 22]. Burgos et al. [22] address the use of e-learning standards such as IMS LD to represent educational games and Marfisi-Schottman et al. [11] propose engineering methods for designing serious games. Other frameworks proposed by *Emergo* [23] and Yusoff et al. [24] are based on UML diagrams to describe and represent game components.

In the current work, UML notations have been selected to represent a game's structural and dynamic view. Class diagrams are an effective way of modeling structural elements such as the characters who participate in the game and the objects that form part of the scenario. Several UML artifacts, such as activity or state diagrams, can help to represent how game characters perform specific actions on certain objects. The current approach is close to the conceptual framework proposed by Yusoff et al. [24] that uses a UML class diagram modeling the main game components such as capabilities, learning activities or outcomes. This class diagram can be complemented incorporating entities to add instructional issues into the game design. For example, to differentiate certain generic capabilities, such as "solving problems" or "supervising teamwork" from more specific instructional contents attached to a specific training area such as a safety protocol. An entity that represents the "box of items" to be collected during the game can be used as a learning outcome and "game conversations" can be part of the activities promoted during the course. To sum up, these entities link learning goals or instructional resources with game elements by means of items such as character scripts, object actions or player roles.

2.3   Game Implementation

Once the main aspects of the instructional game have been designed, these can be implemented by means of prototypes that show how they work in specific training settings. There are several companies that specialize in developing this type of serious games such as *DDigitally*[1] or *PIXELearning*[2] who produce immersive worlds. These products are usually oriented towards 3D complex developments, which are expensive and out of reach of public sector organizations. An alternative way of obtaining affordable products consists of using creative tools either commercial, such as *Adobe*

---

[1] http://www.designingdigitally.com/
[2] http://www.pixelearning.com/

Director™ or *Flash*™ that make it possible to compose simple games or *free software* products adapted to different serious games. In the current work, the main purpose is to implement game prototypes that can be easily tested by instructors to determine their feasibility. After this initial testing and evaluation a decision can be made on whether to take the game development a step further. Several authoring tools were assessed considering these premises for the purpose of creating adventure-based games easily and quickly. In this category there is also a wide range of tools able to generate this type of game. For example, *Adventure Maker*[3] helps to create *point&click* games for web-based environments for users with no programming skills. WME[4] and AGS[5] are similar tools and both require a.NET platform for developing games. *EAdventure* [13] was finally selected as it provides an easy development process using a graphical friendly interface with the option of incorporating didactic objects (e.g., book documents, web pages or video records) and debugging products during the implementation stage. It also provides for the integration of accessible elements that allow disabled players to control the game using a keyboard or enabling audio descriptions of game actions. *EAdventure* can even generate standard specifications, such as SCORM or IMS CP, which can be integrated in e-learning platforms.

2.4   Game Evaluation

The final approach stage deals with the evaluation of developed games and can be viewed from different perspectives, based on either instructional issues or experience features. *Game Object Model* [25] provides a global view of the integration of educational theory and game design complemented by a model of the game's achievements. These achievements can be the link between learning goals and activities formulated in the conceptual game definition, and the game actions that are part of its design and development. Table 1 shows a set of game actions linked to learning goals and associated skills in a public administration context. For example, the collection of objects designed to promote a systematic exploratory ability can be used as a game achievement and is a useful instrument for player assessment. Another example of game achievement can be the number or kinds of conversations started in a game as a way of measuring the player's communication skills. This is critical point in the development and evaluation of serious games, and has been addressed in specific simulation scenarios but it becomes a challenge in achieving generic skills. Event tracking helps instructors to understand how players deal with the game mechanics by obtaining a learner profile describing his game achievements. Serrano et al. [26] implemented a framework "to improve evaluation in educational games" by applying *Learning Analytics* techniques based on the logs produced by the *EAdventure* engine. There are several possibilities for checking relationships between instructional issues and game items to detect if the developed games meet the required training goals. Some

---

[3] http://www.adventuremaker.com/

[4] http://dead-code.org/home/

[5] http://www.adventuregamestudio.co.uk/ac.shtml

studies have also found that games are especially effective for students with poor performance in the domain taught but not all game features improve their learning effectiveness. Wouters et al. [27] propose the alignment of learning outcomes and game types. Games should be carefully designed and evaluated as to their instructional potential in order to have a real impact on learning or training activities [28].

Other issues than instructional aspects can be considered in evaluating a game. Nacke et al. [29] describe several methods of evaluating the *gameplay* experience, by assessing aspects such game system experience, individual player experience and player context experience. The current work focuses on evaluating the player perspective and how he interacts with the game. Since game prototypes are first checked by course instructors, they are considered the main actors in this evaluation process. In this case, eye tracking techniques and mouse tracking analysis can be used to evaluate the player experience from the instructor's point of view. They can then decide not only whether the game mechanics fits the required learning goals, but also whether they can be understood and used by potential players. Usability is a fundamental issue in game evaluation and other aspects, such as playability or accessibility must also be addressed.

3   Developing Game Samples

Several game prototypes were developed to test the proposed approach in a public administration setting. Trials were carried out in *DiVal*, which is a government organization that gives support to local councils in providing services to both the general public and workers. It offers a wide range of services, including training for public employees in several areas. For example, it gives more than 130 courses in life-long learning topics such as risk management and job responsibilities. The first step was to choose the courses that were to take part in the game experience and decide how the proposed approach would later be applied. The conceptual *definition* of these games was based on selecting training scenarios familiar to *DiVal* users. There were a number of candidate courses, and several issues were analyzed to determine whether educational games would be appropriate in their curricula and the transferable skills that could be transmitted by them. The aim was to teach certain knowledge items combined with practical activities, and also to enable the learning of generic skills such as exploratory routines, problem solving, communication abilities and collaboration or negotiation attitudes. Every game application should provide specific outcomes and achievements to make it possible to assess learner performance.

Several sample games were designed under these principles and two prototypes were finally chosen. Figure 1 shows a screenshot of an office-based scenario for a game called *Ergon* (from ergonomics). It can be considered a basic *click&point* product addressed to picking up items from a displayed scenario and promotes basic abilities such as systematic search or promoting inquisitiveness. *Ergon* was developed for a course in *Risk Management*, whose main purpose is to provide information on risk prevention in the workplace and to practice basic safety skills. The *Ergon* prototype concerned teaching ergonomics topics to public employees, among other skills. Figure 1 displays a synthetic view of an office area that contains typical office equipment. For example, the player can examine objects such as lights, chairs or computer devices and then decide on their ergonomic impact (signalled as red square hot spots in Fig. 1). It is important to emphasize the use of a *quiz* metaphor, based on identifying objects with a special meaning, similar to the quizzes for finding the differences between two images. In this way, the *Ergon* game was able to encourage users to systematically explore elements that could be critical to their health thus teaching an additional skill. In the case of the *Ergon* prototype, the game mechanics was rather simplistic since it only required players to collect objects from an office scenario. The narrative began with the instructions and details of how to finish the game (no time limit or deadline was imposed).

Fig. 1. Game display for Ergon and Respon prototypes.

Even in a simple game, such as *Ergon* its formal *design* contributed positively to its further implementation. For example, it enabled game elements and their states to be defined, the operations or methods that could be carried out on the defined elements, or when transitions could be triggered. This design was organized into two main parts: (i) a structural model that represented the main game entities through a UML class diagram, and (ii) a dynamic model of the game behaviour. The diagrammatic representation of the game elements allowed instructors to detect the objects that would be useful in the game and their relationships with its purpose, for example, a *map* for instructions or an *inventory box* to track the game progress. The dynamic model was very useful to represent possible game actions, including when the player decided to quit the game. Figure 2 shows a UML activity diagram displaying some of these actions and highlighting the options that the player can take. For example, the

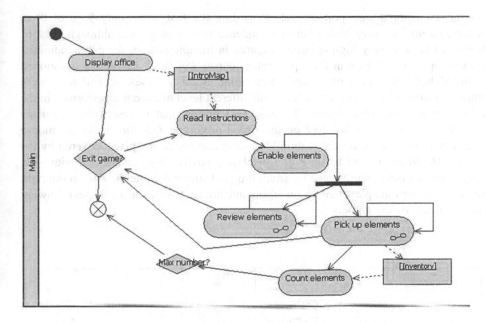

Fig. 2. Ergon activity diagram.

possibility of *examining* or retrieve information from a scenario item or the *take* action of picking up a given element and storing it in the *inventory box*.

The game also contained several scenes and transitions that were carefully designed to cater for the multiple actions the player could be faced with from the interaction among characters. The *implementation* of both games was based on the use of *EAdventure* v1.5, which allows game developers to quickly develop prototypes to be tested by volunteer instructors. *EAdventure* mechanics is rather flexible and enables *point&click* games to be developed from products based on simple object actions to complex interactions among game elements, such as scenario items and characters through conversations and other events. The *Ergon* implementation was also oriented towards accessible features that included voice recordings for every instruction message or object interaction. An additional advantage was the ability to run and test the games inside the authoring environment avoiding the generation of final products every time a change was introduced into the prototype. This feature provided a fast debugging of the game and it enabled to track, for example, the correct increment in the number of collected objects, or to verify the flag values corresponding to certain game states. *EAdventure* was also able to generate learning objects which could be deployed on e-learning platforms such as the *DiVal* Web portal.

The *evaluation* of game prototypes was mainly based on usability tests of the products developed. A questionnaire was also given to *DiVal* instructors in order to obtain their opinion about the use of adventure games in training settings. The questionnaire focused on issues such as the instructor's confidence in game-based learning, the contributions of games to the learning process in administration settings or dealing with the particular impact in their courses. Thirty-two answers were obtained from the instructors using a web polling tool. Regarding the first issue, only 9 % of them reported a high or very high level of confidence in serious games, although most of them had high or very high opinion of games in training courses for public administration topics (65 %) or in their particular courses (59 % of instructors questioned returned high or very high scores). Regarding usability issues, several tests were implemented to check how instructors with different level of expertise performed in the *Risk Management* topic. Figure 3 shows two images that represent the *heatmaps* obtained from the *Odoplus*[6] tool on the *Ergon* prototype. *Odoplus* tracks the mouse clicks performed while an application is running and counts the pixels covered by the player. The image on the left in Fig. 3 displays a novice player interaction with wide dispersion of clicks (represented by small little red squares) while the one on the right in Fig. 3 focuses the player clicks on ergonomic hot spots (red square shapes) showing an expert use of the game.

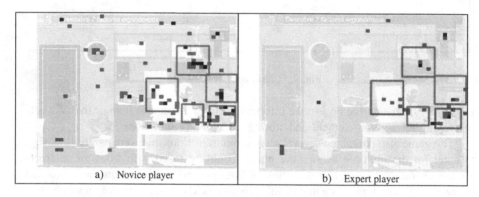

a)   Novice player   b)   Expert player

Fig. 3. *Ergon* user interaction tracking.

4   Conclusions

This paper has proposed an approach that adapts small games for training courses in the public administration context. It combines an ADDIE-based instructional strategy with the use of the *EAdventure* software for rapid game development and testing. The approach was applied in a government organization in the form of several game prototypes, which enabled the acquisition of transferable skills such as exploratory and communication abilities. A questionnaire was completed by the *DiVal* instructors to obtain their opinions of the value of serious games in their training courses. Testing of the game prototypes confirmed the usefulness of *heatmap* and mouse tracking analysis to check player behaviour and to interpret the game achievements. The evaluation outcomes also revealed other issues, such as the need to formalize the analysis of game achievements and their relationship with training goals as well as the need for more

---

[6] http://www.fridgesoft.de/odoplus.php

effective collaboration among practitioners, instructional designers and game developers. The overall experience has shown that much more research is necessary in this field and has also highlighted the difficulties involved in determining how games can support the acquisition of transferable skills in this kind of settings. Further research will be necessary into the use of educational standards and the application of agile engineering techniques in the game development arena.

Acknowledgments. This work is supported by the TEA project (PAIDUPV/2791).

References

1. Kapp, K.M.: The gamification of learning and instruction: game-based methods and strategies for training and education. Ed. Pfeiffer (2012)
2. Ilicsak, M., Wright, M.: Games in Education: Serious Games. Bristol, Futurelab (2010)
3. Bekebrede, G., Warmelink, H.J.G., Mayer, I.S.: Reviewing the need for gaming in education to accommodate the net generation. Comput. Educ. **57**(2), 1521–1529 (2011). Elsevier
4. Stone, R.J.: Serious games and defence medicine. HFI DTC newsletter Frontline, 7 (2007)
5. Caird-Daley, A.K., Harris, D.: Training decision making using serious games. HFI DTC report, reference number HFIDTC/2/WP4.6.1/1 (2007)
6. De Freitas, S., Oliver, M.: How can exploratory learning with games and simulations within the curriculum be most effectively evaluated? Comput. Educ. **46**, 249–264 (2006). Special Issue on Gaming, Elsevier
7. Bookbinder, S.: In adult education, small is beautiful. Digital Media Training (2012). http://dmtraining.net/. Accessed July 2012
8. Gunter, G., Kenny, R., Vick, E.: A case for a formal design paradigm for serious games. J. Int. Digit. Media Arts Assoc. **3**(1), 93–105 (2006)
9. Westera, W., Nadolski, R.J., Hummel, H.G.K., Wopereis, I.G.J.H.: Serious games for higher education: a framework for reducing design complexity. J. Comput. Assist. Learn. **24**(5), 420–432 (2008)
10. Vanden Abeele, V., De Schutter, B., Geurts, L., Desmet, S., Wauters, J., Husson, J., Van Audenaeren, L., Van Broeckhoven, F.: PIMI – A framework for serious game development. Serious Games: The Challenge. K.U.Leuven, Ghent (2011)
11. Marfisi-Schottman, I., George, S., Tarpin-Bernard, F.: Tools and methods for efficiently designing serious games. In: Proceedings of the 4th European Conference on Games Based Learning, Copenhagen, Denmark, pp. 226–234 (2010)
12. Raybourn, E.M.: Applying simulation experience design principles to creating serious games for adaptive thinking training. Interact. Comput. **19**, 206–214 (2007). Elsevier
13. Torrente, J., del Blanco, A., Marchiori, E., Moreno-Ger, P., Fernández-Manjón, B.: < E-Adventure >: introducing Educational games in the learning. In: Proceedings of the 1st IEEE Engineering Conference, Madrid, Spain (2010)
14. Crawford, C.: The Art of Computer Game Design. McGraw-Hill, New York (1984)
15. Pederson, R.E.: Game Design Foundations. Wordware Pub., Sudbury (2009)
16. Molenda, M.: In search of the elusive ADDIE model. Perform. Improv. **42**(5), 34 (2003)
17. Björk, S., Holopainen, J.: Patterns in Game Design. Charles River Media, Hingham (2005)
18. Rouse, R.: Game Design: Theory & Practice, 2nd edn. Wordware Publishing Inc, Plano (2005)

19. Schell, J.: The Art of Game Design: a Book of Lenses. Morgan Kauffman Publishers, Burlington (2008)
20. Michael, D., Chen, S.: Serious Games: Games that Educate, Train and Inform. Thomson Course Technology, Boston (2006)
21. Buendía. F., Díaz, P.: A framework for the management of digital educational contents conjugating instructional and technical issues. Educ. Technol. Soc. 6(4), 48–59 (2003)
22. Burgos, D., Tattersall, C., Koper, R.: Re-purposing existing generic games for ELearning. Comput. Hum. Behav. **23**(6), 2656–2667 (2007)
23. Nadolski, R.J., Hummel, H.G.K., Van den Brink, H.J., Hoefakker, R., Slootmaker, A., Kurvers, H., Storm, J.: EMERGO: methodology and toolkit for efficient development of serious games in higher education. Simul. Gaming **39**(3), 338–352 (2008)
24. Yusoff, A., Crowder, R., Gilbert, L., Wills, G.: A conceptual framework for serious games. In: Proceedings of the 9th IEEE International Conference on Advanced Learning Technologies, Washington, DC, USA, pp. 21–23 (2009)
25. Amory, A., Seagram, R.: Educational game models: conceptualization and evaluation. S. Afr. J. High. Educ. **17**(2), 206–217 (2003)
26. Serrano, Á., Marchiori, E.J., del Blanco, Á., Torrente, J., Fernández-Manjón, B.: A framework to improve evaluation in educational games. In: Proceedings of the 3rd IEEE Engineering Conference, Marrakesh, Morocco (2012)
27. Wouters, P., Van der Spek, E.D., Van Oostendorp, H.: Current practices in serious game research: a review from a learning outcomes perspective. In: Connolly, T., Stansfield, M., Boyle, L. (eds.) Games-Based Learning Advancements for Multi-sensory Human Computer Interfaces: Techniques and Effective Practices, pp. 232–250. IGI Global, Hershey (2009)
28. Egenfeldt-Nielsen, S.: The challenges to diffusion of educational computer games. In: Proceedings of the 4th European Conference on Games Based Learning, Copenhagen, Denmark (2010)
29. Nacke, L.E., Drachen, A., Goebel, S.: Methods for evaluating gameplay experience in a serious gaming context. Int. J. Comput. Sci. Sport **9**(2), 1–12 (2010)

User Profiling: Towards a Facebook Game that Reveals Cognitive Style

Angeliki Antoniou[1(✉)], Ioanna Lykourentzou[2], Jenny Rompa[1],
Eric Tobias[2], George Lepouras[1], Costas Vassilakis[1],
and Yannick Naudet[2]

[1] University of Pelponnese, Terma Karaiskai, 22100 Tripolis, Greece
{angelant,jr,g.lepouras,costas}@uop.gr
[2] CPR Henri Tudor, 29, avenue J.F. Kennedy, 1855 Luxembourg, Luxembourg
{ioanna.lykourentzou,eric.tobias,
yannick.naudet}@tudor.lu

Abstract. This paper presents an innovative approach based on social-network gaming, which will extract players' cognitive styles for personalization purposes. Cognitive styles describe the way individuals think, perceive and remember information and can be exploited to personalize user interaction. Questionnaires are usually employed to identify cognitive styles, a tedious process for most users. Our approach relies on a Facebook game for discovering potential visitors' cognitive styles with an ultimate goal of enhancing the overall visitors' experience in the museum. By hosting such a game on the museum's webpage and on Facebook, the museum aims to attract new visitors, as well as to support the user profiling process.

1 Introduction

Looking for fun ways to attract and engage museum visitors prior to their visit, two main requirements came up immediately: (i) to entertain the future visitor and make her interested in the museum and (ii) to use any information possible to personalize her visit once in the museum. Especially in regards to museums, personalized applications can be a valuable tool in the management of the multi-dimensional museum learning content, as well as an attempt to cover the visit needs of a diverse audience (Gaeta et al. 2007, Muntean et al. 2007, Wakkary et al. 2006). In addition, a typical museum visit lasts a few minutes (Falk et al. 1985, Serrell 1998) and visitors might only visit once. Thus, the personalization processes need to be quick and efficient. For all the above reasons, an increasing number of museums and cultural institutions around the world are using personalized applications. Ardissono and Petrelli (2008) provide a detailed survey of the field of personalized applications in cultural heritage.

To achieve our first goal, i.e. to entertain the future visitor and make her interested in the museum, it was decided to use social networks and particularly Facebook, as one of the most popular networks in Greece (note that the application is developed for a Greek museum), both to approach future visitors and to use the penetration abilities of the network to promote our application. For this purpose, it was also decided to create the application in the form of a game, similar to the popular games played on

© Springer International Publishing Switzerland 2014
A. De Gloria (Ed.): GALA 2013, LNCS 8605, pp. 349–353, 2014.
DOI: 10.1007/978-3-319-12157-4_28

Facebook. Additionally to supporting learning (serious games) or the solving of complex task (games with purpose), games can also provide information on players and their psychological and cognitive profile. The literature on the subject of extracting a user's cognitive style from gaming is very limited and in fact to the best knowledge of the authors this is a novel approach.

For our second goal, i.e. the quick and efficient extraction of user profile information that can be used later on during the actual museum visit, it was decided to implement a Facebook game in order to extract the user's cognitive style. Cognitive style is a person's preference and habitual approach to the organization and representation of information (Riding et al. 1998). Cognitive style provides information on users' behavior and way on thinking rather than on their own personal preferences and can thus be used to infer personalization rules that would fit all users having the same cognitive style. Resulting user stereotypes can be sufficient to provide pertinent personalization. Our postulate is that knowing the cognitive style of visitors gives enough information to personalize their visits, in particular on the kind of (generic or linked to museum's exhibitions) things they like and in which way information should be provided to them. As an example, a cognitive style might tell us whether a user prefers information delivered to her in audio rather than image format, with more or less details, etc.

The work described here is highly novel for two main reasons: (1) It suggests new, alternative and fun ways to gather data needed for personalized interfaces (with the use of a game) and (2) it moves towards the exploitation of rich social network data, provided directly by the user. It is also important to note here, that the novelty of the proposed research imply that the authors have been mainly working with hypotheses, trying to match different gaming aspects to cognitive style dimensions.

In order to assess individuals' cognitive styles, a known, valid and reliable tool is MBTI (Myers-Briggs Type Indicator) (Briggs-Myers et al. 1985). The MBTI is based on Jung's theory of psychological types. Individuals are described using four dimensions: extraversion-introversion (individual's focus of attention), sensing-intuition (the way an individual gathers information), thinking-feeling (the way an individual makes decisions) and judging-perceiving (the way an individual deals with the external environment). The combination of the four dimensions offers 16 personality types. For the different sets of questions that describe the different dimensions, an abstraction procedure was followed, since we tried to keep the elements that best and stereotypically describe the different personality types.

2   The Game

The goal of the player is to create her own museum, populate its exhibitions and decorate it according to her preferences. To do so, the player must collect as many objects as possible, in order to complete the exhibitions. Certain objects in all exhibitions can only be collected from a physical visit at the museum whereas others can be collected by playing mini games such as puzzles, dice throws, etc.

During the first part of the game, the player needs to make some decisions before she can start playing; involving her character in the game and the different tools and equipment she wishes to carry. In particular the player decides about the avatar she wants to use in the game, its traits, the pet following the avatar and the tools she might need. Each character, tool and pet corresponds to different values of the cognitive style. Tools and pets have different abilities that can be used in the game.

After the player has chosen her artifacts for the game, she is directed to her empty museum space that she needs to populate with items and decorate as she pleases. There are three museum templates that the player can choose from, each one corresponding to three different visiting styles. Veron and Levasseur (1989) identified four types of visiting style, based on the visitors' movement in the physical space of the museum. Visitors were placed in the following groups: ant visitors, fish visitors, butterfly visitors and grasshopper visitors. These metaphors showed the nature of the movement, whether for example a visitor approaches exhibits, moves in the centre of rooms, avoids visitor traffic, etc. For the purposes of the game, three different museum templates are designed that the player can choose from. Information about players' visiting style preference can be used later during the players' actual- physical museum visit. Finally, there are also three decoration styles to choose from (i.e. classic, modern, pop). The visitor can choose between a selection of floors and wall papers, a selection of frames for her items, different lights, etc.

In order to collect the items for her museum exhibition, the player can move in front of the empty showcases and frames and complete mini games to win items. Prensky's (2005) classification of games is used here to describe games of low complexity (i.e. mini games). The player can choose between games of different types (i.e. luck, skills, knowledge, memory, brain games, etc.). Figure 1 shows a game avatar moving in the museum and Fig. 2 shows a selection of mini games the player can choose from in order to win an exhibit. The items she can collect if she wins a game are from different thematic categories (i.e. depending on the museum exhibitions the items can be from exhibition number 1, 2, etc.) and the player chooses which one she prefers. The choice of items can also provide some information about the player's interests for the real museum exhibitions and later during her museum visit, the application can guide her accordingly. The game is available at http://apps.facebook.com/mymuseumstory/.

Fig. 1. A game avatar in the game environment.

Fig. 2. Selection of available mini games for an exhibit.

3 Method

There are certain concepts used in the game (i.e. game preference, choice of avatars, pets and tools, etc., all presented below), all of which are hypothesized to be correlated to different cognitive style dimensions. Since the concepts described and used here have not been studied in the past, the design was based on a set of different hypotheses. The player can choose from all the categories described below, allowing us to make assumptions about her cognitive style. In particular, the following choices a player can have in the game might correlate with different cognitive style dimensions: choice of games, choice of avatars, choice of pets, choice of tools, choice of detailed or general view in Gestalt images (Kennedy 1974), choice of game background music, choice of game environment decoration style, choice of fashion items to dress game avatars, number of friends and posts-comments on Facebook.

So far, we tested some of the above hypotheses with a small sample of 51 users, all first year students of the Department of Computer Science and Technology, University of Peloponnese. All our participants were Facebook users and gamers. Students were asked to complete a short version of the MBTI questionnaire in order to identify their cognitive style. After that, students were asked to choose between different aspects of the game that correspond to the different hypotheses. Although this is a particularly biased sample, this was only a pilot study to see whether certain tendencies can be identified, together with possible game problems.

4 Pilot Study Results

From the initial studies it was found that some of the different avatars, pets and tools used could correctly predict different cognitive style dimensions. For example there were very high correlations between the choice of the TV persona and Extraversion axis in Cognitive style, the Engineer and Sensing axis, etc. Other choices were not very good predictors and avatars like Artist and Diplomat did not seem to correlate with dimensions of the cognitive style. Investigating further into the issue, it was realized that avatars, pets and tools need to be accompanied by a small descriptive text to stress the main stereotype they represent.

Similarly, there were indications that different music preferences might reflect different preferences on the Cognitive dimension Judger-Perceiver, with Judgers preferring Classical music and Perceivers preferring Contemporary.

Indications that Perceivers might prefer Adventure and Risk games, Extraverts might prefer Collaborative games) and Introverts might prefer Fantasy games were also found (x^2 (2, 8.130) = Pearson .01.)

Finally, significant results were found between decoration preferences and cognitive style (x^2 (2, 5.883) = Pearson .05.), since Judgers seem to prefer classic decoration style and Perceivers have preferences for more contemporary decoration.

5 Conclusions

So far, we have tested more than half of the different game features against the cognitive style dimensions and important correlations were found, implying that the designed game could indeed reveal players' cognitive styles with the necessary improvements. However, the small and biased sample used only allows for the identification of tendencies which require in depth further studying. The novelty of the described work and the lack of previous studies implied that we have designed game features based on hypotheses. However, if our efforts are successful, then a very promising road opens. The vast numbers of social network gamers implies that there might be immense data available for exploitation; data that could be directly used for the creation of personalized applications. In social networks users voluntarily and over a long period of time, feed their personal space with numerous types of information about themselves. Access to this information might also imply effective personalization for different types of applications, spanning from single use systems (like the one described here) to complex multi use systems of different purposes.

Acknowledgments. The above research is partly funded under the European Union Seventh Framework Program Experimedia project, Contract No. 287966. We would also like to thank the students of the Departments of Computer Science and Technology, University of Peloponnese for participating in the pilot studies.

References

Ardissono, L., Petrelli, D.: UMUAI Special Issue on Cultural Heritage Exploration Preface. User Model. User-Adap. Inter. 18, 383–387 (2008)

Brigges-Myers, I., McCaulley, M.H.: Manual: A Guide to the Development and Use of the Myers-Briggs Type Indicator. Consulting Psychologists Press, Palo Alto (1985)

Falk, J., Korean, J., Dierking, L., Dreblow, L.: Predicting visitor behavior. Curator **28**(4), 249–257 (1985)

Gaeta, A., Gaeta, M., Ritrovato, P.: A grid based software architecture for delivery of adaptive and personalised learning experiences. Pers. Ubiquit. Comput. **13**, 207–217 (2007)

Kennedy, J.M.: A Psychology of Picture Perception. Jossey-Bass Publishers, San Francisco (1974)

Muntean, C.H., Muntean, G.M.: Open corpus architecture for personalised ubiquitous e-learning. Pers. Ubiquit. Comput. **13**, 197–205 (2007)

Prensky, M.: Complexity matters. Educ.T echnol. **45**(4), 1–15 (2005)

Riding, R., Rayner, S.G.: Cognitive Styles and Learning Strategies. David Fulton Publisher, London (1998)

Serrell, B.: Paying Attention: Visitors and Museum Exhibitions. American Alliance of Museums, Washington DC (1998)

Veron, E., Levasseur, M.: Ethnographie de l'exposition: l'espace, le corps et le sens. Bibliothèque Publique d' Information, Centre Georges Pompidou (1989)

Wakkary, R., Hatala, M.: Situated play in a tangible interface and adaptive audio museum guide. Pers. Ubiquit. Comput. **11**, 171–191 (2006)

Quantitative Approach in Measuring Knowledge Convergence in Serious Games

Ariadna Padrós[1](✉) and Margarida Romero[2](✉)

[1] ESADE Universitat Ramon Llull, 08034 Barcelona, Spain
ariadna.padros@esade.edu
[2] Université Laval, Québec, QC G1V 0A6, Canada
margarida.romero@fse.ulaval.ca

Abstract. Collaborative Serious Games (SG) aims to promote knowledge convergence, the process by which two or more people may reach mutual understanding after having interacted together. However, the analysis of knowledge convergence has been mostly developed in the context of Asynchronous Learning Networks (ALN) in a qualitative approach, but has not been investigated in the context of collaborative Serious Games (SG). The present study aims to investigate students' knowledge convergence in the particular case of the SG Metavals, using a quantitative approach. The knowledge convergence results of the dyads playing the MetaVals allows to sustain partially the hypothesis of a better performance and Level of Certainty (LC) (H1), a higher symmetry of knowledge (H2) and a higher shared outcome knowledge (H3), after collaboration than in the initial individual phase of the SG.

1 Introduction

Collaborative learning aims to reunite a group of learners' in order to maximize their own and each other's learning [1] and take advantage of the learners' diversity in terms of their prior knowledge, their learning process and outcomes. Game Based Learning (GBL) takes advantage of collaborative learning through different game dynamics including cooperation and competition [2]. Serious Games, a type of computer-based games with educational purposes, could promote collaboration in two ways "collaboration can either be about the game (and take place in a face-to-face context) or be an integral part of the online game (and take place in a virtual context)" [3]. In this study we aim to analyse the knowledge convergence process as a part of a cooperative learning activity supported by a Serious Game.

2 Knowledge Convergence

In collaborative learning the question raised is whether learners in small groups (2 or 3 individuals) may influence one another and whether they may converge or diverge with respect to their knowledge, by sharing and developing mutual understanding through social interaction and influencing one another when learning together [4, 5]. One of the main aspects of this mutual influence is that knowledge is shared and converges though

© Springer International Publishing Switzerland 2014
A. De Gloria (Ed.): GALA 2013, LNCS 8605, pp. 354–363, 2014.
DOI: 10.1007/978-3-319-12157-4_29

social interaction [6–8]. Peers construct knowledge by working together to solve problems or tasks [9].

In this context of collaborative learning, knowledge convergence is understood as the process by which two or more people may reach mutual understanding after having interacted socially and cooperated together on a task. In other words, it implies an increase in the knowledge all collaborating learners share together, also referred as common knowledge [10]. The knowledge convergence takes place from the reciprocal nature of collaboration. Through this interaction and cooperation, different units of knowledge are exchanged among the learners and it may eventually convergence [7, 11–13] which leads to an increase of similarity in the cognitive representations and knowing of the group members [14].

The result of working and interacting together may be that the individuals cooperating become more similar with respect to their knowledge [13], that is, that there is an increase in the common knowledge that all collaborating partners' participants have [10]. Learners who collaborate may influence one another when learning together [4] as the activities of a learner have an impact on those of their partners, which then in return have an impact on their own activities [7]. The constructivist approach of knowledge of Vygotsky [11] and Brown [15] had previously raised this idea of the impact of the interaction between peers or more knowledgeable others through the mechanisms of peer learning and reciprocal learning.

2.1 Example of the Knowledge Convergence Process

We hereafter exemplify the knowledge convergence process with an image as well as with a description of this process (Fig. 1).

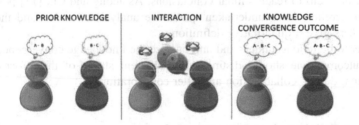

Fig. 1. Knowledge convergence process.

Let us imagine that there are two people working and collaborating together on a task (Player 1 and Player 2 in the context of the serious game MetaVals experience). Player 1 knows A & B and player 2 knows B & C. In this example B refers to the knowledge, or pieces of knowledge, that they have in common on the domain they are working on. Weinberger, Stegmann and Fischer [13] refer to this concept as shared knowledge, where learners have the knowledge on the very same concepts as their learning partners. Jeong and Chi [10] on the other hand, call it common knowledge and define it in a similar way: knowledge that all participants know and refer to the similarities in representations itself. On the other hand, in this example, A and C symbolize the knowledge one dyad has that the other does not prior to interacting and working together in relation to the domain. During the knowledge converging process, their knowledge may converge and ultimately construct similar declarative knowledge. The knowledge convergence outcome achieved after collaboration and interaction implies that, in the end, both Player 1 and 2 know A, B & C. In other words, an increased similarity in the cognitive representations among the group members is achieved as collaborative learners may influence the learning outcomes of their peers [7, 12]. If the amount of common knowledge grows after collaboration, knowledge convergence is meant to have taken place [12].

Even though there have been studies and researches on knowledge convergence in the context of collaborative learning activities involving dyads of learners, we may state that it is yet a topic to be deeply analysed as it entered in the learning sciences not that long ago [10, 16]. Earlier studies [10, 12] presented findings pointing out that knowledge convergence could occur during collaborative learning and some evidences showed that collaborative interaction was facilitating the increase in shared knowledge among peers working together [10]. The assumption is that as a result of such joint construction activities, convergence would arise. Some research [10] observed a correlation between the amount of shared knowledge and learning as seen from a first data analysis. Looi and Chen [14] show in their work how a group of students achieved knowledge convergence and knowledge sharing through participation.

Having said that, studies by some of these same authors, show that cognitive convergence in terms of sharing knowledge following collaboration is typically surprisingly low [17, 18]. Others [19] presented indicators that show that learners in a group may actually become more dissimilar after a joint activity with respect to their prior knowledge as they may benefit differently from learning together.

The difficulty to define the notion of knowledge convergence in a precise manner does not really help to reach similar conclusions. As Jeong and Chi [18] point out, in the past, researchers have undertaken qualitative analysis to understand the process whereas others give a quantitative definition.

In order to be able to understand and analyse the knowledge convergence process, and the outcome, one should distinguish 3 different stages of this process: before collaboration, during collaboration and after collaboration.

2.2 Before Collaboration: Prior Knowledge

There is a widespread agreement that learning is influenced by prior knowledge and that learners build up concepts from prior knowledge [20, 21]. Learners build up concepts from prior knowledge and new knowledge is constructed from old as it determines what we learn from experience.

Prior knowledge influences the learning process, but it may also determine the collaborative learning process within the peers due to the knowledge equivalences and the differences on the specific units of knowledge, considered by Beaton [23] as asymmetrical knowledge, that is, "knowledge that others do not have". One of the most argued advantages of collaborative learning is the transfer of knowledge between those learners who have different levels or units of knowledge [24, 25].

A distinction between knowledge equivalence and shared knowledge must be born in mind. Knowledge equivalence refers to learners becoming more similar to their learning partners regarding the amount of their individual knowledge [13], whereas shared knowledge refers to when learning partners have knowledge on the very same concepts. Weinberger, Stegmann, and Fischer [13] suggest that the distribution of prior knowledge within small groups of learners also influences learning and hence it should be controlled.

A study by Fischer [25] showed dyads with low prior knowledge equivalence acquired more knowledge than those with high prior knowledge equivalence in unstructured discussions.

2.3 During Collaboration: Interaction and Knowledge Contribution

During collaboration and interaction knowledge contribution equivalence represents how much and how heterogeneously learners participate in discourse.

Research based on social perspectives of learning [11, 27] emphasize the idea that learning is dialogue, both internal and with others, and agree on participation being a condition for learning. Hrastinski [28] points out that for nowadays context a learning theory is needed which views online learning as online participation. In this line there is a lot of learning occurring nowadays outside the physical classroom, so that the participation and interaction may not necessarily be a synonym of talking or writing. A clear example is the dynamics followed by students enrolled in fully online learning courses. Some research [29] concluded that online learning was best achieved when learners participate and collaborate and that online participation accomplished better learning outcomes than traditional classrooms as seen in their research. In the MetaVals game dynamics, the interaction and participation of dyads does not necessarily imply physical dialogue aas it can take place by the collaboration in a shared interface where the knowledge decisions of the players are available.

2.4 After Collaboration: Knowledge Convergence Outcome

The resulting outcome of knowledge convergence is an increased similarity in the cognitive representation of the group members [12]. Consequently individuals cooperating may become more similar with respect to their knowledge. The outcome of this collaborative learning may differ depending on whether the knowledge acquired by the individual learners through collaboration is on the same specific concepts (shared outcome knowledge) or whether the outcome refers to individual learners having a similar benefit from working together (outcome knowledge equivalence) [13]. Nevertheless Teasley [26] considers that what really matters is not the amount of shared knowledge, but the dynamics of being able to overcome differences and discover new ones.

3 Research Objectives

This study aims to analyze the knowledge convergence results in small groups playing the Serious Game (SG) MetaVals [30], a domain-independent decision-making customizable game which includes an individual and a collaborative phase [31]. The first research objective aims to analyze the hypothesis of a better performance and Level of Certainty (LC) (H1) after collaboration than in the initial individual phase of the SG. The second and third objectives looks also for better results after collaboration than in the individual phase, in terms of a higher symmetry of knowledge (H2) and a higher shared outcome knowledge (H3).

4 Methodology

In order to analyse the knowledge convergence process in a authentic learning context, we start introducing in this section the quantitative paradigm approach for analysing the knowledge convergence (Sect. 4.1), and after this, the tool developed for applying the quantitative paradigm (Sect. 4.2) and the procedures to measure the (prior/outcome) shared knowledge, the (prior/outcome) knowledge equivalence, and the individual knowledge outcome. The last part of the methodology section introduces the context of the authentic learning task proposed to the students (Sect. 4.3).

4.1 Paradigm and Procedure: Quantitative Analysis of Knowledge Convergence

In order to assess knowledge convergence, we based on Weinberger and colleagues [13] model of study, measuring individual learning outcomes on the 3 different stages: prior, during and following collaborative learning. Their framework on the knowledge convergence process and outcomes has been used in some researches by author authors [16, 17] or it has been conducted similarly by others [18]. These studies have in common the analysis of a task allowing quantifying the units of knowledge achieved after collaboration.

4.2 Instruments: The Quantitative Analysis of Knowledge Convergence in the MetaVals SG

The SG MetaVals has been designed with a research purpose of collecting data during the process of collaborative learning. A part of the data collected by the game could permit analysing the knowledge convergence.

4.3 Context and Participants

The knowledge convergence hypothesis has been testes in an authentic learning task context, playing the MetaVals [30, 31]. The participants were enrolled in management programs provided by ESADE Business School the SG MetaVals was tested with the students using two different modalities, one enrolling dyads formed by two real participants playing collaboratively (named real dyads, thereinafter) and dyads formed by a real participant and a virtual one playing collaboratively, which we name virtual dyads.

Real dyads were created randomly by the instructor before the class, engaging a total of 46 adult learners with an average age of 24 years. Virtual dyads were formed by 31 adult learners with an average age of 31 years. The instructor assigned randomly a novice or expert virtual counterpart to each real student.

5 Results of Analysing Knowledge Convergence in the SG MetaVals

5.1 Results for Individual Knowledge Outcome (H1)

The H1 presumed the performance and the Level of Certainty (LC) achieved individually after collaboration (Stage 3) will be better than the results and performance achieved individually (Stage 1).

A paired-samples t-test was conducted to compare the performance in the individual performance (Stage 1) and the performance after collaboration (Stage 3) in real and virtual dyads' group (Tables 1 and 2).

Table 1. Results of Individual Outcome (IKO) in Real Groups (RG).

Results of IKO in RG	Mean	SD	N	P
Performance Stage 1	4,67	,871	46	0,019
Performance Stage 3	5,02	,954	46	
Level of Certainty Stage 1	32,37	23,832	46	0,010
Level of Certainty Stage 3	35,89	24,243	46	

Table 2. Results of Individual Knowledge Outcome (IKO) in Virtual Groups (VG)

Results of IKO in VG	Mean	SD	N	P
Performance Stage 1	5,29	0,86	31	0,264
Performance Stage 3	5,48	0,81	31	
Level of Certainty Stage 1	31,90	24,142	31	0,140
Level of Certainty Stage 3	36,58	24,783	31	

Both in the performance and LC, all values show an increase, however, in the real dyads' group performance and LC shows significant differences, but not the virtual dyads' groups.

5.2 Results for Knowledge Equivalence Outcome (H2)

The hypothesis (H2) presumes the knowledge asymmetry Coefficient of Variation (CV) will be reduced after collaboration (Stage 3) and hence state if dyads became more similar in respect to their general domain knowledge.

Following Weinberger [14] methodology, it was first of all calculated the coefficient of variation among dyads in order to quantify the symmetry and asymmetry among them. Then, a paired-samples t-test was conducted to compare the coefficient of variation among dyads before (Stage 1) and after (Stage 3) interaction (Tables 3 and 4).

Table 3. Results of Coefficient of Variation (CV) in Real Groups (RG).

Results of CV in RG	Mean	SD	N	P
Performance Stage 1	0,130	0,124	46	0,43
Performance Stage 3	0,108	0,215	46	

Table 4. Results of Coefficient (CV) of Variation in Virtual Groups (VG).

Results of CV in VG	Mean	SD	N	P
Performance Stage 1	0,766	0,646	31	0,038
Performance Stage 3	0,732	0,684	31	

The coefficient of variation among dyads decreases after collaboration (Stage 3) in both groups which leads us to believe that dyads become more similar in respect to their knowledge after collaboration that they were initially (Stage 1). In order words, there is an increase in the knowledge that all collaborating partners have.

5.3   Results for Shared Outcome Knowledge (H3)

The hypothesis (H3) presumes that shared outcome knowledge will increase after collaboration (Stage 3). This analysis can only be carried out with the virtual group due to the current dynamics of the game. A paired-samples t-test was conducted to compare prior shared knowledge among dyads before (Stage 1) and after (Stage 3) interaction (Table 5).

Table 5. Results of Shared Knowledge (ShK) in Virtual Groups (VG).

Results of ShK in VG	Mean	SD	N	P
Performance Stage 1	2,68	2,561	31	0,078
Performance Stage 3	3,032	2,714	31	

Results show that in virtual groups, even though there as an increase on the shared knowledge, results were not statistically significant.

6   Discussion

Analysis carried out corroborate that participants, both in an individual basis and a dyads basis, benefit of working together and that their performance becomes better after interaction with their peers. The analysis of the results allows to sustain the three hypotheses presumed before the analysis although results are not significant for all hypotheses in both real and virtual dyads' groups, which analysis were carried out separately for each of the hypotheses.

H1 is sustained in the context of real groups, which achieved a higher performance and LC after collaboration (Stage 3) and where results were significantly higher. The H1 is not sustained in virtual dyads', where despite the fact that performance and LC are higher after collaboration, it does not show a significant difference. The higher performance and LC in the context of real dyads' could be interpreted in terms of the real interaction developed between the two students' engaged in the dyad. In the context of the virtual dyad, the interaction between the "virtual player" and the real player could be insufficient to increase significantly the performance and LC.

H2 is sustained significantly in virtual groups, but not in real dyads. In both cases the Coefficient of Variation (CV) among dyads decreases after collaboration (Stage 3), leading the students to become more similar in respect to their knowledge after collaboration that they were initially (Stage 1). We interpret the decrease of the CV as an increase in the knowledge that all collaborating partners have.

H3 is not sustained in the context of the virtual dyads', where despite the presumption that shared outcome knowledge increases after collaboration (Stage 3), the difference is not statistically significant. The limits of prior knowledge assessment in the context of real dyads did not allow testing the H3 in the real dyads' groups, which is expected to be carried out in further studies. Both in real and virtual dyads' groups the results were in all cases better in stage 3 after collaboration than in stage 1 in terms of individual knowledge performance and LC (H1), CV (H2) and shared outcome knowledge (H3).

However, and in order to bear in mind the limitation of the study, it must be said that the analysis of knowledge convergence with regard to single concepts does not necessarily imply the convergence of understanding of such concepts nor the convergence of knowledge on knowing how to actually apply them in different contexts. The degree of permanence of the knowledge convergence beyond the single concepts should be explored in future studies and contribute to analyze the knowledge convergence in short and long term tasks. The knowledge convergence process should be continued to be studied using mixed quantitative methods combining both the quantitative approaches applied in this paper based and previous studies [13] and qualitative approaches, in order to better characterize the collaborative learning process, in general [17], and in collaborative GBL activities.

References

1. Johnson, D., Johnson, R.: Learning Together and Alone, Cooperative, Competitive, and Individualistic Learning. Prentice-Hall, Needham Heights (1994)
2. Romero, M., Usart, M., Ott, M., Earp, J., de Freitas, S., Arnab, S.: Learning through playing for or against each other? Promoting collaborative learning in digital game based learning. In: 20th European Conference on Information Systems, 10–13 June 2012. ESADE, Barcelona (2012)

3. Hummel, H.G.K., Van Houcke, J., Nadolski, R.J., Van der Hiele, T., Kurvers, H., Löhr, A.: Scripted collaboration in gaming for complex learning: Effects of multiple perspectives when acquiring water management skills. Br. J. Educ. Technol. (p. 1030) **42**(6), 1029–1041 (2011)

4. DeLisi, R., Golbeck, S.L.: Implications of Piagetian theory for peer learning. In: O'Donnell, A.M., King, A. (eds.) Cognitive Perspectives on Peer Learning, pp. 3–37. Erlbaum, Mahwah (1999)

5. Chen, W., Looi, C.K.: What do students do in a F2F CSCL classroom? The optimization of multiple communications modes. Comput. Educ. **55**(3), 1159–1170 (2010)

6. Barron, B.: When smart groups fail. J. Learn. Sci. **12**(3), 307–359 (2003)

7. Roschelle, J.: Learning by collaborating: Convergent conceptual change. In: Koschmann, T. (ed.) CSCL: Theory and Practice of an Emerging Paradigm, pp. 209–248. Erlbaum, Mahwah (1996)

8. Ickes, W., Gonzalez, R.: Social cognition and social cognition. In: Nyle, J.L., Brower, A.M. (eds.) What's Social About Social Cognition? Research on Socially Shared Cognition in Small Groups, pp. 285–308. Sage, Thousand Oaks (1996)

9. Roschelle, J., Teasley, S.: The construction of shared knowledge in collaborative problem solving. In: O'Malley, C. (ed.) Computer-Supported Collaborative Learning, pp. 69–197. Springer, Berlin (1995)

10. Jeong, H., Chi, M.T.H.: Constructing shared knowledge during collaboration and learning. Poster Presented at the AERA Annual Meeting, Montreal, Canada

11. Vygotsky, L.S.: Mind in Society: The Development of Higher Psychological Processes. Harvard University Press, Cambridge (1978)

12. Roschelle, J.: Learning by collaborating: Convergent conceptual change. J. Learn. Sci. **2**, 235–276 (1992)

13. Weinberger, A., Stegmann, K., Fischer, F.: Knowledge convergence in collaborative learning: Concepts and assessment. Learn. Instr. **17**(4), 416–426 (2007)

14. Looi, C.K., Chen, W.L.: Community-based individual knowledge construction in the classroom: A process-oriented account. J. Comput. Assist. Learn. **26**(3), 202–213 (2010)

15. Brown, A.L.: Design experiments: Theoretical and methodological challenges in creating complex interventions in classroom settings. J. Learn. Sci. **2**(2), 141–178 (1992)

16. Fischer, F., Mandl, H.: Facilitating knowledge convergence in videoconferencing environments: The role of external representation tools. In: Proceedings of the Conference on Computer Support for Collaborative Learning: Foundations for a CSCL Community, CSCL 2002. International Society of the Learning Sciences (2002)

17. Fischer, F., Mandl, H.: Knowledge convergence in computer-supported collaborative learning: The role of external representation tools. J. Learn. Sci. **14**, 3405–3441 (2005)

18. Jeong, H., Chi, M.T.H.: Knowledge convergence and collaborative learning. Instr. Sci. **35**, 287–315 (2007)

19. Webb, N.M., Ender, P., Lewis, S.: Problem-solving strategies and group processes in small groups learning computer programming. Am. Educ. Res. J. **23**(2), 243–261 (1986)

20. Resnick, L.B.: Mathematics and science learning: A new conception. Science **220**, 477–478 (1983)

21. Glaserfeld, E.V.: An introduction to radical constructivism. In: Watlawick, P. (ed.) The Invented Reality. W.W. Norton, New York (1984)

22. Beaton, G.: Why professionalism is still relevant, Professions Australia, p. 9 (2010)

23. Ogata, H., Yano, Y.: Combining knowledge awareness and information filtering in an open-ended collaborative learning environment. Int. J. Artificial Intelligence in Education **11**, 133–146 (2000)

24. Wegerif, R.: The social dimension of asynchronous learning networks. J. Asynchronous Learn. Netw. **2**(1), 16 (1998)
25. Fischer, F.: Gemeinsame Wissenskonstruktion. Analyse und Förderung in computerunterstützten Kooperationsszenarien [Collaborative knowledge construction. Analysis and facilitation in computer-supported collaborative scenarios]. Unpublished Professorial Dissertation, Ludwig-Maximilans-Universität, München, Germany (2001)
26. Teasley, S.D., Fischer, F., Weinberger, A., Stegmann, K., Dillenbourg, P., Kapur, M., Chi, M.: Cognitive convergence in collaborative learning. In: Kanselaar, G., van Merriënboer, J., Kirschner, P., de Jong, T. (eds.) Proceedings of the 8th International Conference on International Conference for the Learning Sciences, vol. 3, pp. 360–367. International Society of the Learning Sciences, Utrecht (2008)
27. Wenger, E.: Communities of Practice: Learning, Meaning, and Identity. Cambridge University Press, Cambridge (1998)
28. Hrastinski, S.: A theory of online learning as online participation. Comput. Educ. **52**(1), 78–82 (2009)
29. Webster, J., Hackley, P.: Teaching effectiveness in technology-mediated distance learning. Acad. Manag. J. **40**(6), 1282–1309 (1997)
30. Padrós, A., Romero, M., Usart, M.: Developing serious games: From face-to-face to a computer-based modality. Elearn. Pap. **25**, 1–12 (2011)
31. Romero, M., Usart, M., Popescu, M., Boyle, E.: Interdisciplinary and international adaption and personalization of the MetaVals serious games. In: Ma, M., Oliveira, M.F., Hauge, J.B., Duin, H., Thoben, K.-D. (eds.) SGDA 2012. LNCS, vol. 7528, pp. 59–73. Springer, Heidelberg (2012)

The 5/10 Method: A Method for Designing Educational Games

Johan Jeuring[1,2(✉)], Rick van Rooij[1], and Nicolas Pronost[1]

[1] Department of Information and Computing Sciences,
Utrecht University, Utrecht, The Netherlands
{J.T.Jeuring,nicolas.pronost}@uu.nl, rick.vanrooij@gmail.com
[2] Faculty of Computer Science, Open Universiteit Nederland,
Heerlen, The Netherlands

Abstract. Serious games may improve understanding, involvement, engagement, reasoning and inquiry, and have been successfully used in schools. Recent studies show that serious games are sometimes misused, and not always easy to integrate in an instructional environment. It is often unclear how a game contributes to student learning, or how it should be used in a course. This paper proposes a method to support the analysis, design, development, and use of serious games in education. The method combines the widely used design model ADDIE with the instructional design method '10 steps to complex learning'. The method is applied in the development of the Moth game, which supports learning optics at the level of high school physics.

Keywords: Serious games · Design methods · Instructional design · Games for physics

1   Introduction

The game River City has been used since 2007 in a game-enhanced science curriculum to teach science to over 8000 students [6]. River City increases the self-efficacy of students and improves student learning. Combining video games and more traditional curricular materials improves the accessibility of the content, and learning is made more relevant to students [10]. A game like River City engages students, which is one of the advantages of using games in education. Autonomy in playing games allows a student to customize gameplay to their personal and cultural norms in a controlled learning environment [2]. A student can disassociate from personal perception of their physical appearance or ability levels, which supports students with low self-esteem or self-efficacy [1]. Using the game Whyville, Kafai et al. [5] show that the gameplay encourages students' participation in scientific arguments and leads to using higher-level vocabulary words. Other research shows that various categories of scientific games support and improve scientific discourse, reasoning and inquiry [1,7,18,19]. More importantly, students from all groups and ages report that they prefer to learn science

© Springer International Publishing Switzerland 2014
A. De Gloria (Ed.): GALA 2013, LNCS 8605, pp. 364–369, 2014.
DOI: 10.1007/978-3-319-12157-4_30

from a game rather than from a traditional text, laboratory-based education, or internet environments [11].

The learning effects of serious games in studies across educational contexts [21] are inconclusive. One of the recommendations is to ensure that game objectives and learning objectives correspond. It is often hard to determine whether or not a game contributes to a student's learning because of a lack of clearly defined learning objectives and outcomes [9]. Furthermore, even though games can be a very powerful educational tool, there is often an integration problem in the instructional environment.

There exist several models that support the design of serious games [4,8,12]. The focus of most of these models is on how to design the gameplay of serious games. In this paper we focus on how to integrate a serious game with the existing curriculum. We propose the 5/10 method: a method that provides guidelines for the design of a game with clearly defined learning goals and objectives, and with a connection to the existing curriculum. The method is a combination of the general design method ADDIE, also used in DODDEL [12], with the instructional design method developed by Merriënboer and Kirschner [14]. We think our method is complementary to existing design methods, and can help to design a game that integrates well in the existing learning environment.

2   The 5/10 Method

This section first briefly describes the ADDIE method and Merriënboer and Kirschner's 'Ten steps to complex learning', and then shows how these two approaches are combined to obtain the 5/10 method for educational game design. The 5/10 method focuses on the instructional system design and largely ignores the design of the artistic components of a game, such as visual, audio and specific level design. While these components are very important for game design, their design is a separate field of research and out of scope for this paper.

2.1   The ADDIE Method

ADDIE (Analysis, Design, Development, Implementation and Evaluation) [16, 20] is a widely used method in product design and especially in instructional system development, such as teaching methods, books and educative games. The ADDIE method provides a good basic skeleton to create an educational method [3]. We use ADDIE as a global framework for the more fine-grained design method using the Ten Steps to Complex Learning [14], which we describe in the next subsection. In the design phase of ADDIE many of the ten steps are used to ensure that a game is designed based on clear learning goals, and that it provides a player with the right information at the right time.

2.2   Ten Steps to Complex Learning

The ten steps to complex learning constitute a holistic method for designing instruction. The method does not separate a complex domain into unrelated pieces, but approaches the problem of learning in a particular domain via simplifying complex tasks in such a way that a learner is confronted with whole, meaningful tasks from the start. The ten steps to complex learning are based on Merriënboer's 4C/ID method [13]. The 4C/ID approach describes blueprints for complex learning by means of four basic components: learning tasks, supportive information, procedural information and part-task practice. Learning tasks include a case that has to be studied, a project that has to be done, a problem that needs to be solved and so on. Supportive information is information necessary to perform non-routine tasks such as problem solving and reasoning. Procedural information is information necessary to perform those parts of a task that are always performed in a similar way. Finally, part-task practice is needed if a learner needs to achieve a very high level of automaticity in part of the task. The blueprint components are developed and designed in ten steps. Of these ten steps, four are design steps, and the other six support these design steps, and are only performed when necessary. The ten steps are:

1. Design learning tasks
2. Sequence task classes
3. Set performance objectives
4. Design supportive information
5. Analyze cognitive strategies
6. Analyze mental models
7. Design procedural information
8. Analyze cognitive rules
9. Analyze prerequisite knowledge
10. Design part-task practice

The ten steps method follows a so-called pebble-in-the-pond model [15], in which the learning tasks represent a pebble thrown in a pond. Each of the subsequent steps grows from that first step like ripples in the water, adding more and more until a full task emerges.

2.3 The 5/10 Method

The 5/10 method combines the ADDIE method with ten steps to complex learning to obtain a method for designing educational games. The design process described in the method is depicted in Fig. 1.

We have used the steps of the 5/10 method in the design of Moth, a serious game for learning optics at the level of high school physics, see Fig. 2. The goal of Moth is to practice optics in the final year of the VWO (Preparatory Scientific Education) level of high school in the Netherlands. We do not have space to describe how we applied the method in detail, but give some of the steps below. Please refer to the MSc. thesis of Van Rooij [17] for further details.

Analyze: The first step consists of four sub steps to determine global learning goals, to analyze the learning material and background, to analyze existing teaching methods, and to analyze related educational games. The learning goals

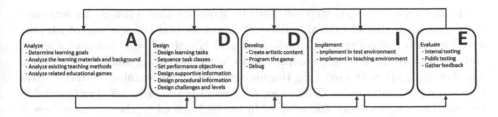

Fig. 1. The 5/10 method

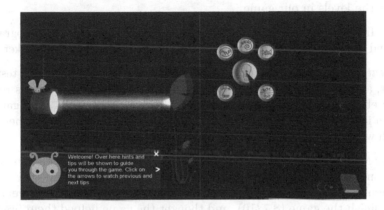

Fig. 2. The interface of the Moth game

for optics are described in a national standard. There are six learning goals, examples of which are: to know and to use Refractive Index and Snellius Law, and to know and to use the lens formula, including being able to calculate and use focus points, lens strength and construction rays for a positive lens.

Design: Now we are ready to start with the design phase of the 5/10 method. In the design phase we design learning tasks, sequence task classes, set performance objectives, design supportive information, design procedural information, and design challenges and levels. These steps correspond to a large extent to the ten steps to complex learning. Some of the ten steps to complex learning are missing here, namely analyze cognitive strategies, analyze mental models, analyze cognitive rules, and analyze prerequisite knowledge. These are the steps supporting designing supportive and procedural information. In almost all cases supportive and procedural information is present in the teaching methods and learning material analyzed in the analysis phase of the 5/10 method. The four omitted analyses have been performed by the developers and authors of the teaching methods and learning material.

To design learning tasks, we look at the learning goals again. It is relatively straightforward to translate the learning goals to learning tasks. For example, for the learning goal: to know and to use Refractive Index and Snellius Law, we directly obtain the learning task: calculate the refractive index, angle of incidence or angle of refraction using Snellius Law.

In the second design step we have to sequence task classes. To sequence task classes we should take the difficulty of a task and the amount of support provided into consideration. Merriënboer and Kirschner [13] advocate a cyclic development of increasingly complex tasks, with decreasing amount of support. Furthermore, often the existing teaching methods and learning material offers tasks in a particular order. The order we present is the order used in the Dutch Newton teaching method, and advised by the high school teacher we interviewed: 1: Law of reflection, 2: Formula of magnification, 3: Lens formula/focus, 4: Snellius Law and refraction, including different wavelengths. We use this order to sequence the levels in our game.

Develop: In the development phase we design the artistic contents, program the game, and debug the result. Moth has been implemented in GameMaker 8.1.

Implement: In the implementation phase, the game is first deployed in a test environment, and then in the intended teaching environment. The game is released on the website https://sites.google.com/site/yarentertainment/. The game has also been installed on the machines of a high school in Zeist (The Netherlands), at which we performed an evaluation of the game.

Evaluate: Moth was played by both high-school students and university students, 12 of whom filled out a questionnaire. Van Rooij [17] gives a detailed description of the results of the questionnaire. On the positive side, players were very motivated to finish the game (8.7/10), and thought the game helped them practicing the material (8.8/10). The difference in difficulty between some levels is far too big (4.3/10), and the user interface needs to be improved (5.1/10).

3   Conclusions

We have developed the 5/10 method: a method for analysing, designing, developing, implementing and evaluating serious games. The method helps collecting the data necessary to design an educational game, and the information a student needs while playing the game. The method combines the ADDIE method and the ten steps to complex learning for the instructional design of serious games. We have developed the game Moth using the method. Moth was designed and developed in a couple of months, and although the evaluations show that it can be improved, much has been achieved in a short period of time.

Acknowledgements. Anastasia Stebakova designed the environments and characters of Moth. Kevin MacLeod (incompetech.com) composed the music of Moth. Anton Bondarenko created an introductory and a concluding movie for Moth.

References

1. Barab, S.A., Dede, C.: Games and immersive participatory simulations for science education: an emerging type of curricula. J. Sci. Educ. Technol. **16**(1), 1–3 (2007)

2. Dieterle, E.: Neomillennial learning styles and river city. Child. Youth Environ. **19**(1), 245–278 (2009)
3. D.J. Grafinger. Basics of instructional systems development. INFO-LINE, 8803 (1988)
4. Gunter, G.A., Kenny, R.F., Vick, E.H.: Taking educational games seriously: using the RETAIN model to design endogenous fantasy into standalone educational games. Educ. Tech. Res. Dev. **56**, 511–537 (2008)
5. Kafai, Y.B., Quintero, M., Feldon, D.: Investigating the whyin whypox: causal and systematic explorations in a virtual epidemic. Games Cult **5**(1), 116–135 (2010)
6. Ketelhut, D.J.: The impact of student self-efficacy on scientific inquiry skills: an exploratory investigation in river city, a multi-user virtual environment. J. Sci. Educ. Technol. **16**(1), 99–111 (2007)
7. Klopfer, E.: Augmented Reality: Research and Design of Mobile Educational Games. MIT Press, Cambridge (2008)
8. Koops, M.C.: The serious gaming lemniscate model for acquiring knowledge through simulation games. In: Proceedings of the 41st Annual Conference of the International Simulation and Gaming Association (2010)
9. Marino, M.T., Basham, J.D., Beecher, C.C.: Using video games as an alternative science assessment for students with disabilities and at-risk learners. SCI Scope **34**(5), 36–41 (2011)
10. Marino, M.T., Hayes, M.T.: Promoting inclusive education, civic scientific literacy, and global citizenship with video games. Cult. Stud. Sci. Educ. **7**(4), 945–954 (2012)
11. Marino, M.T., Israel, M., Beecher, C.C., Basham, J.D.: Student and teachers perceptions of using video games to enhance science instruction. J. Sci. Educ. Technol. **22**, 667–680 (2012)
12. McMahon, M.: Using the DODDEL model to teach serious game design to novice designers. In: Proceedings ascilite Auckland (2009)
13. van Merriënboer, J.J.G.: Training for reflective expertise: A four-component instructional design model for complex cognitive skills. Educ. Technol. Res. Dev. **40**(2), 23–43 (1992)
14. van Merriënboer, J.J.G., Kirschner, P.: Ten Steps to Complex Learning: A Systematic Approach to Four-Component Instructional Design. Lawrence Erlbaum, New Jersey (2007)
15. Merril, M.D.: A pebble-in-the-pond model for instructional design. Perform. Improv. **41**(7), 39–44 (2002)
16. Molenda, M.: In search of the elusive addie model. Perform. Improv. **42**(5), 34–36 (2003)
17. van Rooij, R.: The 5/10 method: A method for designing educational games. Master's thesis, Game and Media Technology, Utrecht University (2013)
18. Squire, K.D.: From information to experience. place-based augmented reality games as a model for learning in a globally networked society. Teach. Coll. Rec. **112**(10), 4–5 (2010)
19. Steinkuehler, C., Duncan, S.: Scientific habits of mind in virtual worlds. J. Sci. Educ. Technol. **17**(6), 530–543 (2008)
20. Wang, S.K., Hsu, H.Y.: Using the addie model to design second life activities for online learners. Tech. Trends **53**(6), 76–81 (2009)
21. Young, M.F., Slota, S., Cutter, A.B., Jalette, G., Mullin, G., Lai, B., Simeoni, Z., Tran, M., Yukhymenko, M.: Our princess is in another castle: a review of trends in serious gaming for education. Rev. Educ. Res. **82**(1), 61–89 (2012)

Balancing Fidelity of Simulation Game Environments to Increase Situational Awareness Skills

Heide Lukosch(⊠)

Delft University of Technology,
Jaffalaan 5, 2600 GA Delft, The Netherlands
h.k.lukosch@tudelft.nl

Abstract. Many working tasks in our complex, technology-based world require active participation in a joint action. Communication and cooperation are basic skills needed for a well functioning team, especially in safety-critical domains like security. In this domain, the ability of a team to cooperate sometimes even decides about life and death. The development of situational awareness and understanding is seen as a prerequisite for effective teamwork. Traditional methods of enhancing teamwork related skills are limited due to their lack of flexibility and their distance to real world challenges. The study aims at exploring whether and how a simulation game should be designed in terms of fidelity to support situational awareness training. Results from usability tests show that realistic virtual environments imply the ability to foster teamwork related skills like situational awareness and communication.

1 Introduction

With simulation games, players can train and probe actions and re-actions in a real-like safe environment, without the risk of real-world consequences. Simulation games provide immediate feedback and help the players to reflect, especially when a proper de-briefing phase is included in a game [1]. They work intrinsically motivating [2] and support knowledge transfer from the virtual to the real world when designed as a so-called "there-reality" including a high level of physical fidelity [3]. Transfer research emphasizes that transfer is effective when the trained skills have similar logical or deep structures in virtual and in real world [4], which is referring to functional fidelity. Military has a long tradition of using simulations for strategy and combat training, because of the chance to clearly illustrate consequences of actions in a safe environment, without risk of injury or other damage [5, 6]. Furthermore, fidelity defines the degree to which a game emulates the real world [7, 8], and has been researched extensively [9, 10]. The results show, contrary to common belief, that there is no linear relationship between level of realism and effectiveness of training. Abstraction and simplification can also lead to excellent training outcomes [11]. For safety and security training in urban environments, however, it is not clear how different levels of fidelity affect training effectiveness, although certain aspects have already been researched. As an example, Visschedijk [12] researched fidelity guidelines of human emotion expressions

© Springer International Publishing Switzerland 2014
A. De Gloria (Ed.): GALA 2013, LNCS 8605, pp. 370–375, 2014.
DOI: 10.1007/978-3-319-12157-4_31

for 3D military serious games. Other research showed that failure to achieve the 'right' level of realism holds the risk that the player adopts a 'wrong' or different strategy than needed in real life [3]. Zielke et al. [13] showed how a serious game could be used to prepare actors for dealing with unknown cultures. Nonetheless, the effect fidelity actually has on processes of situational understanding has not yet been researched properly; to understand this relationship is the major aim of our research.

2 Three Levels of Fidelity in Simulation Games

To gain deeper insights in the role fidelity plays in the design and the effect of simulation games, we developed a framework of fidelity and applied it within a case-study on a simulation game aiming at enhancing situational awareness. For simulation games, we consider three levels of fidelity that could be found in literature [7, 8, 14–17]. Properly balancing the three levels of fidelity means that all three elements should represent enough accordance with the reference system of the game in order to achieve the goal of the game. We summarized the findings to:

1. **Audio-visual or physical fidelity**: This level of fidelity refers to the degree in which the environment of the game, the objects within the game world including their textures, color and movements, the agents in the game and their behavior, and the sound match with the reference system of the game, mostly the "reality".[1]
2. **Functional fidelity**: Functional fidelity refers to the degree in which the roles, processes and tasks of the agents and the players match with roles, processes and tasks of the reference system of the game, mostly the "reality".
3. **Psychological fidelity**: Psychological fidelity refers to the degree in which the emotional and cognitive reactions of the player match with those in reality. It includes the perception of the game play process, the feeling of flow and experience of immersion within the game.

3 High-Fidelity Game Scenarios to Increase Teamwork Skills in Reconnaissance Work

Reconnaissance and close protection of politicians and threatened persons are important security tasks of the police and security services. For police officers in reconnaissance and close protection, it is of crucial importance to interact with suspicious persons to gather reliable information. Additionally to interaction with suspects and other persons in the environment, effective teamwork is of great importance to collect as much environmental information as possible. Very good communication skills are a precondition for proper decision making and action taking. These skills include the interpretation of information, and its processing. Team members have to recognize and

---

[1] We acknowledge the term "reality" is quite controversial, but do not want to involve in this discussion. With "reality", we try to describe the physical world we live in and perceive with our natural cognitive abilities.

interpret hints in the environment, and have to decide on their importance and the way to pass over information to other team members, if needed. This also relates to situational awareness skills, a concept extending communication of information with the relation to past (experiences) and future (prediction). Effective training with a high degree of fidelity is inevitable to prepare teams working in this field. In the following, we introduce three different scenarios that have been developed and show an overview about how these scenarios have been tested with the target group. The tests took place in an experimental setting. All sessions have been observed by two researchers in person and by video. Questionnaires have been filled in before and after playing the game, with regard to expectations and experiences of the players. The de-briefing of the game was also used as part of the qualitative evaluation. The design process of the scenarios is described in detail in [18].

3.1   First Scenario: Trainer-Lead Team Play in an Authentic Virtual City

Five experts played the first game scenario as a trainer-lead game within a Unity-based realistic virtual environment that represented parts of the city center of The Hague. At every game round, two police officers played together in front of two big screens. They formed one team, but were able to navigate their own avatar through the environment. The players could communicate with each other in person, and could use their handheld phone to communicate with the team leader who was located in a different room. One trainer accompanied the team, taking over the roles of virtual persons the team wanted to interact with in the game. The assignment of the game was given after a tutorial within a briefing, structurally based on real briefing situations. The police officers were asked to walk through the virtual city of The Hague along a prescribed route, and to make sure that this route would be safe for a person to be protected afterwards. This means that the police team had to detect suspicious objects and persons. After a short feedback moment, the police team got its second assignment and played a second round within the virtual environment, with a similar objective. The game ended with a de-briefing moment, focused on both the playing experience and the training effect. Based on pre- and related post-questionnaire, combined with observations of the game process, conclusions on the balance of fidelity of this scenario could have been made as follows.

Physical fidelity: The movement of the virtual persons has not yet been realistically enough. Furthermore, the whole scenario did not hold enough details to make clear interpretations of the situation. Relationships between objects and persons are important for interpretation, but have not been clear enough in the game.

Functional fidelity: The virtual agents did not provide enough hints to make any assumptions about the person itself. Clear behavioral signs and with them a fundamental basis for decision making processes lacked in the game.

Psychological fidelity: Players reported that the flow feeling was disturbed by the recurrent switch between in-game action and interaction with the trainer, taking over the role of one of the virtual agents. This also hindered real empathy with the persons and the situation.

3.2   Second Scenario: Self-directed Team Play in an Authentic Virtual City

The outcomes of the first test lead us to the development of a second game scenario, developed with the UDK game engine, and aiming at a self-directed training activity without interaction with a trainer during game play. A slightly different, livelier area of the inner city of The Hague was chosen for the team set-up of the game. The assignment of this scenario was to walk through the environment with three players in a row, each of them confronted with both different and same objects, persons and actions as the other players. Player one had to observe the environment and to pass over information to player two, who had to interpret the scene based on this information and his/her own observations. He/she had to pass over information to the third player, who had to take a decision on an action (whether to let the person to protect walk the observed route or not) based on the information he/she had from his/her colleagues and based on his/her own observations. 16 experts from the field played this scenario. The outcomes of this test can be summarized as follows.

Physical fidelity: In order to enhance the degree of physical fidelity, more objects had been added to the scenario, and number and movements of the virtual agents had been improved.

Functional fidelity: Players made use of the information from prior players, e.g. when recognizing deviant behavior of a virtual person. This mechanism also served as a quality control of each other's work. The player afterwards had to rely on the information he/she received. Thus, when a player observed properly and was able to process and share the information well, he/she enabled the next player doing his/her job properly, too. This refers to work processes in real life.

Psychological fidelity: In self-reflection, the players reported in the questionnaires, that this game scenario was able to address distinct training goals as awareness skills, interpretation and communication skills like information gathering, processing and sharing.

3.3   Third Scenario: Trainer-Lead Single Play in a Generic Virtual City

The third scenario was again developed as a trainer-lead scenario, based on the Unity game engine. This scenario did not take place in the city of The Hague, but in a generic Dutch urban space. The assignment of the game was to accompany a person of public interest (VIP) to an open-air event. The game was divided into the three phases of work preparation, observation and execution of the task. 8 police officers and 8 employees of a private security organization played the game. The police officers were focused on protecting the VIP and detecting deviant behavior of other subjects at the sight, while the employees of the private security organization where focused on the security of objects and buildings. This task distribution mirrors the tasks in real security duties of the two organizations. Two teams of two players, one police team and one team of the private security organization, played each round of the game synchronously. The trainer of the game took over the roles of the virtual persons the players wanted to interact with instead of a user interface. The test results showed the following.

Physical fidelity: The de-briefing of the game showed that players appreciated the generic, unknown virtual environment, because this made them more alert about the situation. The unknown environment forced them to communicate very well with each other, because they could not rely on known mental models or patterns about the surrounding, which is also related to functional fidelity. The environment was very busy, but players still missed clear signs in virtual person's behavior and face expressions.

Functional fidelity: Different to reality, the players within a team couldn't see each other's faces, which minimized their information and ability of interpreting the situation.

Psychological fidelity: The role of the trainer as dialog partner compensated the lack of information from the game environment itself and fostered the flexibility of the scenario, but the players mentioned the fact that this way of interaction always meant a break in game flow.

4   Conclusions

The realistic virtual environment shows the ability to enhance teamwork skills, especially communication skills. Situational awareness can be fostered to a certain limit. Virtual objects could be used for awareness training, but virtual agents of the game scenario's still lack realistic behavior and expressions, thus a higher level of physical fidelity is needed here. The decision for man-machine interaction or a teacher-lead approach, where the teacher takes over the roles of the virtual agents, relates to the balance between fidelity and flexibility of the game. While interaction with the virtual agent produces a more realistic feeling and holds the player within the feeling of flow, a teacher-lead approach supports flexibility of gameplay, but cuts into the degree of psychological fidelity. Regarding the balance of the three levels of physical, functional and psychological fidelity, it showed that functional fidelity is relatively easy to include in a game scenario, when actions and tasks are translated properly. Physical fidelity is much harder to reach, as it takes a lot of effort to create a simulation game environment that is near-to-reality. When game mechanics are developed well, it shows that psychological fidelity as immersion and the feeling of flow reaches a high level. Compared to each other, functional fidelity is mostly appreciated by the players in our study, and when both functional and psychological fidelity are high, it mattered less when physical fidelity did not reach the highest degree. The case study described shortly above showed that all three levels of fidelity should be balanced to a certain degree, but that physical fidelity is less important than psychological and functional fidelity. Future research will include more comparative tests to show how the three levels of fidelity have to be balanced in detail to design as effective simulation games as possible.

Acknowledgments. The Dutch Pieken-in-de-Delta program and the municipality of The Hague supported this work. Alexander Verbraeck, Theo van Ruijven, Linda van Veen and Bas van Nuland of Delft University of Technology also put a lot of effort in this project.

References

1. Kriz, W.: Creating effective learning environments and learning organizations through gaming simulation design. Simul. Gaming **34**, 495–510 (2003)
2. Malone, T.W.: What makes things fun to learn? A study of intrinsically motivating computer games. Pipeline **6**(2), 50–51 (1981)
3. Chalmers, A., Debattista, K.: Level of realism for serious games. In: IEEE Proceedings of 2009 Conference in Games and Virtual Worlds for Serious Applications (2009)
4. Lehman, D.R., Lempert, R.O., Nisbett, R.E.: The effects of graduate training on reasoning: Formal discipline and thinking about everyday-life events. Am. Psychol. **43**, 431–442 (1988)
5. Macedonia, M.: Games Soldiers Play. IEEE Spectr. **39**(3), 32–37 (2002)
6. Bonk, C.J., Dennen, V.P.: Massive multiplayer online gaming: a research framework for military training and education. Technical report, Department of Defense, USA (2005)
7. Alexander, A.L., Brunye, T., Sidman, J., Weil, S.A.: From Gaming to Training: A Review of Studies on Fidelity, Immersion, Presence, and Buy-in and Their Effects on Transfer in PC-Based Simulations and Games. Aptima Inc, Woburn (2005)
8. Harteveld, C.: Triadic Game Design. Springer, London (2011)
9. Feinstein A.H., Cannon H.M.: Fidelity, Verifiability, and validity of simulation: constructs for evaluation. Wayne State University Marketing Department Working Paper 2001-006 (2001). http://sbaweb.wayne.edu/~marketing/wp/008HC.pdf
10. Hays, R.T., Singer, M.J.: Simulation Fidelity in Training System Design: Bridging The Gap Between Reality and Training. Recent Research in Psychology. Springer, New York (1988)
11. Toups, Z.O., Kerne, A., Hamilton, W.A.: The team coordination game: Zero-fidelity simulation abstracted from fire emergency response practice. ACM Trans. Comput.-Hum. Inter. **18**(4), Article 23, 1–37 (2011)
12. Visschedijk, G.C.: The issue of fidelity: what is needed in 3D military serious games? Master thesis, University of Twente/TNO, Soesterberg (2010)
13. Zielke, M.A., Evans, M.J., Dufour, F., Christopher, T.V., Donahue, J.K., Johnson, P., Jennings, E.B., Friedman, B.S., Ounekeo, P.L., Flores, R.: Serious games for immersive cultural training creating a living world. IEEE Comput. Graph. Appl. **29**(2), 49–60 (2009)
14. Kinkade, R.G., Wheaton, G.R.: Training device design. In: Van Cott, H.P., Kinkade, R.G. (eds.) Human Engineering Guide to Equipment Design. American Institute for Research, Washington, DC (1972)
15. Fink, C.D., Shriver, E.L.: Simulators for maintenance training: Some issues, problems and areas for future research. Technical report: AFHRL-TR-78-27. Air Force Human Resources Laboratory, Technical Training Division, Lowry Air Force Base, Colorado (1978)
16. Klabbers, J.H.G.: The Magic Circle: Principles of Gaming & Simulation. Sense Publishers, Rotterdam (2006)
17. Cornacchione, E.B.: Fidelity and game-based technology in management education. Braz. Adm. Rev. **9**(2) (2012). http://www.scielo.br/scielo.php?pid=S1807-76922012000200003&script=sci_arttext
18. Lukosch, H.K., van Ruijven, T.A.W., Verbraeck, A.: The other city? How to design authentic urban environments for serious games. In: Proceedings of the International Conference on Information Systems for Crisis Response and Management (ISCRAM) (2012)

Gaming for Policy Makers: It's Serious!

Josine G.M. van de Ven[1(✉)], Hester Stubbé[1], and Micah Hrehovcsik[2]

[1] TNO, P.O. Box 23, 3769 DE Soesterberg, The Netherlands
josine.vandeven@tno.nl
[2] School of Games and Interaction, University of Arts Utrecht,
P.O. Box 2471, 1200 CL Hilversum, The Netherlands

Abstract. De Burgemeestergame - The Mayor Game - is the result of the research project "GATE Pilot Safety (http://gate.gameresearch.nl/)" (2009–2012). The game provides strategic dilemma training for crisis management scenarios using a serious game format. Since there were no games available that could be used for training policy makers, the valid question at that point was how to develop a serious game that would be used and useful for policy makers. What exactly would such a game look like?

This article explains in more detail the establishment of the learning goals (expert group), the didactic background (self-directed learning) and the development process (AGD Framework) of the Mayor Game.

1 The Mayor Game

The Mayor game consists of a web-based game (small game) that is integrated in a training session (big game) to gain experience, stimulate reflection and awareness and to share experiences between participants. Nothing results in better skill at handling tasks than insight gained from reflecting upon experience [1].

The Mayor game is a dilemma trainer that presents a scenario in eight dilemmas. Dilemmas are introduced with a few lines of text and end with a question (see Fig. 1 below). Participants need to answer this question with 'yes' or 'no'. During crises mayors work with a Policy team; in the game the digital Policy team members are gathered at a table and are available for advice and extra information. Once the dilemma has been answered, the participant is asked to record what information items were important to decide on this dilemma. The game is over when either the time limit has been reached (15 min) or all dilemmas have been answered. The participant is free to choose which dilemma he or she will answer first, although the dilemmas become available in a certain order. The participant can also read all dilemmas before answering any of them. Besides that, extra information and advice from Policy team members is available per dilemma, but it is up to the participant to decide if and when he or she uses this.

Immediately after the game, the participant receives feedback about the choices he or she made. This is done in several ways. First of all, they can read a newspaper article that is personalized according to the choices made. This will give the participant an impression of how the press will write about them the day after. From there the

A. De Gloria (Ed.): GALA 2013, LNCS 8605, pp. 376–382, 2014.
DOI: 10.1007/978-3-319-12157-4_32

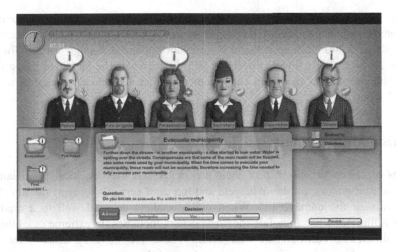

Fig. 1. Screenshot of the game

participant can click through to statistics about e.g. the time needed to answer dilemmas, the number of dilemmas answered, the number of times the advice of the different team members was recorded as important. Last but not least, the participant's answers are related to the three different roles he or she needs to take during a crisis, (1) 'Boegbeeld': taking a prominent role in the media, (2) 'Bestuurder': focusing on the law and administration side of the situation and (3) 'Burgervader': acting as a father/mother to citizens that suffer from the situation. A graph shows how many of their answers can be related to each of the three roles. The feedback focuses on presenting what the participant has done (mirror). The small game does not provide any interpretation or advice.

A typical training session with the game takes 60 min. It starts with a 5 min introduction on the goals and the use of the game. Then a scenario is played, which takes 15–20 min. A clock in the upper left corner counts down from 15 to zero. The remaining time is spent on discussing the thoughts and considerations the participants had while reaching their decision. The actual answers to the dilemmas are not important at all. The responses to real dilemmas can never be right or wrong; only the outcome of the real situation determines, in hindsight, if this was the most effective decision. Therefore, the thoroughness of the decision process is more important. The trainer will stimulate reflection on this process and invite participants to share earlier experiences with similar incidents. Training takes place in a group of 8–15 participants. Each participant plays a pre-selected scenario, individually. It is our experience that most learning takes place in the discussion/reflection phase at the end of the training. Participants quickly experience what dilemmas can occur in relation to specific scenarios. This experience leads to curiosity and a sense of urgency, which increases the effectiveness of the discussion phase (as compared to a case discussion without the game).

At the moment the Mayor game contains 12 scenarios. These are typical scenarios for mayors, focusing on strategic dilemmas for policy makers, and less on the operational choices that have to be made during a crisis. A typical scenario is the pandemic-like incident. Within your municipality two children below the age of ten have died from cerebro-spinal meningitis. Examples of strategic dilemmas in this scenario are: (1) Parents of 5,200 children demand a vaccination, there is enough vaccine for 3,000 children. Do you stay with your decision only to vaccinate the identified risk group of 2,500 children? (2) Do you allow that children are not vaccinated because of religious reasons?

2 Crisis Management and Training

In times of crises citizens expect their presidents and mayors, local politicians and elected administrators, public managers and top civil servants to avert the threat or at least minimize the damage [2]. When policy makers respond well to a crisis, the damage is limited; when they fail, the crisis impact increases. In extreme cases this may be the difference between life and death. These are no easy tasks because the management of a crisis is often a big, complex and drawn-out operation with the mass media scrutinizing and assessing leaders and their leadership. Although policy makers do not deal with this kind of crises on a daily basis, they need to be prepared to take up their role during a crisis. To train Dutch mayors for their role in crisis management, current training focuses on procedures and getting to know the other stakeholders in the Policy Team. These table top exercises usually deal with the first hour after the policy team is assembled during a crisis. The contribution to the professionalization of policy makers in crisis management is limited for several reasons: because of the focus on protocol and cooperation, mayors cannot train the typical dilemmas policy makers face during a crisis. Moreover, the focus on this first hour makes it impossible to train the strategic dilemmas that typically present themselves later on during a crisis and are – mostly – not directly related to the operational activities of first responders.

Trainers find it difficult to develop scenarios that deal with these more strategic dilemmas; their own experience usually lies in operational crisis management. Apart from that they are less familiar with the training methods needed to train strategic decision making. Another issue is, that mayors usually train one to two times a year. Their busy schedules and the logistics needed to arrange a table top training make it hard to increase this frequency. Lastly, mayors are in a position where they need to show they are in control. This attitude often leads to the belief that they do not need more or another training. Although gaming is a popular trend, at the start of the project it was very difficult to convince policy makers and the people around them that serious gaming could be applicable and interesting to them. Apart from the general reluctance to train at all, they feel they have serious jobs and do not like to waste their time on a game.

Our challenge, therefore, was to develop a serious game that would be serious and attractive enough for mayors, that could be played in a short period of time and that would really add to the professional development of mayors. Since this is the first game developed for policy makers, training needs and learning goals were not clearly defined. An expert group of domain experts provided input for these. Our domain experts were individuals involved in training mayors and their Policy teams, looking for alternative methods to do so. Initially, the members of our expert group were actually skeptical about the possibility of using serious games for mayors. Games were not the alternative way of training they were looking for. Throughout the development process we consulted our expert group on learning goals, gaming characteristics, design, and for play testing. They defined the goals as:

- Identifying policy dilemmas
- Reducing training time
- Decision making under time pressure

3   Self-directed Learning

Looking at the characteristics of mayors and the learning goals we meant to achieve, we chose self-directed learning as the educational basis of the training method. Self-directed learning is a way of learning that most adults use in work or hobby-related situations. In their meta-review on self-directed adult learning, Stubbé and Theunissen [3] concluded that the characteristics of adult learning match with the elements of self-directed learning. An important characteristic of self-directed learning is that the learner takes control over his/her own development and education [4]. Training developed to support self-directed learning should therefore allow the learner to take control. The training is based on the five elements of self-directed learning as described by [3]:

(1) Learner control. Ideally, a self-directed learner has control over all educational decisions.
(2) Self-regulating learning strategies. To gain control, a learner needs to use learning strategies like setting goal, planning and monitoring their planning.
(3) Reflection. The reflection element contains two aspects: (1) assessing their own performance in relation to goals, and (2) evaluating the learning process itself.
(4) Interaction with social environment. Cooperation and collaboration with others.
(5) Interaction with physical environment. Training should be based on work-related situations and dilemmas and allow learners to practice and experiment.

Below we will describe how these elements have been integrated in the game:

(1) Learner control is implemented by allowing the learner to choose which dilemmas he/she would like to answer first. Moreover, learners can decide for themselves whether they ask for extra information and advice from their policy team. The feedback is give personally and individually. Learners can decide for themselves whether they want to share the feedback with others or not.
(2) Self-regulating learning strategies have not been fully implemented in the game. To set goals, plan how to reach them and monitor progress, learners need access to their results. Anonymity and safety were deemed to be more important. Therefore results are deleted at the end of every day, making it impossible to use them for further learning.
(3) Reflection is supported by the feedback that is provided in the Mayor game and by the trainer.

(4) Social interaction is supported by the fact that training takes place in a group of 8–15 learners with similar learning goals. During the reflection afterwards the participants interact with each other, learning from each other.

(5) All scenarios and dilemmas are based on situations that have occurred in reality, thus creating an authentic learning environment. Learners can experiment with scenarios they might have to deal with in the future and gain experience. They can also try out new solutions for a situation they have encountered before. The way in which the scenarios and dilemmas are presented resemble reality.

4   Right or Wrong?

Some people may argue that the Mayor game is not a real game, because the player cannot die or score any points and it lacks a hall of fame. Moreover, the game play relies on a rather static presentation of the member of the Policy team and a textual presentation of the scenarios and dilemmas. Interaction is based on 'point and click', allowing the participant to access pre-defined text elements. The rationale behind these choices is the following. During a crisis, mayors and their Policy team assemble in an office and receive information in text or by phone. Portraying the Policy team at a table resembles reality and allows for the seriousness mayors are looking for in a game. Moreover, mayors are not known for their gaming abilities; using a point and click system provides easy access to the game dynamics.

Scoring was one of the issues that we debated extensively. A score implies that there is a 'best solution' and that you can do well or badly. Crisis management itself is an area in which the best solution can usually only be determined in hindsight. The fact that we have focused on strategic dilemmas in crisis management only strengthens the fact that there is no 'best solution'. Apart from that, our experts indicated from the start that it would be inappropriate to calculate a baseline on the basis of a group of participants. Since mayors feel they are doing quite well, feedback that implies they could have done better would lead to a rejection of the game. We needed to look for other ways to nudge them towards further development and professionalization. Lastly, when piloting the game we have seen that a 'yes' or 'no' can be based on exactly the same arguments and considerations. In the discussion phase the answer itself becomes less important; it only serves as an accelerator to stimulate deep thinking. Talking about their thoughts, using case-based reasoning helps the participants to learn more about the conditions and signals that must be considered in any future decision on a similar topic.

A 'yes' or a 'no' answer to a dilemma can be related to one of the roles a mayor can take during a crisis (Boegbeeld, Burgervader, Bestuurder). It reflects the preferred style of a mayor during a crisis. The profile based on the type of answers provides food for thought (see Fig. 2). The participant is invited to question if this role was appropriate for the situation at hand. This can lead to a further discussion about roles, and increase the mayors' ability to switch between roles as a result of enhanced role awareness. Currently, the relation between the dilemma answer and the role performed is defined by experts.

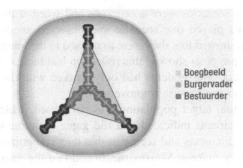

Fig. 2. Example of feedback on three roles

5 The ADG Framework

"Making a good game is hard. Making a good serious game is even harder" [5]. Knowing your target population, learning goals, appropriate didactics and context does not lead automatically to a good serious game. To avoid the well-known pitfall of designing a very serious but boring game, we have applied the AGD Framework (see http://gamedesigntools.blogspot.kr/2013/05/2cat-framework-for-applied-game-design.html). This Framework was developed at the *University of Arts Utrecht*. The AGD framework is meant as a tool for game designers. The designer must first build awareness about the different game design domains and how their demands affect the design of a game. The designers in this project worked together with the expert in the domain of crisis management, a didactic specialist, and a game designer. They worked together for several sessions before a paper based version of the game was developed. Using the paper based version of the game, the game mechanics were tested with students in crisis management and our expert group. Based on their feedback changes were made and the game feedback was designed as described before.

Described in terms of gameplay elements, game elements used in The Mayor Game were story comprehension, information management, time pressure, and prioritization. The tone of the game has a light dramatic feel that is oriented towards typical modern Dutch cultural themes. Visually, the game is a stylized 3D-rendering, comparable to cartoony game styles such as Tintin© and Blue Toad Murder Files™. The goal of the game-play experience is to create tension by challenging the player's ability to prioritize conditions within the decisions, filter information, and make critical decisions while under the pressure of time.

6 Results

During and after the development of the Mayor game we have collected various types of results. Because of the specific characteristics of our target population – mayors – we were not able to carry out an experiment in which progress was measured using pre-posttest. The paper-based version was tested with 25 students of Integral Safety Management, aged between 20 and 44. The aim of this test was to determine whether the game play worked, the scenarios were appropriate and whether the didactics supported reflection. The students played one scenario and observed another student playing a scenario. Observations showed that they were immersed in the game. A questionnaire on self-directed learning (pre-post) showed that reflection had increased, but not enough to be statistically significant. The students had only worked with the game for one hour, which was probably too short to see improvement.

A test with the actual target population was performed, which also resulted in a positive reaction. Participants indicated that the game gave them the opportunity to practice responding to dilemmas and scenarios that they recognized as true to their role and experience as policy makers. Mayors mentioned that the game 'really made them think!' and triggered them to look at dilemmas from a different perspective. Following the game experience, mayors have initiated more contact with mayors from other cities and explored legislation in certain areas. This indicates that the Mayor game stimulates gaining experience, awareness and reflection. Coming from a population that was not interested in training or gaming, this is a very strong result.

The training is currently available through the IFV (Institute for Safety) who function as a distributor. Trainers can buy 'tickets' for their training. The Mayor game can only be used by licensed trainers. IFV also provides train-the-trainer courses. The game became available for the public on 1 April 2012. Since then 30 trainers have obtained their license and half of the mayors in The Netherlands have been trained with this game. The number of tickets sold indicate that the Mayor game is used every week, with an average of one group of eight people per week. These training sessions are extra: the current training programme is still followed. This shows that the frequency of training has increased. The adoption rate (50 %) also shows that we managed to design and develop a game that was accepted and taken seriously by our target population.

Acknowledgements. We would like to thank the Nederlands Genootschap van Burgemeesters (Dutch Association of Mayors), people of the veiligheidsregio's (Dutch Security Regions) and trainers who have given their time and advice to this project.

The project was funded by ICTregie (http://www.ictregie.nl/).

References

1. Rodgers, C.: Defining reflection: another look at John Dewey and reflective thinking. Teach. Coll. Rec. **4**, 842–866 (2002)
2. Boin, R.A., 't Hart, P., Stern, E., Sundelius, B.: The Politics of Crisis Management: Public Leadership Under Pressure. Cambridge University Press, Cambridge (2005)
3. Stubbé, H.E., Theunissen, N.C.M.: Self-directed adult learning in a ubiquitous learning environment: a meta-review. In: Proceedings - Special Track on Technology Support for Self-organised Learners During 4th EduMedia Conference 2008 "Self-organised Learning in the Interactive Web" - A Change in Learning Culture? Salzburg, Austria, June 2008
4. Collins, J.: Education techniques for lifelong learning: principles of adult learning. RadioGraphics **24**, 1483–1489 (2004)
5. Winn, B.M.: The design, play, and experience framework. In: Ferdig, R.E. (ed.) Handbook of Research on Effective Electronic Gaming in Education. Information Science Reference, Hershey, PA (2009)

Serious Game Design for Vehicular Language Learning Addressing Work Needs

Hariklia Tsalapatas[1(✉)], Olivier Heidmann[2], Rene Alimisi[2],
Spyros Tsalapatas[1], Spyros Kourias[1], Martin Sillaots[3],
Bernando Hourmat[4], Michela Tramonti[6],
Steffan Oie[5], and Elias Houstis[2]

[1] University of Thessaly, Argonafton & Filellinon, 38221 Volos, Greece
htsalapa@uth.gr
[2] Institute for Research and Technology Thessaly, 1st Industrial Area,
38500 Volos, Greece
[3] Tallinn University, 25 Narva Road, 10120 Tallinn, Estonia
[4] European Welding Federation, Av. Prof. Dr. Cavaco Silva,
2780-998 Porto Salvo, Portugal
[5] Hist Contract Research, E.C. Dahls gt, 7004 Trondheim, Norway
[6] Università degli Studi "Guglielmo Marconi", Via Plinio, 00193 Rome, Italy

Abstract. In today's open business environment peer communication across borders is the norm. It is commonplace in face-to-face interaction as well as on-line communities that facilitate work related collaboration of cross-border teams. To effectively work in these international surroundings, individuals resort to commonly understood, vehicular languages. In work-related contexts, impeccable use of a language is less important than effective communication towards addressing common goals. This work departs from typical professional language learning approaches by introducing a serious game for building language and cultural communication skills in a lingua franca. The game exposes professionals to typical deployment of a lingua franca by native and non-native speakers. Learners build communication competence through situated learning approaches that draw inspiration from the real world, which is both multilingual and multicultural. At the same time they become aware of the cultural wealth that is manifested in the individualized uses of vehicular languages by individuals with diverse backgrounds.

1 Introduction

The development of international teams that collaborate towards common business or other goals is commonplace in the current global business environment. Cross-border collaboration activities range from work in the context of formal international projects or frameworks to informal interaction for addressing professional or broader interests. It facilitates information sharing, networking, and know-how exchange. To effectively communicate in this diverse cultural environment individuals spontaneously resort to so-called "vehicular languages", namely ones that are commonly understood by individuals whose mother tongues differ.

A. De Gloria (Ed.): GALA 2013, LNCS 8605, pp. 383–389, 2014.
DOI: 10.1007/978-3-319-12157-4_33

The use of vehicular languages, or otherwise called "lingua franca", is not new. Vehicular languages have played a unifying role throughout history in cultural crossroads where diverse groups meet for trading or generally for conducting business. The term "lingua franca" emerged in the eastern Mediterranean during the renaissance years where a commonly understood tongue based primary on Italian with influences from Old French, Greek, Arabic, Portuguese, Occitan, and Spanish was used as a language of commerce 1.

Given the different use of languages even among native speakers it may be argued that there is not one single correct use of a particular language. For example, English speakers in the UK, USA, Australia, and beyond have different pronunciations, spell words differently, and use different expressions in everyday communication. To take this argument a step further, consider the use of English by Indians. A population of over 700 m speaks English in a characteristic manner that is globally recognizable making Indian English as valid as that of native speakers.

When communicating in a lingua franca the main objective is to understand the co-speaker and to become understood. The use of a language in a manner that follows exact use by native speakers becomes of secondary importance. This is particularly the case in the context of business communication in which meeting work objectives is the primary goal.

This paper presents a serious game developed in the context of the siLang project [2] for vehicular language learning that addresses work needs. siLang departs from traditional professional language training approaches aiming to build communication and cultural skills in vehicular languages with the objective of facilitating professional cross-border collaboration. Based on the observation that language skills are more effectively developed through exposure to real-life communication the siLang serious game immerses users to typical deployment of vehicular languages in diverse cultural environments through situated learning that draws inspiration from actual professional processes and every day activities.

2   A Review of Serious Games Used in the Context of Language Education

Gaming approaches are well accepted and used in language learning. Off-line games may engage learners in role-playing, conversation, and in communication exercises aiming to increase exposure to and use of a foreign language.

The idea of using digital games for learning purposes is not new. The potential educational value of digital games in educational settings is under exploration ever since recreational digital games emerged in the software applications market. Related applications have been developed both for commercial purposes and for other reasons, for example for military or health sector training 15. Games offer a good opportunity to build language and communication skills before being called to use them in the real world. By simulating real life, games offer a cost-effective training method for skill building by immersing users to characteristic interaction situations and related exercises. Vocabulary, syntax, and broad communication skills can be practiced through educational, serious games.

The Tactical Language Training System (TLTS) 3 is a serious game that aims at building language and culture skills. The game targets military personnel; however the game principles could be adapted to cover broader learning requirements, for example towards building language skills for business. The TLTS game is task-based encouraging users to 'carry out tasks in a foreign country such as introducing themselves, obtaining directions, and meeting local officials'.

Another example of a language learning game is Manolo's Business Trip 4, an interactive language learning course with virtual characteristics that aims to build English language skills for professional communication. The main character is Manolo, a professional with 'a flexible professional/personal background' who goes through numerous episodes with increasing difficulty level aiming to build transversal and specific language skills.

With the emergence of mobile apps innovative software is introduced for supporting language and vocabulary building skills. This includes the Knowji mobile application 5 that uses spaced repetition algorithms to help users build vocabulary.

Finally, language learning services and communities that apply gamification principles can be accessed through the web. These include the Livemocha commercial language learning community 7 which in addition to providing educational content networks learners so that they can practice speaking through conversations, tutor each other, and help each other learn. The busuu.com community 6 offers interactive content while bringing individuals together for practicing language skills through communication.

3 How the siLang Language Learning Game Differs from Traditional Language Learning Software

siLang stands apart from related activities in the broader sector of language education through its main focus and educational objective, which is the development of communication skills in vehicular languages. The project addresses the needs of a multilingual and multicultural world contributing to the development of communication capacity, as opposed to the perfection of language form. This is in-line with communicative approaches to language education 1112 that steadily gain ground as the research and instructional communities shift focus from mainly practicing correct application of language elements such as syntax to enhancing the ability of learners to communicate.

siLang embraces the cultural wealth that is evident in the diverging uses of vehicular languages by individuals with rich backgrounds. This view of language as a communication tool reflects perceptions in today's global communication practices: professionals rarely criticise mother tongue influences that peers unconsciously introduce into conversation. Effective communication is the objective as it allows diverse teams of workers to focus on joint goals promoting competitiveness and productivity.

In terms of software, and specifically serious game, design towards language skill building siLang introduces innovation in a number of design principles:

- Implementing in practice the objective of exposing users to diverse uses of a lingua franca, non-playing characters in siLang introduce transfer effects manifested in pronunciation, syntax, and expressions
- Similarly, authentic voices of individuals with diverse backgrounds are recorded and associated with non-playing characters. In earlier sections this is referred to as localization of the siLang game
- siLang is adaptive with respect to the background of the user and the location in which the user will be called to use a vehicular language. If the user, for example, indicates that she wants to practice using English in Estonia, non-playing characters will be assigned voices of Estonian nationals
- siLang is adaptive in terms of professional role with the conversation being adapted to the professional role the user which she has the opportunity to indicate upon entrance into the game
- The game allows the user a certain degree of control on the unfolding of the storyline through choices that the user can make at critical points in the game scenario. While this design choice may increase the cost of game implementation a foldback story structure 10 helps contain development resources
- siLang is designed for standalone use by learners who have the opportunity to enhance their language skills through game play anytime, anywhere; however, it can also be used in a classroom by instructors as a complementary language learning tool
- The game supports touch screen interfaces further promoting broad adoption and flexible use
- While emphasizing the development of communication capacity and exposing learners to broad uses of vehicular languages the siLang game also provides opportunities for users to enhance their knowledge on basic language elements, such as vocabulary and syntax, through task-based approaches

4 Design of a Serious Game for Vehicular Language Competence Building Addressing Work Needs

The design of the siLang serious game applies situated learning methodologies 1214 promoting vehicular language learning through exposure to typical use by native as well as non-native speakers 89. Situated learning is based on communicative approaches 1112 that have been gaining ground in language education departing from more traditional drill-based learning plans. It immerses users to learning scenarios that draw inspiration from typical business collaboration. A learning-by-doing, active skill development methodology enables learners to build language and cultural skills by engaging with rich characters in the context of game play. The target audience includes professionals, vocational workers, and higher education students.

The siLang serious game validates the proposed situated learning methodologies towards building capacity of professionals to communicate in global English. However, the siLang game design is generic; design principles can be transferred towards developing serious games for building capacity in other vehicular languages.

siLang is a point and click game. It is a first person view game where the main character, who is the game user, is not visible. The user interacts with avatars that are introduced through the game scenario through interactive prompt dialog. Compelling features are the light-hearted and engaging storyline and humorous content integrated into the scenario.

The siLang game player is profiled upon login with the objective of adapting the game tasks to specific professional interests related to language and cultural communication. Adaptation of the game story in terms of user background, target environment for language deployment, and, to a lesser degree, professional role facilitates higher learner engagement.

Profiling and adaptation enables the tailoring of activities to personalized learning objectives. For example, being aware of the background and mother tongue of the user allows the introduction of tasks that address specific difficulties that the user may be faced with in language communication. Knowing the environment in which the user aims to communicate professionally in a vehicular language allows the adaptation of dialogs enabling the user to gain experience on transfer effects that might be introduced by peers of a different cultural background. Finally, information on the user's professional role can help link the game scenario to user interests and enhance game relevance to user goals.

The siLang game is designed with a backbone story line that includes all characteristics of the basic game plot including all possible branches of the foldback story structure. At this initial stage the user can have a first level of control on the instantiation of the storyline. Localization of the story line refers to adapting the game in terms of user background and target environment for language use. The basic story is enriched with non-playing character (NPC) voices recorded using authentic speakers with a background from different countries and specifically Greece, Norway, Estonia, Italy, and Portugal. In addition, it is enriched with transfer effects, i.e. common mistakes, which the NPC's introduce into the dialog. The user has further control on the unfolding of the storyline through choices at critical events through which she can choose among mutually exclusive paths of the foldback story. Through these choices the user controls the path of the storyline evolution.

The siLang storyline follows a young professional as she maneuvers the business world. Through the storyline the user is exposed to typical business activities such as responding to a job posting, going through an interview, participating in an international meeting, socializing with peers in an afterhours relaxed setting, and developing a report. What is considered most important than the storyline itself is the game play, i.e. the interaction of the user with the game non-playing characters and the tasks that she is involved with. Interactive activities include:

- Responding to listening comprehension exercises
- Self-recording
- Acting according to information received through game characters
- Filling-in text gaps with correct vocabulary or correct syntax
- Writing a text in response to specific directions; the activity allows practicing of written skills, syntax, and vocabulary

- Matching pronunciation to specific characters
- Matching images, words, sounds, and more according game-play information
- Dragging and dropping the correct answer into text

5 Instead of Conclusion

The siLang serious game is under development following the design herein. The game will be evaluated in real-life contexts engaging professionals, vocational workers, and higher education students in Greece, Portugal, Norway, Estonia, and Italy. Evaluation will be pursued through qualitative approaches that deploy participatory observation of researchers in learning experiments during which stakeholder representatives will be exposed to the game. Embedded evaluation approaches will further be explored for collecting information on the learning experience of users and the perceived learning benefits.

Acknowledgements. This work is funded with the support of the European Commission. This publication reflects the views only of the authors and the Commission cannot be held responsible for any use which may be made of the information contained therein.

References

1. Lingua franca, Wikipedia. http://en.wikipedia.org/wiki/Vehicular_language. Accessed 27 June 2013
2. The siLang project. http://www.si-lang.org
3. Johnson, W.L., Vijhjalmsson, H., Marsella, S.: Serious Games for Languag eLearning: How Much Game, How Much AI, USC Center for Advanced Research in Technology for Education
4. Manolo's Business Trio. http://wat.iavante.es/blogs/etp/manolos-business-trip
5. Knowji. http://www.knowji.com/apps/
6. Busuu.com. http://busuu.com
7. Livemocha. http://livemocha.com
8. Tsalapatas, H., Heidmann, O., Alimisi, R., Houstis, E.: A serious game-based approach for situated learning of vehicular languages addressing work needs and cultural aspects. In: 7th International Technology, Education and Development Conference, Valencia, Spain, 4–5 March. IATED (2013). ISBN: 978-84-616-2661-8
9. Tsalapatas, H., Heidmann, O., Alimisi, R., Houstis, E.: English language learning through innovative ICT solutions that promote enculturation and role playing. In: Future of Education Conference, Florence, Italy, 13–14 June 2013
10. Adams, E.: Fundamentals of Game Design, 2nd edn. New Riders, Berkeley (2009)
11. Canale, M., Swain, M.: Theoretical bases of communicative approaches to second language teaching and testing. Appl. Linguist. **1**(1), 1–47 (1980)
12. Hymes, D.H.: On Communicative Competence. University of Pennsylvania Press, Philadelphia (1971). Extracts available in Brumfit, C.J., Johnson, K. (eds.): The Communicative Approach to Language Teaching, pp. 5–26. Oxford University Press, Oxford (1979). ISBN: 0-19-437078-X

13. Brown, J.S., Collins, A., Duguid, P.: Situated cognition and the culture of learning. Educ. Res. **18**(1), 32–42 (1989). Killroy, D.A.: Problem-based learning (2004). http://emj.bmj. com/content/21/4/411.full.pdf
14. Oliver, R., Herrington, J.: Critical Characteristics of Situated Learning: Implications for the Instructional Design of Multimedia. Edith Cowan University, PDF (1995). Accessed 20 April 2006
15. Ulicsak, M., Wright, M.: Games in education: Serious Games (2010). http://media.futurelab. org.uk/resources/documents/lit_reviews/Serious-Games_Review.pdf

Harmonizing Interoperability – Emergent Serious Gaming in Playful Stochastic CAD Environments

Z. Kosmadoudi[1], Theodore Lim[1], James M. Ritchie[1], Y. Liu[1],
R. Sung[1], Jannicke Balsrud Hauge[2], Samir Garbaya[3],
Robert E. Wendrich[4(✉)], and Ioana A. Stanescu[5]

[1] Heriot-Watt University, Riccarton, Edinburgh EH14 4AS, Scotland, UK
{z.kosmadoudi,t.lim,j.m.ritchie,r.c.w.sung}@hw.ac.uk
[2] Bremer Institut für Produktion und Logistik (BIBA), Bremer, Germany
baa@biba.uni-bremen.de
[3] Arts et Métiers ParisTech, UMR CNRS 6306, LE2I, Paris, France
samir.garbaya@ensam.eu
[4] University of Twente, 7500 AE Enschede, The Netherlands
r.e.wendrich@utwente.nl
[5] National Defence University "Carol I", 50662 Bucharest, Romania
ioana.stanescu@adlnet.ro

Abstract. Computer-Aided Design (CAD) applications often promote memorable experiences for the wrong reasons. Coupled with complex functionality and poor user experience the learning curve is often steep and overwhelming. Invoking design creativity remains limited to conveying established geometry. Gameplay conversely excels in memorable and formative experiences and could spur intuition and natural creativity. If games are profoundly imbued for purposeful play, thriving on tacit and explicit user knowledge, a CAD system carefully stylized with ludic mechanisms could potentially be highly productive. An emergent serious game (SG) and CAD system may then hold promise. Preliminary feedbacks suggest a game-CAD environment incorporating interoperable mechanisms of CAD and SG systems to exchange creation improves user interactions resulting in better evolution of the workflow. The emerging scenarios presented reports a transformative approach to understanding of relationships in CAD use, learning and play mechanisms that enhance creativity and innovation.

1 Introduction

Product design is a complex set of activities beset not only by the limiting enablers but also by the unwitting impact of mediocre designs. Small errors in the early design phases may not be apparent until it becomes too late. Consequently, co-design ideation spaces, where product ideation is first developed and designs are potentially central for the development cycle, innovation and creativity [1, 2]. Ideation is the "ability one has to conceive, or recognize through the act of insight, useful ideas" [3]. However, current CAD systems (enabler) are governed by rigid rules and predetermined "canonical" procedures that limit user/designer creativity.

© Springer International Publishing Switzerland 2014
A. De Gloria (Ed.): GALA 2013, LNCS 8605, pp. 390–399, 2014.
DOI: 10.1007/978-3-319-12157-4_34

Gaming, though, has extended beyond its natural boundary of entertainment and is now associated with the process of problem solving and even questioning of scientific viewpoints through active game-play. The rules of game interaction or game mechanics include the concepts of usability and playability which are focused in a less stringent environment which provides a more intuitive user experience (UX). The transition from masses to user centered design paradigms sees engineering creativity being compromised. One reason is that the problem-solution space is challenging, a complex balance between representation, generation, and search of a design space in pursuit of original design solutions.

This paper presents the notion of playful CAD environments as a transformation technology to address current drawbacks such as complex menus, limited interactive assistance during the design task, informal conceptual design tool and the fixation on design routines that stifle users' creativity and intuitive notions.

2 The CAD-Game Conundrum

Research has showed that CAD users spend more time in learning the CAD system than actually using it [4]. The most important challenges facing novices are: the ease of learning, memorization and error-free use. The hypothesis is that such skills can be acquired much faster by experiencing product design in a gaming world. User experience and "interactional intention" are fundamental in design process; however, they are not easy to formalize in standard CAD systems. Games though provide enhanced cues and/or error notification instantaneously. This contrasts with CAD where users themselves judge errors.

A game is an abstract control system [5] where state-change during play and progress are controlled by rules [6]. In comparison, CAD (e.g. SolidWorks, Catia, ProE) operates via variations of sets of parametric functions. This approach creates a gap between the user and the CAD system where user experience, learning threshold, system functionality, performance and productivity are directly influenced and constrained (Fig. 1a). Design tasks instead become one of finding alternative event structures. Not surprisingly engineers' perception and UX have been compromised by the system's functionality and step-by-step evolution (for example the function structures of Pahl & Beitz) [7]. In "Digital Natives, Digital Immigrants" [8], Marc Prensky cites a case where mechanical engineers learned CAD software by playing an FPS-like game called "The Monkey Wrench Conspiracy." Then, perhaps enriching CAD environments by applying gaming techniques and mechanisms may improve the efficacy of design and productivity while enhancing user experience (memorable and formative). Digital gaming systems are complex and comprise interactive technologies, media, and simulation technologies [9], often with a story/plot. Games could provide a context for creativity coupled with challenges ranging from decision-making and problem solving strategies through to action reflexes [10].

A game architecture can be approached using the tetrad of Schell [11]: aesthetics, mechanics, technology and storytelling. However, as Church [12] cites, "The design is the game; without it you would have a CD full of data but no experience." Games and their design approach are different compared to traditional design and productivity domains such as CAD. Games actively encourage a variety of experiences while CAD strives for consistency at all times. Design is often viewed as a transformation from function to form, while the process of synthesis is the creation of a form that meets functional requirements. To create a synthetic CAD-game eco-system both game design and design synthesis methods must be extrapolated to allow metacognition to be triggered and enhanced through enriched visualization of the design/process flow.

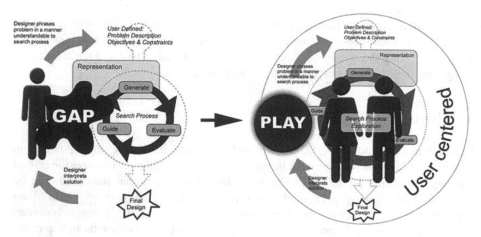

Fig. 1. (a) Identification of gaps in user experience in CAD systems [18]. (b) User centered playground with stochastic CAD eco-system.

3   User Centered Playground with Stochastic CAD Eco-System

A design solution space is always infinite and includes past, present, and future design states. If this space is describable to a computational game-based eco-system, then the challenge is to effectively find, search, and explore the solutions that best meet the demands of the design problem. A game-like environment has the potential to directly and positively reinforce the user experience and its creativity, as well as enhance new insights in understanding and learning. This design solution space enables the challenging task to target the problem definition in direct assimilation with the possible solutions that are emulated and represented by the CAD-Game System (CGS) (Fig. 1b).

Furthermore, the CAD-Game System could introduce some randomness in finding neighboring solutions preventing to become trapped in a local neighborhood. The CGS nudges (Fig. 2) the CAD-players to keep on creatively tracking and backtracking to iterate and re-iterate in the design solution process to provide more than one final design outcome. The general consensus is that bringing product design as CAD play and SG mechanisms/concepts together is fundamental to the future development of next generation intuitive design environments.

4   CAD-Game for Enhanced Creativity and Motivational Design

A game is an effective and engaging environment that is accessible anywhere, at any time, on demand, at your leisure and to your liking. Game playing offers learners motivation for acquiring new skills and/or to enhance the current skill-sets to improve individual capabilities [4, 13]. Games can be a cost-effective solution (savings) to support just-in-time ideation and/or creative design with periodic or continuous feedback. The ubiquity of games thus provides rich resource for improvement and adaptation in contextualized environments to communicate design. Since communication is a critical component of any design process, it fundaments the premise of using a game-infrastructure for CAD in support of users.

Some games are very difficult to play, not least to master. The demands for the user(s) are based on a serendipitous combination of skills (i.e. awareness, hand-eye coordination, tacit knowledge, creative cognition, etc.). The various levels of complexity and challenges are dominant features of game environments and are interoperable with CAD Game Eco-systems.

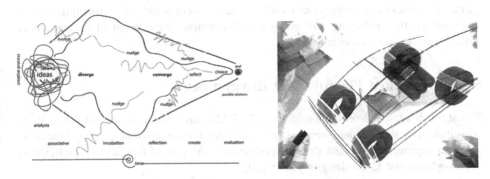

Fig. 2. (a) Scenario for Game-based CAD [16]. (b) Possible collaborative interactive solutions.

Koestler's [14, 16] view of creativity considers the externalization during the early stage of the design process, wherein the ideational concepts stemming from the mind's eye (inner visions), metacognitive aspects, imagination, mental divisions and distractions are transformed and represented. Design intents are fused together to create content through this in the creative act. The creative act initiates with a complete and boundary-less attitude towards inner and outer space. As with state changes in game play a current design state and context has no bearing until a cognitive nudge (Fig. 2) forms a solid representation. From this point on the challenge is to complete the design task at hand by bringing possible conclusions with iterative solutions. To paraphrase Dalcher [15] we concur that design is neither orderly nor linear; it implies a continuous and active search to resolve trade-offs and satisfying constraints.

Initial CGS research [16, 17] in Figs. 2 and 3 show how the creative human capability (imagination and inspiration) and capacity to playfully collaborate in design

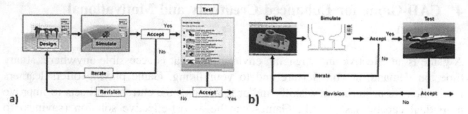

Fig. 3. Comparative game-CAD design and simulation scenarios [17]. (a) CAD-game. (b) Conventional CAD.

processing coincide with the intuitive natural human ability to interact, communicate and challenge conventional thinking.

When a CAD system is designed to accept input with the user defining the rules in comparison with the game system, is it possible for the game UX to be transferred to fit a CAD system? If so, could gaming make the user design process in CAD more interactive and meaningful? Many studies providing a useful list of game-relevant issues and cognitive models that aid the understanding of the outcome of the experience [18, 19] yet none has been able to evaluate which game mechanics or set of game mechanics cause engagement with a system. There is lack of statistical models to evaluate whether engaging and enjoyable interactions have taken place and under which specific game mechanics.

5   Implemented Playful CAD Environments

To establish a trace about the usefulness of a CAD-game environment and UX, a study with industrial stakeholders were asked to optimize the design of an existing bracket to meet an engineering product design specification. As part of this activity participants used a parametric CAD design system [20].

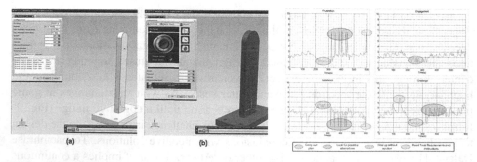

Fig. 4. UI of bracket design experiment. (a) Conventional UI/CADT. (b) Game-like UI/CADG. (c) Affect response of design task in CAD-game environment [20].

Each session comprises two different user interface (UI) settings (Fig. 4a and b) with no time restriction for task completion. Analyzing the psycho-physiological signals and action data, an interaction model was established identifying which of the proposed game mechanics contributed the most to enhance the user experience and to relay gain and winnings to the user's efforts (rewards & achievements). The affective response (Fig. 4c) indicated a clear preference of CGS over conventional CAD.

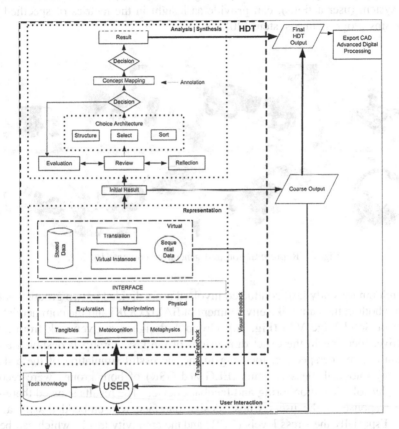

Fig. 5. Flow diagram of user-centered hybrid CAD environment embedded with fuzzy and logic mode [16].

The approach towards a boundary free Playful CAD environment to author and build hybrid design tools is to create blended virtual environments (Fig. 5). Designers are tethered to virtual digital realities where tools are developed and designed by system engineers and software programmers. It is apparent that loss of control, manual dexterity and intuitive interactions surface as a result of this mismatch [21]. Virtual reality environments are also eluding, and to paraphrase Lanier [22], users are reduced to conforming to the system rather than demanding the system be adaptive.

Meta-cognitive aspects, creativity and intuitive user interactions are measurable. By observing the creation of mental models of objects (representation) and design creation (generation), an analysis of how well an iterative outcome (solutions) meets the design goals and constraints (evaluation) can be understood [23]. Feedback on improvements to the design for the next iterative sequences (performance feedback & status) provides further subjective and objective groundings (Fig. 6).

Emergent progressions towards such environments have already been conducted to investigate how game mechanics are implemented in CAD UI and how a new model with psychological relationships (engagement) mapped to the user interactivity with a system (user actions), can provide an insight in the metrics of specified game mechanisms progress in a system [20].

Fig. 6. Representation and generative content [16, 21].

A preliminary study [20] conducted involved users divided in two groups - A & B - designing both in the game-like environment of BAMZOOKi and the commercial CAD package of Solid Edge V20 (Fig. 7a). Group A designed a given task from a CAD perspective, focusing in the exact dimensions of the task. Group B designed a given task from a game perspective, focusing in the successful simulation of the task. The psycho-physiological measurements (EEG and GSR) of both groups were recorded, through physiological monitoring and feedback device. The results showed there was a positive response of the users whose design interface was embedded with a game element. Especially the stress levels (GSR) and the creativity levels, which can be seen with an increase of theta waves (EEG), differed from the users who designed a task without the game element and who didn't show any significant changes in their emotional responses (Fig. 7b).

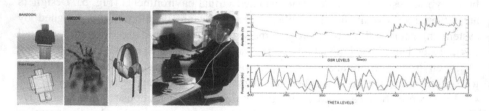

Fig. 7. (a) Design parameters: CAD-game vs. conventional CAD. (b) Behavioral and neurophysiological response in CAD-game and conventional CAD [20].

Design apart, assembly activity represents over 60 % of the manufacturing costs therefore a system whereby engineers can build mental models for assembly planning in VE could be beneficial for the conceptualization/ideation stage and the products' competitive route to market. In this respect it is important to meet the requirements of design for manufacturing and assembly (DFMA) [24], Fig. 8.

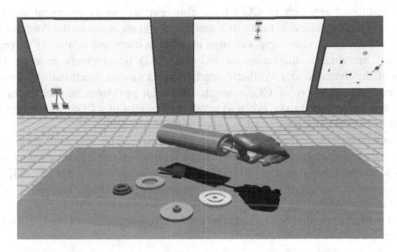

Fig. 8. Assemblability testing and generation of assembly plans in virtual environments [24].

The integration of sensory feedback, such as haptics and audio, has already shown to enhance user performance [25]. However, there is limited reported research that includes SG in virtual assembly environment [26]. The generation of assembly sequence is a task that requires building mental models to develop strategies necessary to obtain not only feasible assembly sequence but also the most feasible sequence or optimum assembly sequence. The potential of including SG in assembly design and planning would provide important assistance to the operator in making decisions on which part should be assembled first in order to build the product. Operation sequencing via assembly trials for which the operator get notified about his performance with reference to the optimum assembly plan could enhance his skills by building mental models of assembly operations.

6   Conclusions

For CGS, as with the design and development of SG, it is important to integrate the game aspects into the CAD Eco-system, i.e. supporting the co-creative product development process; this will contribute to a stimulated and improved user-experience. Employing game mechanisms as pointed out above in conjunction with a multi-disciplinary and cross-domain approach can create an enriched stochastic design space. Contextual knowledge and content developed using a CGS would document and present to users an immediate insight to understanding the design process in a superfluous and engaging way.

This means users acquire a full understanding, have real-time access to data, get instant-rewards and rich iterative content for future ideation and work.

Initial implementation and testing the usefulness of experimental CGS environments have been conducted. The measures of meta-cognitive aspects, creativity and intuitive user interaction indicate the benefits of CGS in terms of gaining user experience.

The results of research in CGS have also revealed many emergent issues and challenges. These manifest in many different forms and areas across the domains of SG and CAD. The rapid technological change impacts on users and influences perceptions of uptake. Sustainable adaptation of SG and CAD development requires further insights of the dynamic and synthetic mechanisms to avoid functional redundancies. Awareness and adoption of CGSs within industrial environments continues to be limited, and actions need to be taken to reveal the benefits of a CGS oriented approach not only in industry but also in education.

Interoperability is fundamental to CGS deployment. The transition from process base to knowledge embedment in engineered products mean industries now require formats to unobtrusively capture and externalize knowledge for reuse [27, 28]. However, a means of evaluating design quality, engineers' confidence levels and solution integrity is not trivial.

The research presented herein show promise and evidence that SG in CAD supports this direction.

Acknowledgments. This project is partially funded under the European Community Seventh Framework Programme (FP7/2007 2013), Grant Agreement nr. 258169 and EPSRC/IMRC grants 113946 and 112430.

References

1. Hesmer, A., Hribernik, K., Baalsrud Hauge, J., Thoben, K.-D.: Supporting the ideation processes by a collaborative online based toolset. Int. J. Tech. Mgt. **55**(3/4), 218–225 (2011)
2. Cross, N.: Developments in Design Methodology. Wiley, Chichester (1984)
3. Vaghefi, M.R., Huellmantel, A.B.: Strategic Management for the XX Century. CRC Press, Boca Ranton (1998)
4. Kosmadoudi, Z., Lim, T., Ritchie, J., Louchart, S., Liu, Y., Sung, R.: Engineering design using game-enhanced CAD: the potential to augment the user experience with game elements. CAD **45**(3), 777–795 (2013)
5. Grünvogel S.: Formal models and game design. Int. J. Comp. Game Res. **5**(1) (2005)
6. Tabuada, P., Pappas, G.J., Lima, P.: Compositional abstractions of hybrid systems. Discrete Event Dyn. Sys. **14**(2), 203–238 (2004)
7. Pahl, G., Beitz, W.: Engineering Design: A Systematic Approach. Springer, London (2005)
8. Prensky, M.: Digital natives, digital immigrants part 1. On the Horizon **9**(5), 1–6 (2001)
9. Narayanasamy, V., Wong, K.W., Fung, C.C., Rai, S.: Distinguishing games and simulation games from simulators. Comp. Ent. **4**(2), 9 (2006)
10. Lindley, C.: Game Taxonomies: A High Level Framework for Game Analysis and Design. Gamasutra. http://www.gamasutra.com/features/20031003/lindley_01.shtml
11. Schell, J.: Art Game Design – A Book of Lenses. Morgan Kaufmann, Burlington (2008)

12. Church, D.: Formal Abstract Design Tools. Gamasutra. http://www.gamasutra.com/features/19990716/design_tools_01.htm

13. Sivanathan, A., Lim, T., Louchart, S., Ritchie, J.: Temporal synchronisation of data logging in racing gameplay. Procedia Comp. Sci. **15**, 103–110 (2012)

14. Koestler, A.: The Act of Creation. Hutchinson & Co., London (1964)

15. Dalcher, D.: Consilience for universal design: the emergence of a third culture. Univ. Access Inf. Soc. **5**(3), 253–268 (2006)

16. Wendrich, R.: The creative act is done on the hybrid machine. In: Proceedings of 19th International Conference on Engineering Design (ICED2013) (2013)

17. Sung, R.C.W., Ritchie, J.M., Lim, T., Rea, H.J., Corney, J.R.: Automated capture of design knowledge using a virtual creature design environment. In: Proceedings of 40th ISAGA Conference 110007 (2009)

18. Wendrich, R.E., Tragter, H., Kokkeler, F.G.M., van Houten, F.J.A.M.: Bridging the design gap: towards an intuitive design tool. In: Proceedings of the ICSID World Design Congress (2009)

19. Jennett, C., Cox, A.L., Cairns, P., Dhoparee, S., Epps, A., Tijs, T., Walton, A.: Measuring and defining the experience of immersion in games. Int. J. Hum. Comp. Stu. **66**, 641–661 (2008)

20. Liu, Y., Kosmadoudi, Z., Sung, R., Lim, T., Louchart, S., Ritchie, J.: Capture user emotions during computer-aided design. In: IDMME Virtual Concept Conference (2010)

21. Wendrich, R.E.: Multimodal interaction, collaboration, and synthesis in design and engineering processing. In: Proceedings of the 12th International Design Conference, DESIGN 2012, pp. 579–588 (2012)

22. Lanier, J.: You are Not a Gadget. Vintage, NewYork (2010)

23. Bellotti, F., Kapralos, B., Lee, K., Moreno Ger, P., Berta, R.: Assessment in and of serious games: an overview. In: Advances in HCI 2013 (2013)

24. Garbaya, S., Colado, U.Z.: Modelling dynamic behaviour of parts in virtual assembly environment. In: Proceedings of the ASME WINVR 09 (2009)

25. Lim, T., Ritchie, J., Sung, R., Kosmadoudi, Z., Liu, Y., Thin, A.G.: Haptic virtual reality assembly – moving towards real engineering applications. In: Advances in Haptics (2010)

26. Yu, H., Lim, T., Ritchie, J., Sung, R., Louchart, S., Stănescu, I.A., Roceanu, I., de Freitas, S.: Exploring the application of computer game theory to automated assembly. Procedia Comp. Sci. **15**, 266–273 (2012)

27. Assuring the future of manufacturing in Europe. Strategic Research Agenda (2006)

28. Manufuture Report EC. Manufuture Platform Strategic Research Agenda (2006)

A Diagnostic Tool on Time Perception
of Children with ADHD

Pongpanote Gongsook[1(✉)], Janneke Peijnenborgh[2],
Christian Sallustro[1], Erik van der Spek[1], Jun Hu[1], Francesco Bellotti[3],
Matthias Rauterberg[1], and Jos Hendriksen[2]

[1] Department of Industrial Design, Eindhoven University of Technology,
5600 MB Eindhoven, The Netherlands
{p.gongsook, c.sallustro, e.d.v.d.spek, j.hu,
G.W.M.Rauterberg}@tue.nl
[2] Kempenhaeghe, Center for Neurological Learning Disabilities,
5591 VE Heeze, The Netherlands
{PeijnenborghJ, HendriksenJ}@kempenhaeghe.nl
[3] ELIOS Lab – DITEN, University of Genova, Via Opera Pia 11/a,
16145 Genoa, Italy
franz@elios.unige.it

Abstract. ADHD is among the most common childhood developmental disorder which may affect the school achievements. Children with ADHD may show symptoms of time perception problems. Although ADHD is a clinical diagnosis with several approaches, no diagnostic tool has been designed to detect the symptoms of time perception problems in ADHD children. A computer game can be a powerful tool to be used as part of the psychological assessment and yield better accuracy in ADHD diagnosis. In this paper, we present our concept of a diagnostic tool on time perception for children with ADHD-symptoms.

Keywords: ADHD · Diagnostic tool · Serious game · Time perception

1   Introduction

Attention Deficit Hyperactivity Disorder (ADHD) has been widely researched in the past decades. Several hypotheses have been formulated on the causes of this disorder, as it could be derived both genetically and environmentally [1]. Some researchers have already proposed a tool targeting the cognitive functions for ADHD diagnosis [2–4].

Children with ADHD may have difficulties in processing, reading and telling time [5, 6] and a diminished functioning of reaction time and information processing speed [7]. Therefore, for an alternative to general cognitive measurements, we are interested to investigate the question on whether a computer game on time perception may contribute to a diagnostic process for children aged 4-8 years old. In this paper, we briefly describe what ADHD is and approaches to the diagnosis (Sect. 2), as well as why the diagnosis on time perception using computer games is of importance for our current design and development (Sect. 3).

© Springer International Publishing Switzerland 2014
A. De Gloria (Ed.): GALA 2013, LNCS 8605, pp. 400–405, 2014.
DOI: 10.1007/978-3-319-12157-4_35

2 Attention Deficit Hyperactivity Disorder (ADHD)

ADHD is a behavioral and developmental disorder identified by the Diagnostic and Statistical Manual of Mental Disorders, Fourth Edition (DSM-IV) [8]. Its symptoms must be present before the age of seven, persist for at least six months, must be maladaptive for the development of the child, inconsistent with the person's developmental level, and severe enough to impact daily functioning across several environment settings [9]. They reveal subtle but clear impairments in several complex functional systems such as selective attention, memory, motor speed and visuomotor ability, inhibitory control, and working memory [2].

Despite that we have DSM-IV guidelines for ADHD, no absolute methods for diagnosis have been defined. Moreover, it is difficult to diagnose ADHD since this developmental disability can not be diagnosed until children are six years of age, when they are exposed to classroom learning of academic tasks [10]. There are some computer games designed for ADHD diagnosis for example IntegNeuro [11], and Groundskeeper [12]. IntegNeuro is designed to assess people aged 6–96 years old, while Groundskeeper has been designed to target people from 6–17 years old.

We agree with Greenberg [13] that there is no such game that fits all age groups, the diagnostic game should be tailored to match the specific age group. The target age group of children in our project is 4–8 years old, the reason for choosing this age range complies with what Kalff [14] stated: (1) there is a limited amount of research conducted with children 4–8 years old, and (2) The symptoms that can be diagnosed as belonging to ADHD are not obviously shown but will gradually emerge when the children grows up.

3 A Diagnostic Tool on Time Perception

Time perception is a conceptual understanding that enables us to predict, anticipate, and respond to events occurring in the environment [15]. Children with ADHD may have deficits in working memory, that is related to time perception [16]. In addition, we know that children with ADHD may have brain abnormalities in some regions such as the pre-frontal cortex, basal ganglia, striatum, corpus callosum, nucleus caudatus, globus pallidus and cerebellum [17]. Those regions relate to the conceptual understanding of time [18]. Moreover, unlike other symptoms that could decline when the child grow up, time perception problems still remain even when the child becomes an adult [19]. This makes time perception a suitable factor for diagnosis. Therefore, we contend that if we have a better understanding of time perception in children with ADHD, we can train time perception, which contributes to the treatment of attention problems in children with ADHD.

3.1 Game as a Diagnostic Tool

Computer games offer players with intense and often relentless action, immediate rewards, challenging, and appealing stories, which seems to be something the brain of children with ADHD eagerly desire, and they hardly get from the everyday life outside the digital world [20]. The game we are creating is well fitted to the term of serious game [21]. It is designed specifically for diagnostic purposes with immersive environments, and multimodal interaction.

We aim at giving them the feeling that they are playing instead of being tested. Computer games could give an advantage over a plain psychological test because it does not induce a type of the Hawthorne effect [22], where kids behave differently when they know they are being studied. Using a game could therefore improve the ecological and external validity of ADHD diagnosis.

3.2 Current Project Approach

We have formed a collaborative and multidisplinary working team of computer scientists and designers from Eindhoven University of Technology, and psychologists from Kempenhaeghe, center for neurological learning disabilities. The development of the diagnostic tool is roughly divided into three phases in each iteration: design, implementation, and evaluation, with a spiral model [23, 24]. In the design phase we applied participatory design model (PD) [25] and user-centred design (UCD) [26]. We working with psychologists for their requirement, and re-design the diagnostic tool regarding to their feedback and comments. Children have been involved and observed do they understand our designed user-interaction, and asked how the non-player control characters in the game should looks like (see Fig. 1).

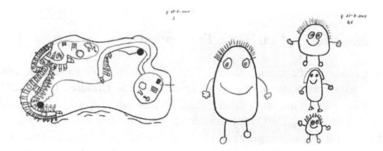

Fig. 1. Sample design of game scene and non-player control characters by a child

According to Zapata-Rivera and Bauer [27], there are some important items that should be taken into account when designing the game: (1) avoid to construct irrelevant content which need knowledge or skills on the player's side that are unrelated to our assessment goal, (2) limit other types of user interaction, but do not make the game boring or repetitive, (3) if we need more cognitive processing in working memory, we must introduce high interactivity and engagement, (4) players need support from in-game tutorial to become familiar and know how to interact with the game environment, and (5) provide formative feedback to the players.

Fig. 2. Sample screenshot of the diagnostic tool

The diagnostic tool will be used with a supervision from a psychologist. It is a single player game display in first person view using 23 inch LCD touch screen. Duration for diagnosing with our tool is set to the maximum of 30 minutes per session so the child will not feel too much fatigue. The diagnostic tool has a controlled linear story to secure that every child who plays our diagnostic tool will experience the same story progression. We have designed mini games to test specific aspects of time perception and related aspects such as time estimation, reaction time, and waiting time behavior.

Figure 2 shows one of the mini games which testing on children inhibition with go-nogo signals, the child has to clean banana peels from the pathway but the cleaning will be successful only when the monkey is hiding behind the leftmost banana trees. We believe that children who perform worse in the mini games have more possible deficits in the relevant executive functions. We already had a small evaluation test with normal children and received very positive feedback.

4 Future Work

We would like to explore whether information of time perception does contribute to an understanding of children with ADHD. Before going to conduct a clinical experiment with children, we will conduct a pilot test to get qualitative data and observations from children's behaviors to assess key game features such as usability, usefulness play-fulness and attractiveness.

5 Conclusion

ADHD is a developmental behavior disorder which impedes the learning achievements of children. Psychologists use a combination of various approaches to diagnose ADHD. But there is no existing computer game which is designed extensively to diagnose possible deficits in time perception which we know is associated with ADHD.

In this paper we present our concept of a diagnostic tool, and mini games. We strongly believe that a computer game on time perception will definitely contribute to the diagnostic process for children aged 4–8 years old. We are not yet receiving the confirmation, but from the evaluation feedback we consider that we are getting closer to receive the answer soon.

Acknowledgement. This work was supported by the Erasmus Mundus Joint Doctorate in Interactive and Cognitive Environments (ICE), which is funded by the EACEA Agency of the European Commission under EMJD ICE FPA n 2010-0012. We are also very grateful for the collaboration with Dr. Jos Hendriksen, Prof. Dr. Hans Vles, Prof. Dr. Bert Aldenkamp, and Janneke Peijnenborgh MSc. from Kempenhaeghe, Center for Neurological Learning Disabilities, and Christian Sallustro from the User System Interation (USI) program, Eindhoven University of Technology.

References

1. Attention-Deficit/Hyperactivity Disorder: Causes of ADHD. http://www.webmd.com/add-adhd/guide/adhd-causes
2. Gualtieri, C., Johnson, L.: ADHD: Is objective diagnosis possible? Psychiatry (Edgmont). **2**, 44–53 (2005)
3. Elwood, R.W.: MicroCog: assessment of cognitive functioning. Neuropsychol. Rev. **11**, 89–100 (2001)
4. Gualtieri, C.T., Johnson, L.G.: Reliability and validity of a computerized neurocognitive test battery, CNS Vital Signs. Arch. Clin. Neuropsychol. **21**, 623–643 (2006)
5. Hurks, P.P., Hendriksen, J.G.: Retrospective and prospective time deficits in childhood ADHD: The effects of task modality, duration, and symptom dimensions. Child Neuropsychol. **17**, 34–50 (2010)
6. Barkley, R., Koplowitz, S.: Sense of time in children with ADHD: effects of duration, distraction, and stimulant medication. J. Int. Neuropsychol. Soc. **3**, 359–369 (1997)
7. Leth-Steensen, C., Elbaz, Z.K., Douglas, V.I.: Mean response times, variability, and skew in the responding of ADHD children: a response time distributional approach. Acta Psychol. (Amst) **104**, 167–190 (2000)
8. American Psychological Association: Diagnostic and Statistical Manual of Mental Disorders, Washington, D.C. (1994)
9. Goldman, L.S., Genel, M., Bezman, R.J., Slanetz, P.J.: Diagnosis and treatment of attention-deficit/hyperactivity disorder in children and adolescents. JAMA J. Am. Med. Assoc. **279**, 1100–1107 (1998)
10. Glascoe, F.P.: Early detection of developmental and behavioral problems. Pediatr. Rev. 21, 272–279, quiz 280 (2000)
11. New breakthrough in diagnosis of ADHD. http://sydney.edu.au/news/84.html?newsstoryid=4501
12. Montini, L.: CogCubed Is Using Games to Help Diagnose ADHD. http://www.health2con.com/news/2013/04/16/cogcubed-is-using-games-to-diagnose-adhd/
13. Greenberg, B.S., Sherry, J., Lachlan, K., Lucas, K., Holmstrom, A.: Orientations to video games among gender and age groups. Simul. Gaming **41**, 238–259 (2010)

14. Kalff, A.C., Hendriksen, J.G.M., Kroes, M., Vles, J.S.H., Steyaert, J., Feron, F.J.M., van Zeben, T.M.C.B., Jolles, J.: Neurocognitive performance of 5- and 6-year-old children who met criteria for attention deficit/hyperactivity disorder at 18 months follow-up: results from a prospective population study. J. Abnorm. Child Psychol. **30**, 589–598 (2002)
15. Toplak, M.E., Rucklidge, J.J., Hetherington, R., John, S.C.F., Tannock, R.: Time perception deficits in attention-deficit/hyperactivity disorder and comorbid reading difficulties in child and adolescent samples. J. Child Psychol. Psychiatry **44**, 888–903 (2003)
16. Barkley, R.A., Murphy, K.R., Bush, T.: Time perception and reproduction in young adults with attention deficit hyperactivity disorder. Neuropsychology **15**, 351–360 (2001)
17. Wassenberg, R., Hendriksen, J.G., Hurks, P.P., Feron, F.J., Keulers, E.H., Vles, J.S., Jolles, J.: Development of inattention, impulsivity, and processing speed as measured by the d2 Test: results of a large cross-sectional study in children aged 7–13. Child Neuropsychol. **14**, 195–210 (2008)
18. Toplak, M.E., Dockstader, C., Tannock, R.: Temporal information processing in ADHD: Findings to date and new methods. J. Neurosci. Methods **151**, 15–29 (2006)
19. Biederman, J., Mick, E., Faraone, S.V.: Age-dependent decline of symptoms of attention deficit hyperactivity disorder: impact of remission definition and symptom type. Am. J. Psychiatry **157**, 816–818 (2000)
20. Bioulac, S., Arfi, L., Bouvard, M.P.: Attention deficit/hyperactivity disorder and video games: a comparative study of hyperactive and control children. Eur. Psychiatry **23**, 134–141 (2008)
21. Bellotti, F., Berta, R., De Gloria, A.: Designing Effective Serious Games: Opportunities and Challenges for Research. Int. J. Emerg. Technol. Learn. (iJET) **5**, 22–35 (2010)
22. McCarney, R., Warner, J., Iliffe, S., van Haselen, R., Griffin, M., Fisher, P.: The Hawthorne Effect: a randomised, controlled trial. BMC Med. Res. Methodol. **7**, 30 (2007)
23. Boehm, B.: A spiral model of software development and enhancement. Computer **21**, 61–72 (1988)
24. Rauterberg, M., Strohm, O., Kirsch, C.: Benefits of user-oriented software development based on an iterative cyclic process model for simultaneous engineering. Int. J. Ind. Ergon. **16**, 391–410 (1995)
25. Read, J., Gregory, P., Macfarlane, S., Mcmanus, B., Gray, P.: An investigation of participatory design with children – informant, balanced and facilitated design. In: Interaction Design and Children, pp. 53–64 (2002)
26. Rauterberg, M.: User centered design: what, why, and when. In: Graefe, E. (ed.) tekom Jahrestagung, pp. 175–178. Gesellschaft fuer technische Kommunikation e.V, Wiesbaden (2003)
27. Zapata-Rivera, D., Bauer, M.: Exploring the role of games in educational assessment. In: Clarke-Midura, J., Mayrath, M., Robinson, D. (eds.) Technology-Based Assessments for Twenty-First-Century Skills: Theoretical and Practical Implications from Modern Research, pp. 147–169. Information Age, Charlotte (2011)

Author Index

Printed in the United States
By Bookmasters